THE GIFTED
Developing Total Talent

Publication Number 770

AMERICAN LECTURE SERIES®

A Monograph in

The BANNERSTONE DIVISION *of*
AMERICAN LECTURES IN SPECIAL EDUCATION

Edited by

MORRIS VAL JONES, Ph.D.
Speech and Hearing Center
Sacramento State College
Sacramento, California

THE GIFTED
Developing Total Talent

By

JOSEPH P. RICE, Ph.D.

*Chief, Bureau of Special Education for Educationally
Handicapped and Mentally Exceptional Children
California State Department of Education
Formerly
Consultant in Education of the Mentally Gifted and
Co-Director, California Project Talent*

With a Foreword by

Max Rafferty, Ed.D.

*Superintendent of Public Instruction
California State Department of Education*

CHARLES C THOMAS · PUBLISHER
Springfield · Illinois · U.S.A.

Published and Distributed Throughout the World by
CHARLES C THOMAS • PUBLISHER
Bannerstone House
301-327 East Lawrence Avenue, Springfield, Illinois, U.S.A.
Natchez Plantation House
735 North Atlantic Boulevard, Fort Lauderdale, Florida, U.S.A.

With THOMAS BOOKS *careful attention is given to all details of manufacturing and design. It is the Publisher's desire to present books that are satisfactory as to their physical qualities and artistic possibilities and appropriate for their particular use.* THOMAS BOOKS *will be true to those laws of quality that assure a good name and good will.*

Printed in the United States of America
C-1

FOREWORD

EVERY schoolman is ruefully familiar with the parent who is positive that her offspring is a genius. I am using the feminine possessive pronoun deliberately here, because Dad somehow is apt to have a few more doubts than does Mom about Junior's intellectual kinship with Leonardo da Vinci and Sir Isaac Newton.

If Junior in fact turns out to be just a smarter-than-average youngster—and the odds are terrifically in favor of this being the case—then Mom's insistence on special instruction and advanced seminars down in the third grade can be a real headache for the harassed school administrator. But suppose the one-in-a-million chance comes true. What happens in our schools to the lone—and lonely—genius?

First of all, he is all too apt to go unrecognized. My own state happens to have tax-supported machinery by which the gifted pupil can be at least identified, but it is one of very, very few which make even this gesture. After recognition is achieved, however, it is up to the individual school, and more importantly to the individual teacher, to develop methods of helping the child who dwells in the strange, enchanted world of the supremely bright.

We know a few things about the gifted. Their IQ is up above 130. They tend to be stronger, taller, heavier than their less-talented classmates. Contrary to the popular caricature of the bespectacled bookworm, they top their peers in such social graces as popularity and attractiveness, too. Among the mentally as among the financially successful, "them that has, gets."

We can understand what makes a gifted individual gifted. Those of us who boast normality of intellect are in exactly the same relation to the 140-IQ mind that the low-grade moron occupies in relation to us. If you would like an uncomfortable insight into one of the problems of giftedness, try to imagine yourself living in a world in which everyone around you had an intelligence quotient of 60.

There is considerable resistance on the part of many taxpayers and the legislators who represent them to do anything which costs money to help the gifted youngster in school. One of them recently unburdened himself to me of the following sentiment:

> "Millions of dollars to set up special classes for the gifted? What for? Those kids are smart enough to make their own way in life without any help from me."

This, of course, is exactly as sensible as saying that people with superior minds do not need to hire a guide when they go hunting in the North Woods.

A chance to whet their magnificent brains against those which are their equals—a teacher who is herself gifted, access to the great minds of the past and the masterworks which they produced or the finest books, tapes, and films which our civilization has to offer—these are the things the gifted need in our schools. Too few of them get even a glimpse of this kind of education.

But I have been speaking of the gifted. At least we have a pretty good idea of their needs. The true genius is another story. He may be as different from the merely intelligent as we are different from the unfortunate imbecile. His mind works in ways which we cannot even begin to fathom; indeed, by the very nature of his superiority to us, we may never understand him.

In times gone by, how many of these tormented titans perished at the stake, or quietly starved, or beat their priceless brains out against the walls of some madhouse cell?

We must do better than this. At present, we educators do not know how to educate a genius. But we do know how to educate the gifted. Our problem is to convince the rest of America that this seed corn of our nation is worth some special cultivation.

Dr. MAX RAFFERTY
Superintendent of Public Instruction
California State Department of Education

PREFACE

CAN students with diversified talents realize their potentialities within the framework of our prevailing American philosophy of education? When existing educational programs are investigated, one discovers widespread inadequacies in provisions for talented students.

The problem of unequal education for talented students appears to be rooted in two sociopolitical dilemmas. First, in spite of unequivocal historical records of the contributions of human genius, the realities of individual differences in human potentialities and rates of productivity are not well understood nor realistically incorporated into educational program planning. Second, our democratic society, which alternately values cooperative versus individual excellence has yet to amalgamate the concepts of equal political rights for opportunity and freedom with the deeply philosophical mission of Western Man—the development of the individual man to his highest levels of expression, talent, and productivity.

Many states, including California, have established special educational programs for certain types of talented youngsters, usually the so-called academically or mentally gifted. However, no agency has yet envisioned a program with sufficient complexity and differential program possibilities to meet the needs of diverse types of talented students. Although the programs for the academically or mentally gifted are needed, such programs represent only a beginning.

In this book the author has attempted to summarize the basic ingredients of sound educational program development for the talented. Program goals and student identification procedures are linked to evaluation processes. Studies of actual student opinions and needs are related directly to curriculum planning. In eclectic fashion, several developmental models for understanding and educating the gifted child are presented for the readers ultimate selection.

A composite classification of talent is elaborated upon. While academic, creative, and leadership talent potentials are shown to be generally related to vocational and professional outlets, more specific talents, such as athletic or performing art talents, are also discussed. Differential diagnosis of talent potentials and appropriate education program placement is emphasized.

This book was written for teacher trainees as well as practitioners. An effort was made to include materials relevant to the work of teachers, guidance workers, and administrators. Although pedological in tone, the book should be of interest to parents of the gifted. Parents, in the final reckoning, bear the heavy burdens of taxes, personal sacrifice, and anxiety in the rearing of the gifted. They should be interested in recommendations for more adequate education of their talented offspring.

It is apparent that successful educational programs for the academically talented are now a reality. Now we must try out unique educational approaches with the promise of appeal for the creative student, the potential leader and the technically competent. The social sciences offer a reservoir of ideas for new "brain storming" techniques, special seminars, and open forums for the expression and stimulation of innovative ideas. In order to reach and encourage the skillful performer and the master technician, we will need to fight a whole constellation of snobbish attitudes which artificially place higher premiums upon the purely academic, scholarly, and professional preparations as opposed to the athletic, manual, technical, and performing art skills. At this point, we must begin to think in terms of master plans for total talent development utilizing more generous classifications such as those developed in this text.

JOSEPH P. RICE

CONTENTS

TABLES

THE GIFTED
Developing Total Talent

Chapter 1

THE GOAL OF TOTAL TALENT DEVELOPMENT

A S part of our democratic heritage, we believe that all children should be educated. At the same time, we recognize the limitations placed upon some of them by their handicaps. We are painfully aware of the vast intellectual differences among children. The issue is further complicated because our society values, simultaneously, both unity and diversity. On the one hand, we support egalitarian cliches which presume that all students may benefit, more or less equally, from an equivalent general education. Contrariwise, we lament our national paucity of intellectuals, scientists, and creative artists. Before effective programs for the talented are realized, we must somehow resolve these contradictions in our collective philosophical outlooks.

Believing that it is possible to educate all of our children, while at the same time designing programs for the development of individual potentialities, the National Education Association has stated

> ... the instructional program cannot be the same for all. Provision for individual differences should be made by qualified teaching personnel through diagnosis of learning needs and through appropriate variety of content, resources for learning, and instructional methods.[1]

The National Education Association has described "the essential objectives of education" as follows:

1. learning how to learn, how to attack new problems, how to acquire new knowledge;
2. using rational processes;
3. building competence in basic skills;
4. developing intellectual and vocational competence;
5. exploring values in new experiences;
6. understanding concepts and generalizations.[2]

The modern public schools' role in the overall cultivation of our talented students will be determined by the manner in which we are able to resolve historically controversial issues. Can we reconcile the egalitarian or Jacksonian concept of democracy with the strategic necessity to prepare scholars, leaders, and creative artists? Will our educational establishment sponsor creative innovation? Will educators continue to maintain the *status quo* of traditional knowledge and outmoded teaching techniques?

---

[1] National Education Association Projects on the Instructional Program of Public Schools: *Schools for the Sixties.* New York, McGraw, 1963.

[2] *Ibid.*, p. 9.

3

The subtitle of Gardner's book on *Excellence* asks the question, "Can we be equal and excellent too?"[3] After citing such theoreticians as Whitehead and James, Gardner concluded that "Free men must set their own goals . . . they must do it for themselves."[4] Recognizing that "excellence implies more than competence," Gardner emhasized our national need for the encouragement of "individual excellence in all its forms."[5] Should we encourage individual excellence through the recognition, development, and utilization of each man's unique gifts? If so, we must recognize the differences in capability among men.

BACKGROUND OF CONTROVERSY

Two disparate philosophical outlooks currently compete for adoption by modern schools. The more aristocratic viewpoint stems from antiquity and argues that special elites are a naturally occurring phenomenon. Such thinking has much historial precedence; stemming from Plato's discussion of the "Golden Men," educators have assumed that intellectual elites exist and should be educated separately and differentially. The modern twist to this trend seems to be an emphasis upon fulfillment through individual excellence in one's field of endeavor. In the United States, this point of view became highlighted, perhaps exaggerated, in the late 1950's with the realization that other societies possessed the capability for great achievement which might, through the process of history, surpass or even overwhelm us.

Persisting since the social revolutionary thought of France in the eighteenth century and culminating in America with the statements of the so-called progressive educators, there has evolved an entirely different educational viewpoint. These educators promote awareness of the social skills of citizenship, group and cooperative interaction, and general development of all students disregarding capability. One finds little discussion of measurable individual differences in capability among writers of this later school of thought.

As extremes of social utopianism may lead to an unrealistic educational program actually suited for no one and leading to no concrete results, so an education based upon elitism leads logically to a society which is part aristocratic and part slave. All modern educational programs, therefore, will need to generate differential definitions of moral, social, political, religious and intellectual rights, commonalities, and differences.

It is possible to practice political and religious egalitarianism. However, it is difficult to envision egalitarian absolutism in the intellectual realms without sacrificing the gifts of the few to the overall cultural detriment of the many.

---

[3] Gardner, John W.: *Excellence.* New York, Harper, 1961.
[4] *Ibid.*, p. 161.
[5] *Ibid.*, p. 162.

Faust attempted to reconcile the special educational provisions for bright children in terms of their individual rights and societies benefit by noting that "society cannot afford the loss entailed upon it by the incomplete development of its most able and competent members." He went on to emphasize: "on the individualistic side every child, whether subnormal, normal or supernormal has a right to that kind of education which is best suited to his powers and needs."[6] A reasonable justification for the development of talent is that society has a strategic requirement for such development. The development of individual talents accrue toward the overall betterment of society.

Unfortunately, we must take into consideration the seemingly inevitable tendency of mankind to group themselves according to classes, castes, or subsocieties. Thus, there is an ever-present danger of new elites, however essential they may be, aspiring to general social and political roles of ascendency to the detriment of groups not included in their category. Bettelheim has speculated that intellectual elites, so-called white collar elites, will come to replace existing socioeconomic, racial, and political groupings if an emphasis upon special education for such groups is continued:

> . . . highly educated peoples of all colors. Their education, their manners and outlooks on life will set them apart. They will live and think, act and interact in their own distinctive fashion, permanently separated from the rest of the population by educational rather than by social or racial barriers.[7]

It is encouraging to note that many of our liberal leaders have emerged through private schools and upper-class circles. For example, two of our recent presidents, namely, Franklin D. Roosevelt and John F. Kennedy, were exposed to remarkably similar styles of upper-class schooling and parental indoctrination. The record appears to indicate that such background did not lead to the development of elitism in these men but actually seems to have stimulated progressive political, social, and economic outlooks on their parts.

Some have felt that prolonged debate over the issues of social egalitarian versus elite policies of education has not led to constructive outcomes. For example, Freehill has noted that while

> . . . restrained and limited controversies seem to produce desirable results, prolonged debate of these issues may engender attitudes which limit free interchange of ideas . . . and probably delay progress in solving the educational problems of the gifted.[8]

---

[6] Faust, Clarence H.: Why the new concern for educating the gifted? *School Review,* 65:12, Spring 1957.

[7] Bettelheim, Bruno: Segregation: new style. *School Review,* 66:264, Autumn 1958.

[8] Freehill, Maurice F.: *Gifted Children, Their Psychology and Education.* New York, Macmillan, 1961, p. 24.

Still, such controversies must inevitably be resolved within given school settings before meaningful programs for talent development can be established.

Other authors have noted the tendency toward a one-sided controversy which results in general neglect of the gifted and talented student. For instance, Cutts and Mosely have noted

> . . . some teachers and administrators think it undemocratic to give bright pupils special attention, and still more undemocratic to segregate them in special classes. There are also some who object to any identification of a pupil as bright. They think this smacks of class distinction. . . .[9]

Teachers may resent the superior child's competency and unconsciously enforce egalitarianism in the curriculum as a sort of equalizer.

Other authors have alluded to the waste of our "nation's greatest resources." While warning us not to be "scared into action," Abraham has noted stark statistics indicating widespread waste of intellectual talent. He noted that among our top 25 percent of high school graduates, half do not finish college; aspiration toward higher degrees such as the Ph.D. is lacking; or, higher educational facilities for the preparation of teachers for the talented are scarce.[10]

The cyclical development of special educational provisions for gifted children is of interest since it may underscore our national ambivalence for these programs. As we study the historical development of programs for the gifted in this country, we note a basic philosophical dichotomy between those educators who attempt to supplement existing curriculums as opposed to those who stress the need for special settings such as special classes.

Borrowing from a number of sources, it is possible to set down some of the notable events in the history of programs for the gifted:[11]

1779—Thomas Jefferson advocated special education provisions and settings for students of more able learning capability over the entire range of schooling as part of his "School Plan for Virginia."

1800-1900—Private schools copied the "European type" of education. Exclusive schooling for socioeconomic and intellectual elites proliferated, especially in New England and the South. Upper-

---

[9] Cutts, Norma E., and Mosely, Nicholas: *Teaching the Bright and Gifted*. Inglewood Cliffs, Prentice-Hall, 1957, p. 18.

[10] Abraham, Willard: *Common Sense about Gifted Children*. New York, Harper, 1958, p. 5-11.

[11] See for example, Witty, Paul: *The Gifted Child*, Boston, Heath, 1951, p. 1-9; or Durr, William L.: *The Gifted Student*. New York, Oxford U. P., 1964, p. 1-13.

class traditions amalgamated into an educational emphasis upon taste, cultivation, and intellectual discipline.

1868—The first systematic plan for providing special educational programs for gifted in the public school setting was implemented. The St. Louis schools developed a system of flexible promotions utilizing annual, semiannual and shorter intervals of advancement instead of rigid grade-level promotions.

1869—Publication of *Galton's Hereditary Genius* amplified the differences among men with reference to their intellectual endowment and familial heritage. This volume excited strong interest in individual difference and the development of modern psychological and statistical concepts of deviation.

1886—In Elizabeth, New Jersey, the public schools divided their classes into rough homogenous groupings based upon academic achievement. The high achieving group was stimulated to progress more rapidly through the curriculum.

1890-1900—The so-called Three-Track Plan began to be utilized in a number of larger city school districts. For example, in 1898 the Santa Barbara, California, schools began to group all of their bright students together in order that they might benefit from broader educational experiences. It is notable that in Santa Barbara and other districts, acceleration was discouraged and ability grouping was thought to be a logical substitution for advanced placement.

1900—The New York City Schools established what may have been the first homogenously grouped special classes for gifted students. These special classes were designed to permit acceleration through the existing curriculum at a faster pace.

1901—As a logical sequence to the evolution of special ability grouping, the first known separate special school for the gifted was organized in Worcester, Massachusetts. Still, the main objective was acceleration of academic progress.

1902—Additional special schools for the gifted were established in Baltimore and New York City which opened the Stuyvesant High School for high achieving boys. However, only selected subject matter areas were offered.

1915—The Los Angeles schools tried out experimental classes for the gifted in order to provide a more enriched general education as opposed to mere acceleration.

1920—The Cleveland, Ohio, schools, sensing the need for broadened enrichment established the so-called Cleveland Plan, also known as the Major Work Program, which is still in operation after half a century.

1920-1930—More combinations of diverse practices were started. It has been estimated that only about four thousand children, nationwide, were enrolled in special programs during this period. Nevertheless, programs reflected possibilities for acceleration, enrichment, special settings, and unique combinations of these various program prototypes. Historically, the states of Ohio, New York, and California have the lead in the development of these programs.

1920 to the present—Louis Terman began the now classical Stanford studies of genius (see *Genetic Studies of Genius:* volumes I through 5. Stanford Univ. Press). Terman discovered and intensively studied a group of fifteen hundred gifted individuals (IQ in excess of 140). The original gifted group is still under study. These studies formed the basis for most ensuing California special programs.

1930-1950—As a possible contaminate of the depression era, acceleration programs came to be emphasized due to their economy. Many inaccurate generalizations which prejudice us against acceleration stem from this period.

1950-1960—School districts in California, Illinois, and New York began to emphasize experimental programs and program evaluation. Emphasis was placed upon program validity in terms of measurable outcomes derived from student exposure to particular curriculums, settings and programs. In 1957, Russian scientific achievements stimulated critical controversy over possible educational lag.

1960—The United States Office of Education inaugurated special "project talent" programs with emphasis on the discovery and development of our nation's human resources. Conant studies and criticizes the modern American high school emphasizing the need for better teacher training and the development of more sophisticated curriculums.

1960 to the present—Special programs for gifted children with state level reimbursement were pioneered in California, Illinois, and New York. Renaissance of the private school setting for the gifted child and much public awakening may be noted. At least forty other states have inaugurated plans for the establishment of various types of talent development programs.

TALENT BROADLY DEFINED

Experts writing in the field of talented or gifted students generally acknowledge the multidimensional nature of talent. Yet, they tend to restrict their recommendations to those students possessing specific qualities such as intellectual or academic giftedness. For example, DeHaan and Havighurst, while accepting that giftedness is a "broad area," nonetheless restricted their consideration of candidates for educational programs to "children in the upper one-tenth of one percent" who are called, "first order or extremely gifted"; the remaining children in the upper 10 percent in a given ability were considered "second order gifted."[12]

After indicating that intellectual ability is the "outstanding manifestation of giftedness," DeHaan and Havighurst listed "creative thinking, scientific ability, social leadership, mechanical skills and talent in the fine arts" as other "important aspects of giftedness."[13] "Giftedness was viewed as a singular quality with diverse manifestations. In like fashion, Gallagher noted that the "definition of gifted children has changed and expanded over the last few decades . . ." but proceed to state that the individual intelligence test is "the best method" for identifying gifted children.[14]

While current writers appear to recognize the existence of diverse forms of human talents, they seem somewhat reluctant to formalize their observations into multidimensional classifications of talent. Witty seemed to sum up this tendency when he stated, "Although much of the experimental work with gifted children has dealt with the verbally or academically gifted student, a beginning has been made in other areas."[15]

Ward has noted that children endowed with superior abilities have been alternately termed "superior and talented, able and ambitious, academically talented and other familiar designations."[16] Ward proceeded to single out the "clearest among these qualities of giftedness" by designating general intelligence and specific aptitudes as main qualities of giftedness:

1. general intelligence, usually manifest in high IQ scores, and
2. specific aptitudes (or talents) as measured by valid tests appropriately designated, or as evidenced through remarkable insights and skills in particular areas of knowledge or human endeavor.[17]

Dereday and Lauwerys have made a scholarly survey of the historical and current definitions of the gifted child and have found four alternative theories "corresponding to differences in the way the gifted child is de-

---

[12] DeHaan, Robert, and Havighurst, Robert: *Educating Gifted Children*. Chicago, U. Chicago, 1961, p. 15.

[13] *Ibid.*, p. 18.

[14] Gallagher, James H.: *Teaching the Gifted Child*. Boston, Allyn & Bacon, 1964, p. 20-21.

[15] Witty, Paul: Current concepts concerning the superior student. In Shertzer, Bruce (Ed.): *Working With Superior Students: Theories and Practices*. Chicago, Science Research Associates, 1960, p. 24-37.

[16] Ward, Virgil S.: Basic concepts. In Barbe, Walter B. (Ed.): *Psychology and the Education of the Gifted: Selected Readings*. New York, Appleton, 1965, p. 45-50.

[17] *Ibid.*, p. 46.

fined."[18] These alternate theories describing the ways in which giftedness may be identified are summarized below:

1. Stemming from Galton's and Terman's assumptions that the primary factor determining potential achievement is the innate endowment of intelligence, some, particularly British psychologists, define the gifted child on the basis of the IQ as determined by tests of general intelligence.

2. American theorists, led by Thurstone and his work on the primary mental abilities, has led to a broader and more generous type of definition. While still considering tests of general intelligence as good screening devices, such theorists aim to discover as wide a variety of talent as possible. Modern tests, such as the differential aptitude tests, reflect this tendency to differentiate among various kinds of mental abilities.

3. Some theorists have recognized two main groups of the gifted including those who are generally endowed and those who are specifically gifted. Such theorists still reserve the term "gifted child" to refer to children of high intelligence as determined by tests of general intelligence. But, they also recognize a separate group of the specially gifted, who possess specific aptitudes as determined by separate tests or manifestations of skills. This group may not possess a high IQ.

4. Certain theorists, borrowing the egalitarian doctrine of the French materialists of the eighteenth century, have rejected the innate capability theories and have sought to define giftedness in terms of achievement as acquired through one's interaction with his environment. This theory is exemplified by the assumptions made by the American behaviorists who maintain that any healthy infant could be trained to become any type of specialist one might select. This point of view may form the basis for the current impetus of creativity into the classroom as a substitute for general intelligence when interpreting the potentialities of students.

New approaches to the identification and development of talent need to be envisioned. Havighurst began this process by advocating an "increase in the pool of talent."[19] Havighurst noted that "children become superior through a combination of being born with superior potential and being raised in a superior environment." He proceeded to discuss talent from the point of view of a broad definition: "Talent is superior performance in any area of complex human activity." He did not restrict himself to discussion in intellectual areas only but referred to talent in the "arts and other complex forms of activity." This concept of a "talent pool," which represents a pooling together of many different kinds of potentiality with a

---

[18] Bereday, George G., and Lauwerys, Joseph: *The Gifted Child: The Yearbook of Education.* New York, Harcourt, 1962, p. 5-6.

[19] Havighurst, Robert J.: Increasing the pool of talent. In Bereday and Lauwerys, *op cit,* Sec. III., pp. 353-360.

view toward selective development, will be utilized as we explore the dimensions of talent development programs.

Of course, any discussion of talent development within a school setting must be tempered by the realities of available selection techniques and competent examiners. Also, administrative considerations, such as program costs, the availability of specialists to conduct programs, and the general level of sophistication of the teaching staff, must be taken into account. Although a more complex classification of talent will be presented, we must accept the reality that school personnel are most acquainted with the characteristics of the academically or intellectually talented.

Our suggested classification of talent includes seven categories: academic, creative, psychosocial, performing, kinesthetic, manipulative, and mechanical-technical.

The academic, creative, and psychosocial categories may be considered general talents in the sense that (1) they tend to be general predictors of success in a wide range of productive endeavors, and (2) they tend to be related to or correlated with other more specific talents.

The performing arts represent a composite category for the classification of a diverse variety of manifest talents which are difficult to relate to any measureable aptitudes. The dramatic performer possesses verbal expressive skills which the musical performer may not necessarily possess.

The category of kinesthetic talent includes a variety of physical endowments and bodily skills which are probably less related to the general measures of talents such as intelligence than are any of the other categories listed.

A preliminary discussion of our suggested classifications of talent follows.

1. *Academic Talent.* Validity studies have shown that general academic talent can be predicted from high scores of general mental ability. The classification of academic talent may be further defined in terms of particular achievement or competence. We might state that a given student is academically talented in science, mathematics, the humanities, social science, the literary arts, linguistics, or the fine arts. It is apparent that academic talent is highly prized within the school setting. It is typically associated with and restricted to the so-called mentally gifted.

Since this category of human talent has been studied more than any other category, it follows that the major portion of any discussion of talent must be devoted to this group. Most of the special program prototypes to be discussed, such as acceleration, enrichment, or special classes, have been developed specifically for this group. When this type of talent is properly motivated it usually manifests a level of scholarly behavior culminating in such designations as "honors student."

2. *Creative Talent.* Other authors have clearly demarcated creative from gifted children. For example, Getzels and Jackson have questioned

the meaning of giftedness and proposed an expansion of the concept to include "other potentially productive groups" such as a group "which may score high on measures or observations of creative performance and not necessarily in the area of general intelligence."[20]

Our category of creative talent will include those students who may be selected on the basis of experimental measures of creative performance, those displaying clear creative capabilities as witnessed by their productivity and those who are deemed by professional judgment to be inventive or innovative. However, this category, in particular, should not be restricted to students selected by rigid identification procedures. This category includes diverse groups ranging from conforming types such as inventors, theorists, and critics through to extraordinary types such as revolutionaries, avant-garde poets and creative writers.

3. *Psychosocial Talent (Leadership).*—Our understanding of leadership potential will be based on the simple concepts of influence upon others. Hence, this category is quite broad and can include those who influence others in intellectual, social, religious, political, or military ways. It is apparent that we do not fully understand all of the dimensions of psychosocial talent. We have few valid ways of measuring it. However, when psychosocial talent manifests itself in our midst, it is unmistakable.

Some of the qualities of the leader seem to be intuitive and social, rather than intellectual. The leader may be a person serving others in social or religious ways, or he may be a commander such as a business executive, politician, or military leader. All leaders seem to possess a capability for empathy which enables them to anticipate the reactions of others and behave accordingly. Psychosocial talent may be viewed as the vehicle through which other kinds of talent may be expressed or perpetuated through social communication.

4. *Talent in the Performing Arts.* In contrast to the other suggested categories of talent which are based upon aptitudes, this category is mostly empirical in its conception. Here, we can include those skillful and complex sorts of behavior such as singing, musicianship, dramatics, or the creative dance. These complex behaviors involve skilled performance as well as aesthetic values and motivations. In this category we have the opportunity to include some culturally valued kinds of talents which, though imprecisely understood, nonetheless possess the capability for entertaining, affecting, and influencing vast audiences. For example, allowing ourselves some imaginative latitude, we might include such diverse performers as the comedian or the choreographer.

5. *Kinesthetic (Athletic) Talent.* Athletic prowess has probably had

---

[20] Getzels, J.W., and Jackson, P.W.: Concepts and concerns about giftedness: The meaning of giftedness—an examination of an expanding concept. In Barbe, Walter B., *op cit,* Chap. 2, pp. 40-41.

more historical "ups and downs" than any of the other suggested categories for human talent. Some societies, notably the Greek, have elevated the physical capabilities to a prominence parallel with the spiritual and intellectual realms. Other societies have tended to narrowly interpret and apply the bodily capabilities in terms of sheer power as for application to war making. For example, current examples from the Germanic culture or historical reference to the Assyrian culture should underscore this point.

Americans seem to have mixed reactions to this category. They alternatively elevate athletes to higher status or caricature athletic prowess by relegating it to the position of gladiatorial exhibition. This kinesthetic category should be treated in the same manner as the category for the performing arts. Utilizing our observation and imagination, we should include those devoted to the expressive dance, gymnastics, physical culture, or even modeling. Also, we should fully appreciate the relationship of this category to productive physical work.

6. *Manipulative Skills.* In this category we place tactual skills related to measurable aptitudes. These skillful performances are usually referred to as the "psychomotor capabilities." Of particular importance to this kind of talent is the ability to coordinate what the eye observes with what the hand produces. The complete list of occupational and professional positions requiring manipulative talent would be virtually endless. The craftsman, painter, or sculptor represent obvious cases. Less obvious cases might include such work categories as master chef, tailor, or carpenter. Again, we find great disparity among cultures in terms of the way in which the manipulative talents are valued. In modern Mexico we find that the folk arts are nationally subsidized; along the major western highways in the United States we find that the American Indian must sell his handicrafts in a manner bordering on professional begging.

7. *The Mechanical-Technical-Industrial Complex of Skills.* In This category we include all of those aptitudes and skills highly prized by the industrial-business complex. Of course, this category could be further broken down into such subcategories as technical skills, computational skills, scientific-technical skills and the like. However, all of these categories share in common specific aptitudes which are perceptual and special in nature. Moreover, an analysis of the work tasks involved in the manifestation of this talent complex indicates a high loading of mechanical aptitudes. While the master mechanic, machinist, draftsman, or computer programmer are highly valued by industry after they leave school, there is a tendency to neglect this sort of talent within the public school setting.

Within a public school setting, the concept of a general talent pool might be maintained. Into this general talent pool would be placed potential candidates from one of four main kinds of identification sources including

1. those who possess high general intelligence (two or more standard deviations above the mean intelligence on a test of general intelligence or mental ability);
2. those whom teachers and other experts observe in actual productivity such as creative writing, invention, or other creative endeavor;
3. those who demonstrate their ability to influence their fellow students in school or extracurricula activities;
4. those possessing measurable aptitudes for future performance of culturally-valued areas such as the performing arts, the crafts, athletics, or mechanical-technical-industrial skills.

These main categories of talent are summarized in Table 1. Such a classification of talents should motivate schools to maintain two broad kinds of talent development programs including (1) programs for general education and cultivation designated by such labels as "enrichment programs" and (2) programs which are highly specialized such as seminars, special classes, advanced placement possibilities, and counseling sessions for all kinds of talented students. Schools establishing general talent pools will ordinarily discover that from 10 to 30 percent of their student population will ultimately be included.

This concept of a general talent pool obviates the need for arbitrary labels such as "mentally gifted students." Literally, each student included in a general talent pool is a unique diagnostic entity. There is no need to label him with any operationally meaningless title. It is sufficient for this student to realize that he has certain endowments or skills which may enable him, with education or training, to contribute to his society in certain specific productive ways. Furthermore, an avoidance of singular labeling of students may eventually discourage the prevailing tendency to place a

TABLE 1

MAIN CATEGORIES OF POTENTIAL AND MANIFEST TALENT

GENERAL TALENT POOL OF POTENTIALITY

"g" Intelligence—Verbal	*Kinesthetic Prowess*
Specific Aptitude Complexes	*Manipulative Skill*
Creativity	*Mechanical Ability*
Aesthetic Sensitivity	*Group Leaders*

PRODUCTIVE BEHAVIOR THROUGH EDUCATION

Scholarship	*Community Leadership*
Innovation—Invention	*Artistic Performance*
Professional Attainment	*Craftsmanship*
Technical—Industrial Output	*Artistic Performance*
Literary Productivity	*Specialized Complex Behavior*
	(e.g. actor, musician)

TABLE 2

STATES OF TALENT

GIFTEDNESS	ACHIEVEMENT	PRODUCTIVITY
Possession of skill, ability	Accomplishment through learning	Invention, work, change
Potentiality	Scholarliness, application	Innovation, release
Endowment, hence limited	Learning, hence unlimited	Imaginative, unlimited
A candidate	A student	Productive writer, craftsman, etc.

hierarchy of value judgments upon different kinds of talent. Our current obsession with the academically gifted tends to infer that other kinds of talent, such as leadership, are somewhat less valued. Of course, this is not the case when students enter the competitive world of work. It is to be hoped that through the course of a thorough education, students of widely diversified capabilities will interact. From this relationship should develop mutual respect.

As each student is placed into a general talent pool, his case study ought to consider a variety of factors including the following:

1. the dimensions of his talent including descriptions of general intelligence as well as specific capabilities, aptitudes, and skills;

2. comparative ratings of these capabilities with meaningful norm groups as well as a personal profile;

3. projected outcomes including prognostications and expectancies;

4. thorough consideration of non-intellectual characteristics which affect his behavioral, motivational, attitudinal, and personal predispositions.

Talent may also be viewed in terms of different states of existence. Conventionally, we tend to view talent as a gift, that is to say potentiality for future performance. It is because educators stop at this level of understanding that they sometimes observe great disparity between the measurement of giftedness on the one hand and its manifestation in achievement on the other. Instead, we can envision at least two other states of talent: talent as manifest achievement or scholarly accomplishment and, in its highest state, talent as productivity or creative innovation. The three developmental states of existence of talent, in summary, may be viewed as giftedness, achievement, and productivity. These states of talent are summarized in Table 2.

This interpretation of talent is flexible and developmental. In the first instance, the task of the school is to discover various kinds of giftedness and treat such gifts as potentialities for future performance in given mental, physical, or creative areas of endeavor. Subsequent placement into talent development programs ought to lead to manifest achievement as witnessed by meaningful and productive work. If our diagnosis of potentiality has been accurate and if the student is placed into programs which will enhance his gifts, then we ought to observe indices of productivity as the student enters his life's work.

In summary, newer classifications for talent must distinguish between general versus specific aptitudes, capabilities, and states of being. For example, mental ability, creative expressiveness, and leadership capability appear to be general variables which affect the condition and output of any talented person. Contrariwise, athletic skills, handicraft ability, or mechanical ability are specific traits which will enhance one's performance in circumscribed endeavors only. Moreover, some talents, which are highly prized by modern society, are based upon inherent aptitudes, while other talents represent the expression of complex personality variables.

The scholar, master craftsman, or skilled technician owes much of his unique talent to acquired mental and physical attributes. On the other hand, the actor, politician, or jazz musician, while possessing unique aptitudes, still must in addition possess that rare combination of emotional, mental, and psychosocial attitudes to cause the unique kind of vocational expression he chooses.

A composite classification of talent, to be useful in an operational way as schools plan educational programs, should be based partly on inherent capability and partly on culturally-valued societal roles.

In order to stimulate educational master programs which are truly oriented toward total talent development, it will be necessary to institute some classification of potential talents, however rudimentary this classification may be at first. The classification outlined above is, admittedly, basic and sketchy. Obviously, as our sophistication with talent development programs grows, we will be in a better position to diagnose unique talents more finely and prescribe more specialized educational programs.

Within any classification of talent, recognition should be given to at least three stages or levels of talent. For example, among performing artists, craftsmen, or skilled technicians, it is possible to distinguish among those with raw aptitude, skill, or potential, those with acquired achievement, performer status, or premium skills, and those who excel in expression, creative inventiveness, or have achieved master status. It is lamentable that all too often the academically or mentally gifted student is measured and classified with no provisions made for his development through the higher stages of manifest achievement and manifest creativity through scholarly contribution. The emphasis among any and all programs of talent development should be upon "development" rather than "discovery."

BASIC GOALS OF TALENT DEVELOPMENT PROGRAMS

Three broad philosophical alternatives seem apparent as educators contemplate special educational programs for gifted students in public schools:

1. Educate them within the framework of a general education model exposing gifted students to the same basic curriculum as other students and attempt to instill the same range of acceptable social and democratic values.

2. Focusing upon their superior mentalities, design an educational program that is uniquely different than the program offered for ordinary students because it is (a) designed to include content of more advanced nature and (b) it emphasizes the discovery, development, and utilization of the intellectual skills of problem solving, criticism, and invention.

3. A compromise between equal and separate education is possible by conceiving of subgroups within regular classroom settings. For example, in the elementary school cluster grouping is now widely practiced. A subgroup of from five to fifteen students may be placed in a classroom of more able learners. Duing the school day a class may be subdivided into various discussion and/or learning sessions in the same way that teachers now segregate remedial readers for special instruction.

Advocates of general education would tend to support educational programs of subject matter enrichment within the regular classroom and programs of widespread cultivating exposures. Special classes, out-of-school trips, or various kinds of advanced placement would be possibilities advocated by those believing that intellectually superior individuals require separate and unique education.

Table 3 summarizes the differences between the goals of modern and traditional education as presented by Roger Revelle in a paper prepared for the U.S. House of Representatives Committee on Science and Astronautics, January 26, 1966. The goals of modern education seem quite suited for the gifted student.

TABLE 3

A COMPARISON OF GOALS OF MODERN AND TRADITIONAL EDUCATION

Modern Education Strives to Give	*Traditional Education Leads To*
Problem Solving Ability	Rote Learning
Belief in Experimentation and Empiricism	Acceptance of Authority
Love of Innovation	Love of Tradition
Creativity	Regimentation
Self-Confidence	Search for Security
Optimism	Fatalism
Ability to Continue Learning Throughout Life	Terminal Education
Bringing Out Individual Abilities	Uniformity of Training
Self-Discipline in Work	Imposed Discipline in Classrooms
Coordination Between Hand and Brain	Rejection of Handwork
Public Morality and Responsibility	Family or Group Morality and Responsibility
Management and Decision Making Ability	Avoidance of Decisions
Ingenuity and Inventiveness	Following of Routine or Accepted Ways of Doing Things

TABLE 4

SEVENTEEN POSSIBLE GOALS OF A PUBLIC SCHOOL

Brief Form	Description
Academic Guidance	provides counseling and guidance for students with academic problems.
Adult Education	provides a broad program of adult education including an evening division beyond high school.
Aesthetic	promotes the discovery, development, and use of aesthetic skills and encourages appreciation and enjoyment of aesthetic outlets such as music and art.
Basic Skills	teaches and places emphasis upon those subjects which include the basic skills necessary for everyday living.
Creativity	emphasizes the discovery and exploitation of creative talents and encourages unique expression including the appreciation of uniqueness in others.
Democratic Life	promotes the democratic way of life emphasizing the study and perpetuation of democratic institutions.
Formal Education	provides preparation for further formal education and background.
General Guidance	provides general orientation and guidance programs for all students.
Homemaking	prepares young people for homemaking and family life.
Intellectual	emphasizes the use of the intellect and promotes critical thinking.
Mental Health	promotes self-understanding and good mental health habits.
Peace	promotes international understanding and peace.
Personal Guidance	provides help for the student in solving personal adjustment problems.
Social Maturity	promotes social development and adjustment to everyday society, helping the student to gain poise, self-assurance, and mature social bearing.
Spiritual	helps the student discover and develop sound moral and spiritual values.
Vocational Education	provides specific vocational education preparing the student for employment in specific skilled areas.
Vocational Counseling	provides counseling and guidance based on an objective assessment of a student's ability, interests, and needs in order to help him choose his life's work.

For the purpose of considering the general goals of education with reference to all children, Table 4 contains a list of objectives which might be used as a summary. The list was synthesized from many sources using statements of philosophy contained in school district philosophies of education as primary sources.

The general objectives contained in Table 4 will be used to compare the educational outlooks of the gifted with other groups in a subsequent chapter (Chap. 5).

In contrast, Virgil Ward has advocated "an axiomatic approach" to the education of the gifted.[21] Ward maintains that the arguments for specialized education for the gifted rests upon two main propositions including "the biological superiority of the individual and the fact that he can therefore manage a more difficult curiculum, and (secondly) the particular functions

---

[21] Ward, Virgil S., *Educating the Gifted—An Axiomatic Approach*. Columbus, Merrill, C.E., 1961, p. 240.

which he is, on the whole, destined to accomplish in his culture emphasizing the fact that he needs a different curriculum."[22]

Ward has proposed a number of propositions which might be thought of as foundations "from which the principles of instruction derive and . . . the overall organizational aspects of the school system" depend.[23] These general principles represent the thinking of the current school of thought which advocates unique and different educational experiences for the gifted:

Ward's propositions state

1. that the educational program for the intellectually superior individuals should be derived from a balanced consideration of facts, opinions based on experience, and deductions from educational philosophy as these relate to the capacities of the individuals and to the probable social roles which they will fill;

2. that a program of education for the intellectually superior should be relatively unique;

3. that the curriculum should consist of economically chosen experiences designed to promote the civic, social, and personal adequacy of the intellectually superior individual;

4. that teachers of intellectually superior children and youth should be among those of the greatest general excellence to be found in the profession;

5. that the education of the gifted individual should contain considerable emphasis on intellectual activity;

6. that the educative experience of the intellectually superior should be consciously designed as generative of further development, extensively and intensively, along similar and related avenues;

7. that the education of the gifted child and youth should emphasize enduring methods and sources of learning, as opposed to terminal emphasis upon present states of knowledge;

8. that the instruction of intellectually superior individuals should emphasize the central function of meaning in the acquisition of fact and principle, and the varieties of reflections of meaning in the developed communicative devices of man;

9. that the instruction of the intellectually superior should include content pertaining to the foundations of civilization;

10. that scientific methods should be applied in the conception and in the execution of the education for personal, social, and character adjustments of the intellectually superior individual;

---

[22] *Ibid.*, p. 80.
[23] *Ibid.*, p. 81.

11. that instruction in the theoretical bases of ideal moral behavior and of personal and social adjustments should be an integral part of the education of intellectually gifted individuals;

12. that the concomitant factors under control of the school should be positively controlled so that they contribute to sound personal, social and character development.

Here is the way in which a gifted seventh grader recently interpreted giftedness: "a gifted kid is one who's got something everybody else seems to want . . . except the kid!" Investigation revealed that well-meaning but misguided educators had substituted brutal routine for intellectual stimulation; pedantic acquisition of knowledge for scholarliness; and disciplinary pressure for natural motivation for learning.

By contrast, a fourth grader in a more healthy educational setting has observed that her special classroom differs from other classrooms in the following respects: "Kids are on their own more, they can read many books, study many subjects, go to many exciting places; they can ask all kinds of questions and find many different answers to their questions; they think all the time and they are allowed to solve problems on their own; and, they can work on special projects that will help them to feel important." Inherent in this answer we find the basic ingredients for a sound gifted-child educational program, specifically the following general goals should be implemented in any sound program for gifted students:

1. *Scholarliness.* Advanced and diversified subject matter should be presented sequentially at all grade levels. Gifted students are ready and willing to learn and apply advanced subject matter disciplines much earlier than the normal population. For example, some well-designed curriculums for gifted students at intermediate grade levels include such diversified subject matter as mathematical logic, economics, geometry, one or more foreign language, scientific methodology, and aesthetics.

2. *Cultivation.* Gifted pupils tend to become the intellectual leaders of their communities. Our intellectuals of the future must develop sufficient enlightenment to deal with the international problems of a world shrunk by intercultural communications. Refinement has been confused with snobbery or elitism. As a consequence we tend to neglect the cultural elements in education; we tend to produce too many individuals lacking the capability for aesthetic appreciation or the refined tastes. Implementation of this goal requires movement on many cultural and educational fronts. The school must begin to acquire cultural embellishments. Exposure to the fine arts should become an everyday experience for the young child. Tastes, styles, and trends should be matters of everyday discussion.

3. *Rationality.* Intellectual excellence is achieved through cognitive

growth and effectiveness, not by scholarly achievement alone. Our potential intellectuals must develop significant capabilities for solving new problems and thinking critically about outdated solutions. It is essential that the school introduce exercises in thinking, abstract reasoning, and critical discrimination as soon as the child demonstrates a capability for utilizing his higher level mental processes. If the school succeeds, the student demonstates problem-solving capabilities early. He discriminates ideal from reality, evidence from hearsay, propaganda from documented fact and belief from empirical evidence. In essence, he becomes a rational man.

4. *Creativity*. The individual should reach a stage in his life complimented by productive and creative output. The process of creation involves a deep longing in the intelligent mind for fulfillment. The school must tolerate true discovery, invention, and the application of new ideas. The creative personality tends to clash with an environment which attempts to indoctrinate him or inhibit his tendencies toward criticism, challenge, and change. This continuing battle between society and men of genius has been an uneven fight; the men of genius usually win. Rigid cultures become overwhelmed by the flood of new ideas and are supplanted by more vital cultures. Unfortunately, there can be no compromise with creativity. It can only flourish in an environment which is free and tolerant, yet critical and challenging.

5. *Ethical Systems*. History has shown us that the final test of a man may be measured by his moral convictions. By exposure to competing systems of thought and the disparate beliefs of others, our future intellectuals may develop internal ethical guidance systems. In a society dedicated to the principles of integration without surrender of political, religious, or group beliefs, there is need to stress the individual man's development and defense of his personal system of values. At the same time, he must tolerate disparate value systems in a plural society. Education should identify conflicting systems of values which exist in the student's immediate environment. The student should learn that it is his "inalienable right" to emerge with his personal philosophy of life with its unique configuration of values. The gifted individual is likely to exert leadership influence both in his area of professional attainment and in the social-political arena. Since the talented leader can influence others out of proportion to his representative membership in the larger society, it is imperative that he acknowledge the accepted ethics of his social and political systems. Intolerance or disregard for the ideas and contributions of others may lead to a closed intelligentsia or an aristocratic society.

Social responsibility has acquired disproportionate importance as a core ethic due to the capability of modern intellectuals, especially scientists, to contribute inventions to society with or without social, moral, or political controls. Through comparison with the goals of society the talented individual must weigh his contributions against the possible misuse, misinterpretation, or misapplication of his products.

6. *Self-Actualization.* In order to realize one's total potentialities, it is necessary to understand one's self thoroughly, learn to make and evaluate decisions, allow for self-expression, and engage in self-modification. In a literal sense, educators do not create nor develop talent; the talented individual understands and actualizes his own potentialities through a complex process of self-understanding and self-expression. No person of worth has emerged from the process of living without defeat as well as success. Through processes of societal feedback and self-criticism, the talented individual can develop toward self-realization.

The goal of self-actualization may be thought of as paramount. Therefore, a more thorough discussion of the concept of self-actualization follows.

UTILIZING SELF-ACTUALIZATION AS A MODEL FOR EDUCATIONAL GOALS FOR THE GIFTED

Carl Jung, Eric Fromm, and A. H. Maslow, among others, have maintained that a psychology which emphasizes the study and description of the crippled, immature and pathological personality can only lead to a warped understanding of universal human nature. These authorities have pointed out that the healthy individual is deserving of a separate, and more appropriate, study of his natue and characteristics. Hence, A. H. Maslow has adopted the term "self-actualization" to describe a syndrome of human behavior which characterizes the most healthy, most productive, and most self-fulfilling of human beings. The self-actualizing individual may be defined as one having "an absence of neurosis, psychopathic personality, psychosis, or strong tendencies in these directions." (The discussion of self-actualization which follows was adopted from Maslow, Abraham H.: *Motivation and Personality.* New York, Harper, 1954, pp. 200-234.) The self-actualizing individual may be thought of as one who "fully uses and exploits his talents, capabilities and potentialities." Such individuals have generally gratified their emotional needs for safety, belongingness, love, and self-respect to the extent that they are free to pursue higher level needs for knowledge, understanding, self-expression, and creativity.

Thorough understanding of the healthy personality should be essential to educators working with the gifted and talented. The concept of self-actualization may be used as a model of excellence toward which the gifted individual may aspire. Through study and emulation of self-actualizing individuals, the gifted student may incorporate into his personality those attributes and mechanisms indicative of self-actualizing individuals. Furthermore, teachers may utilize a model of self-actualization as a standard against which to match their own behavior as well as that of their students. The model of self-actualization may be used as a teaching device with which to impart to students the nature of self-fulfilling maturity as well as acquainting students with the hierarchy of values to which persons of eminence subscribe.

The following list of characteristics, compiled by Maslow, was based upon a sample of subjects, both historical and contemporary figures of eminence, who were judged to be self-actualizing in their lifetimes. Self-actualizing individuals possessed the following characteristics:

1. *More Efficient Perception of Reality and More Comfortable Relations With Reality.* They possessed capability for judging people accurately and efficiently; they were unthreatened by thoughts of the unknown and could tolerate the ambiguous and the unstructured; postponement of decision making did not result in doubt or uncertainty but rather was reviewed as a stimulating challenge.

2. *Acceptance of Themselves, Others, and Nature As They Exist.* Self-actualizing individuals can acecpt their own nature, with its inevitable shortcomings, as it exists; they eschew falsification and fantasy; other human beings are accepted on their own terms; they do not color or distort their perceptions of others or nature; their lives are characterized by a lack of defensiveness or feigned sophistication; they tend to disdain artificiality, guile, or hypocrisy.

3. *Spontaneity.* Their behavior "is marked by simplicity, naturalness, and conversely, by a lack of artificiality or straining for effect"; behavior tends to be related directly to the immediate experience; they do not feel bound by ordinary conventions; they appear to be free to develop more fully in their own style; they develop rather than strive.

4. *Problem Centering.* Self-actualizing individuals view problems in objective terms; they avoid personal involvement in problem-solving activities; they tend to view problems apart from themselves; work tasks tend to be unselfish and concerned with the general good; they tend to be concerned with basic issues, eternal questions, or philosophical and ethical concerns; they avoid petty or local conflicts or problems.

5. *Quality of Detachment, Autonomy.* These individuals "positively like solitude and privacy . . ."; this detachment is not withdrawal and may be resorted to, reluctantly, in order to find time for the thinking processes; this detachment enables the self-actualizing individual to concentrate on inner problems, feelings, and thoughts; they do not appear to be primarily dependent upon environmental factors for plotting their destinies; rather, they depend on their own knowledge, personal develop-

ment, potentialities, and latent resources; self-actualizing individuals appear to be "inner-directed" as opposed to "other" or "outer" directed.

6. *Continued Freshness of Appreciation.* They seem capable of appreciating the basic pleasures and sensory impressions which life offers as fresh experiences; their daily experiences are not perceived as "ordinary, workaday or drab"; they may find beauty and satisfaction in everyday experiences which seem mundane to others.

7. *Capability for Mystic Experience, the "Oceanic Feeling."* A feeling of unity with nature and the universe is sensed; self-actualizing men and women are exhilarated and strengthened, not exhausted, by work and accomplishment; the essentially emotional reaction accompanying the "mystical experience" may be stimulated by scientific, aesthetic, or religious awareness; the "mystical experience" is variously described as "awesome, revealing, or overwhelming."

8. *Gemeinschaftsgefuhl.* Adapted from Alfred Adler, this word roughly means feeling for mankind such as empathy. Self-actualizing individuals possess deep feelings of identification and affection for mankind; of course, they may experience occasional and normal anger, impatience, or disgust for their fellows; "they have a genuine desire to help the human race"; a sense of universal brotherhood pervades their relationships with mankind.

9. *More Profound Interpersonal Relationships.* As a logical outcome of their empathy for mankind, they are capable of "greater love, more perfect identification, and more obliteration of the ego boundaries separating themselves from other people . . ."; due to the depth of the self-actualizing love relationship, their circle of close friendships may be small; self-actualizing individuals characteristically attract admirers, friends, disciples, or worshipers even though they may find this devotion to be embarrassing.

10. *Democratic Character Structure.* Maslow has found all of his self-actualizing subjects, "without exception," to be "democratic people in the deepest possible sense." A self-actualizing person avoids authoritarianism and puts great stress on dignity or prestige; they de-emphasize social, political, or other artificial status.

11. *Discrimination Between Means and Ends.* In their ethical dealings, they display moral standards and tend to support the accepted "right" as opposed to what the society considers "wrong"; of course, "their notions of right and wrong are often not the conventional ones"; as problems are analyzed, methods and results are clearly distinguishable for those people; "in general, they are fixed on ends rather than on means, and means are quite definitely subordinated to these ends"; it must be stressed, however, that ethical and moral consideration is always applied to the methods or means to be applied.

12. *Philosophical, Unhostile Sense of Humor.* Interestingly, their sense of humor "is not of the ordinary type"; they do not engage in hostile humor at the expense of hurting or humiliating another; nor, do they prize "superiority humor"; they are capable of "poking fun at themselves"; noting Abraham Lincoln's joke-making, he rarely made a joke that hurt anyone else but tended to poke fun at the pompous or the foolish, sought humor for its own sake, attempted to educate by humorously treating the parable or fable in a joke; he poked fun at those, including himself, who had for the moment lost track of their own place in the universe.

13. *Creativity.* "This is a universal characteristic of all self-actualizing individuals"; there is no exception; such creativity or originality may take the form of inventiveness, productivity, or intellectual output; however, this creativeness may also appear in the form of expressing their own healthy personality by projecting it outward toward the world as example; this creativity is unrestricted; these individuals lack inhibition, constriction, or a sense of boundaries.

14. *Resistance to Enculturation.* In the same sense of being "well-adjusted" by virtue of superficial approval and identification with the culture, self-actualizing people may not be "well-adjusted"; since they seek more profound and meaningful interpretations of their culture, they may feel the need to resist enculturation and to "maintain a certain inner-detachment from the culture . . ."; yet, they do not tend to stray beyond the limits of conventionality in choice of clothes, language, or other customary behavior; they are rarely long-term discontents; they tend to "identity" with movements and organizations of wider scope; they do not feel restricted or bound by nationalistic or regional mores, manners, or rituals.

It should be stressed that the process of self-actualization is subject to individually differential growth rates. Self-actualization may be considered to be a sort of "ego-ideal" state. It is improbable that any human being attains full self-actualization. As Maslow has noted, it is an ordinary mistake to portray the "good human being" in such an extreme way as to make him appear to be a caricature. Every human being possesses shortcomings and eccentricities. Self-actualizing individuals are no exception. The key concept necessary to understand self-actualization as a process of human development is its stress upon the psychologically healthy personality. A self-actualizing personality is capable of utlizing its potentialities more efficiently and effectively.

Implicit in our discussion of self-actualization has been the assumption that such individuals possess a set of values which provide them with a philosophical reference. The self-actualizer incorporates into his system of values, feelings of worth for human nature, love of his natural surroundings, and assumption that life is essentially good. Such a system of values is bound to culminate in such cognitive outlooks as intellectional objectivity, honesty, and a basic respect for human nature. Also, the self-actualizing individual is apt to be unbiased in spite of the peculiarities of his society or culture. His world view is, therefore, more open and accepting of cross-cultural differences. His overall understandings of the world, nature, and the universe would tend to be typified by general or universal explanations, theories, and feelings.

The characteristics of self-actualizing persons may be used as developmental goals in the education of the talented. These goals, as enumerated above, synthesize the "affective and cognitive domains" into a unified set of operational standards. The concept of self-actualization is clearly influenced by the Judeo-Christian tradition. Man is viewed as imperfect, yet he strives for perfection and excellence; man is pictured as capable of self-help—he can literally change himself and thereby influence his destiny. Therefore, a practical application of this model might involve the direct imparting of the characteristics of self-actualization to students through direct instruction. This application is not unlike the teachings of religious schools which utilize the lives of saints as exemplary examples of human behavior toward which the faithful are urged to strive.

A more subtle use of the model of self-actualization might involve the development of unique curriculums and teaching techniques designed to create environments in which the qualities of self-actualization are caused to naturally emerge. For example, concerning content, the needs of the self-actualization seems to call for more study and contact with nature, philosophical frames of reference, social science, or key concepts and theories. Encouragement for the qualities of self-actualization might be implemented with more time for individual study and contemplation, endeavors involving service to others, or physical exposure to the out-of-doors. Also, distinct implications for teaching techniques may be implied; for example, "lecture or directive" methods seem to be unconducive to self-actualization processes. Small group discussions, individual study or instructional-counseling programs would seem to encourage self-actualization processes.

When building curriculums for the talented, the model of self-actualization should prove useful as the basic statement of overall program goals: specifically, the curriculum should include methods, contents, and environments designed to enhance the process of self-actualization in students. Likewise, self-actualization might serve as a point of departure for in-service teacher training programs. Teachers are exemplars. If their behavior exemplifies the qualities of self-actualization, it may be assumed that most students will attempt to emulate this behavior.

Chapter 2

TOWARD A CLASSIFICATION OF TALENTS

IT is easy to speak of monolithic subpopulations such as "the gifted." However, human nature is too complex to lend itself to overly simple classifications or understandings.

When we study those with superior potentialities, we need to consider many complicated variables: potentiality as opposed to manifest behavior; general versus specialized capabilities; or talent as product, service, or creative endeavor. Intellectual, psychosocial, and creative talents are general in the sense that they may be found to be, more or less, universally possessed by those who succeed in school, occupation, and productivity. Other valued talents, such as the ability to work skillfully with one's hands, are comparatively less related to the universal abilities.

Any classification of talents should be flexible and open to revision. As society selects new skills and capabilities to value, so our classifications should reflect newly acknowledged talents. Any classification of talent should be viewed as tentative. Candidates ought to be viewed as *potentials* rather than *members* of a chosen elite group. The difference between potentiality, as measured by prognostic tests, and actual performance, witnessed by one's achievements, creative products, and success, must be continually reemphasized. It would be unrealistic for schools to expect a one-to-one relationship between candidates in their *talent pools* and ultimate attainment as judged by achievement, professional accomplishment, or creative outputs. On the other hand, unless their identification programs have been unduly restrictive or inaccurate, there certainly should be a relatedness between the talent pool of a school and the eminent performance of students after leaving school.

All students in a talent pool may not produce eminent accomplishments; some students never noticed nor included while in school may achieve and accomplish. We must recognize that our selection procedures and identification techniques will probably never be absolutely perfected. This reality should not deter us from building programs for talent development which should include greater numbers and varieties of students.

Since academic giftedness will be shown to be the most reliable general indicator of potential achievement, we will view such giftedness, as determined by tests of mental ability, as being a prime criterion for including a student in a talent pool. At the same time, we will advocate the inclusion of any student demonstrating particular aptitude into a general talent pool. Our objective will be to develop all sorts of human potentiality toward levels of attainment, productivity, and self-actualization.

We Americans enjoy coining phrases and inventing terminology. As a result, various professional groups have invented classifications to describe disorders, gifts, or differences. Some classifications are confusing and misleading. It is amusing to observe professional meetings at which participants are unable to communicate with one another because they have developed dissimilar classifications to describe the common phenomena they have observed.

The tendency to concoct terminology may be partly due to unwillingness to study human nature as it exists. Instead of objective study, teachers may attempt to describe human behavior in terms of their own fantasies. Instead of quantitative terms, teachers may use emotionally loaded terms such as "delightful, pleasant or nice" to describe children. As a result, they expect creativity, love, and good behavior from all children.

The grouping together of dissimilar characteristics and the reclassification of human attributes in such a way as to obscure their real qualities may result. For instance, the co-mingling of such disparate characteristics as abnormality, defectiveness, excellence, and disability under the general umbrella of "exceptionality" has occurred.

We must critically analyze existing definitions for human characteristics, reject terminology which is useless, and continually formulate new descriptions of human behavior based upon objective observation. When describing mental superiority, we must be particularly careful to distinguish potentiality from productivity.

Classifications attempting to encompass dissimilar subgroups of students will be avoided in this book. We are studying the talented, the mentally superior—those with reserves of culturally valued attributes. The author can find few meaningful relationships between the talented and the handicapped. To group them together adds little to our understanding of either group.

INTELLIGENCE AND MEASUREMENT

The broad concept of intelligence is at the foundation of an understanding of talent, creativity, and genius. We still speak of "intelligence" as if it were a single factor. This is because the various mental abilities tend to be highly correlated; we tend to find universally high mental abilities in the same people. Of course, exceptions to this generality are to be found. Some individuals possess certain high mental abilities while having only mediocre endowment in other areas. However the general tendency is for "positive characteristics to correlate positively." Unfortunately "negative characteristics also correlate positively."

Classically, three notions describing the basic nature of intelligence have been proposed:

1. it is the native ability to solve novel problems with or without prior training;

2. it is the ability to learn rapidly and retain what one learns over a long period of time; and,

3. it is the ability to adapt one's behavior appropriately to accommodate changing environmental conditions.[1]

General tests of intellectual ability commonly contain verbal, numerical, and spatial items. Recent theories have significantly increased the number of possible separate mental abilities. For example, what we normally call "thinking or reasoning ability" may consist of a series of separate capabilities such as analogic reasoning, sequential reasoning, judgment, and other subsumed reasoning capabilities.

An interesting example of the way in which the list of primary mental abilities has expanded since Thurstone's time is indicated in Table 5 which appears below and is taken from work by Thurstone, Shartle and Guilford and borrowed from Super.[2]

In addition to the "primary mental abilities," a number of complex abilities such as "social intelligence" must be considered. The concept of intelligence is certainly not a simple one. We view "intelligence" as if it were a general ability. However, when measuring intelligence, we are really adding together and averaging a whole constellation of differential abilities. Since most of us have taken "intelligence tests," it should not be difficult to recognize that the items represented different kinds of thinking, problem-solving, and learning abilities.

Tests and measures may be confused with the actual quality being assessed. For example, laymen tend to use such terms as "IQ, intelligence, stanine, or ability," more or less synonymously. Of course, terminologies such as "IQ, percentile, or stanine," are statistical or descriptive terms. Such terms merely express a person's standing upon comparison with individuals presumably like himself as measured by items the particular test includes. Such terminologies as "talent, ability, intelligence or aptitude," on the other hand, represent theoretical potentialities that we may or may not be able to measure directly. A "test" performance is nothing more than a selective sample of a person's behavior. Any test result can only estimate an individual's total ability to solve problems, learn, or adjust himself to real problems.

Test companies invest large sums of money to be sure that their instruments are both "valid" and "reliable." They ordinarily attempt to prove that a test is valid in one of two main ways: (1) they show that the test

---

[1] Freeman, Frank S.: *Theory and Practice of Psychological Testing.* New York, Holt, 1951, p. 68.

[2] Super, Donald E.: *Appraising Vocational Fitness.* New York, Harper, 1949, p. 63.

TABLE 5

THE EXPANDING LIST OF PRIMARY ABILITIES ACCORDING TO THURSTONE,[a] SHARTLE,[b] AND GUILFORD[c]

Thurstone 1938	USES (Shartle 1945)	A.A.F. (Guilford 1947)
Spatial	Spatial	Spatial Relations I
		Spatial Relations II
		(Right-Left Discrimination)
		Spatial Relations III
		(Unknown)
		Visualization
		Mechanical Experience
Perceptual Speed	Symbol Perception	Perceptual Speed
	Spatial Perception	Length Estimation
Number	Numerical	Numerical
		Mathematical Background
Verbal Relations	Verbal	Verbal
Word Forms		
Memory Span		Paired Associates Memory
		Visual Memory
		Picture-Word Memory
Induction		
	Intelligence	General Reasoning
Reasoning or Deduction	Logic	Analogic Reasoning
		Sequential Reasoning
		Judgment
		Planning
		Simple Integration
		Complex Integration
		Adaptive Integration
	Speed	
		Psychomotor Speed
	Aiming	
		Psychomotor co-ordination
	Finger Dexterity	Psychomotor Precision
	Manual Dexterity	
		Kinesthesis
		Carefulness
		Pilot Interest
		(Active-Masculine)
		Social Science Background

[a] Thurstone, L.L.: Primary mental abilities. *Psychometrika;* —(No. 1):   , 1938.

[b] Shartle: Factor analysis of occupational aptitude tests. *Educ Psychol Measmt,* 5:147-155, 1945.

[c] Guilford, J.P. (Ed.): Printed classification tests. *AAF Aviation Psychology Report,* No. 5. Washington, D.C., Government Printing Office, 1947.

is correlated with an already established instrument, thereby demonstrating that it measures the same sort of quality as the more venerable test or (2) they attempt to show that it will predict good adjustment or high performance in tasks known to be related to the abilities they are measuring. For example, if a test purported to measure "mechanical ability," then the publisher might demonstrate that high scores on this device predicted which persons could perform real mechanical tasks with proficiency, such as work on motors.

In addition, the test would have to be shown to be reliable. For example, individuals who scored high on the test should also score high when the test is readministered; conversely, subjects scoring low should score low upon repeated administrations. Of course, many other considerations such as practicality, economical efficiency, and other factors must be considered before a test is used by schools. Unfortunately, many tests on the market today have not been proven valid nor reliable. A volume entitled *Mental Measurements Yearbook* edited by Buros summarizes the validity and reliability findings on most published tests in America.[3] It is an excellent resource when one wishes to ascertain the usefulness, dependability, and background on given tests.

The American Psychological Association has developed "technical recommendations for psychological tests" in order to provide test users with "standards of professional judgment in selecting and interpreting tests."[4]

The document describes four types of validity:

1. *Content validity* is evaluated by showing how well the content of the test samples the class of situations or subject matter about which conclusions are to be drawn. Content validity is especially important in the case of achievement and proficiency measures.

In most classes of situations measured by tests, quantitative evidence of content validity is not feasible. However, the test producer should indicate the basis for claiming adequacy of sampling or representativeness of the test content in relation to the universe of items adopted for reference.

2. *Predictive validity* is evaluated by showing how well predictions made from the test are confirmed by evidence gathered at some subsequent time. The most common means of checking predictive validity is correlating test scores with a subsequent criterion measure. Predictive uses of tests include long-range prediction of intelligence measures, prediction of vocational success, and prediction of reaction to therapy.

3. *Concurrent validity* is evaluated by showing how well test scores correspond to measures of concurrent criterion performance or status. Studies which determine whether a test discriminates between presently identifiable groups are concerned with concurrent validity. Concurrent

---

[3] Buros, Oscar K.: *The Sixth Mental Measurements Yearbook.* Highland Park, Gryphon, 1965.

[4] *Technical Recommendations for Psychological and Diagnostic Techniques.* Prepared by a Joint Committee of the American Psychological Association, American Educational Research Association and National Council of Measurements Used in Education. *Psychol Bull,* vol. 51, No. 2, Part 2, March 1954. Publishd by American Psychological Association.

validity and predictive validity are quite similar save for the time at which the criterion is obtained. Among the problems for which concurrent validation is used are the validation of psychiatric screening instruments against estimates of adjustment made in a psychiatric interview, differentiation of vocational groups, and classification of patients. It should be noted that a test having concurrent validity may not have predictive validity.

4. *Construct validity* is evaluated by investigating what psychological qualities a test measures, i.e. by demonstrating that certain explanatory constructs account to some degree for performance on the test. To examine construct validity requires both logical and empirical attack. Essentially, in studies of construct validity we are validating the theory underlying the test. The validation procedure involves two steps. First, the investigator inquires—From this theory, what predictions would we make regarding the variation of scores from person to person or occasion to occasion? Second, he gathers data to confirm these predictions.

Current misunderstanding of intelligence may be traced, in part, to the inability or unwillingness to understand the nature of testing, and yet, most of the judgments we make in life are based upon formal or informal "tests." For example, the measurement of a room with a yardstick involves a test administrator, an instrument, and a subject. The accuracy of our measurement will probably be very close to actuality, but not absolutely exact. This measurement will probably be very reliable, although other persons attempting the same measurement might vary by as much as one-eighth of an inch. If we pooled all of the measurements made by a great number of measurers, we would come up with an average measurement which would probably be closer to the real measure than any single measurement made by any one person. Psychological testing, although far more inaccurate, also becomes more reliable the more scores we collect.

Most predictions are stated in terms of "probabilities." For example, a weatherman will state that there are "two chances out of ten for the occurrence of showers." Some have ridiculed such statements; but, we must realize that there is no other intellectually honest way to state a prediction. In effect, many psychological test scores, especially intelligence test scores, are statements of prediction. They are attempts to predict how an individual will perform. Many of the newer intelligence tests are appropriately called such things as "tests of learning potential." The test developer has found that his instrument can predict with higher probabilities than by chance alone which individuals will later succeed in certain kinds of learning tasks.

Nevertheless, no test score with its implied prognostications is ever absolutely certain. Teachers must take into account "errors of measurement," such uncontrollable factors as the condition of the testee or the possibility that the instrument being used does not happen to measure the particular qualities the individual being tested possesses. Remember that a test is nothing more or less than a sample of behavior. An individual may have a vocabulary of from twenty to fifty thousand words and more, yet no vocabulary test would be feasible for practical use unless it contained fewer than one hundred words.

Moreover, it is always possible that the items chosen for the test have some built-in bias. For example, during the Korean War it was found that examinations for student exemption were "passed" more often by students from Ivy League colleges. Did this imply that state college students were less endowed? Probably not. Analysis of the examination indicated an abundance of items from such knowledge areas as mythology, ancient history, poetry, and other culturally loaded fields.

We must be certain that any instrument which purports to measure human abilities is rigorously validated, interpreted properly, and periodically reevaluated and revised to measure changing populations. Such intricate instruments as tests can never be perfect. It is probable that an individual's scores on similar kinds of tests will vary from testing to testing. However, some pattern of central tendency will usually emerge. The best advice to educators concerning the use and interpretation of tests might be to

1. design testing programs which include a variety of instruments measuring different qualities (e.g. aptitude as well as achievement);
2. repeat the program periodically, at least every three years;
3. place more emphasis upon counseling and interpretation of tests to students than upon the actual testing situation; and
4. view each student's resulting "profile" as an individual case deserving of unique explanations.

Utilizing the standard deviation, it is possible to demarcate "deviation categories" of intellectual functioning based on scores from tests of mental ability. Table 6 presents such a suggested classification for the intellectually talented. It is possible, in this manner, to distinguish among at least three subgroups of the *mentally gifted* including *potential able learners* (plus 1 to plus 2 SD units); *gifted potential* (plus 2 to plus 3 SD units); and *highly gifted potential* (plus 3 or more SD units). Moreover, it is possible to generalize typical learning programs for the resulting subgroups. We would expect the regular curriculum to be suitable for students between minus 1 and plus 1 standard deviation units from the mean as measures of general intelligence. We would expect students deviating one or more SD units to require subject matter content of differing kinds.

Viewing the upper extreme end of the intelligence scale, only about

TABLE 6

SUGGESTED CATEGORIES OF INTELLECTUAL DEVIATION BASED UPON THE STANDARD DEVIATION

Standard Deviations	−3	−2	−1	0	+1	+2	+3	
Deviation I.Q.'s	55	70	85	100	115	130	145	
Deviation Categories	Defective	Retardation	Learning Deficit	Learning Low Normal / Average Learning Ability	High Normal	Able Learner	Gifted	Highly Gifted
Grouping Possibilities	Individual Custodial Care	Special Class	Homogeneous "Z" Group	Homogeneous "Y" Group	Homogeneous "X" Group		Special Class	Individual Instruction or Tutoring
Typical Special Learning Possibilities	Corrective Training	Special Subject Matter	Remedial Instruction	Regular Academic Program	Enrichment	Advanced Subject Content	Specialized Curriculum	Individual Program

seven out of every thousand human beings will be found to have an IQ in excess of 160; therefore, group programs seem to be impractical.

IQ's, percentiles, and stanine scores are popular ways of reporting test results. However, they are quite different in terms of what they express. The IQ is a simplified mathematical expression of one's mental age divided by his chronological age, multiplied by one hundred. An IQ of 100 is precisely "normal." Approximately two thirds of all human beings obtain scores between an IQ of 90 and an IQ of 110.

Percentiles do not measure in direct relationship to the normal distribution described above. Percentiles merely describe what proportion of the population scores below a given result. While percentiles seem easy to understand, they may obscure the issue. Human capabilities do not distribute themselves in the way that percentiles would seem to indicate (i.e. in rectangular fashion). Also, percentiles do not emphasize rarity and so are not as useful for the discrimination of extremes of talent or retardation.

Stanines, ranging from one to nine, may be more useful since they are more closely related to the normal distribution. For example, a person scoring somewhere in the ninth stanine would be in the upper four per cent of the population. Some school districts are beginning to use T-scores which are directly related to a normal curve. In order to highlight rarity, the IQ seems to be best measure yet developed.

During the past fifty years, extensive studies have indicated that intelligence as expressed in an IQ score is fairly constant throughout one's lifetime; an individual will tend to score in the same relative position every time he is tested. When we say that his "IQ is constant," it must be emphasized that the individual is being compared to the same peer chronological group. As they develop in an absolute way, so does he. Scores such as the IQ do not indicate absolute or "power" comparisons. For example, an individual with a high IQ at age six, should not be directly compared with persons older than himself even though they have the same IQ. Obviously, their mental ages will be higher than his own.

Single references to "intelligence," such as the IQ, are further complicated by a multitude of hereditary, environmental, developmental, and physiological factors which may affect a person's intellectual functioning. Psychologists have differed considerably throughout the years as to the relative influence of such factors as heredity and environment upon the developing intelligence of a human being. Animal studies have tended to indicate that intelligence is an inheritable characteristic. Specially bred animals can be shown to be able to learn, adjust, or perform predictable tasks. Likewise, experiments have indicated that such factors as early sensory deprivation causes dull animals (or dull children) to develop. Perhaps the interrelationship between heredity and environment could be stated as follows: *An individual is endowed with certain genetic potentialities. These genetically determined potentialities may be viewed as "ceilings." They are the absolute limits to which an individual may develop providing he is exposed to proper and adequate developmental and environmental conditions.*

During infancy, physical variables such as nutrition can profoundly affect adequate maturation of the brain and other tissues. Later, environmental forces in the form of learning, exposure to sensory impressions, and succorance can cause these genetically determined mental abilities to be used or to atrophy. The whole story, therefore, is not entirely on the side of "heredity" nor is it on the side of "environment." A more complex concept, which takes into account the interaction of an individual with an environment must be contemplated. Probably, every human being has an absolute limitation imposed by heredity. However, it is doubtful that most of us ever come close to the fulfillment of these potentialities.

INTELLIGENCE OR MULTIPLE APTITUDES

Our discussion of general intelligence notwithstanding, there is still considerable controversy concerning the nature of intelligence. Traditionally, psychologists have viewed intelligence as a single general factor. Beginning with Spearman's[5] work, statisticians have consistently found positive intercorrelations among the various mental subabilities thought to constitute intelligence. This observation caused Spearman to suppose that most of the mental abilities share in common a general factor or "G" factor.

In recent years, intelligence has come to be viewed as a multidimensional aspect of human behavior. Among the first to recognize the apparent fact that intelligence is composed of more basic abilities was Thurstone.[6] Thurstone developed a theory of "primary mental abilities." Six "primary" abilities were distinguished through factor analysis. These six primary mental abilities included

1. the number factor which enabled individuals to work with numbers with speed and accuracy;

2. the verbal factor which involved the capability to comprehend words and was related to such measures as vocabulary;

3. space factor which enabled individuals to imagine dimensionality in space and can be demonstrated in such tests as those involving mechanical ability;

4. a word fluency factor which enables the individual to connect or associate words or concepts with great speed;

5. a reasoning factor which enables the individual to discover rules or

---

[5] Spearman, C.: *Ability of Man.* New York, Macmillan, 1927.
[6] Thurstone, L.L.: Primary mental abilities. *Psychol Monogr*, No. I, 1938.

principles which explain how series or groups of letters are related or form a series; and

6. a rote memory factor involving the ability to memorize quickly.[7]

Certain modern test batteries such as the Differential Aptitude Tests (Psychological Corporation, 1947) have incorporated Thurstone's notion of primary mental abilities into separate aptitude tests. The Differential Aptitude Tests include

a *Verbal Reasoning Test* (involving Thurstone's verbal factor) purporting to measure ability to generalize and to think with words utilizing verbal analogies for the purposes of measurement;

a *Numerical Ability Test* (incorporating Thurstone's numerical factor) which tests the student's understanding of numerical relationships and measures the student's capability for manipulating numerical concepts;

an *Abstract Reasoning Test* (involving Thurstone's reasoning factor) which includes problems of a spatial nature calling upon the student to discover an underlying principle to explain a series of changing geometric figures;

a *Space Relations Test* (incorporating Thurstone's space factor) in which the student must visualize, in three dimensions, how complex objects would appear after being rotated as well as visualizing objects from patterns;

a *Mechanical Reasoning Test;*

a *Clerical Speed and Accuracy Test;* and

a *Language and Usage Test* involving spelling and sentences.

Perhaps the most ambitious modern example of the way in which the multiple aptitude concept of intelligence has been applied is the work of Flanagan and his associates in the development of the Flanagan Aptitude Classification Tests (referred to as the FACT battery).[8] The FACT battery is of interest to us since it attempts to make differential predictions concerning aptitude for professional level jobs. The tests are listed in Table 7. Flanagan's work has been elaborated in Project Talent and supported by the Cooperative Research Branch of the U.S. Office of Health, Education and Welfare.[9]

The objectives of Project Talent are ambitious and include (1) an in-

---

[7] Thurstone, L.L., and Thurstone, T.G.: *The Chicago Tests of Primary Mental Abilities. Manual of Instructions.* Chicago, Science Research Associates, 1943.

[8] (Refer to four manuals) Counselor's Booklet, Examiner Manual, Student's Booklet, and Technical Supplement, *Flanagan Aptitude Classification Tests.* Science Research Associates, 1957.

[9] Flanagan, J.C.; Diley, J.T.; Shaycoft, M.F.; Gorham, W.A.; Orr, D.B., and Goldberg, I.: *Designing the Study.* Technical Report to the U.S. Office of Education, Cooperative Research Project No. 566. Pittsburgh, Project Talent Office, University of Pittsburgh, 1960.

TABLE 7

THE FLANAGAN APTITUDE CLASSIFICATION TESTS

Fact No.	Name of Test	Measures
1	Inspection	ability to spot flaws or imperfections in a series of articles quickly and accurately.
2	Coding	speed and accuracy of coding typical office information.
3	Memory	ability to remember the codes learned in Test 2.
4	Precision	speed and accuracy in making very small circular finger movements with the hands.
5	Assembly	ability to visualize the appearance of an object from a number of separate parts.
6	Scales	speed and accuracy in reading scales, graphs, and charts.
7	Coordination	ability to coordinate hand and arm movements.
8	Judgment and Comprehension	ability to read with understanding, to reason logically, and to use good judgment in practical situations.
9	Arithmetic	skill in working with numbers—adding, subtracting, multiplying, and dividing.
10	Patterns	ability to reproduce simple pattern outlines in a precise and accurate way.
11	Components	ability to identify important component parts of a complex whole.
12	Tables	performance in reading tables, numbers, and tables of words and letters.
13	Mechanics	ability to analyze mechanical movements based on understanding of mechanical principles.
14	Expression	knowledge of correct English for purposes of getting ideas across in writing and talking.

ventory of current American human resources based on a sample of 440,000 high school students who will be extensively tested over a long period of time; (2) the creation of a set of standards for educational and psychological measurement based upon the voluminous data collected; (3) increasing the possibility for comprehensive counseling guides based upon patterns of aptitude and ability which are predictive of success in various careers; (4) based on follow-up studies during the next twenty-five years, a better understanding of how young people choose their life's work; and (5) a better understanding of the educational experiences which prepare students for their life work.[10]

The Project Talent Aptitude and Achievement Tests include *information tests,* including tests of vocabulary, literature, music, social studies, mathematics, physical science, biological science, aeronautics and space, electricity and electronics, mechanics, home economics, screening (including questions of basic knowledge), and total scores on the information tests; *language aptitude and ability tests,* including tests of memory for sentences, memory for words, disguised words, English tests, spelling, capitalization, punctuation, English usage, effective expression, and total scores for En-

[10] Flanagan, J.C., *et al.: The Project Talent Data Bank.* University of Pittsburgh, Project Talent Office, March 1965.

glish, word functions and sentences and reading comprehension; *complex intellectual aptitude tests,* including tests of creativity, mechanical reasoning, visualization tests, visualization in two dimensions, visualization in three dimensions, and abstract reasoning; *mathematics test,* including tests of arithmetic reasoning, introductory high school mathematics and total and part scores in mathematics with a special test in advanced high school math with subjects such as plane geometry, solid geometry, algebra, trigonometry and elements of analytical geometry and introductory calculus included; and, finally, *clerical and perceptual aptitudes tests,* including arithmetic computation, table reading, clerical checking, and object inspection.

In addition to these comprehensive results, Project Talent will collect interest inventories based upon student activities, behavior, and general attitudes. Later, data will be collected concerning student vocational and professional placement. Intricate statistical manipulations will isolate out predictive factors. This ambitious study should answer many of the validity problems concerning the predictability of aptitudes for later performance in vocational and professional callings.

More sophisticated statistical analyses of subtest information sometimes reveal spuriously high intercorrelations among subtests of mental ability total scores. Moreover, restructuring of mental ability tests may have caused authors to load the general factor into so-called verbal subtests. For example, a recent longitudinal study of the primary mental ability tests revealed that the "verbal meaning subtests predicted achievement most effectively with the total score ranking second."[11] This well-constructed study included a sample of one hundred eighth graders on a test-retest basis at the eighth and eleventh grades. It was further found that "the relative position of students on the Primary Mental Abilities Test is fairly well maintained over time. . . ." This evidence adds to the collection of findings indicating that group measures of mental ability are reasonably reliable over time.

Bradway and Robinson[12] began their important follow-up study in 1931 utilizing the Stanford-Binet scale. They administered the Stanford-Binet on a preschool basis to a group of 212 San Francisco Bay area youngsters. Follow-up occurred in 1937 and 1956. Among other significant findings, the authors found that "a correlation of .59 between preschool Stanford-Binet IQ's and adult IQ's could be reported . . . a correlation between adolescent and adult IQ's obtained in 1941 and 1956 for the same group

---

[11] Meyer, J.S., and Bendig, A.W.: A longitudinal study of the primary mental abilities test. *J Educ Psychol,* Feb. 1961.

[12] Bradway, K.P., and Robinson, H.B.: Significant IQ changes in 25 years: A follow-up. *J Educ Psychol,* April 1961.

was .85. . . ." These findings corroborate those of Terman. There seems little question that the IQ, when considered as a composite single score, is consistent and reliable. These authors did discover, interestingly enough, that the intellectual growth of their subjects continued well past adolescence and did not cease at the approximate age of sixteen as had been previously believed.

As far as the validity of general intelligence tests is concerned, the classical results of Terman have clearly indicated that intelligence, as expressed through the IQ, is closely related to future academic and professional performance. Most researchers continue to find positive relationships between academic performance and intelligence as measured by tests of mental ability. For instance, Holland[13] found that a student sample obtained randomly from the National Merit Scholarship finalists mostly included students whose grades were high. However, when studying the relationships between criteria involving creative performance and personal, demographic, and parental variables, the author's results suggest that "creative performance at the high school level occurs more frequently among students who are independent, intellectual, expressive, asocial, consciously original, and who have high aspirations for future achievement." Also, Holland found that "students who are persevering, sociable, responsible and whose parents hold somewhat authoritarian attitudes and values, are more frequently academic achievers." These results based on a large sample of 9,868 high-scoring merit scholarship finalists indicate that, at the high aptitude level, achievement versus creative performance is more determined by attitude and environmental consideration than by basic mental ability. However, it must be underscored that all of the students studied had the prerequisite high mental ability.

It cannot be doubted that there are definite discernible differences among groups of children with low, average, and high IQ's. For example, an interesting study recently conducted by Klausmeier and Loughlin[14] found definite differences among groups of children with low, average, and high IQ's as they solve problems deliberately graded in difficulty to their present achievement levels. That is to say, the dull children worked on less difficult problems while the high IQ children worked on more difficult problems. The authors reported that

> . . . the high IQ children showed a greater incidence than the average and the low, and the average a greater incidence than the low, in noting and correcting mistakes independently, verifying solutions, and using a logical approach. . . .
> The low IQ group showed a greater incidence than the average and the high,

---

[13] Holland, J.L.: Creative and academic performance among talented adolescents. *J Educ Psychol*, June 1961.

[14] Klausmeier, H.J., and Loughlin, L.J.: Behaviors during problem solving among children of low, average and high intelligence. *J Educ Psychol*, June 1961.

and the average a greater incidence than the high in nonpersistence, offering an incorrect solution, and using a random approach. The high IQ children were superior to the low in efficiency of method, as ascertained by the ratio of number of moves made to the least number required for solution of problem.

The pupil of low intelligence typically used a method which we could describe as "random approach." The pupil of high IQ typically utilized learning strategies and methods involving "logical approaches." These findings were noted in spite of the fact that the problems were simplified for the pupils with low IQ and made more difficult for pupils with higher IQ. Thus, the IQ, as a composite total score, still seems to differentiate among children of different intellectual capabilities as to how they think, achieve, and solve problems.

Thus, the concept of general intelligence, in addition to being simple and practical, also has considerable credibility. Over the past fifty years, voluminous studies have been conducted to relate general intelligence to job performance, school achievement, and intellectual productivity.

Resorting to "common sense," McNemar has said ". . . all intelligent people know what intelligence is—it is the thing that the other guy lacks."[15] In a more scholarly fashion, McNemar has thoroughly reviewed the claims and counterclaims of the general intelligence advocates and the multiple ability advocates. He has found that those who have constructed multiple aptitude batteries ". . . never bothered to demonstrate whether or not multi-test batteries provide better predictions than the old-fashioned scale of general intelligence." McNemar has concluded "that the concept of general intelligence . . . still has a rightful place in the science of psychology and in the practical affairs of man."

Human potentiality is complex; contradictory theories cannot be avoided. It is easy to arbitrarily categorize human beings into oversimplified subgroups. We can rate or rank people in many ways: socioeconomically; racially; intellectually; physically and so forth. Unfortunately, such arbitrary classifications may have very limited meaning. Thorough understandings of human nature must be predicated upon a thorough analysis of all of the attributes we can observe. Hence, we should avoid superimposing labels on children prematurely. Instead of saying about a child "he is gifted," we should rather say, paraphrasing Terman, "he demonstrates potentiality for possible gifted intellectual performance." The identification of a child with particular talents is literally never completed. At any given point in his education, we can only state with assurance that he has already produced or achieved, the rest is prognostication and subject to change as new conditions develop.

We have referred to three generic terms: *talent, intelligence,* and *crea-*

---

[15] McNemar, Quinn: Lost: Our intelligence? Why? *Amer Psychol,* 19(No. 12): Dec. 1964.

tivity. Each of these "global" capabilities may be broken down into subsumed abilities. Thus, we speak of musical, artistic, or mechanical talent; we acknowledge verbal, numerical, or spatial intelligence; we refer to various kinds of creativity in terms of the product produced.

The terms "talent" and "intelligence" are very close in meaning. We will use "talent" when referring to manifest capability, and "intelligence" to refer to innate, latent, or potential capability. Wechsler's summary definition of intelligence seems useful for our purposes:

> Intelligence is the aggregate or global capability of the individual to act purposefully, to think rationally and to deal effectively with his environment.[16]

Stoddard[17] views intelligence as "the ability to undertake activities that are characterized by (1) difficulty, (2) complexity, (3) abstractness, (4) economy, (5) adaptiveness to a goal, (6) social value, and (7) emergence of originals and to maintain such activities under conditions that demand a concentration of energy and a resistance to emotional forces."

We must continue to distinguish between intelligence as potential and intelligence as a useful capability for social or practical performance. Dewey has stated, "Intelligence becomes ours in the degree in which we use it and accept responsibility for consequences. It is not ours originally or by production."[18] Another way of distinguishing between mere intellectual potential and actual performance is in terms of adjustment: "The well-adjusted person is one who has learned to apply his intelligence to the effective solution of the problems of living."[19]

THE VARIETIES OF TALENT

In general usage, the word "talent" is used in two main ways: (1) to denote general mental superiority and (2) to refer to specific gifts or skills. From Webster, we note that talent is "preeminent aptitude; superior intelligence and ability . . . or . . . a natural capacity or gift; as musical talent. . . ." Thus, we sometimes use "talent" synonymously with "mental giftedness," while at other times zeroing in on a highly specific skill, aptitude, or performance.

We will reserve the term "mental (or academic) giftedness" to refer to those with significantly high intelligence as determined by general tests of mental ability. Thus, mental giftedness is but one kind of potential talent. The term "talent" will be construed to be more generic than intelligence including a great variety of skills, abilities, aptitudes, and perform-

---

[16] Wechsler, David: *The Measurement of Adult Intelligence.* Baltimore, Williams & Wilkins, 1949, p. 3.

[17] Stoddard, G.D.: *The Meaning of Intelligence.* New York, Macmillan, 1943, p. 4.

[18] Dewey, John: *Human Nature and Conduct.* New York, Random, 1957, p. 314.

[19] Symonds, Percival M.: *Dynamic Psychology.* New York, Appleton, 1946, p. 389.

ance capabilities. Therefore, the term "talent" should be preceded with a descriptive adjective (e.g. academic talent, musical talent, athletic talent).

When we analyze the nature of human talents, we discover many confusing variables. For example, one person may possess native skill for performing musically (e.g. sense of timing, accurate tone, discrimination) but never be afforded the opportunity to benefit from training. Another may possess less spectacular endowments but be exposed to near ideal educational settings. The resultant combination of environmental benefits and native aptitudes may cause less endowed individuals to perform more skillfully than those whose native ability was greatest at the outset.

In order to plan appropriate educational programs for various kinds of talented individuals, we need to consider some sort of system of classification of talents. Two main approaches might be considered: (1) inspect the kinds of productivity the society prizes or (2) analyze the main varieties of human aptitude.

From a practical point of view, the people can and do choose among their fellows on the basis of manifest capabilities. Moreover, they are minutely discriminating when choosing the exact kind and style of talent they wish to revere. Thus, we note wide intercultural differences with reference to the sound quality of the singing voice most admired or the variety of craftsmanship most prized. In fact, within a given culture, styles change, fads disappear—the crooner of yesterday may have to find skill for folk singing. At any given time and place, therefore, it is possible to design a classification of human talent based upon observation of the culture, picking out those kinds of mental and physical performances which are admired, fostered, subsidized, praised, respected, or emulated by the people. Of course, our list of talents would be long, painstakingly specific and useful only for a limited period of time since different varieties of talent might be prized tomorrow. Perhaps such an approach to the classification of talent could be made more lasting by comparison with the historical evolution of special talents. In this way, talents with a heritage of acceptability could be distinguished from those with but fleeting regard.

A more fruitful approach to the classification of human talents might be based upon a study of human aptitude. At this point, we would do well to study some of the terminology used, sometimes interchangeably, to refer to talent. Some of these terms refer to innate capabilities (e.g. aptitudes) while others refer to acquired traits (e.g. achievement). Some terms are more useful for understanding physical manifestations of talent (e.g. skills), while others describe mental or contemplative capabilities (e.g. giftedness). Some terms are generic (e.g. talent, intelligence), while others are specific (e.g. special aptitudes or skills). As these terms are used to describe students, we must bear in mind that some refer to hereditary endow-

TABLE 8

A COMPOSITE CLASSIFICATION OF TALENT

Talent	*Exceptional Characteristics*	*Evaluation Assessment Observation*	*Educational Program Possibilities*
Academic	Retentive memory Abstract vocabulary Thinks with logical systems Long attention span	Mental ability tests (esp. verbal components: vocab., reasoning, analysis) (WISC, Binet, WAIS) Achievement tests School grades	Acceleration Special classes Advanced classes Enrichment
Creative Inventive Innovative Revolutionary	Ability to elaborate Tolerance for unconventionality, difference and change Unexplained insightfulness Unfettered thinking Fluency, flexibility, originality	Torrance's tests Guilford's tests Teacher nomination	"Brainstorming" periods Special seminars (open forums for expression of new ideas)
Kinesthetic Athletic Dance	Coordination, balance, stamina Time sense, physical prowess, endurance Healthy, reserve of energy	Objective ratings by physical educators Athletic prowess Competition	Physical culture classes Athletic competition Creative dance Subsidized participation in Olympics
Manipulative Craftsmanship Tailor crafts Cooking	Extraordinary hand-eye coordination General psychomotor control Spatial sense Views materials as amorphous	Judgement of crafts Measurement of hand-eye coordination Nomination for shop, craft, art teachers	Special classes: carpentry, tailoring, sculptor, crafts, etc. Subsidized projects (building, sculptoring, etc.)

Psychosocial Political Social Professional Intuitive	(Usually) tolerance for other points of view Capability for sympathy, empathy Sense of humor (socially acceptable social-emotional traits) Gregariousness Intuitive grasp of situations, times, people Understands compromise	Evaluation of sociometric data collected by teachers Objective classroom observation Analysis of extracurricula activities	Academic legislatures, courts, senates Debating societies, classes Encouragement for service societies Leadership seminars
Performing Arts Art Music Drama	Rare combination of skills which cut across mental, physical, psychomotor lines Can relate affective mental	Auditions Teacher nominations competitive selection by artist	Special classes Tutoring, coaching Subsidized performances
Mechanical Technical Industrial	Relates measurement to spatial dimensions 2 & 3 dimensional visualization Views materials as tools, having fluid dimensions	Tests of mechanical, spatial, or scientific aptitude	Technical shop classes Industrial apprenticeship programs

ments, others environmentally acquired traits; some are general, some specific; and some terms refer to physical or motor performance skills, others to perceptual or mental abilities.

Vernon[20] has studied and analyzed results from varied test batteries administered to representative samples of adolescents and adults in order to discover the "main general and group factors underlying tests relevant to educational and vocational achievements." These factors are presented, diagrammatically in Table 9A. Utilizing this empirical classification of factors as a guide, it is possible to envision a tentative taxonomy of talent based upon measured capability (see Table 8).

It can be seen, then, that talent is a very broad concept encompassing many subcategories of special aptitudes, traits, and capabilities. Talents are not only immensely diversified but also unequally distributed among groups of persons and within the same person. The possibilities for individual differences are enormous and underscore the need for intensive, individual testing and diagnosis when planning educational programs for talented children. For example, the so-called underachieving student may suffer from severely uneven aptitudes complicated by related uneven achievement. Such a student may be relatively deficient in those verbal skills areas necessary for written or oral communication of his ideas; hence, teachers may actually be rating the student's inability to communicate well rather than any actual deficiency in achievement.

Still another set of variables to consider when thinking about talent are those related to time and fruition. It has been noted that Terman was well aware of these factors when he referred to gifted children as "potential geniuses." Essentially, we should think of talent in the following developmental ways:

1. In the first analysis it is talent or gift; biological, or inborn capability.

2. Next, what is done to develop the talent through achievement, scholarliness? What is done to exploit or nurture one's endowment?

3. Lastly, what does the person do with his talent in terms of productivity, change, work, or creativity?

As we discuss talents, we will reserve the term "gifts" for potential or mental skills without training or education. Terms like "scholar or performer" are more appropriate when referring to those who have benefited from formal training or education and are capable of producing important works. Terms such as "genius" should be reserved for those whose capabilities, as modified by their unique experiences, have produced or created illustrious ideas, works, or products.

---

[20] Vernon, P.E.: *The Structure of Human Abilities,* 2nd ed. London, Methuen, 1961.

Bryan[21] feels that most kinds of giftedness or talent can be encompassed in four categories: academic talent, creative talent, kinesthetic talent, and psychosocial talent. If we add to these the categories listed in Table 8, such as "performing talent" (e.g. musicians, artists), we may have a more functional classification of human talent for which schools can make special provisions. Table 8 summarized these categories of talent in terms of their definition, some characteristics, ways in which they may be identified or assessed, and examples of vocational or productive outcomes which may result as these talents are developed.

Table 9B represents the suggested placement of the operational categories of talent contained in Table 8 with the main factors underlying educational and vocational achievement as presented in Table 9A. For the sake of further simplicity, schools might think in terms of four *main talent pools:*

1. *Mentally gifted:* students with high general intelligence (+2 SD's above mean). Given students may possess special subject area proficiencies in any academic area.

2. *Performing artists:* including all students displaying manifest capability in drama, dance, music, or athletics.

3. *Craftsman:* those with demonstrable manipulative skill including artists, sculptors, woodcarvers, tailors, cooks.

4. *Skilled technicians:* all those with technical and mechanical skills, including those inclined toward business or industrial careers. This mixed category includes those with a combination of aptitudes (e.g. mechanical or clerical) with accompanying marketable competency (e.g. mechanical ability or technical know-how).

In this four-way classification, "creativity" would be thought of as the key general factor affecting every other category. Each category might contain three types of individuals:

1. *Mentally gifted*
    those with measured potential (high IQ)
    those with manifest achievement (high grades)
    those with manifest creativity (scholars, writers)

2. *Performing artists*
    those with demonstrable skill
    those with performer status (acknowledged actors, musicians)
    those with master status (celebrated performers or creative artists)

3. *Craftsmen*
    those with raw aptitude (measured aptitudes)

---

[21] Health, Education and Welfare Indicators. *Education for the Gifted.* April 1964. Washington, Superintendent of Documents, U.S. Government Printing Office.

TABLE 9A

MAIN GENERAL AND GROUP FACTORS UNDERLYING TESTS RELEVANT
TO EDUCATIONAL AND VOCATIONAL ACHIEVEMENTS

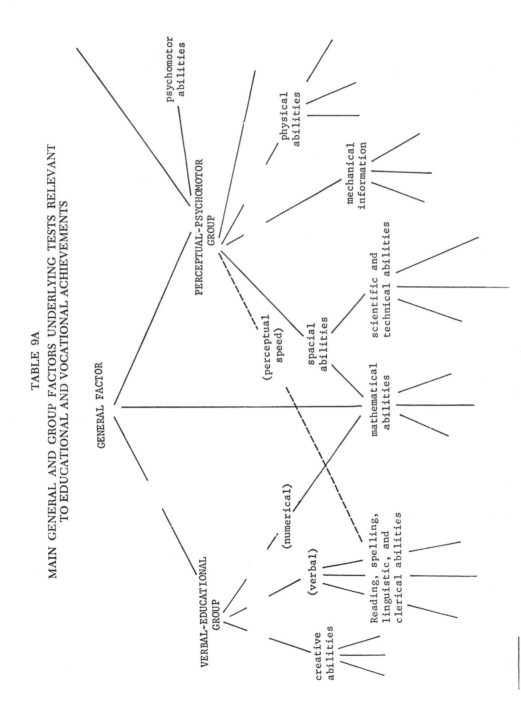

Adapted from P.E. Vernon: *The Structure of Human Abilities*, 2nd ed. London, Methuen, 1961.

TABLE 9B

MAIN GENERAL AND GROUP FACTORS UNDERLYING TESTS RELEVANT TO EDUCATIONAL AND
VOCATIONAL ACHIEVEMENTS INTEGRATED WITH A COMPOSITE CLASSIFICATION OF TALENT

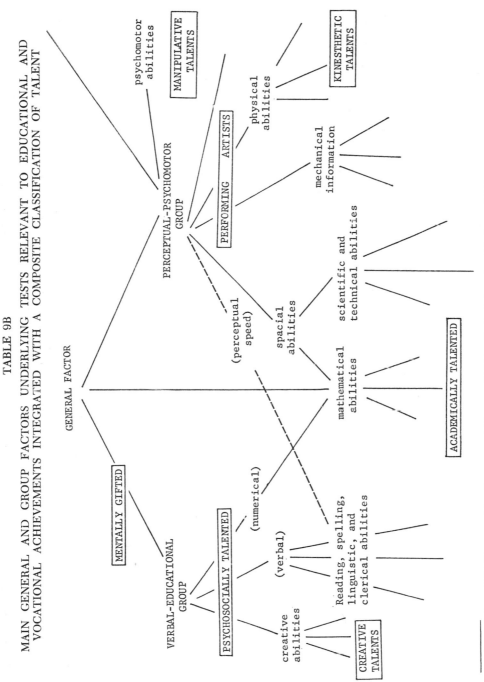

Adapted from P.E. Vernon: *The Structure of Human Abilities*, 2nd ed. London, Methuen, 1961.

those with acquired skill (marketable skills)
those producing creative products (art works, etc.)

4. *Skilled technicians*
   those with aptitude
   those with premium skills
   those who excel and invent

Also, the "psychosocial category" would be thought of as general and apply to any of the four performance categories as individuals who have attained eminence.

It is notable that schools design programs, or at least supplemental outlets, for most of these talent categories right now; but often such programs are afterthoughts. Begrudgingly, we admit that the prowess of the athlete is backed by specialized abilities, but we oftentimes caricature athletic talent by allowing it to be perverted to ulterior ends such as "spectator sports." Instead, we must cultivate the special nature of every talent emphasizing self-fulfillment and excellent performance. If schools would consider a diversity of talent development programs in the psychomotor, performing, leadership, and creative areas of endeavor, as well as the traditional academic areas, our current tendencies to make unfounded value judgments concerning the differential worth of disparate talents might be circumvented. For example, would the comparison between school grades and later performance in jobs be so disparate for top-grade mechanics, if we really supported programs for excellence in industrial skills? Would parents of children with performing talents have to seek out private schools or neglect musical or artistic talents in their children if schools offered specially designed tracts for such students?

We know a great deal about the student with "academic talent," so much in fact that we may have a tendency to misapply some of this knowledge if we do not keep the concept of individual variability constantly in mind. Remember, all talent is, at the outset mere potentiality. It is likely, even probable, that a student with high general intelligence and a good memory will be an above average student (as indicated by grades and performance) but it is not certain. Background, motivation, adjustment to particular educational settings—all must be considered in the equation before we prognosticate as to whether not a particular individual with academic talent will be a good student.

Ginsberg[22] has found that graduate students with academic promise (those who are fellowship recipients), all culminate in the "two highest rungs of the occupational ladder." Without exception, the 342 students Ginsberg studied ended up in professional or managerial positions.

---

[22] Ginsberg, Eli: *Talent and Performance.* New York, Columbia, 1964.

Interestingly, half of the group of graduate students entered into and practiced independent professions (e.g. law, business). Seven out of ten earned a doctorate within twelve years after completing undergraduate work while most married and maintained "normal family patterns." This study, along with many others, would indicate that we can select our academically promising students with a high degree of efficiency. Such students become what we expect them to become—scholars, teachers, professionals—our intellectual doers.

It is when we try to differentiate the creative from the academic group that we encounter confusing recommendations and theories from the literature. For now, we will differentiate between "creative" and "academic" talent on the basis of behavior and actual products. The behavior of the creative student tends to be independent, to a point of unconventionality; he is not restricted by the boundaries society has constructed to limit thought. Hence, his mental and physical products (ideas and actual works) tend to be inventive, differentiated, and in the extreme, revolutionary. It is interesting how educators purporting to work with creativity avoid the rather apparent relationship between creativity and revolutionary thought, behavior, and works. The creative tend to criticize and challenge the *status quo*. They are constructively (or destructively) discontent with theories or precedents which do not apply or explain new situations and problems.

The creative component in human personality is not exclusively mental. It is a composite quality incorporating special capability, strong motivation, sharp interests, and insightful awareness of existing inadequacies. Like general intelligence, this creative complex is a general, as opposed to a special, quality. That is, it must be considered in terms of, and related to, other qualities. We should look for greater or lesser amounts of both academic and creative potentialities in all children identified for talent development programs. Obviously, the less academic potential we find, the less will be the possibilities for advanced training; just as obviously, the fewer indications of creative ability, the less will be the prognosis for production of unique, inventive, or innovative work.

The category of psychosocial talent is also quite general in the sense of overlap with other categories. It is apparent that we can think of leadership in social, intellectual, physical, or performing outlets. In order to sharpen our focus, we might concentrate on those experiences of leadership which affect or influence others in everyday social affairs: political or social leadership. Within this meaning, we are able to differentiate a rather clear dichotomy between political versus social leadership.[23]

---

[23] See Spranger, E.: Types of Men. As presented in Alpert, Vernon, and Lindsey: *Manual: A Study of Values*. Boston, Houghton, 1960, for a discussion of different values of political and social men.

The political leader, influenced by the nature of power, may be more coldly logical in his attempt to understand and control others. The social leader, interested more in human welfare as opposed to control, may rely heavily upon his emotional reactions such as empathy for others when determining how he can best lead them. A study of the words "political" versus "social leaders" use to influence others might be helpful in differentiating between them. Our political leaders tend to call upon us to "sacrifice, strive, endure"; our social leaders to "build, enjoy, fulfill." Probably, the way others feel about their political and social leaders is also quite different. The political leader (e.g. senator, businessman, executive) may be held in awe, respected, but with elements of fear. The social leader (e.g. service club president, clergyman) may be respected, but with elements of tenderness, love, and close personal identification.

Kinesthetic, manipulative, mechanical, and performing talents can be viewed as reasonably "pure" talents from the point of view of outcomes. The athlete, craftsman, master toolmaker, and trumpet player are all valued for unique and different outputs. When we analyze the underlying aptitudes and skills, however, we find considerable overlap. For example, the physical attributes of high energy level, endurance, coordination and spatial visualization seem generally applicable to all of these categories. Other aptitudes or skills such as time sense may be more important to some talents (e.g. musician, athlete) than to others (e.g. mechanics, craftsmen).

The performing arts category is, perhaps, the least "pure." Obviously, performers (in the sense of actors or musicians) have extensively complex combinations of talents which may even include psychosocial components. However, it is administratively useful to consider this category separately since the sorts of programs we establish can easily be designated in terms of specific performing arts.

While we will include those with exceptional scientific aptitude with the academically gifted, it is apparent that many scientific pursuits involve loadings of mechanical aptitude (e.g. biology) or mathematics (e.g. astrophysics). Just as clearly, all scientific abilities involve varying amounts of verbal, numerical, and spatial capability.

Those with technical-industrial skills and aspirations have suffered an unfortunate socioeconomic identity with "lower class" work. This has led to a tendency to downgrade this type of talent, in spite of the economic gains made by the mechanically talented through the rise of industrial priorities for these skills. The psychological effect of merely paying some attention to mechanical skills in the school setting cannot be overemphasized. Ingenious designs and completed shop projects should be rewarded with equivalent value as are scholarship or the performing arts.

Perhaps the most neglected talent category in the twentieth century

American life is that of manipulative talent. Sometimes scorned, sometimes indulgently equated with the compensatory capability of the (otherwise) retarded, it is consistently relegated to lower positions of eminence in our society, with the possible exception of the sculptor. Those who prize individual craftsmanship must look abroad for elegant crafts (e.g. Scandinavian furniture). Our cultural downplay of beauty and perfection has caused historically valued talents to be dramatically downgraded. This is one area where educators can assume a truly meaningful service. By supporting the craftsman, displaying an appreciation of the products of craftsmanship, and by providing the programs, we can reverse this unfortunate trend. A boy displaying obvious and exceptional skill in carving, for example, might postpone or substitute practice at his skill, for say, spelling lessons.

What about kinesthetic talent? Again, we are dealing with a misunderstood, sometimes perverted, type of talent. Contrast, for example, the difference between perverting athletic prowess for the purposes of brute sports (e.g. boxing) with the development of the body for the purposes of beauty and personal fulfillment (e.g. creative dance, gymnastics). Of course, certain organized sports involve clear application of kinesthetic skill (e.g. basketball, track, wrestling).

Perhaps we should reach back to antiquity for a concept of the "total man" involving physical, intellectual, and spiritual development (the Greek triangle). We need to consciously seek a level of civilized development for all of our human potentials.

SUMMING UP SOME NEW DIMENSIONS

We have discussed giftedness, creativity, intelligence, and talent. We may wonder if it is wise, in view of the abundance of unsettled issues, to even consider an entity of "giftedness." But, guided by practicality, we recognize the need to place students into educational programs most apt to meet their broad educational needs. Moreover, some generalizations have held up reasonably well. General mental ability does persist as the only reliable predictor of academic success, professional attainment, and intellectual productivity.

The problem is that we may be tempted to exclude too many students. If we view those with above average intelligence as *potential producers* and take into consideration indices of specific aptitudes as well as manifest demonstrations of capability, we could think of *talent pools*. Such pools should include from 10 to 20 percent of the students in a school district rather than the 2 to 5 percent commonly sought.

Some terms as "academic giftedness" could be applied to those demonstrating, through test performance, that they possess general potentiality. Their final attainment will depend upon many other factors such as motivation, stability, or preferences.

There are other sorts of talent which correlate, but not highly, with intelligence. Some of these talents society values (e.g. leadership or performing arts); some we have not made up our collective minds about (e.g. creativity); and other talents have been depreciated, neglected, or snubbed due to association with lower socioeconomic classes (kinesthetic, mechanical, or manipulative talents). Most of these talents show themselves in the early behavior of children. Talent can be tentatively identified through objective observation alone. Standardized devices are unnecessary to measure them. Total programs of talent development cannot be restricted for the academically gifted alone, although this group includes the largest single pool of potential talent.

Throughout the rest of this book, we will concentrate upon describing and prescribing programs for academic, creative, and psychosocial talent. These categories are generic, cutting across other subclassifications of tal-

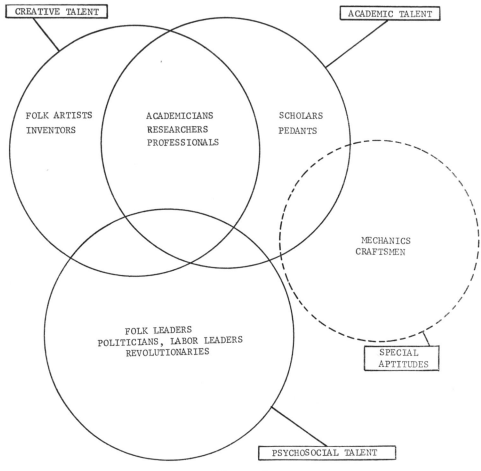

FIGURE 1.

ent. They represent the sorts of talent thought to be most needed in our modern world. Schools are in a position, without considerable further implementation, to offer special programs. The relationship of academic, creative, and psychosocial talents overlap; the same students may appear in all programs. However, certain students may manifest very specific talents as outlined in Figure 1.

The overlap between academic and creative potential is probably very great; between psychosocial and the creative-academic complex there is probably considerable unilaterality. Hence, enrollments in special programs for academically or creatively gifted students should largely coincide. Important exceptions should be deliberately searched for. Enrollment in leadership preparation programs, while including a loading of academically able students, will also include many students displaying manifest or latent leadership capability without necessarily being otherwise gifted.

Our concentration on academic, creative, and psychosocial talent not withstanding, schools should maintain individualized settings for specially talented students. It is hazardous to generalize about the extent of leftover talents, since these will vary markedly. Regions inheriting cultural bias for the fine arts will find need for special programs in music, art, and literature. Districts within regions will be influenced by socioeconomic realities causing more stress to be placed on programs for students with mechanical, technical, and computational skills.

However a given school defines its indigenous *talent pool,* it will have to recognize degrees of difference within that pool. Therefore, static *talent pools* should be avoided; static pools tend to become caste systems. Finality can be avoided by the use of adjectives such as *potential* to refer to candidates.

Talent development programs should allow participation of well-motivated candidates, who, for technical reasons, might otherwise be unselected. The concept of *trial periods* might be utilized allowing participation of any student, who after guided self-examinations, believes he belongs in a given program. Continual *talent searches* should be undertaken to screen the largest number of prospective candidates in programs.

Talent discovery and development programs should distinguish among *potentialities, achievement,* and *productivity.* Programs of *selection* ordinarily find and describe *potentialities; identification* alone may bear little relationship to *achievement* or *productivity.* This fact is often disconcerting to teachers who may note wide discrepancies between *psychological diagnosis* of giftedness and actual *classroom performance* of the child.

Achievement should be continually reassessed and indices of extracurricular activities included in the evaluation of a student's overall performance.

Productivity should be differentiated from mere duplicative achievement. Teachers should recognize and reward true departures, creations, inventions, and new interpretations by their students.

No researcher has systematically ruled out the existence of a general intelligence factor which still appears to be the best single predictor for academic promise, higher level professional attainment, and intellectual productivity later in life. Therefore, we will speak of gifted students in this book as being those who score above criterion scores on tests of mental ability.

Occasionally an individual is found who possesses singular exceptional aptitudes without accompanying high general intelligence. Therefore, we will recommend that programs of talent development, while concerned primarily with the academically gifted, should include supplemental programs for unique talents.

There are areas of human performance for which no standardized tests exist. Some of these talents display themselves in such a way as to be unmistakable. For example, the child possessing great musical or artistic skill will generally display such ability through his actual behavior if given an opportunity. Therefore, schools must not rely upon standardized testing devices exclusively as a basis for including students into talent development programs. Traditional methods of observation such as the *audition* along with objective observation in the classroom should uncover many talented children otherwise missed by tests alone.

Since the real goal of teachers is the individual development of each student, the maintaining of *case study records*, with unique entries and explanations for each student, is basic to any program of talent development.

The main emphasis of any program is to develop the talent to its fullest potentiality. The child must become aware of the rewards and responsibilities of talent and be guided toward useful, productive, satisfying, and creative tasks.

Do not expect all gifted children to be universally talented. Also, a given child's maturity may be eccentric with certain aptitudes and skills appearing early, while others emerge much later in his development. Therefore, periodic reevaluation is essential.

Ultimate individual worth, both to one's self and to society, is not determined by the mere possession of raw gifts. Talent must be treated as a personal asset, in a matter-of-fact way, without creating artificial hierarchies among students based upon certain talents which teachers may happen to admire. In an advanced civilization, multiplicity of talent should be encouraged by finding outlets for all of the disparate kinds of gifts children possess. Our tendency to search for *the* program which will suit all talented pupils must be checked. As these students are multivaried and complex, so our programs must be capable of customized accommodation to each student.

Many of the glib generalities we have evolved in education to describe normal children simply do not help us to understand gifted children. Unfortunate results might ensue if a teacher enforced daily drill with a musical instrument for *any* child; but, there is no other proven way to teach the child motivated and talented enough to become a great musician.

It is clear that we can accept no simple-minded definition for talented children. We will need to deal in complex terms when discussing identification or educational programming for the talented. We will speak of differential diagnosis because insofar as possible the program for a complex, multitalented child must be individualized.

Many talents overlap; intellectually gifted students will tend to possess many socially valued capabilities. But, the overlap is not certain. Moreover, certain capabilities, such as kinesthetic or manipulative gifts, may be comparatively less related to general intelligence. Hence, there is need to consider these talents separately. Every ability could represent a separate category for education program development. The academic, creative, and psychosocial categories will tend to overlap. The performing arts, athletic, mechanical, and manipulative gifts may include a large proportion of students with specialized aptitudes not necessarily well correlated with general intelligence.

Chapter 3

IDENTIFYING THE GIFTED

SINCE the academically and creatively gifted encompass the great majority of persons who reach levels of meaningful productivity, we will concentrate upon the characteristics of these groups. Scientific selection procedures for the psychosocially gifted or the performing artist are not well established. In order to identify these groups, we must retain such traditional approaches as the audition, objective observation, and the use of expert judgment. Specialized talent, such as mechanical ability or manual skill, can be easily diagnosed through standard testing procedures. In order to ultimately identify all forms and levels of talent in a given population, the school must establish differential screening procedures which allow for candidate nominations from

1. child guidance and testing centers;
2. experts, specialists, professionals in the community;
3. classroom teachers, consultants, and administrators;
4. parents;
5. self-referral by students;
6. work settings in business and industry; and
7. formal screening programs (e.g. annual test batteries, teacher ratings, peer referrals by sociograms).

At the basis of sound identification procedures is the building of intensive case study forms. Useful case study data may be divided into the following data categories:

1. *Developmental Information*
    Home and family background, activities
    Health and physical audition
    Social-emotional maturity
    Diversity of interest, involvement and productivity
    Record of manifest talents
    Awards, competitions, honors
2. *Psychometric and Academic Data*
    Summary of grades, ratings, performance
    Academic achievement tests and exams—all areas
    Mental ability scores IQ
    Survey of aptitudes, skills
    Interest, value inventories
    Assessment of personality functioning

3. *Self-Inventory*
    Aspirations, ambitions, plans
    Doubts, inhibitions, anxieties
    Expressions of self-understanding, insight
    Inventory of acknowledged educational needs
4. *Professional Prognostications*
    Summary of anecdotal records
    Recommendations for special program placement
    Warnings for anticipated developmental problems, conflicts
    Projections of expected training educational needs
    Predictions from community experts (e.g. music teachers)

Case study data should include diagnostic descriptions of relative weaknesses as well as strengths. Many programs for the gifted fail to include remedial aspects, thereby restricting enrollment to high scholastic achievers only. Contributions to the case study record should be obtained from teachers, psychologists, parents, specialists working with the child in the community as well as the candidate himself. It is illuminating to have several parties rate similar characteristics of the same candidate in order to obtain different viewpoints. In this manner, explanations for apparent problems may be a by-product. For example, high academic ratings by teacher and pupil accompanied by low ratings by parents may reveal overbearing parental attitudes which may help to explain the pupil's social-emotional handicaps.

Since the primary goal of identification procedures ought to be the selection of the widest possible range of gifted candidates, it follows that selection committees ought to be composed of a variety of professional and talented members. General identification committees in schools certainly should include teachers from various subject disciplines, administrators, school psychologists, and specific community experts as indicated. Most professional educators in the school ought to be in contact with the talent selection committee at some time since (1) nominations should be openly competitive, (2) screening procedures should be circulated to all teachers during annual survey periods, and 3) in-service training for diagnosis and talent development should be open to all teachers.

The composition of a school's talent selection committee might follow the outline for "the classification of talent" presented in the last chapter and include a general committee to certify academic and creative potential candidates and special subcommittees for certification of specific talent potentials: a leadership committee, athletic committee, crafts and manipulative skills committee, business and industrial committee, and a performing arts committee.

Identification committees perform five main functions: (1) they describe the characteristics sought in prospective candidates in behavioral terms, (2) they design nomination forms and case study folders, (3) they supervise the collection of all available data and prescribe additional tests and examinations, (4) they review each case and certify a candidate's *potential* for participation in a special sequence of educational programs, and (5) they continue to collect evaluative data and change the candidate's program as indicated.

Some of the problems which inhibit talent selection programs might be avoided if educators planned to disseminate community information well in advance of program inception. The public is not as acquainted with the varied nature of talent, as they are about the handicapped. Resentment for talent development programs could be reduced by intensive public information promotions. A related problem is that of sharing academic and psychometric data with parents and students. Schools have an obligation to translate test findings in meaningful terms for parents and students. In general, all the information discussed in this chapter should be shared with parents.

SCREENING OUT THE GIFTED

We have accumulated considerable information describing the characteristics and behavior of intelligent children in the classroom. In a congenial educational setting, gifted children are likely to be

curious;
interested in words and ideas;
manifest a keen sense of humor;
display the ability to make logical associations;
demonstrate an ability to do original research; and
display considerable drive to accomplish their goals.

They may, at times, display characteristics that teachers deem to be undesirable. They are particularly prone to displease teachers when they are placed in a setting calling for repetitious or superficial activity. For example, a teacher may call upon the pupil to repeat rote memory exercises already well established and understood by the pupil. In such a circumstance, the child may become restless, inattentive, disinterested, and unmotivated. He may react more aggressively. He may conjure up ideas of his own to occupy the time he has gained by ignoring the assignment. In the earlier years of childhood, he may be outspoken and critical of other classmates and the teacher. As he develops independent attitudes, he may inadvertently alienate himself from his classmates and his teacher who expect more conforming behavior.

It is possible for teachers to accurately rate the intellectual functioning, interest patterns, physical development, social development, and emotional development of gifted children by utilizing rating techniques along with adequately defined categories. For example, a 5-point rating scale ranging from "Little if any" through "Outstanding" could be used to rate a given youngster's growth as follows: *1.* Little if any; *2.* Below average; *3.* Average; *4.* Above average; and *5.* Outstanding. Almost any human characteristic could be rated on such a scale providing definitions are given, comparison groups are described, and teachers are adequately trained in rating techniques.

The characteristics listed below have been used by teachers to rate nominees for talent development programs:[1]

1. *Knowledge and skills:* possesses a comfortable knowledge of basic skills and factual information and uses these skills appropriately for the solving of problems.

2. *Concentration:* is not easily distracted; can focus his attention on a problem for sufficient periods of time to reach solutions.

3. *Enjoyment of school:* enjoys academic pursuits and assignments.

4. *Persistence:* has desire to follow through on assigned work; completion of a work task becomes an important goal.

5. *Responsiveness:* is easily motivated; responds positively to adult suggestions and questions.

6. *Intellectual curiosity:* gains satisfaction through the process of answering questions himself; generates questions on his own.

7. *Response to challenge:* is not frustrated by moderate challenge; on the contrary, enjoys the challenge of more difficult problems, assignments, and issues.

8. *Perceptiveness:* is alert and observant beyond his years; is aware of the forces and stimulations that cause him to respond.

9. *Verbal facility:* uses many words easily and accurately; is interested in word derivation; makes unusual but logical and coherent verbal associations.

10. *Ideational volubility:* produces many rather than few ideas; does not become bogged down in fruitless ideas; can easily adapt or revert to newer, more powerful concepts.

11. *Ability to focus on a problem:* does not allow his personal biases to obscure problems; is able to view a problem from the point of view of other persons or disciplines.

12. *Originality:* uses novel or unique methods for the solving of problems; continually recombines old ideas in new ways; produces works of unusual quality.

---

[1] This list of characteristics adapted from *California Project Talent Case Study, 1964,* developed by author and staff through support of Cooperative Research Project, No. D-072 (Contract OE-10-109).

13. *Imagination:* thinks on his own; produces new patterns of mental images and reports these; relates his images to reality rather than fantasy.

14. *Ability to reason:* tends to expand concepts that are given to him into broader relationships; perceives pieces of data given to him in relationship to the whole of which they are a part; is eminently logical.

15. *Ability to apply scientific methodologies:* can define problems, formulate hypotheses, test ideas, and arrive at valid conclusions.

16. *Independence in thought and action:* inclined to follow his own ideas and organize appropriate activities accordingly; more direct thought and action follows; he evaluates results.

17. *Appreciation for different values:* enjoys and is responsive to various impressions including aesthetic, economic, scientific, religious and social experiences; is tolerant of differential value orientations in others.

18. *Universal interest patterns:* shows interest in participating in variour studies; interest patterns may include art, dramatics, handwriting, spelling, reading, written expression, mathematics, music, physical activities, science, and social studies.

19. *Physical development:* is on a par with or ahead of other children in such functions as coordination, timing, agility, and the ability to satisfactorily participate in organized games; has sufficient resources of vigor for carrying on most physical activities.

20. *Popularity and acceptance by others:* in spite of his precociousness, others enjoy his company; he relates well to others and they mutually seek one another out for play.

21. *Social status:* assumes roles of leadership; is comfortable with power or status.

22. *Social concern:* is willing to work with others cooperatively; is sensitive to the needs and feelings of others; properly observes the rules of social conduct; enjoys serving others.

23. *Sense of well-being:* appears self-confident, happy and comfortable in most situations; displays ability to laugh at himself, if necessary, indicating a keen sense of humor; problems do not cause anxiety and worry but are faced and solved as they occur.

24. *Relationships with adults:* is capable of communicating with adults such as teachers and parents; usually relaxed and communicative in the presence of adults.

25. *Emotional stability and control:* expresses his feelings with moderation and appropriateness; is capable of adjusting to daily changes without emotional outbursts or tantrum activity.

26. *Acceptance of others and self:* comprehends the role of other people in his life; is able to view himself in terms of his limitations; does not excuse, but tends to be tolerant of shortcomings in himself and others.

27. *Views conformity in a social context:* while his behavior tends to be independently motivated, he is nonetheless sensitive to the needs of others; appropriate behavior is usually the expectation, but occasional nonconformity is well justified.

No inventory of characteristics would be complete without some assessment of the activities that the home provides for the child which, in turn, affect the child's cultural growth patterns. What kinds of trips do the family plan? Do these trips include visits to museums, galleries, plays, concerts, and other cultural pursuits? To what extent does the bright child contribute recommendations for family activity and an evaluation of this activity? What supplemental materials such as books, records, magazines, and pictures are available in the home for the child's scrutiny and use? Does the child require or ask for special lessons, training, tutoring, or other learning opportunities outside of the school? To what extent are the parents aware of the child's hobbies and special interests? Are sufficient funds set aside for the purchase of special materials and supplies for the development of such hobbies? Is the child given an opportunity to participate in truly creative activities in the home, such as helping with the redesign of the interior decor of the home or planning for the utilization of unused floor space for hobby activity?

No definitive summary of characteristics can possibly encompass the wide range of attributes possessed by gifted children; but perhaps the "expanded understanding of characteristics of gifted children" presented in the film *Understanding the Gifted* (produced by Churchill Films) comes close when it is stated, "Gifted children" generally display the following characteristics:

> ability to perceive and identify the significant;
> interest and pleasure in intellectual pursuits;
> desire to search for truth and apply concepts;
> power to logic, ability to develop systems;
> high level of retention;
> high vocabulary level; facility in verbal expression;
> intellectual curiosity;
> critical ability;
> persistent, long-ranging interests;
> need for freedom and individuality in study; and
> high energy, intense application, power of concentration.

IDENTIFICATION OF THE CREATIVELY GIFTED

"Creativity," notes Guilford, "is a magic word. . . . It catches immediate attention. . . . The term is a kind of catchall label, too loosely employed; only when we break it down into its several manageable implications are

TABLE 10

STRUCTURE OF INTELLECT SHOWING INTELLECTUAL OPERATIONS ADOPTED
FROM GUILFORD

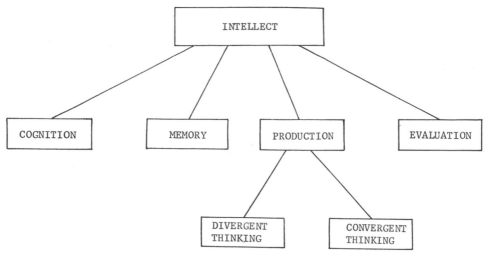

we able to do much—creatively—about it."[2] Table 10 represents a simple
general scheme of the structure of the intellect as described by Guilford.

Table 11, adopted from Frank Williams' work with creative teachers,
summarizes the way in which creative intellectual factors such as ideational
fluency can be integrated into an overall classification of higher mental
processes. The creative abilities can be largely subsumed under the higher
level mental operations of "divergent thinking" and "evaluative ability."

Others have attempted to differentiate among the various levels of creative mental activity. For example, Taylor has attempted to distinguish
among the various levels of creativity by postulating the following categories of creative activities:

Expressive creativity—independent expression in which skills, originality, and quality are relatively unimportant.

Productive creativity—in which the individual produces intellectual
products by way of mastery over some portion of the environment.

Inventive creativity—involving ingenuity in visualizing new uses for
old parts where no new basic idea is involved.

Innovative creativity—involving significant alterations in the basic foundations of the principles of a theory or situation in which the individual
needs to possess and apply highly developed abstract skills of concep-
tualization.

Emergentive creativity—ability to absorb the experiences which are

[2] Guilford, J.P.: Creative thinking and problem solving. *CTA Journal,* 60:(No. 1):8-13,
Jan. 1964.

TABLE 11

CREATIVE ACTIVITIES CLASSIFIED INTO THE HIGHER MENTAL PROCESSES[3]

I. *Cognitive Ability:* discovery, recognition, comprehension, awareness, understanding.
   Activities that: generate curiosity, provide rediscovery, require comprehension, cause awareness.

II. *Memory:* storage and retention of knowledge—what has been cognized; ability to recall information when needed.

III. *Convergent Thinking:* redefinition, transformations, recognized best or conventional solution, improvizations.
   Activities that: transform, redefine, improvise. Ability to pick best of choice of several alternatives.

IV. *Divergent Thinking:* scanning stored information, searching for many possible solutions, thinking in different directions, ability to go off in new and untested directions, deferred judgment.
   A. Fluency: quantitative—emphasize rate within classes.
      1. Ideational fluency—generation of a quantity of IDEAS, words, titles, responses, phrases, sentences, uses, consequences, productions (drawings, pictures, designs, or other sense stimuli).
      2. Associational fluency—completion of relationships—production of relations; generation of synonyms, analogies, similarities, problems of likeness.
      3. Expressional fluency—new ideas to fit a system or structure organization into systems or logical theories; sentences, verbal ideas, question responses.
   B. Flexibility: quantitative—variety.
      1. Spontaneous flexibility—variance of kinds of responses into classes; number of considerations of properties, attributes, or inherent characteristics of problem or product; number of shifts of category responses, versatility.
      2. Adaptive flexibility—number of detours, freedom to make changes, number of approaches or strategies used in seeking solutions; number of changes of interpretations, changes in direction of thinking.
   C. Originality: qualitative—unusual, remote, clever, uncommon, infrequent, remote associations. verbal, figural, symbolic transformations as uncommon objective unusualness—statistically infrequent—subjective choice as clever, far-fetched, novel, different from standard or norm.
   D. Elaboration: production of detailed steps, variety of implications and consequences; quantitative measure.

V. *Evaluative Ability:* goodness, suitability, adequacy, determination of fit, ability to determine if produced solution fits the problem (search model).
   Activities that: produce conceptual foresight, raise pertinent questions, cause sensitiveness to problems, require curiosity, noticing defects or changes, seek improvements to social customs, institutions, behavior, noting defects in objects or ideas, evaluating implications, observations of imperfections or inadequacies, constructive discontent, flexibility of critical-mindedness, purposeful judgment.
(Memory, item II, is normally operable in all individuals; all other abilities listed are those used by all *creative* individuals.)

commonly provided by the environment and from these conventional experiences to produce something entirely new.[4]

Unfortunately, research attempts to replicate, validate, or isolate such variables as fluency or elaboration have met with little tangible success. For example, Bereiter attempted to study verbal and ideational fluency by administering a battery of eighteen reference tests involving such factors as verbal fluency to a large sample of academically superior tenth grade

---

[3] Taken from Williams, Frank: *The Search for the Creative Teacher. CTA Journal,* 60, (No. 1):14-16, June 1964.

[4] Taylor, Calvin: The creative individual: A new portrait in giftedness. *Educational Leadership,* Act. 1960, pp. 7-11.

students.[5] Tenth grade girls emerged with replicable reference factors or verbal fluency, word fluency, associational fluency, and expressional fluency. However, for the boys, only a general verbal fluency factor appeared. Moreover, even among the girls, "The verbal factors obtained . . . suggested certain simplifications in the definition of previously identified factors. The factors obtained in the area of nonverbal ideational fluency abilities indicated that such a domain of fluency abilities does exist and it is accessible to measurement; but the important dimensions of that domain did not appear to have been isolated."

Other researchers have attempted to link Guilford's description of the intellectual functions to known qualities of the human intellect. The results have been discouraging. For example, Harootunian and Tate attempted to "estimate the importance of problem recognition, word fluency, ideational fluency, closure, judgment, test intelligence, and reading ability in problem solving."[6] They found that "The most important of the seven predictor variables were reading, test intelligence, judgment and problem recognition." Such variables as "closure, word fluency, and ideational fluency made little independent contribution to the variance of the criterion." It was interesting to note that, when the influence of the other variables were statistically controlled, the correlation of ideational fluency with problem solving was negative.

In another research study by Piers and others, "Seven of Guilford's creativity tests . . . were administered to 114 seventh and eighth grade students of above average intelligence and school achievement, and the results were compared with teacher ratings of their students' creativity. . . ."[7] It was found that tests of originality correlated more highly with IQ and with teacher ratings than did tests of ideational fluency. Teacher ratings of creativity proved to be an inconsistent criterion due to the vagueness of the concept of creativity.

Thus, we would do well to move slowly before adopting newer concepts of the nature of the human intellect. As indicated by current research, new conceptions of the human intellect either correlate so highly with our existing notions of general intelligence, achievement, and reading capability as to be indistinguishable or do not correlate in any meaningful fashion with manifest intellectual productivity.

Recent research findings are complicated by the fact that the researchers use criterion groups of subjects who are all high in mental ability to start

---

[5] Bereiter, C.E.: Verbal and ideational fluency in superior tenth grade students. *J Educ Psychol,* Dec. 1960.

[6] Harootunian and Tate: The relationship of certain selected variable to problem solving ability. *J Educ Psychol,* Dec. 1960.

[7] Piers, E., *et al.:* The identification of creativity in adolescents. *J Educ Psychol,* Dec. 1960.

with. Ordinarily, we think of correlating samples of individuals which are randomly selected. Hence, we would expect the correlations to be low or meaningless. Many of the researchers, in dealing with groups which are intellectually superior to begin with, are inferring that the relationship between creativity and intelligence can be assumed.

The studies of Getzels and Jackson seemed to demonstrate clear distinctions between groups of students who were in the upper 20 percent in measured intelligence but in the lower 80 percent in measured creativity as compared with students who were in the upper 20 percent in measured creative ability but in the lower 80 percent in measured intelligence.[8] They reported that these two groups were equivalent in achievement, indicating that whatever creativity is, it must have contributed to manifest capability.

However, closer scrutiny indicates that both groups of students were clearly superior in both intelligence and achievement when compared with the general population from which they were taken. Other researchers have indicated clear lineal relationships between traditional measures of achievement and intelligence and the newer notions of creativity. Anderson has postulated an interesting "ability-radiant theory" which states that "IQ could be expected to have an effect on academic achievement up to a certain threshold IQ level, where further increases in IQ would have no further effect on achievement, but where creativity would begin to have an effect."[9]

Cicirelli tended to support the conclusion that the relationship between creativity and achievement "was weaker than some previous studies suggested...."[10] However, "no maximum IQ thresholds were found for reading and arithmetic achievement . . . there was some evidence for a maximum IQ threshold at the IQ level 130-139 for language achievement." Moreover, he found that the relationships among IQ, achievement and creativity tended to be additive and lineal instead of interactional or involving clear-cut thresholds.

Thus far, we have explored the nature of creative giftedness as if it were exclusively an intellectual characteristic. Perhaps creativity is a composite characteristic of personality involving a combination of unique attitudes, values, and motivational patterns.

Barron has conducted extensive studies of the personality characteristics

---

[8] Getzels, J.W., and Jackson, P.W.: *Creativity and Intelligence: Explorations With Gifted Students.* New York, Wiley, 1962, p. 242.

[9] Anderson, J.E.: The nature of abilities. Taken from Torrance, E.P. (Ed.): *Talent in Education.* Minneapolis, U. of Minn., 1960, pp. 9-31.

[10] Cicirelli, Victor G.: Form of the relationship between creativity, IQ and academic achievement. *J Educ Psychol,* 56(No. 6):303-308, Dec. 1965.

of creative individuals who have actually produced products others have deemed to be creative.[11] Barron has suggested a simple dichotomy between "complex and simple" persons which may enable us to distinguish the creatively productive from the unproductive individual:

The complex person
1. is artistic,
2. has unconventional friends,
3. occasionally is visited by an impractical idea . . .
4. would rather be creative and neurotic than normal and ordinary,
5. is politically somewhat radical and can be militantly opposed to such occurrences as racial prejudice,
6. is aware of present imperfections and
7. welcomes and has faith in future (as opposed to past or present) developments.

In stark contrast, the simple person
1. does not like modern art,
2. particularly values kindness and generosity (including) feelings that are properly filial in sentiment . . .
3. feels that a citizen should support his country, right or wrong, and that disobedience to the government is never justified . . . prefers a team effort to individual competition,
4. prefers symmetry to asymmetry . . . prefers straightforward reasoning to metaphors in the search for analogies,
5. has clear-cut plans for the future (and appears to look for simplicity in ideas as he accumulates more information) . . . and,
6. (tends to avoid thinking about problems or situations which would worry him) . . .[12]

Barron compared the highest scores on composite indices of originality with the lowest scorers on these same measurements. Those with high originality

1. were verbally fluent, conversationally facile;
2. had a high degree of intellect;
3. communicated ideas clearly and effectively;
4. cathected intellectual activity;
5. were effective leaders;
6. were persuasive people;
7. were concerned with philosophical problems in the meaning of life; and
8. tended to take an ascendant role in their relationships with others.

Low scorers on composite measures of originality
1. were conforming, tending to do that which was prescribed;

[11] Barron, Frank: *Creativity and Psychological Health.* New York, Van Norstrans, 1963.
[12] *Ibid.,* p. 196.

    2. were stereotyped and unoriginal in their approach to the solution of problems;

    3. had narrow ranges of interests;

    4. did not become involved in things and events;

    5. lacked social poise and presence;

    6. were unaware of their social stimulus values;

    7. were permissive and compliant to authority;

    8. lacked confidence in self;

    9. were rigid and inflexible; and

    10. lacked insight into their own motives and were unable to make decisions.

Barron also found that professional raters tended to use adjectives such as "clever, imaginative, poised, resourceful, reflective, enterprising, energetic, determined, logical, rational, shrewd, mature, versatile, efficient, organized, and fair-minded" to refer to high scorers on measures of originality. In contrast, low scores on measurements of originality were rated as being "dull, commonplace, simple, slow, apathetic, rigid, unassuming, and conventional."[13]

MacKinnon has indicated that creative potentiality may be a characteristic which can be understood only by comprehensive study of the total personality.[14] Generalizing from MacKinnon's writings and personal interviews with him, we might summarize the nature of creative individuals as follows:

1. *Unique Characteristics of the Creative Person*

    He is intelligent.

    He is effective in making applications; he possesses cognitive flexibility.

    His responses are original and the quantity of his responses are positively related to their quality.

    He is independent in thought and action.

    He is open to experience which is felt from within or is perceived as part of the outer world although he leans toward the perceptive attitude, integrating his inner feelings into a synthesis with what he observes in the outer world.

    He has an intuitive nature.

    He possesses strong theoretical and aesthetic values.

    He has a sense of destiny; he appears to know who he is, he has identity, and he seems to know what universal processes he is involved in.

---

[13] *Ibid.*, p. 218.

[14] Read for instance: MacKinnin, Donald W.: Personality and the realization of creative potential. *Amer Psychol,* 20 (No. 4): April 1965.

2. *Unique Characteristics of Creativeness Itself*

It is a novel response, fresh and distinctive.

It tends to be adapted to reality and therefore tends to solve pending problems and explain away contradictions.

It generally involves elaboration toward the total development and explanation of a concept.

It is a beautiful response with definite feelings of an aesthetic nature involved.

3. *Process of Creativity*

There is a period of preparation during which the creator poses problems to himself.

This is followed by a period of concentrated effort in which the individual displays tension, but tension which helps him release the energy necessary to produce the effort with which he can solve the problem.

This energetic period is followed, paradoxically, by a period of seeming withdrawal from the problem which might be termed "incubation." Actual escape from the problem may occur during this period with various kinds of diversions monopolizing the attention and time of the individual. It may be that during this period of incubation unconscious mental and motivational processes are at work.

Suddenly, a period of unusually vivid insight occurs.

This period is accompanied by emotions of elation. Rapid thinking occurs during this period and a high energy level is regained.

A final period of creativity culminates with verification and elaboration upon the insights discovered and developed. Usually, practical applications are suggested at this stage.

4. *Interesting or Unusual Notes Concerning the Personal Lives of Creative individuals*

Their families tend to move more often than those of other families. Among groups of architects and scientists studied, for example, families were found to be living abroad more often than we would commonly expect.

Personal family life allowed more freedom of behavior for the growing creative child than is customarily found in other families. This led to life styles on the part of creative individuals which were independent and exploratory as opposed to conforming and safe styles of living.

Creative individuals tend to report that their families did not pressure them to make professional choices. Apparently, the were allowed considerable freedom in choosing their own intellectual as well as vocational outlets.

Creative individuals tended to receive strong ethical teachings from their family and friends even though, interestingly, two-thirds or more of the creative individuals studied by MacKinnon report that they are "not religious."

Creative individuals tend to identify with both of their parents with equal intensity or they may choose father or the mother with no particular pattern. This identification with a parent must be contrasted with the tendency in our society to identify with the mother.[15]

GENERAL IDENTIFICATION PROCEDURES

Recent developments in the education of talented pupils are calling for close cooperation between guidance personnel and curriculum consultants. We have come to realize that no single group of educators can function autonomously. The developers of curriculum must have knowledge concerning the nature of the learner, just as the academic counselor must have intimate knowledge concerning all aspects of the curriculum. In order to deal effectively with the differential needs of the gifted pupil, we should be able to provide the differential means and plans for educational programming.

In a program that calls for the identification of a small percent of the population, the diagnostic and evaluative procedures must be precise, reliable, and sophisticated. As many as half of the cases of "giftedness" are not clear-cut. Contradictory evidence must be sifted and properly evaluated by professional workers before a stable judgment and diagnosis can be made. The process of identifying gifted pupils is complex and involves most of the crucial events elaborated upon below.

Guidance, curriculum, and administration personnel must agree upon the criteria to be used in selection, as well as the motives of the program and goals to be attained. A philosophy of education must be developed which, by its nature, will describe the type of learner sought for and the kinds of experiences he will be exposed to.

Typically, the teacher or school principal nominates the pupils. The teacher is usually provided with a list of criteria and attempts to match appropriate candidates with these selection criteria. Many educators find that the successful nomination plan developed by Terman is still useful.

After a group of nominees has been submitted, a guidance worker must screen those from a more critical and psychologically oriented viewpoint. From the data submitted on a thorough nomination form, the consultant can usually eliminate those candidates who do not specifically match up with the criteria developed in the philosophy of a given school district.

An adequate examination includes the development of a thorough and

---

[15] This summary is based upon conversations with MacKinnon held during 1965.

descriptive case study. The examination and case study processes should yield the following kinds of personal data:

1. *Academic history.* An analysis of grades, teacher ratings, cumulative records, and extracurricula activities needs to be made.

2. *Achievement.* A complete survey of the pupil's test records needs to be assessed. Of particular importance are the pupil's reading ability, which should be several grades in advance of his peer group, and his skill in the language arts and mathematical areas.

3. *Intelligence.* It has been found useful to describe specific intellectual levels of "giftedness." Most school districts would define a gifted child as one with a total intelligence quotient of 130 or above.

4. *Interests.* Teacher ratings, pupil self-ratings, and standardized interest inventories should be surveyed. Unfortunately, many of the interest assessment devices currently used lack adequate sophistication in discriminating among the infinitely variable maturity levels of interest. The interests of the talented child are typically precise within a particular interest category and yet diverse in the sense that the gifted pupil may have a much wider universe of interests.

5. *Personality Assessment.* By utilizing interviews, standardized tests, and in some cases projective techniques, it is possible to develop a description of the pupil's functional personality as well as his potentialities. Of particular importance is the study of any personality characteristics which might obviate the pupil's participation in a given kind of program. For example, it is conceivable that an otherwise well-qualified pupil may possess serious inhibitions and doubts about himself which would obviate his participation in an acceleration program. Social maturity and awareness are also important factors to be considered.

6. *Counseling.* Following the examination of the pupil, some counseling is usually needed. The pupil should have developed questions concerning the proposed program he is to participate in, as well as his adequacy. The pupil's parents may need guidance as concerns the nature of the program proposed for the pupil or a discussion of any special problems the pupil may have or anticipate. The parent should be intimately involved in the entire case study process. Any disagreements should be resolved by an objective study of the evidence collected. Before a pupil is assigned to a given program, the pupil's nominating teacher, an administrator, a guidance consultant, and the pupil's parents should discuss the data which have been collected and decide whether or not this pupil would benefit from any of the programs the district offers. Also, they must decide which kinds of evaluation follow-up and special educational implementations are needed in the given case.

7. *Placement.* Following his examination, case study, and certification,

the pupil needs to be placed in a program or programs best suited to meet his individual academic requirements. The timing of his placement may be crucial to the stimulation and motivation of the pupil. Any placement should be considered tentative, and periodical follow-up should be made concerning his progress. The certification committee cannot consider its job complete when it has placed the pupil in a program. An extensive follow-up and evaluation process should be described and implemented during the following months. This follow-up process typically utilizes attitude scales, indexes of satisfaction, objective tests, and other measurements of the pupil's growth in academic proficiency and other talents.

8. *Evaluation.* In a document entitled *The School Psychologist and the Education of Gifted Children,* the Gifted Child Committee of the California Association of School Psychologists has stated, "The school psychologist has a responsibility to guard against repeated application of group tests directed toward the qualification of as many children as possible. A line must be drawn between legitimate evaluation and reevaluation on the one hand and exploitation on the other. Planning for a gifted child must be based upon accurate information regarding exceptional educational needs insofar as possible. In some instances, the psychologist should discourage as well as encourage placement of a mentally gifted minor in a specific program." Of course, no amount of prescribing can instill the ethical spirit necessary for the complete success of an academic program for the gifted. The process of identification is complex and expensive. Minimally, the process of identification needs to include well thought-out nomination and screening procedures, thorough examination techniques, detailed case study, and the availability of expert counseling for parents, pupils, and others.

As with all new classifications, definitions may be vague, evaluation possibilities may be too new to be practical or useful, and competing categories may tend to obscure the original intentions of the program. The category of "mental giftedness" is artificial because it is arbitrary; the point at which you cut off the subpopulation is open to much difference of opinion. Therefore, flexibility in diagnosis and placement should be the guiding principle of identification.

The Process of Identification

Identification must be a "process" rather than an "act." It is not static. Literally, it is never completed. Its development must be punctuated by frequent and periodic data-gathering situations. As these new data feed back into the general case study of a pupil, modifications must be introduced into the pupil's program. Since the gifted pupil is, by definition, significantly deviant from the general population in some if not all intellectual categories, he must be supplied with an educational program uniquely designed to complement his intellectual differences.

Typically, the gifted can function faster and more accurately than others. This indicates the need for more quantity and diversity of curriculum materials. Also, they tend to think in ways qualitatively different from their normal age peers. For example, whereas normal primary children typically employ trial-and-error methods, this child will already be applying various methodologies for problem solving. Approaches to problem solving utilizing sophisticated scientific methodology, sampling techniques, various logistic approaches, and the use of mathematical logic would actually be more "practical" for his use in the early grades. The process of identification becomes integral with the operation of program planning and curriculum construction. The case study should include specific recommendations for curriculum planning.

Purposes for Identification and Case Study

Every school district will need to generate definitions, rationales, and philosophies of education which are consistent with the social forces in their particular communities. The all-encompassing purpose for identification of a select group will need to stem from a genuine desire to meet disparate individual needs with diverse and differentiated educational programming.

The practical purposes for establishing and conducting identification procedures include the following:

1. *Certification.* A committee of professional workers, having been provided with operational criteria, will need to certify the fact that certain individuals conform to these criteria and are bona fide candidates. This certification, unfortunately, has a certain finality built into it. Therefore, such certification must be based upon accurate, extensive, and varied data.

2. *Placement.* Identification should lead to appropriate placement of the individual into new program patterns or sequences theoretically better suited to his unique characteristics. Such placement must be justified by the nature of the case history gathered and the prognosis made. For example, placement into an acceleration-type program must be justified by the presentation of unambiguous data indicating that the child is emotionally stable, socially acceptable to older groups, physically sound and superior as well as being intellectually precocious.

3. *Anticipation of Problems.* During the identification, problems as well as potential difficulties must be accurately anticipated. Of particular importance is the study of the child's social and cultural milieu. Do his

parents plan realistically for his future? Do his parents or his siblings misunderstand, envy, or in any way disparage his capabilities? Would his placement into a "prestige" program place him in an untenable position with his friends?

4. *Prognosis for Success.* Many program alternatives must be considered in every case. Tentative estimates of success should be entertained about every alternative even though the individual is placed in only one of the alternative programs. For example, most broad program alternatives could be divided into the following four categories: (a) advanced placement of some sort, (b) special grouping or segregation, (c) special counseling or instruction outside of the regular school day, or (d) enriched activities in the regular classroom. A differential prognosis based upon the available data might be made for each of these four alternatives. Variables which mitigate against special grouping or advanced placement would need to be specified. Contrariwise, data which would tend to support these alternatives should be clearly postulated.

5. *Systematic Follow-up and Evaluation.* A main purpose of the case study aspect of the identification process should be to continue to collect data on a systematic and periodic basis in order to provide feedback for program modification and a basis for pupil progress evaluation. Such data provide for individual pupil evaluation and collectively form the basis for total program evaluation.

Outline for the Identification Process

Ideally, the identification process should begin in kindergarten and continue the entire school career. A breaking point in this process occurs at the time of certification. Prior to certification, the identification process tends to be historical. Data are collected concerning the individual's development and a thorough assessment is made of his various potentialities with particular focus upon his mental abilities. Subsequent to certification, the identification process becomes more or less synonymous with the accumulation and use of a case study.

The first time a pupil is considered for possible certification and program placement, the following steps might be followed:

Step 1. Survey-Screening

Some form of group device such as a mental ability test might be used to select individuals who score in a significantly deviant fashion. Candidates who do not score can be easily eliminated from further consideration on an efficient and logical basis, or teachers might be asked to determine the top two or three candidates in each room: children leading others; pupils who excel in academic work, etc.

Step 2. Nomination

Subsequent to the screening procedure, a list of possible nominess becomes available. From this list of potential nominees, principals, teachers, and others may attempt to match candidates with appropriate selection criteria provided by their school district and based upon the education philosophy of the district. Nomination forms can be designed to include definitions and criteria for selection. In a sense, the nomination forms become the actual identification instruments since they will call upon the person who nominates to supply valid criteria as justification for their nominations.

Step 3. Intensive Examination and Case History

A qualified person such as a school psychologist should assess the intellectual abilities, personality functioning, past achievement, social and emotional adjustment patterns, developmental history, and specimens of productivity of the nominee. A case study form can be designed for this purpose and includes questions pertaining to the pupil's attitudes, motivation, special skills, talents, interests, future plans, social maturity, educational background, health and development, home and family relationships, and other significant data. The case study should be designed in terms of kinds of questions we will want to answer about a student's potentiality for inclusion in various program patterns. For example, certain of the areas such as attitudes, motivation, and social maturity may be more significantly related to the problem of advanced placement.

Step 4. Certification and Placement

A committee of professionals preferably including teachers, psychologists, and administrators should study all of the data collected with a view toward placing the pupil in an appropriate program pattern. As a part of this certification, case conferences should be held with the parents in order to acquaint them with the data collected and reflect their viewpoints in the final determination. The placement procedures should not be viewed as final. This decision must be constantly subjected to revision following the collection of more information. The pupil himself should play a key role in the placement procedure. Should the pupil, for any reason, not wish to accept a given placement, his wishes should be respected.

Step 5. Periodic Follow-up

Perhaps every thirty-six months the entire case study record should be reassessed in the light of new evidence that has accumulated in it. Among the new data should appear the following: mental ability and achievement test results, general aptitude test results, indications of vocation interests, academic records of performance, anecdotal notes by teachers, discipline records, opinions and attitudinal changes of parents, and periodic self-evaluation and reappraisal by the student himself.

Evaluation of two sorts needs to occur for ultimate program success. Each pupil needs to be evaluated on a yearly basis with reference to his academic increment of growth, interest in the special program, and general development in areas other than achievement. At a group level, general increments of academic growth need to be measured and compared with those gains recorded for similar or matched groups. Also, the institution needs to weigh such intangible factors as general faculty morale, public acceptance of the program, general cultural contribution of the program, and usefulness and adaptability of techniques and materials for general curriculum development.

STRUCTURE OF THE CASE STUDY

Between the period of nomination and certification of candidates for placement into appropriate programs, a thorough case study should be gathered by school psychologists and counselors in cooperation with teachers, parents, and other persons directly involved with the education of the nominee. Three main kinds of data are collected: developmental information, psychometric and academic data, and a self-inventory from interviews with the student. When these data are gathered and analyzed, a placement committee should summarize and recommend suitable programs for the child based upon this study. Of course, certain data will be more significant for given types of gifted students than will other data.

Developmental background information should be collected by guidance workers who are familiar with the techniques of structural interviews and can comprehend and analyze multidisciplinary data. The information should be collected during structural interviews with parents and teachers. Supplementary forms may be sent to physicians and teachers, as indicated, for the collection of health data, physical descriptions of condition, and educational history.

Home and family background can be gathered during interviews with parents utilizing structural questions and checklists of activities, like the following:

> Summarize your impressions of the quality of the child's education to date. Describe ways you have supplemented the child's education in the home. State educational levels achieved by parents, occupational levels, special interests. Discuss family unit, sibling relationships, rivalries, any conflicts. Summarize early development, speech, walking, interests, reading.

Check activities family participates in or encourages (e.g. travel, concerts, museums, listening to music, instrumental, television, camping, arts and crafts, reading).

Note special talents or skills child has demonstrated in the home. Compare your educational and vocational expectancies with your knowledge of the child's aspirations and goals. List general cultural materials available for the child in the home (e.g. encyclopedia, magazines, phonograph records, library, art works).

Summarize the child's opportunities for extracurricular training. List child's significant interests, hobbies, activities. Discuss child's attitudes toward school, home, future.

Check the following items (1) (Little) to (5) (Much) to describe your child as you view him disregarding any ratings such as school grades.

The following lists may be rated independently by teachers and students in addition to parents, in order to provide comparative rating of these developmental qualities.

Psychometric and academic data should be collected by guidance workers and teachers by studying all past cumulative records and administering current tests, examinations, and ratings when the record is unclear or incomplete. At the end of this case study, the following kinds of information should be available in unambiguous form:

1. summaries of all academic grades, ratings, exam scores, and teacher anecdotal records;

	Little 1	2	Moderate 3	4	Much 5
(1) Enjoyment of school. Enjoys academic pursuits; likes school.					
(2) Persistence. Desire to follow through on work; concern with completion.					
(3) Intellectual Curiosity. Questions the common, ordinary, or the unusual; generates questions of his own.					
(4) Perceptiveness. Is perceptive, interpretive, and observant beyond his years.					
(5) Sensitivity to Problems. Is aware of problems and inconsistencies that others may not see; is ready to change existing situations and suggest improvements.					
(6) Originality. Often uses original methods of solving problems; creates products of unusual character or quality.					
(7) Aesthetic Appreciation. Enjoys and is responsive to beauty in the arts or nature.					
(8) Independence in Thought. Inclined to follow his own ideas, values.					

(9) Independence in Action. Able to initiate direct action, follow through.					
(10) Physical Ability. Coordination, timing, agility, and ability to participate in games, sports.					
(11) Physical Stamina. Available resources of energy, stamina, endurance.					
(12) Popularity. Others enjoy being with this child.					
(13) Acceptance of Others. Relates to others with genuine interest and concern.					
(14) Social Maturity. Willing to work with others, sensitive to needs and feelings of others; observes rules of social conduct.					
(15) Sense of Humor. Ability to laugh at himself; laughs easily and comfortably.					
(16) Emotional Stability. Is able to cope with normal frustrations of living; adjusts to change with minimum of difficulty.					
(17) Enthusiasm. Enters into most activities with eagerness and whole-hearted participation.					
(18) Self-Acceptance. Seems to understand and accept self; able to view self in terms of limitations.					

4. scores from all achievement, intelligence, and aptitude tests;

5. where indicated, scores from currently administered individual intelligence and other performance tests, auditions, examinations, or objective ratings;

6. descriptions of manifest skills, competencies, talents, and work habits;

7. conclusions from psychological analysis of personality functioning, interest orientations, and value patterns;

8. analysis of any developmental problems such as daydreaming, unpredictable or uncontrolled behavior, anxieties, preoccupations, or learning disabilities; and

9. descriptions of the child's creative products, inventions, other useful work outputs; specimens of actual products should become part of record.

The student self-inventory should be obtained by a guidance worker during personal counseling interviews following the collection of background and academic information. The questions asked should be similar to those put to parents during the collection of home and family background information. In addition, the following types of questions should be asked of the student.

The academic record might be summarized in a table combining indices of interest, performance, and test or grade level data as follows:

Subject Area	Interest					Performance					Level
	Little		Moderate		Much	Low		Aver.		High	of Capability
	1	2	3	4	5	1	2	3	4	5	
ACADEMIC											
Art											
Foreign Language											
Handwriting											
Mathematics											
Music											
Oral Expression											
Reading											
Science											
Social Science											
Spelling											
Written Expression											
ARTISTIC PERFORMANCE (Specify Kind)											
ATHLETIC											
Dance											
Physical Development											
Sports											
CREATIVE OUTPUT (Specify)											
DRAMATIC EXPRESSION (being in plays, acting)											

After explaining the nature of special programs, tentatively being considered for him, ask the student how he feels about the proposed placement. Help to eliminate doubts by providing objective assessments of programs proposed in terms of the student's assets.

The student should assess his strengths and predict probable future performance in more challenging settings. Expressions of inadequacy should be carefully noted.

Subject Area	Interest					Performance					Level of Capability
	Little 1	2	Moderate 3	4	Much 5	Low 1	2	Aver. 3	4	High 5	
LEADERSHIP											
Honors											
Offices, appts.											
Student Activities											
MANIPULATIVE (Construction with hands)											
Arts and Crafts											
Categorical Shop Experience (Specify)											
MECHANICAL (Work on autos, shop)											
(Specify)											
MUSICAL PERFORMANCE											
(Specify)											
PERFORMING ARTS											
Art (Specify)											
Drama											
Music (Specify)											

Total educational and vocational plans should be outlined and tested against the realities of location, means and abilities depending, of course, upon the age of the child.

Definitions for motivation, aspiration, values and related terms, should be provided. The student should estimate his own levels in these areas. Comparisons with the ratings of teachers and parents are made; discrepancies are explained through further study.

The student should inventory his habits, hobbies, cultural activities, and creative endeavors with a view toward efficient use of time. Any proposed increase in work load should be integrated into existing schedules realistically.

Typical styles of personal interaction and work habits should be discussed. Does he prefer to work alone, in groups, or with a project-oriented approach? Attention span, endurance, and relative intensity of interests should be analyzed.

The student's relationships with adults ought to be explored in some depth. Does he respect the professional status of his teachers? When critical of adults, does he offer constructive alternatives?

The student should be afforded the opportunity to speculate about ideal educational plans. How would he design the ideal school setting? What courses would he schedule his time among the many pursuits attracting his attention? What practical suggestions does he have for specific changes in the schools talent program offerings?

Talent Development Programs
CERTIFICATION AND SUMMARY FORM

Pupil's Name _____ School _____

Pupil's Age _____ (M) _____ (F) _____ Grades Completed: K 1 2 3 4 5 6 7 8 9 10 11 12

Parent _____ Siblings (number) M_____ F_____ (ages) M_____ F_

Address _____ Phone _____ Date _____

CHECK OR FILL IN ALL ITEMS THAT APPLY:

Factor	Tests or Source of Information	Scores or Ratings	Recommendation for Participation			Needs Further Study		Includ. in Case Study		Comments Reservations Data
			Yes	Undec	No	Yes	No	Yes	No	
Academic										
Grades										
Teacher Ratings										
Cum. Data										
Achievement Tests										
Reading										
Arithmetic										
Other ( )										
Total Scores										
Intelligence										
Group Test										
Indiv. Test										
Programs										
Arithmetic										
Arts and Crafts										
Drama										
Leadership										
Music										
Physical Devel.										
Reading-Lit										
Science										
Social Science										
Writing										
Other ( )										
Personality										
Interview										
Tests Used										
Other ( )										
Maturity Ratings										
Teacher Ratings										
Parent Ratings										
Objective Ratings										
Other ( )										
Other Factors										
( )										
( )										
( )										

Identified as mentally gifted: Yes____ No____ Date Certified as mentally gifted _____ I.Q._

Identified as creatively gifted: Yes____ No____ Other Talent Category _____

We certify and approve _____ for participation in the following
(pupil's name)

type(s) of special programs _____

_____   _____   _____   _____
(Teacher)   (Administrator)   (Guidance Consultant)   (Parent)

A *professional summary* should be made by a placement committee composed of teachers and guidance workers who have contributed to the case study. The summary should act as a checklist of factors to assure that all pertinent data has been collected. The summary can facilitate review of all data pursuant to certification of the candidate and placement into appropriate educational programs or sequences.

On a minimal basis, the summary should summarize all records collected, make recommendations for special program placement, elaborate upon any developmental problems, set down a projected educational plan and include all prognostications for future achievement.

A sample certification and summary form appears on the facing page.

Chapter 4

REARING AND EDUCATING GIFTED CHILDREN

THE rearing of intelligent children is difficult. While we patiently enforce the basic rules for everyday living, abstract concepts such as the principles of Western Man should be interpreted to intelligent children. It is an arduous, trying, and unrelenting task to raise and educate a gifted child properly.

Most parents provide the essential ingredients for child rearing. Abundant time, resources, and energy are expended in the process, but such ingredients are seldom analyzed. Ultimate outcomes may become subordinated to contemporary demands or satisfactions. Thoughtless cliches such as "Let them have their childhood" may obscure many of the real intellectual and disciplinary needs of gifted children.

Parents and teachers of talented children must recognize that adequate education includes intellectual, cultural, moral, and religious aspects. Gifted children will be influenced by the tastes, cultural interests, love of learning, and respect for self-discipline of adults. Since the gifted child is precocious, parents and teachers must act and influence with dispatch; they cannot afford to vacillate or shrink from the responsibilities of educating and cultivating the talented child.

There are no magical formulae for determining who gifted children are. Current psychometric standards are not very accurate. Some "experts" restrict their consideration of the "gifted" person to rigid IQ limits. However, their collective lower cutoff points for determining giftedness may range from a high of 150 IQ down to a low of 110 IQ.

Our understanding of intelligence is largely based upon tests and measurements which possess the built-in errors of all measuring instruments. Perhaps we need to consider a more empirical viewpoint concerning intelligence. True intelligence will manifest itself in academic achievement, scholarliness, and intellectual products. A professor of statistics once stated, "If you smell smoke and see flames do not bother running for a thermometer." Likewise, if the intellectual products of a given child are superior, we need not concern ourselves with measuring devices.

Of course, reality must be faced. It is a fact that human intelligence is widely varied. We should not disregard psychometric data describing intelligence. However, when such data is contradicted by performance, we should place more credence upon our observations of actual performance. For practical purposes, we might consider an IQ of 115 to be the lower limit for what we shall consider to be "potentially gifted children." Remember,

84

we should place children in "talent pools" as they are revealed through five major measures: (1) general intelligence, (2) creativity, (3) psychosocial skill, (4) specific aptitudes, and (5) manifest products.

A scientifically oriented school ordinarily schedules examinations and planned observations on a systematic basis. Since children are known to develop erratically, intellectual assessment should be a continuous operation. Also, no educator should ever discount such broad factors as motivation or personality when analyzing a given child's intellectual output.

Degree of excellence in any human products should be interpreted in terms of the historical context in which they were created. Also, we must be careful to assess the developmental maturity of the producer. We are ethically responsible to apply the highest current standards for judging the intellectual products at hand. It is a disservice, even to a child, if we fail to acquaint him with the prevailing standards of his culture. If the child is to finally produce creative products of his own, he needs to know the prevailing cultural developments from which he must depart.

While the child is encouraged to express himself freely, he should never be deluded into believing that he has excelled when he has not. He should be able to relate his products to existing cultural developments. This sort of reality orientation does not inhibit gifted children. On the contrary, it excites their curiosity and competitive motivation. The child will construct his own theories, products, and reforms from the educational background we give him in ideas, science, and law.

We must beware that our quest for excellence does not degenerate into passionate recitations of sorry slogans. To discover, encourage, and nurture talent is commendable. To expect to find general excellence in everybody, everywhere, is unrealistic. While we should expect most people to respect excellence, we must also respect the limitations placed upon each man by his own inadequacies.

Thus, our quest for excellence in children must be tempered by the reality of their mental endowment. We should provide adequate cultural criteria in order for the child to determine for himself which intellectual products are worthy of notice. No products will be forthcoming from a child who lacks motivation. While nurturing talent, there is no place for impatience. Even highly intelligent children may take considerable time to emerge. Childhood is developmental in nature; it should not be artificially accelerated.

OBLIGATIONS OF PARENTS

Parents and their vehicle, the home, have always formed the foundations of civilization. Societies in which the family has succeeded have generated codes and freedom, heritage and innovation, and individuality and cooper-

TABLE 12

DEVELOPMENT OF THE GIFTED

Developmental Stage	Age Ranges	Typical Developmental Problems for Parents	Expected Products
I. *Impulsive-Acquisitional* (Early Childhood birth to 3) Integrated willful personality emerges early; self-control well established but complicated by impulsivity, early interest in "older toys," colors, sounds, other senses. Possession and accumulation are key values; imagination already active; demonstrates more tenacity, purposeful behavior.		Finding suitable playmates; providing presocial experiences; finding toys that challenge; keeping occupied; resolving developmental discrepancies (e.g. willfulness may retard toilet training); reading myths, poems may be interpreted more literally than expected.	Precocious, walking, talking, symbolization, comprehension, social awareness; establishment of foundation values (e.g. self-concept, trust friendship, possession, local community).
II. *Duplicative-Expressive* (Childhood 2-6) Unlike normal children, words are understood apart from concrete experience-opening possibilities for duplicative, complex and abstract behavior; experimentation with diverse media may be confused with true creativity; unlike normal children, synesthetic experience is sought; expressions are related to ideas rather than mere impulsive outbursts.		May emulate adult mannerisms too convincingly (e.g. "little man" or pseudo adult behavior). Hyperactive flow of questions; unauthorized "explorations" (e.g. disassemble clocks, roam); motivation to learn may outstrip physical endurance; social-emotional maturity may show marked lag; compulsivity sometimes confused with lack of creativity.	Precocious; ability to abstract, codify, reason; drawings, speech demonstrate diversity of interests and ideas; inherent recognition of form, harmony, proportions are apparent; ability to estimate, judge, calculate with rudimentary number systems.
III. *Practical-Productive* (Late Childhood 5-10) Perceives key conceptual relationships rapidly; applies ideas and solutions of others with accuracy; uses precedence, proven formulae by choice; almost abnormal development of values of independence, power, utilitarianism—lends credence to notions they may be snobbish elites; sense of humor well developed, but "wisecracks," may annoy others.		Sex role differentiation less pronounced, girls, boys continue to share common interests; first indications of rejection by his peer group based upon intellectual inequalities; pompousness, exaggerated self-assurance; short-term obsession with given subjects, projects; outspoken, indifferent to social niceties.	Exaggerated interests in science, empirical subjects; inventions having concrete rather than conceptual form. Scholarliness bordering on pedantic; self-reliance, confidence.

IV. *Stereotypic-Critical* (Adolescence 9-16) Intellectual break with childhood first appears as criticism characterized by cynicism, doubt, hostility for adult conventions; sentimental identification with intellectual or historical figures may occur rather than normal adolescent subcultural identities; or social need for identity may result in compensatory playing of "average guy" role; end of period may witness sudden spectacular emergence of leadership, productive qualities.	Defense mechanisms (e.g. rationalization) more effective, convincing due to verbal ability, may cause parent to slacken essential discipline; seeming discrepancies in maturity most pronounced. In our society, comparatively unproductive stage; highest incidence of personal maladaptation occurs here; perseverance, scholarliness and work habits may retrogress; incidence of interpersonal conflict high; danger of vexation in this period.	Battleground for resolution of most basic adult values, beliefs, attitudes; first formulation of brilliant insights, ideas, theories occur; catharsis; theorizing, though wildly overgeneralized, may contain genuinely valid innovative ideas.
V. *Assertive-Creative* (Youth, 15 to Adult) General qualities of self-actualization should emerge (e.g. objectivity, independence, etc.). Emergence of the "universal man" with intercultural values, awareness. Personal strength to weather "the slings and arrows of outrageous fortune." Clearly-defined mission in life.	Societies suppressive reactions in form of antiintellectualism, demands for conformity; finding bases for productivity throughout comparatively long educational processes (as college); maturity to accept offspring's surpassing of parents.	Whole spectrum of human products depends upon unique value orientation of individual. Genuine contributions to posterity beyond the previous achievements of man.

ation in delicate balances. Societies in which the family has failed have led to extremes such as intolerance, indifference, and absolutism.

The ancient family relied upon traditions to prescribe codes of parental conduct. These traditional recipes resulted in predictable prejudices, attitudes, and behavior. The acculturation of the young tended to be rigid, ritualistic, and highly predictable.

Modern parents realize that petrified knowledge does not maintain a civilization. Modern societies do not perpetuate themselves in unmodified form. We have come to realize that each generation of men must interpret their heritage afresh and modify it accordingly. Therefore, our designs for parenthood need to include knowledge of the psychological development of children, the modern needs of society, and provision for self-understanding on the part of the parents themselves.

Some modern designs for parenthood emulate existing fashions and aim to rear children who are average or normal. Unfortunately, such designs may lead to personal waste and societal mediocrity. If a gifted child learns to set his goals in terms of "average expectancies," then it follows that his aspirations will be mundane and his intellectual products will be uninspired.

From biographies of illustrious men, we find that men of eminence ordinarily come from homes which foster standards of excellence.[1] Such homes ordinarily use heritage as a point of departure. An excellent home, like an excellent school, establishes the rationale, methodology, and setting for free inquiry and productivity.

Parents and teachers should expect gifted children to eventually produce worthwhile intellectual products. However, intellectual productivity may take different forms. While it may lead to scholarship and the pursuit of truth for its own sake, it may also culminate in tangible contributions to society such as inventions, literature, artistic products, or social service. Such disparate outcomes may be largely determined by what the gifted person has learned to value. Childhood exposures to a unique variety of men and ideas will determine what the individual finally comes to value. Limited experiences will produce limited men.

It is well that society caricatures the occasional genius who cannot make judgments outside of his specialized field or competency. He may be the creature of an oppressive and narrow environment. Fortunately, most geniuses can and do make judgments of marvelous variety and complexity.[2] Such men report that their own parents allowed latitude with reference to

---

[1] See for example, Goertzel, V.G., and Goertzel, G.G.: *Cradles of Eminence.* Boston, Little, 1962.

[2] See for example, Einstein, Albert: *Out of My Later Years.* New York, Philosophical Lib, 1950.

the learning and discussion tolerated in the home. Childhood was usually filled with travel, study, contemplation, social interaction, work, play as well as a variety of emotional experiences. Such men, as children, tended to view life and death, joy and sorrow, or pleasure and pain as these conditions exist in real life. Therefore, their unique system of personal values developed in a context of reality. They were not artificially sheltered in the home, or later, in the school. Interestingly, most men of eminence report that they learned to value excellence in others before they could objectively discriminate it in their own intellectual products.

Paramount among the obligations of parents of gifted children is that of preparing them for emotional maturity. Emotionally unstable or immature men do not produce worthwhile intellectual products. They remain too involved with themselves. Many parents and teachers fail to understand that there is only one "norm" for emotional maturity and that is the individual child. Too many parents and teachers equate emotional maturity with conformity. They expect the "emotionally mature" child to be unaffected, courteous, and unassuming. Of course, such a child may be simply withdrawn.

Parents and teachers should establish social settings in which the child can express, yet control, his emotions. The child should learn to admit guilt and yet be able to rationalize such guilt for his own well-being. All the while, parents and teachers must be careful to avoid overly-disciplined situations in which the child's yearnings, impulses, sentiments, and feelings cannot be adequately expressed.

Assuming that parents and teachers want gifted children to reach creative stages by adulthood, they might trace the development of a gifted child through the following stages and supply appropriate support:

TIMETABLES AND EXPECTATIONS

Hopefully, the timetables for rearing and educating intelligent children will be flexible. Rigid or unilateral adult timetables for the development of children usually culminate in frustration and failure. The child may perceive threatening expectations and react with hostility, evasion, and developmental arresting. As we chart the development of an intelligent child, we must de-emphasize his conformity to our expectations and emphasize objective observation of his unique development. As we observe new growth, we should modify or scale down our expectations accordingly. While it is natural for parents and teachers to expect scholastic success from intelligent children, they must realize that such success is based upon a complex combination of motivation, endowment, and preparation. Also, even though the intelligent child is ordinarily accelerated from the start of his school career, yet his education will have to extend over a longer period of time demanding extended planning. Influential adults must constantly remind themselves that intelligence in children is but a potentiality —a hope. In order to encourage intellectual products, the environment must be planned in such a way as to challenge the innate intelligence of the child. Preparation of rational timetables of appropriate educational and cultural experiences will insure such environmental exposure.

Actually, two timetables are involved: (1) the actual observed growth processes of the child including social, physical, mental, and emotional qualities; and, (2) the adult-planned schedule of events and experiences to enhance educational and cultural growth. The adult schedule ought to be based upon a sympathetic understanding of the developmental growth timetable. In this fashion, the superimposed cultural experiences will be relevant to the developmental readiness of the child. In order to observe individual child growth accurately, parents and teachers should avail themselves of child study training. Since most of the available developmental studies of children describe "normal" children, the child study training of adults who want to study intelligent children will have to draw upon the latest research which describes the characteristic developments of intelligent children.

Intelligent children characteristically reach criterion stages of development earlier. In addition, they will continue to develop over a longer period of time. Therefore, in a quantitative way adult schedules will have to provide more experiences for younger children and continue to provide a vast array of cultural experiences over a longer period of time. In a qualitative sense, adult timetables should include activities which reflect abstract content and cultural enrichment. For example, normal children might be exposed to classical music in early childhood, but the intelligent child may express a qualitatively different understanding of the music and demand to know such content as forms of music, composition, or historical context of music.

Most parents and teachers would agree that no child should be driven or overworked. But, would they also agree that no child should be forced into an arbitrary slow schedule or artificially held back in his intellectual development because of artificial grade level standards? A psychologically healthy intelligent child ordinarily demands challenge in his everyday work tasks. Such "challenge" does not consist of a burden of more work in the quantitative sense. On the contrary, the intelligent child should be scheduled for no more schoolwork during the course of the day than is a normal or slow child. However, that work which he is scheduled to perform, ought to be composed of sufficiently challenging content in the qualitative sense of being intellectually challenging and abstract in concept formation. A growing body of research is accumulating to indicate that bright students, particularly boys, can be artificially truncated in their intellectual growth by exposure to curriculum content which is tedious, uninteresting, and un-challenging.

Even in infancy and early childhood, intelligent children can be expected to excel their peers both quantitatively and qualitatively. The quantitative gains, such as vocabulary, are particularly spectacular. In a qualitative way, young intelligent children tend to think for themselves almost as soon as they acquire the capability for verbal communication. The intelligent early child is capable of gaining prodigious amounts of knowledge very rapidly. For example, there is evidence to show that by the age of three, intelligent children have a capability for such complex learning tasks as typewriting; speaking a foreign language as well as the mother tongue; primary school level reading; completing simple arithmetical tasks such as addition and subtraction; telling time and scheduling their day accord-ingly; understanding the generalization or concept involved in simple myths or folk tales; or, appreciating an abstract value such as aesthetic ap-preciation of art or music.

While normal children formulate fundamental morals in childhood, the intelligent child codifies such morals and may even construct corollary systems of ethics to complement basic moral principles.

While normal children form primitive "pal" relationships in early child-hood, the intelligent child may have intuitively recognized many of the dynamics of group behavior already. His analysis of group behavior may have established a leadership role for himself. Since he can interpret and anticipate the behavior of other children, he is in a logical position to lead them. Due to group pressures, he may choose to disguise his intellectuality as early as childhood. Even though he applies an abstract understanding of group behavior, yet he may communicate with the group in terms of their own vocabulary and folkways. This simulated "folksy" behavior may cause objective observers to misinterpret the child's actual potentiality. This is why individual intellectual assessment of potentially gifted children is so important.

Average primary school children may content themselves with memoriza-tion, emulation, and ritualistic study habits. In contrast, intelligent children will concoct, apply, and analyze various methodologies. Facts alone do not satisfy them. They want to know how facts were derived. They are more concerned with experimentation, research models, and the solving of their own intellectual problems.

In short, intelligent children are a different breed, and their mark is made early. Therefore, a schedule of educational and cultural activities for childhood should not utilize descriptions of normal children as its proto-type. Moreover, the timetable should not lag but rather should excite the imagination of the intelligent child on an everyday basis. Early childhood should include the widest possible exploratory exposures to art, music, nature, cultural heros, current events, basic skills, and the elements of computation. Even games and play should be built around rules and more complex activities which will excite his intellectual curiosity. The late childhood development of the intelligent child should witness tremendous gains in the content of knowledge. Therefore, vast storehouses of potential knowledge such as books, records, travel opportunities, and other research tools should be available. Educationally, the childhood of the intelligent boy or girl should include appropriate amounts of acceleration and exposure to qualitatively different and advanced subject matter.

Some intelligent children may seem to slow down in development as they approach adolescence. Perhaps some of this phenomenon will be due to the fact that other youngsters are catching up with them, particularly in social and emotional development. Our society does place considerable premium upon social development in adolescence, and so, we tend to exaggerate the significance of the acquisition of sophisticated mannerisms or superficial social intercourse. In point of fact, the intelligent adolescent will still be functioning years ahead of his peers. However, his behavior may become more private, introspective, and sensitive during this stage. The gifted adolescent may appear to have more problems, simply because he understands more. He may tend to perceive the transitional, physiological, and psychological changes of adolescence with more intensity than does an average youngster. Fortunately, he will typically possess sufficient background and thinking ability to formulate solutions to the inevitable problems that adolescence brings.

Negligent parental or educational guidance during the adolescent period may be particularly devastating. For example, some parents and counselors may prescribe ambiguous advice during this period. Ambiguous, evasive, or permissive advice giving during this period may be particularly harmful. As in the case of all adolescents, the youngster may become rebellious or lazy during this period. Such ill-conceived advice as "Let him alone, he'll grow out of it," may result in the tragedy of an intelligent "dropout." Records clearly indicate that the high school "dropout," be he intelligent or average, becomes the nonentity of tomorrow. An adequate program of group and individual counseling may be part of the answer to such a problem. This is the stage in life where thorough record keeping would be most utilized. In general, symptoms of underachieving, rebelliousness, or lack of motivation occur sporadically earlier in the student's academic career. The importance of diagnostic guidance clinics, supplemented by counseling facilities, cannot be overemphasized.

There may be some tendency in our era for average and intelligent men alike to avoid the great issues of life and death, identity and oblivion, God and man, history and meaning. However, it is next to impossible for an intelligent youth to be unaware of such problems. If he is to grow to intellectual stature, he must sooner or later grapple with the contemplation of such problems. The intelligent youth may worry his parents and instructors because he seems to contemplate such problems "too deeply." The more conservative adults may become alarmed at his tendency to act out or act upon the inevitable conclusions to which his contemplation brings him. Unconventional, sometimes radical, behavior may be expected from a large proportion of intellectual youths. Their tendency toward activism may be exaggerated if their adolescence and childhood consisted of severe middle-class restriction. The insightful, empathetic adult can play a crucial role during this period of turbulent youth. A mature adult role can only be played if the adult possesses a genuine sense of history and a philosophical commitment to individual freedom.

WIDENING CULTURAL EXPOSURES

Lack of adequate cultural exposure, even before formal schooling begins, can lead to tragic human waste. Recent studies of "culturally deprived or disadvantaged children" indicate how much children need broad cultural exposure before they come to school. Of course, it would be impossible to expose even the most brilliant child to the sum total of all of the aesthetic, intellectual, historical, and literary accomplishments of Western Civilization. Therefore, the guiding parent or teacher should make judgments concerning the worthwhileness of certain cultural exposures over others. No child will be found to be innately capable of making sensible cultural choices without first being informed of existing cultural criteria, the collected wisdom of the race, and the limitations placed upon his search for knowledge by the existing mores and laws of the civilization. A selective yet representative exposure to his cultural heritage will provide the child with the background necessary to make future judgments and to finally develop a unique cultivated outlook of his own.

During an era that may be overemphasizing "social adjustment and conformity," it may be difficult for the sensitive adult to reinforce aesthetic, literary, historical, and natural learnings by way of sufficient cultural exposures. It must be borne in mind that while cultural experiences may be shared during activities, they are more likely to be considered private perceptions by the intelligent child. Such perceptions will involve meditation, study, and critical comparison. Although the intelligent child will incorporate group values and appraisals into his overall cultural viewpoint, it is to be hoped that his final sense of cultivation will be private and unique.

Each generation of men appears to consider itself to be the apex of civilization, and our generation is no exception. However, even a cursory inventory of the American scene will indicate an overemphasis upon scientific and technological progress. It may be that the critical analysis of history will determine that in certain areas we may have retrogressed. For example, the generations immediately preceding us have emphasized the fine arts, philosophy, mathematics, logic, and a certain elegance in the communication skills including mastery of several languages. We have tended to relate all art and science to purely practical applications. This has caused our young people to divorce a sense of the aesthetic from the study of subject matter such as mathematics or philosophy.

Study of existing elementary school curriculums will usually show conspicuous absence of aesthetic exposure or training. Where aestheticism is nurtured, only primitive or simple forms may be used. One is likely to witness the playing of folk music records, paper cutting, finger painting, or similar unskilled activities at the elementary school level. However, listening to various forms of music or systematic exposure to the various art forms for the relating of aesthetic values to other intellectual experiences is not presented. It may be that the marked aversion of many of our intelligent youth toward aesthetic forms results from this paucity of experience at the elementary school level. In general, elementary school faculties ought to reestablish systematic exposure to the various forms of music, painting, sculpture, architecture, drama, and other fine arts. Such a reemphasis upon aestheticism may reinstate aesthetic values to their former prominence in our overall cultural viewpoints in the next generations.

The systematic exposure to aesthetic forms must not end with the rote learning of series of musical scores or art histories. Rather, the child should learn to distinguish and value various forms according to internalized criteria of worth. Aestheticism will not form as a core value unless it is associated with the ability to critically discriminate among the complex emotional and intellectual variables which affect aesthetic choice.

Adequate and natural exposure to the fine arts cannot be confined to any one environment. The home, school, and community at large should cooperate for the development of a community-wide program of aesthetics. We can expect children to reject the fine arts if they are presented in stuffy, pedantic, or esoteric settings. Aesthetic appreciation will develop only if pleasant associations from childhood have been established with art forms. Therefore, rooms in the home and the school should reflect, to the extent that we are financially capable of doing so, aesthetic taste. It is notable that some European nations cultivate the same attitudes on the part of their children toward opera or the drama that we engender toward sports or science. A balanced cultural diet should include reasonable amounts of exposure to aesthetic forms in a context of other learnings.

Among the important cultural exposures must be listed linguistic and literary pursuits. The reading of great literature, the study of languages, the study of methodology and folklore, and the achievement of a personalized style of writing should not be artificially postponed. Since it is well known that intelligent children manifest verbal skills quite early in childhood, it follows that varied linguistic and literary experiences are logical. It would be hard to estimate the wasted time involved in the postponement of learning a foreign language. It has been long recognized that the acquisition of a foreign language not only heightens the individual's appreciation for the literary use of words but also enhances the mastery of his mother tongue.

Even before the intelligent child can thoroughly understand selected works of great literature, he may benefit from hearing such materials read to him. For example, teachers and mothers of intelligent children report that they listen intently to such varied readings as poetry, mythology, folklore, or selected works of certain historical novelists. While the child may not comprehend the total meaning of a poem by Milton, they may learn to recognize such factors as meter or style. Later, when they mature toward conceptual understanding of the work, they will recognize and be comfortable with it due to their earlier experience.

In order to be comfortable with his cultural heritage, the intelligent child needs to study his historical identity. History should provide the intelligent child with models and examples. The child can reject or copy historical models, depending upon the way in which he evaluates them. Therefore, the essential ingredients of a systematic study of history are twofold and include the acquisition of that vast body of knowledge we collectively call "history," in addition to methodologies and frameworks with which to interpret, apply, and modify this history for the future.

In particular, it is the hero within an historical context which will provide the model upon which the child may develop his own self-image. Certainly, there is considerable historical eivdence to indicate that men of eminence themselves compared, modified, or copied their own styles of living from heroes they chose from history. Since most heroes were subject, in their own time, to controversy, it becomes important to provide intelligent children with suitable methods for ascertaining fact from fiction, myth from reality, propaganda from fact, or national bias from a world view. Our young hero in the making must avoid the pitfall stated succinctly by Santyana "Those who disregard the lessons of history are doomed to repeat them."

Of course, a study of one's historical heritage can never be entirely objective. It is almost impossible to sift out the contemporary heroes and villains in terms of one's own nationalistic sentiments. Still, we should try to sift reality from fiction. Uninformed men, however honorable they may have considered their convictions to be, have been known to destroy themselves and their civilization. It is to be hoped that modern educators will introduce sufficient historical examples, readings, and methodologies to insure that the intelligent child will form his own moral convictions about the progression of history.

Problems and controversy may be encountered when the intelligent child pursues his quest for historical understanding to the study of worldwide culture. The child may not easily conform to our national prejudices. Just as the child in the fable insisted that the "Emperor was naked," so the astute child in our time may proclaim that a given cherished governmental policy is barren.

The intelligent child may single out obvious differences in value orientations among existing world cultures before his teacher perceives them. He may choose to identify, for a time, with the foreign value orientation. Some of the more common differences in value orientations he may observe include time orientations which may focus upon the present, past, or future; natural outlooks which may view man as subordinate to nature or man as the master of nature; man may be viewed with reference to God as dependent or independent, subservient or equal, close or apart; and, cultures may place differential emphasis upon social, material, political, aesthetic, scientific, or religious values.

A working understanding of the different value orientations of men may result in tolerance for the viewpoints of foreign peoples. Tolerance, in this case, will not be equated necessarily with acceptance. While he tolerates, the intelligent child does not necessarily incorporate the foreign value into his own way of life.

As the intelligent child becomes more cultivated, we will expect him to understand himself in terms of the heritage he has studied. In addition, we should expect to find more respect, admiration, and tolerance for foreign cultural heritages. The understanding of foreign cultures may result in healthy competitive comparisons with one's own culture. Such comparisons may result in internal cultural absorption and refinement of the cultural developments of others.

Finally, we should expect the intelligent adolescent to speculate about his philosophy of life. He should interrelate such notions as man's relationship to nature into his philosophical scheme of things. It is interesting to note that persons of equal intelligence may come to diametrically opposed conclusions because they differ in their personal value orientations. For example, when proposing solutions for such common problems as highways versus natural parks, some men may never equate nature with beauty and choose utility and economy instead, while others emphasize spiritual and aesthetic values in preference to economical or utilitarian considerations. Intelligent children should have ample opportunity to discuss, perhaps in seminar settings, the interrelationships of the natural world with spiritual, philosophical, and aesthetic interpretations.

REFINEMENT REVISITED

A cultivated man ought to acquire attributes and characteristics which typify him and distinguish him from other men. An exhaustive list of such personality traits would be encyclopedic. However, it may be possible to discuss the cultivated man in terms of simplified historical and modern classifications of the cultivated man. Classical societies valued four main characteristics in the cultivated man including the qualities of aestheticism, intellectuality, refinement, and taste. Modern men have come to prize more modern characteristics including adaptability, creativity, emotional stability, historical perspective, objectivity, and a system of personal values. Discussion of these traits should indicate specific directions which instruction or guidance should take in order to aid the intelligent child in his development toward appropriate cultivated habits and attitudes.

Little philosophical depth can be reached without some contemplation of the essential qualities of beauty. Moreover, aesthetic men claim that their aestheticism enables them to experience a closer harmony between their emotions and their rationality. Aestheticism must involve appreciation. Therefore, a wide exposure to musical and artistic experiences is imperative. Study of the definitions, modalities, and form of beautiful works must also be carried on. Each in his own life space must define beauty for himself. Such a definition will be enhanced by thorough and systematic study and experimentation with form, symmetry, harmony, and rhythm in all of the aesthetic modes.

Intelligence may be innate, but intellectuality certainly is not inborn. The "dropout records" of many intelligent students bears grim testimony to this statement. Intellectuality must be nurtured. At first, the more natural tendency of man to react first and rationalize later must be substituted with the learning and utilization of logical approaches and methodologies for the solution of problems. To be "intellectual" as opposed to being merely "intelligent," one must learn to use his mind as a tool. This process involves degrees of mental discipline. The solving of mental problems is not always easy nor is it fun. Intricate rather than simple, difficult rather than easy solutions must often be chosen. Therefore, intellectuality must be developed systematically. Even the preschool child should become accustomed to solving certain of his own personal problems.

Refinement, of course, would include all of the qualities being discussed. Yet, it may be viewed as the culmination or end product of the process of culturation. It is incumbent upon parents and teachers to provide models of refined behavior for the child in his everyday environment. As a matter of fact, a codified set of refined manners differentially fostered on the playground, in the classroom, and at the eating table. Early establishment of a refined set of manners will form the skeletal structure for the more complex code of refinement of the cultivated adult.

"Taste" might be thought of as the ability to distinguish those objects and conditions which are excellent. The patience to appreciate a beautiful impression, the judgment based upon an understanding of historical development, and the ability to discern degrees of good quality are but a few of the specific attributes of a person who possesses good taste. To some extent, modern American society may have confused good social manners with good taste. For example, the ability to judge artistic performances is lacking in many communities. High school and college performers rarely have the benefit of honest criticism. Poor acting or mediocre performances are often accepted simply because the performers "did the best that they could." Perhaps, their best performance was lacking in talent or finish. This is not to say that good taste should be accompanied by cruelty or bad manners. Still, the process of upgrading the arts is strategically dependent upon the existence of honest, fair, and impartial judgmental criticism. In order to develop good taste the child needs to be presented with suitable standards for the evaluation of himself and the performance of others.

Adaptability may have been equated by some moderns with conformity. As a consequence, many young intellectuals may have interpreted adaptability to mean the institution of flexible behavior in the face of social demands. However, adaptability should be considered something more profound. The thinking individual must reconcile himself to the fact that environmental conditions are constantly undergoing change. Even the most rigid standards must lend themselves to modification or be destroyed. The quality of adaptability implies a capability for adjustment to changing conditions.

It should be noted that the process of adaptability may cause as many changes in the environment as it does in the individual. As the adaptive individual generates new models of behavior, others may adapt these models, and so change themselves. Instead of blind conformity, adaptive behavior may be viewed as one of the ultimate expressions of will. The new adaptive behavior will be a matter of individual choice. An intelligent individual must learn to contemplate all of the conditions leading up to a proposed new adjustment. Also, he must project his tentative solutions in such a way as to envision all the possible outcomes of his proposed adaptive behavior. Still, he must bear in mind that some situations in life cannot be adjusted to if we are to maintain our moral integrity. Therefore, the individual must develop the courage to be unadaptive when the conditions of life warrant resistance.

The creative behavior of the cultivated man tends to be general rather than specific. All aspects of life, including his own impulsive life, are of interest to him. He has learned how to express his unique ideas in ways that are rewarding to himself and palatable to society. The truly creative act is a perfection of discipline. It represents the harnessing of deeply impulsive forces. The creative individual strives to appreciate the unique ingredients in every episode of his life. He rehearses daily his ability to formulate fresh descriptions of the sensory impressions he receives. He exploits his natural gift for expressing such sensory data in new forms. He may be distrusted by society because some of his ideas may revolutionize thought. Consequently, he must be capable of surviving in ambiguous states of existence. He must frequently grapple with the inner reality of his own unique understandings of the world along with the outer reality of a conservative and uncomprehending society.

COOPERATIVE EDUCATIONAL PLANNING

The education and cultivation of intelligent children is dependent upon a continual input of appropriate learning activities. The intellectual development of the child may be viewed as a corporate endeavor even though we sometimes artificially demarcate the home from the school, the church from the home, or the community cultural activities from all of the other institutions. All of these institutions ought to cooperate and coordinate their cultural activities toward the end of broad social, cultural, and moral education.

While the main influences upon intelligent children will be manifest in their home and school, yet the community at large with its libraries and other cultural facilities will also greatly impress and affect his development. The home will provide the basic attitudinal orientations which will orient the child for a lifetime. Also, the family will lay the groundwork for his core values. One cannot overestimate the effect of the cultivation process in the home during the first five years of life. Through an emphasis upon programs designed, presumably, in terms of modern learning theory, the school will attempt to provide a broad spectrum of learning experiences through exposure to well-trained and intelligent teachers in order to provide the student with the tools with which he can express his attitudinal and value orientations in real service or output. The agencies of the home and school may not have the resources to carry out a full program of cultivation. Therefore, the community at large must be considered as a fountainhead of broad cultural outlets and experiences. Often, families and schools have been blamed for failure to turn out a significant number of cultivated boys and girls, when in reality it may have been the culturally impoverished community which failed to exploit the interests of these students by providing adequate outlets in the arts, drama, and other cultural activities.

A more definitive treatment of the topics of home and school will be attempted later. At this point, it may be useful to survey a few of the major contributions of the home and the school to the nurturance of intelligent children.

While rearing intelligent children, families need to foster certain cultivated and intellectual attitudes as well as providing essential physical embellishments in the home. Following are some of the considerations families might consider as they plan the early childhood development of intelligent children.

The entire family, including parents and siblings, should *participate in broad educational planning for all of the offspring.* For the intelligent child, such planning must begin quite early in childhood, since by definition, the child is precocious. Parental guidance may be far more important in the early years with reference to intelligent children than for normal children since they are already in a position to make decisive judgments concerning their future even at an early age. Also, unusual intellectual activities may be carried on by intelligent children by a very tender age. For instance, in spite of any indoctrination, or lack of it, intelligent children will have a propensity to read by the age of three and challenge most philosophical or legalistic interpretations made for them. Therefore, some master plan of approaching such learning activities should be discussed by the family.

Men who become great and eminent have learned to make choices and held decisive opinions. Such outlooks did not develop in a home typified by a vacuum of opinion and discussion. Therefore, it behooves the families of intelligent children to *discuss even controversial matters in decisive, direct, and reflective ways.* Evasive statements, rationalizations, and false values which allow the suppression of discussion on the basis that "it isn't nice or proper," should have no place in the home environment of the intelligent child. Literally, no area of discussion is sacred to the child whose mind is apt to probe deeply into any and all problems of human existence.

The intelligent child will tend to respect his parents, even if they have strong but opposite convictions. He will tend to evaluate his parents in terms of the way they reflect their convictions in terms of their lives rather than by the way in which such convictions may conflict or oppose his own. Stimulating, exciting conversations should occur often in the family circle of the intelligent child. The child will learn that controversy, differences of opinion, or advocacy are healthy competitive exercises. Obviously, the developmental level of the child must be taken into consideration. There will be no need to overwhelm the child with the sophistication of esoteric arguments before such time as he is able to comprehend them. The important principle for the family to adhere to is that the child must be allowed to develop opinions and points of view of his own in a context of intellectual honesty and freedom.

The home and family must *provide the models of excellence toward which the young intellectual will aspire.* We know that men of eminence tend to come from families where the "love of learning" was a way of life exemplified in every family experience. While the child may not emulate the specific model of one or both of his parents, yet these parents will provide him with the abstract principles upon which to base his own developing image. If the child lacks the habits of scholarliness or intellectuality later in his school career, it may be largely because the family did not prize these characteristics in his early development.

Insofar as it is financially possible, *the home should represent a cultural microcosm.* The artifacts of art, music, sculpture, literature, and other cultural embellishments should adorn the home. In the case of the arts, the child will appreciate beauty, form, and style if his early experiences included firsthand exposures to original artistic products. Certainly, in a time when original pieces of art can be purchased at very modest prices, there is little if any excuse for the barrenness of some modern homes. One cannot overemphasize the effect of having great literature available to the child within the home setting. A wide range of literary products including poetry will go far toward stimulating the child later in his life to pursue literary activities.

The family must provide the examples for the core values that the child will be expected to incorporate into his own personality structure. Perhaps a wide exposure to differential value orientations will both interest the child and allow him to identify with those values most closely related to his own propensities. Again, exposure to a variety of personalities and reading may be accomplished through traveling, visits by interesting and stimulating guests, or exposure to different literary forms.

The parents of intelligent children particularly ought to *stimulate community betterment by way of support of the cultural life of the community.* Particularly in smaller communities it may be necessary to aggressively pursue the encouragement and support of the performing arts and other cultural programs.

It is important that the parents of intelligent children *interact with other families having gifted children.* Already there exists chartered organizations for the parents of such children. Unfortunately, such organizations are often affiliated with larger agencies which obscure their specific reason for existence. The specific reason for such organizations ought to be the intimate interaction of parents of intelligent children toward the end of discussing, implementing, and producing unique, home, school, and community activities for intelligent children. In so doing, such parents should not only discuss but actually enter into the demonstration, research, study, and creative productivity of imaginative programs of learning for their children. One example of such a movement is the Monterey Association for the Gifted, which conducts summer cultural programs for gifted children in which such activities as the pursuit of music, drama, ballet, and the arts is carried on utilizing qualified teaching staff as well as interested and specially trained parents.

The parents themselves may want to *avail themselves of specialized educational training, cultural enrichment, and the acquisition of specialized techniques* for dealing with their intelligent children. Therefore, such parents need to support lectures, seminars, adult educational enrichment activities, and other educational opportunities in their own communities. It might be a wise idea to consider a kind of "learning partnership" with their children. For example, in some communities seminars have been established for parents, teachers, and intelligent children meeting together as a group.

It has been indicated that the main influence of the family upon the gifted child is in the attitudinal and value formation areas. The need for decisive planning, guidance, and demonstration of parental value orientations for emulation by the child have been stressed. It is apparent that the main influence of the environment upon the gifted child will shift once he enters the formal school setting. Therefore, it is of utmost importance that a coalition of parents, educators, and community leaders think seriously about the broad spectrum of learning experiences which gifted children must be exposed to.

The school, as an institution, must consider its commitment to a philosophy of individual differences as implemented by way of educational programs which offer a broad spectrum or learning experiences along with exposure to well-trained and intelligent teachers. Of course, the school cannot function in a cultural vacuum. The community must provide the cultivating experiences necessary for the full actualization of the potential of the gifted child. More definitive treatments of the specific contributions of the home, school, and community will be elaborated upon later. At this point, we might consider some of the general educational conditions necessary for an adequate program of development for gifted children.

Schools must *provide for broad sensory, learning, and cultural experiences* beginning at the kindergarten and preschool levels with general exposures and narrowing toward more specific experiences later in the educational career. For intelligent children, nursery school education should definitely be considered as an educational opportunity. At the nursery and kindergarten levels, gifted children will be ready to hear children's literature and poetry and learn some rudimentary symbols such as traffic signs, key words and phrases, and more complex operations such as time telling or telephone dialing.

By the time the intelligent child reaches the first grade, formal education already has begun. Typically, the intelligent child will approach the first grade with considerable proficiency in the basic skills areas such as arithmetic judgment, reading, general oral expression, block letter writing, and the assimilation of certain bodies of knowledge such as folklore, mythology, and other information. It is remarkable to note that gifted children are capable of learning several languages from a very early age. At the primary level, gifted children are usually already prepared to approach special subject matter areas with considerable scope and depth. Departmentalization of subject matter content, if not classrooms, might be considered for gifted children by the fourth grade level at the latest.

High school education for gifted children must emphasize highly specialized subject matter content in view of the vast stores of knowledge with which such students approach the high school. Advanced placement to college and introduction to useful research endeavors should begin by the early high school level for gifted students.

Schools must *consider two main dimensions of growth* when planning for the education of intelligent and gifted children. Specifically, such children are precocious and may require advanced placement and, secondly, their level of learning sophistication at any given age will far excel that of their age peers and therefore much thought must be given to the scope and content of curriculum offered.

Early entrance to the first grade may not be "acceleration" in the strict sense of the term. Rather, educators may be placing a child with a peer group more like himself in developmental ways. Perhaps such an advanced early entrance placement might be termed "proper developmental placement." Many states have enacted laws enabling younger children to be placed from the kindergarten into the first grade (e.g. California, Connecticut, Pennsylvania). This technique seems to be sensible since it avoids the skipping of blocks of subject matter. Early entrance to the first grade enables the child to be placed in a educational setting in which the children are more like himself in physical, social, and mental ways. The research evidence indicates clearly that such children adjust well and are indistinguishable from their older grade peers after a year or so placement in the advanced program. It has been recommended that early entrance be considered for all intelligent children with IQ's in excess of 120.

It must be emphasized that early entrance, or advanced placement at a later time, cannot be considered a total program. Even though the child is placed with older peers, he will still require curriculum content planned in such a way as to incorporate subject matter content of more challenging concept levels.

School must *provide specialized and differentiated educational programs* for gifted students along the entire educational continuum. Such educational planning might be called "master programming." All of the various program possibilities, including such choices as enrichment units, acceleration, or special classes, ought to be considered as placement possibilities for every gifted child at all educational levels. However, knowledge of such children indicates that acceleration and enrichment program possibilities are popular choices early in the educational career and especially during the primary grades. The upper elementary and junior high school levels lend themselves to programs including special seminars, special counseling opportunities, and special classes. The high school and college levels lend themselves to advanced placement, special classes, special lecture and career opportunity exposures to experts outside of the school, and individual research.

In order to implement the aforementioned programs adequately, schools must *provide specialized staff, materials, and building space.* While the professional staff need not be technically "gifted," they should be respectful of the scholarly propensities of the children with whom they must work. Moreover, such teachers and other professional workers should display interest in academic pursuits in their own collegiate and research training.

Thus far, only private schools have experimented with special building settings for the education of gifted children. Logic alone would dictate that precocious children require school plants sufficiently flexible in their structure to be used for laboratory settings even in the early elementary school. Likewise, little if any curriculum research has been devoted to the development of specialized materials for gifted children. Currently available materials are frequently rejected by gifted children because they are boring. While the profession awaits the development of specialized learning materials for gifted children, they will need to consider the development of specialized curriculum models within the individual school setting.

Lastly, in order to coordinate all of the various institutional influences upon the gifted child, schools must *foster a philosophy of education which is eclectic, experimental, and pragmatic.* The school system must allow its own staff sufficient freedom for real educational experimentation. In order to attract and keep such a well-prepared staff, the administration of the school must be tolerant of differing educational philosophies.

In summary, the total process of rearing and educating gifted children involves intellectual and cultural inputs from a diversity of agencies and institutions. Before adolescence, it is apparent that the family and the school, in that order, will have the most influence upon the child. If the home has provided value orientations which foster intellectual habits and an appreciation for cultural pursuits, then the school will be in a better position to implement this attitudinal beginning with appropriate educational programs. If the programs of the school lack the intellectual and cultural stimulation necessary to excite the intelligent child, then such a child may become one of the "intellectual casualties" of our age. The key to understanding a total program for gifted children is the understanding that the home and the school must act as interrelated stimulations in the life of the child. Such cooperation should include free interaction among teachers and parents in the educational process. For example, just as we expect teachers to supplement the emotional development of the child with appropriate nurturance, so we expect the home to implement the intellectual development of the child with appropriate cultural embellishments and intellectual stimulation.

PLANNING SCHOOL PROGRAMS

As educators plan special educational programs for talented students, three main considerations ought to be discussed: (1) the commitment of teachers to a philosophy of individual differences, (2) the school's readiness for establishing "differential programming" to meet the individual learning requirements of talented students, and (3) the professional staff's willingness to design "master programs" for each child which include pupil assessment and diagnostic teaching along with school-community involvement.

"Differential programming" for pupils implies that a school district has established a wide range of program possibilities into which pupils with varying learning needs may be placed. Different programs such as special classes, acceleration, special tutoring, counseling, special lectures, seminars, and advanced placement to higher educational institutions are but a few of the possibilities for differential programming.

When designing "master programs," school districts must consider at least two important dimensions for curriculum planning: (1) orderly sequence of knowledge and concepts, and (2) scope and depth of material. In order to include a sufficient variety and difficulty of learning materials to challenge and satisfy the pupil, teachers must record activities accurately and plan years ahead. Also, programs designed for intelligent children should be continually reevaluated by collecting specimens of pupils' work and comparing program outcomes with results from other program types. Difficulties may develop when school district personnel bog down in discussions of the types of programs they should offer. Picayune differences are sometimes presented as strategic reasons for not including certain kinds of programs. Special classes and acceleration programs are particularly susceptible to unwarranted and prejudicial attack.

All programs for gifted youngsters have to be designed to stimulate abstract thinking capabilities. Educational materials which are clearly advanced both in grade level and conceptual content will need to be used.

Suitable programs for intelligent pupils are likely to be unsuitable for other pupils. Therefore, it is curious that school personnel frequently reject some types of programs because they are not useful for "all students." Of course, it is possible to rewrite and translate many content areas into more concrete terms for pupils of lower intelligence. In fact, this is the great challenge of the so-called enrichment types of program. If an enrichment program is properly constructed and taught, it is the most difficult program to administer due to the complexity of levels of learning that must be synchronized.

Initially, before actual programs are prescribed, a talented child should be identified on the basis of all available data. On a minimum basis, intelligence tests, records of achievement tests, case history items, assessments of emotional and social maturity, and recommendations from the classroom teachers should be collected and analyzed. Based upon this assessment, a child can be placed into a special program sequence best suited to meet his learning needs. The adequate identification of talents must be viewed as a process rather than a static act. Literally, it is never completed. A case study should be developed and continually added to with data describing changes in classroom performance, additional tests, changes in attitudes, and new insights into the child's personality characteristics. Since the intelligent child can function faster and more accurately than others, there is need to collect a diversity of materials that he produces.

Actually, the identification of talented children should begin before the child reaches kindergarten. The parent will note many instances of precocity in the child's first years of life. The parent will find that an intelligent child begins to talk early, comprehends and follows instructions, plays and organizes activities with other children, dresses and cares for himself, engages in coordinated activities such as bike riding, and manifests moral judgement and advanced decision making. During nursery school and kindergarten, he will want to learn how to read, write, tell time and engage in other intellectual tasks not participated in by other children.

Once formal schooling begins, it is possible to collect and maintain a more thorough "case study" for the child. The first time a pupil is considered for possible inclusion in a special program, the following kinds of information might be collected: (1) a nomination endorsement from his classroom teacher which includes anecdotal records substantiating the teacher's belief that the child is intelligent and suggesting possible program patterns; (2) background information including historical and developmental records; (3) health and medical records including estimates of the child's stamina and physical capabilities; (4) results of standardized tests of mental ability, achievement, and aptitudes; and (5) a written summation by a professional worker such as a school psychologist with hypothetical prognostications of the child's success if he were placed in differential program possibilities.

A case study should be maintained for any child placed into special program settings. As new data is channeled into the case study on a systematic basis, feedback is translated into program modification and becomes a basis for evaluation of the pupil's progress. The collection of periodic examination data from subject matter areas will indicate rather clearly to what extent the pupil is accepting the challenge of his new program pattern.

New educational programs might be developed by the following stages:

Step 1. Planning the Program

Using as its guiding philosophy the concept of differential programming," a district would focus upon individual pupils and their special needs rather than groups. Of course, the district would need to consider the background and history of its community before specifying definite program possibilities. Open meetings of the Board of Education or other public meetings might serve as an opportunity for the assessment of community wishes. The district would also need to make an inventory of community resources, teaching resources, availability of special learning materials, library facilities, special equipment, classroom and plant space, and the availability of specialists such as psychologists, subject matter specialists, and curriculum consultants.

Step 2. Program Development

A committee, preferably composed of lay and professional members, should be supplied with a set of purposes as set forth by the school district's philosophy. The committee would then design specific academic activities for pupils which would need to be supplemented by adequate new curriculum development. This curriculum development should incorporate methods for unleashing pupil potentialities, creativity, and productivity. As the curriculum develops, it should be accompanied by specifications for the particular kind of student sought for in a particular type of differential program. Such practical considerations as the cost of extra materials should be thoroughly analyzed by this committee. A well thought-out program would include descriptions of educational objectives, educational activities, special supplemental curriculum, the necessary materials, the specialized staff and services, and the specific methods of evaluation for each type of differential program.

Step 3. Selection and Placement of Appropriate Pupils

The whole objective of designing special educational programs is to place pupils with special learning needs into programs best designed to meet these needs. The description of a prospective pupil should "match up" with the program proposed for him. Any adequate program of selection and placement must involve some means of following the student and evaluating his progress. The whole identification sequence should be based upon a differential outline of human talent.

Step 4. Administration and Supervision of the Program

The district should provide coordination for all aspects of the differential programs. Systems of classroom supervision and teacher evaluation should be developed and expedited by trained supervisors. Teachers need to be exposed, from time to time, to educational opportunities themselves. Such advanced training may be provided by a local college, by inviting guest lecturers to address teachers, or by providing in-service educational opportunities for teachers in their own classrooms and schools. Professional staff-members, such as research specialists, should be assigned the reponsibility for overall program evaluation. By collecting independent measurements of achievement, attitudes, and examination scores, the researcher would be able to come to objective conclusions concerning the worthwhileness of total or parts of programs. Since a slate of programs should include special instructional possibilities for the whole range of human talents, it may be necessary to maintain up-to-date reference files containing the names and specialties of community resource teachers, consultants, and lecturers.

Special program opportunities for talented children may be developed as supplemental units for the regular curriculum offered by the school. Or, special programs may take the form of a total redesign of a school district's curriculum. The curriculum can be reconstructed in such a way as to incorporate more abstract conceptual materials. An example of a "master program slate" involving many differential program possibilities follows:

I. *Special Grouping Possibilities*
   A. *Special Classes.* Highly intelligent pupils, for whom ordinary educational programs may be totally inappropriate, may be placed with other gifted youngsters into a special full-time classroom.
   B. *Cluster Grouping.* Small groups of from five to ten bright youngsters may be placed into a regular classroom setting. During special activities programs such as library reading, this group can engage in more specific study activities.
   C. *Homogenous Grouping.* A school district may structure all of its classrooms in terms of intellectual ability. Less intelligent children, when grouped together, may benefit from specialized instruction such as remedial reading. The more average groups of pupils will receive a balanced educational program. The brighter groups of youngsters will be exposed to materials and teaching techniques which challenge them more fully.
II. *Enrichment in the Regular Classroom*
   A. *Pupil Projects.* Special projects for advanced study and research

may be planned for all subject matter areas in order to enable pupils to study particular aspects of the curriculum in much more detail and scope.

B. *Supplemental Learning Kits.* Sequential grade level materials such as classroom reading libraries, science kits, study habits exercises, programmed learning materials, and audiovisual language materials may be provided in the regular classroom for individual pupil study.

C. *Special Subject Matter Units.* In given subject matter areas such as the fine arts, mathematics, science, or the language arts, special units which reflect higher level mental processes and advanced methodologies can be introduced into the regular classroom for brighter children.

D. *Utilization of Teacher Specialists.* Teachers with specialized subject matter background can cooperate with teachers possessing different backgrounds and form a teaching team approach. For example, a teacher with a background in science can visit different classrooms on a rotational basis and across grade levels while another teacher with dissimilar backgrounds rotates simultaneously teaching in her specialized area.

E. *Small Group Activity.* Small groups of pupils with similar interests and capabilities can meet periodically during the week to discuss reading materials and other forms of study. This seminar type activity can be supervised by a teacher or consultant other than the the classroom teacher.

F. *Large Group Activity.* Many learning activities such as television instruction, audiovisual demonstrations, guest lecturers, and simulated public activities lend themselves to large group organization. Two or more classrooms full of children can meet in larger quarters. Certain demonstrations in civics and citizenship lend themselves to large group activities. For example, simulation of a courtroom, United Nations meetings, and legislative deliberations may be demonstrated by the participation of large groups of youngsters.

III. *Acceleration and Advanced Placement*

A. *Advanced Classes.* Even at the elementary school level, advanced subject matter classes can be offered to qualified pupils.

B. *Ungraded Classrooms.* Particularly at the primary level, it is possible to allow bright pupils to advance through subject matter materials at their own pace. The artificial barriers of grade levels become immaterial. A child may enter the fourth grade after leaving kindergarten in from one to four years depending upon how rapidly he develops and masters his skills.

C. *Utilization of the Summer School.* Summer school sessions may be used for substitute grades. For example, properly qualified children may take a substitute third grade summer school directly from the second grade and enter that fall into the fourth grade. Also, summer schools may provide opportunities for studying subject matter areas, such as the fine arts, which may be neglected during the regular school year because of the press of other subject matter areas.

D. *Early Entrance.* Intelligent and literate children may be placed into the first grade before the age of five. Special programs may be designed to combine a half-year kindergarten experience with a half-year first grade experience. The actual acceleration of the pupil would occur when he is placed into the second grade one year or more earlier.

E. *Grade Combinations.* A school district may combine two or more grades during the regular school year. This type of program necessitates the rewriting of the entire curriculum. For example, the curriculum materials ordinarily offered in the fourth, fifth and sixth grades may be rewritten in such a way as to be presented in two years.

F. *High Ceiling Curriculum.* Many school districts hesitate to actually accelerate pupils by advancing them in actual grade level. However, they make it possible for the pupil to utilize materials two or more years in advance of his actual grade level. In such a program, the teacher must be particularly cognizant of her responsibility to record the actual level of achievement a given pupil arrives at in order to avoid duplication the next school year.

G. *Simple Double Promotion.* Grade skipping, although it has fallen into disrepute, is still practiced by many school districts. Providing that ample study has been made of the pupil it may be a simple way to achieve better adjustment into a more challenging classroom setting.

H. *College Classes.* Certain qualified high school pupils may be placed into college classes for credit. Such programs enhance motivation. Advanced placement into college may also be accomplished by examination procedures in which a pupil may "challenge" an introductory college class by taking an appropriate examination.

IV. *Opportunities for Placement into Special Settings*

A. *Special Seminars.* Opportunities for discussion of subjects in depth outside of the regular classroom may be offered even to elementary pupils. Small group seminars afford the pupil an opportunity to explore concepts in considerable depth and scope. Seminars may be planned to articulate with the curriculum offered in the regular classroom.

B. *Special Lecturers.* Scientists, authors, college professors, and other resource persons from the community can be utilized at any level for the embellishment of the curriculum offerings of the school. Lecture activities are most successful when planned in such a way as to coordinate with the curriculum offered during the regular school day.

C. *Individual or Small Group Counseling.* Even at the elementary school level, school districts may provide opportunities for counseling for educational, vocational, and personal concerns. A counselor with special training in group dynamics may be an appropriate leader for seminar activities designed to probe the meaning for various concepts presented in the classroom.

D. *Tutoring Opportunities.* Interested teachers, professionals from the community, and specially educated parents may provide tutoring activities for that occasional child whose interests and capabilities are so esoteric as to be difficult to provide in the regular school setting.

E. *Field Trips.* An imaginative teacher can schedule a series of trips to cultural activities, museums, industries, and other places of interest in order to supplement the curriculum with live experiences.

F. *Travel.* Summer travel to points of interest and even to other cultures is highly desirable. There can be no substitute in the life of a cultivated person for the insights gained by travel and interaction with peoples in other countries.

V. *Specialized Instruction for the Development of Unique Talent*

   A. *For the expressive arts* (e.g. dance, music, drama)

   B. *For the fine arts*

   C. *For the manual arts and crafts*

   D. *For the literary arts* (particularly creative writing)

   E. *For the industrial arts* (particularly higher level skills such as toolmaking)

   F. *For linguistics*

Such a master program might encourage enrichment activities for all grade levels. Advanced placement and acceleration opportunities might be preferred for the early grades and late high school. Special settings such as travel to foreign lands and extensive field trips might be more feasible for the higher grades and during the summer. Occasionally, a pupil will be found to be so far advanced as to require individually designed program possibilities at the outset. Other talented pupils may require only enrichment activities for their whole school career; their maturity levels might contraindicate advanced placement or placement into special settings.

As we invent, try out, and refine new programs for their benefit, we must infuse these programs with liberal amounts of in-service training for teachers, school officials, and parents. There is no easy way to understand the needs of the intellectual child. Literally, all of us engaged in this teaching process must ourselves be scholars and learners.

SOCIETY AND CULTIVATION

Collectively, schools constitute a key institution for the cultivation of modern men. But, it would be delusional to think that schools are the only agency for the education and cultivation of men. The works and cultural embellishments of civilizations in the forms of architecture, statuary, art, music, drama, literature, and machines profoundly influence the cognitive styles of the observer. The institutions of the family, church, and state probably exert greater influences upon the ultimate ideals of men than does the school. Moreover, too many great scholars have been shown to be completely uninfluenced by schools for us to assume that schools are the only agency for the formal teaching of knowledge. Therefore, it is appropriate to consider the cultivation process in the broader context of the civilization.

Civilizations mold the intellectual, esthetic, technological, and spiritual aspects of the emerging personalities of men. Paradoxically, civilizations may stultify the growth of individual men. Civilizations which have succeeded in bending all individuals have culminated in tradition-bound states which were unsuitable for survival in a dynamic world. Civilization must adapt to survive. Those civilizations which have prevailed were able to combine massive doses of historical lessons with sufficient tolerance for the changes that tradition must undergo.

Civilizations represent the sum total of our collective intelligence. That the emerging intelligent child should be exposed broadly to this heritage has never been seriously questioned. The extent to which the intelligent child may probe, challenge, and attempt to change this heritage has been seriously questioned.

How does our society cultivate its young? If our society, disregarding the lessons of history, proceeds to indoctrinate rather than educate, it will destroy its capability for flexible adaptation in a changing world. On the contrary, if it fails to provide its young with models of excellence, traditions, and the accumulated knowledge of the race, it will destroy itself in one generation. It will have produced men who are ignorant and sterile of ideas.

During the process of rearing children, we concern ourselves with nurturance. We allow the child to enjoy the privilege of expressing himself because we know that all too soon he will be confined by the standards which societies have developed for the regulation of men. As we watch the child develop, we concern ourselves with his selfish needs. We search for the motives which help to explain his behavior. We try to understand the child fully. Although we discipline him, we are more prone to excuse his mistakes.

Societies, however, care little for motives and do not cherish or pay attention to individual expression. Society concerns itself with products, work, utility, conformity, and stability. Most societies do permit reasonable amounts of departure from accepted behavior. Particularly, societies are tolerant of departures which lead to useful applications. As a consequence of societies expectations, the child must be introduced to reasonable amounts of discipline. The individual must convert his impulsivity into usable creative energy. There is no easy formula for this transition. Models for mental discipline may be viewed by the merging personality as environmental hurdles which are insurmountable. The more healthy individuals will view these hurdles as challenges. They will develop adaptive mechanisms to both overcome these hurdles and contribute to society new models of behavior.

No worthwhile cultural innovation builds upon nothing. Creative productivity must have a background of traditional knowledge upon which to build the new imaginative forms that we call "creative products." Most of the products we call "creative" are based upon established facts which have been transmuted or translated into new forms. Of course, it is true that some generations of men do develop creative ideas with sufficiently radical departure to be called "completely novel." Such radical departures are most apt to occur when the creative individual, such as an Albert Einstein, perceives that "motivation develops from a dissatisfaction with existing states." The prevailing attitudes and mores of societies can either place limitations upon the expression of man or open vistas of exploration heretofore never imagined.

It is not logical to assume that human societies will automatically welcome intellectuals and innovators. Societies normally operate within the boundaries of traditional mores, folkways, and values. Most folkways tend to be intolerant of individuals who are unpredictable, eccentric, or independent. Yet, the intellectual may have to behave in ways that other more simple folk would consider "odd."

Moreover, societies pass from states of barbarism to levels of civilization with uneven progress. As societies evolve, they may retain many of the attributes of their savage forebears. As societies codify their patterns of behavior and transmit these through language, they may retain many of the ancient beliefs and standards disguised in such a way as to be more palatable for modern men. Tyrannical insistence upon ritualistic kinds of cooperative behavior, distrust for men who deviate by being more intelligent and profound, and a fundamental belief in the magic inherent in forces of nature around them are but a few of the primitive outlooks that modern men retain. Generally, the ancient beliefs of the people tend to be in opposition to the empirical findings of the intellectual.

The majority of the people still react to the outer controls of society and the inner urges of unfulfilled needs without the slightest attempt to understand their behavior through rational means. Moreover, a cross section of the population, from any modern society, will reveal behavior ranging from that of a savage up to that of a highly organized human being. If we properly rear and educate an intelligent child, he must be appraised of this societal condition.

The young intellectual will invariably find himself surrounded by agonizing dilemmas. If he is too far ahead of his time, no one will understand him or heed him. If he does not produce ideas and useful work, committees consisting of retired admirals and senile educators will ridicule and harass him because he is not "living up to his potential." If he goes through to a graduate school eduaction and becomes a "working professional," he will become dissatisfied with himself because he is not producing creative and novel ideas. How can we advise such an individual? One way to begin, is to recapitulate the development of man. The follies or the successes of other intelligent men may serve as a model for his own intellectual emergencies. In order to acquaint the budding intellectual with the cultural accomplishments which are his heritage, societies should support institutions and supplemental cultural activities other than the school.

The following list of cultural activities is not intended to be exhaustive. Moreover, any such list is presumptuous. The making of a "list" indicates a kind of prescription for the dissemination of culture. This is not the spirit in which the following list is offered. This list should serve as a checklist of some of the cultural activities modern societies need to support in addition to schools in order to fully convey its heritage:

1. *Architecture.* Few civilizations have equaled the variability of form to be found in our architectural heritage. Western Civilization has not only evolved unique symmetries of its own but has absorbed an extensive array of ancient and Oriental forms. Some of our large cities do have specimens of truly great architecture. Even small cities could develop some sort of an architectural style. If we conduct a survey of the architecture in our area, we are bound to find college campuses, occasional buildings, or industrial complexes which reflect various architectural styles. For example, some of the buildings designed by the late Frank Lloyd Wright might be catalogued and shown to children. We should petition appropriate governmental agencies and planning commissions to design and build structures equivalent to our historical capabilities and opulence.

2. *Community Educational Enrichment.* We have every right to expect our schools to offer supplemental activities outside of the regular school day to complement their regular educational programs. Lecture series, special interest seminars, adult education, recreational instruction and activities, industrial and vocational displays, and general cultural activities such as recitals and art showings are but a few of the activities that a good school system should offer the public.

3. *Festivals.* A visit to any public meeting place for young people, should convince most skeptics that the human race has not lost its need for the festival. The vestal virgins still dominate our "cultural" activities through the new medium of the beauty contest and pregame pageant. Yet, we seem to be a self-conscious people. Every festival must be disguised and seem to be something else. There are signs that more festive activities are beginning to emerge on the cultural scene.

Unfortunately, because adults rarely participate in these activities, they tend to be primitive and sexual in character. "Folk song festivals," for example, seem to have adopted some of the song forms and general activities from past days and have injected healthy amounts of new forms and usages; but these new activities have developed by default because adults have failed to provide adequate festival activities for young people. We possess the traditional prescriptions for the practice of holidays. Reinstitution of the festival is only a matter of planning and earnest participation. Religious holidays, foreign folk festivals, fairs, or seasonal festivals are a few of the possibilties for festive occasions.

4. *Fine Arts.* Because of their particular importance, architecture, music and the theater will be discussed separately. If history is any judge, then the appreciation of the fine arts is one of the most important ingredients in the maturity of a cultivated human being. A few random exposures to objects of art is not enough to excite the imagination of an intelligent child. Exposure to the fine arts must be incessant, sequential, and developmental. An everyday environment which contains examples from the fine arts should be maintained.

Of course, exposure to the fine arts must not be forced upon a child. Art appreciation should consist of exemplary exposures. Tasteful art should be seen every day, in the background, in the home, or in the school. Displays of painting, drawing, sculpture, and other manual arts can be supported by business and community interests.

5. *Libraries.* Although it seems obvious that libraries should be included in a list of cultural activities for the intelligent child, it must be emphasized that the mere existence of a building that we label a "library" is not enough. To satisfy the need of the intelligent human being for literature and bibliographical resources, the community libraries must

be efficiently linked with other libraries in order to offer the widest possible variety of books and documents.

There are signs that brilliant young people are arriving at colleges with little if any exposure to great literature. Tracing backward, one finds that this predicament is caused by a reluctance on the part of school officials and parents to demand exposure to our great heritage of literature, even though it does not meet with the requirements of the bigot. A countermilitancy must be generated. Libraries must offer the widest possible variety of literature for the consumption of intelligent minds. The philosophy of libraries must defend a point of view which reflects complete freedom to read, think, and analyze all past and current literature. A legitimate scholar should have complete freedom to explore. Libraries and bookstores should be habitual visiting places for the growing intelligent child.

6. *Music.* The ancients realized the importance of music in the life of a cultivated human being. Music was usually incorporated with the major curriculum. In recent times, music has been equated with effeminacy and degeneration. Music, of course, can convey all things to all men. Possibly this has been the reason for both its past glory and its recent downfall. The fact remains that few men of eminence deny that music constitutes a great source of enjoyment for them.

As with other forms of the fine arts, music must be understood at some level to be fully appreciated. Music needs to be understood through disciplines of its own. Therefore, the school needs to offer many levels of exposure to music including training in musicianship.

Communities should insist on and support private and public musical teaching facilities; encourage participation in and support of local musical groups; insist upon a wide variety of musical exposures for children in homes, schools, and community activities; tolerate and support musical festivals; and offer financial and moral support for FM radio stations and educational television stations when they program satisfying musical events.

7. *Natural Surroundings.* Perhaps the most frequently overlooked ingredient in the life of a cultivated man is that of his natural surroundings. Our age has the distinction of being liable for more destruction of natural resources than all of the tyrants and pestilences of history put together. If contemplation in serene natural surroundings is a prerequisite to the development of ideas, then it is no wonder that we despair for the lack of new philosophers in our generation. The tendency for urban areas to utilize every square inch of ground for buildings, parking lots, or streets must be reversed.

The presentation of state and national parks might be a beginning. In addition, urban communities should reassess their "stripping" practices which leave cities devoid of natural beauty. Ideally, the child should be exposed daily to the beauty of nature. Our schools should be built in such a way as to enclose and be surrounded by living things.

8. *Sports and Athletics.* This is one category in which modern American society does offer considerable cultural outlets. However, while such competitive sports as baseball or football are highlighted, other athletic activities may be wholly neglected. No great peoples, since antiquity, have been known to neglect the physical nature of man. All of the fine attributes of the human spirit may be evoked in an athletic performance.

Community support for healthful athletic activities might take the following forms:

A. encouragement of excellent physical development in the schools through greatly improved physical education programs;
B. introduction of a much wider range of athletic contests in order to facilitate a wider range of kinesthetic abilities;
C. discouragement of brutal, dangerous, or destructive "sports," such as boxing;
D. more public support for gymnasiums, stadiums, and playing fields; and
E. more emphasis upon awards and honors for physical excellence as well as competition.

9. *Theatre and Other Live Performances.* Perhaps the most neglected of the cultural outlets is that of the performing arts. Although many amateur groups have been organized, professional performing societies are becoming a rarity. Professionals complain that they find little support when they visit the hinterlands. A casual assessment of any typical suburban or rural area will reveal little if any live performances of the dance, of poetry readings, or of plays. Some say that television has come to substitute for many of the performing arts. However, the intelligent child deserves the opportunity to observe live performances. The school ought to be a place where the child can experiment with live performances of his own. However, the student needs to learn the standards of excellence in performance which can only be gained by direct observation of skillful performers.

All too often, educators view the school as a training institution. Education is equated with conditioning or indoctrination. In order to avoid such an unfortunate interpretation of the educational process, we have discussed schools in the broader context of cultivation. While the school administrator plans a new program for talented children, he should bear in mind that the "program design" he works with is only a model. The model must be related to cultural products. What purpose would be served by an acceleration program if the accelerant failed to attend college and excel in a scholarly profession? Why bother with an "enrichment program" in the fine arts unless we obtain evaluative findings to verify that the students actually add aesthetic qualities to their everyday living?

Chapter 5

INTERESTS AND OPINIONS OF THE GIFTED

A S we rear and educate gifted children, we may become obsessed with
such factors as achievement to the neglect of other factors as inclination. The child tends to take his ability for granted; he is far more concerned
with his desires, needs, predispositions, and interests. As programs for the
gifted are evaluated, it is regrettable to note that little time is devoted to
talking with the children themselves. It will be shown that gifted children
are capable of providing school planners with insightful evaluations of the
effectiveness of programs, as well as sound suggestions for program improvement.

We have previously equated "giftedness" with "potentiality for productivity" and "talent" with "manifest productivity." The most reliable indicator of giftedness is still the IQ, representing a general pool of potential
talent. The direction in which a gifted person develops will depend heavily
upon his inclinations (e.g. interests and values). Can it be doubted that the
great violinist is first of all a gifted child, who chooses to express the intelligence through the medium of music?

The act of becoming a mature person may be traced, in part, by studying
changes in basic inclination. From the emotionally loaded interests of
childhood will develop the intellectualized values of the youth. Complexes
of values later form the missions of the productive man.

We cannot react passively to the development of values in the gifted. The
very survival of civilization may depend upon the integration of social,
political, and scientific values. Since values appear to be exclusively environmentally determined, we can profoundly influence them through educational intervention. The absurdity of indoctrination has been verified by
the failure of totalitarian governments to control their intellectuals. The
democratic ideal calls for the free exposure of all points of view; judgment
is reserved for the individual. Schools have an obligation to objectively expose the student to the diversified values of mankind. From this array, the
gifted individual will choose his unique set of values upon which he will
develop his own philosophy of life.

Fortunately for posterity, the gifted tend to be constantly involved in
the evaluation of their personal philosophies. This is the main reason why
counseling programs should be included in master program sequences for
the gifted. Most of the material collected for this chapter was based on
actual interviews with gifted children and youth in group counseling sessions.

119

In one study, random samples of gifted, normal, and retarded pupils were studied in terms of their interest patterns. It will be shown that the interests of the gifted tend to be uncorrelated with any other group, including "bright" youngsters. Indeed, each intellectual level appears to have its unique interest configuration. This finding should suggest the possible need for separate activities. This notion will be suggested, later, when it will be demonstrated that the gifted actually prefer segregated experiences and classes.

In another study, 119 gifted secondary students were interviewed to obtain their personal recommendations for academic program changes. They preferred (a) more freedom in course selection; (b) more variety in "heavy" courses such as foreign language, mathematics, literature, and social science; (c) more opportunity for intellectual criticism; (d) discussion of "real" controversial issues (as opposed to the contrived issues sometimes presented by teachers); (e) more recognition for their work; and (f) selected types of classroom segregation.

Amalgamating the viewpoints of gifted children and youth, it may be noted that they are concerned with "becoming an intellectual" as well as the "responsibilities of intellectual leadership." An attempt will be made to analyze these maturational processes with a view toward constructive recommendations for supportive adult roles.

ACADEMIC INTEREST PATTERNS

The academic interests of gifted children are of special importance since they will influence his adaption to school and, later, his choice of a profession. One of the more dangerous assumptions made by schools is that all children share similar academic interests, or lack of them. Academic interests are, on the contrary, extremely variable and associated with intelligence. If a school constructed a curriculum based upon the academic interests of normal children, and regrettably many schools do, they might hold the attention of average and dull pupils, but they would fail to challenge the bright and gifted. It has been known for a long time that bright children are more interested in academic pursuits such as reading or calculating than are duller children. This tendency involves more than being able to perform. The constitutional endowment of the intelligent child causes him to apply thoughtful methods to all of his pursuits, whereas the more limited child will content himself with rote learning and random observation.

In the study which follows, random samples of pupils from exceptional and normal groups were studied with reference to their academic interest patterns. In general, it was found that the more highly talented pupils display significantly more interest in academic areas, particularly reading, science, and arithmetic. It was found that most groups are uninterested in writing and social studies. The interest areas showing the most deviation from group to group included interest in class activity, science, and arithmetic.[1]

Some generalizations that could be inferred from this study included (1) each group seemed to be unique in its particular interest configuration, (2) gifted pupils' interests differed most from those of other groups with no particular patterns of deviance, and (3) the interests of average and less talented pupils were more closely related than the interests of gifted and more talented pupils.

Plan of Study

Children in the intermediate grades (grades 4 through 6) were chosen for study by assigning random numbers to all pupils in these grades and selecting subjects from a table of random numbers. Excepting teachers for the mentally retarded, no teacher filled out more than three interest questionnaire forms. Since the pupils were selected for study at random, smaller samples could be used. Approximately thirty pupils from each academic group were chosen since this figure represented typical class size.

The pupils were selected from the population of a California unified school district which practices homogenous grouping of pupils. In this district "homogenous grouping" involves the differential placement of pupils at a given grade level into one of five levels of classroom including (1) gifted classes, (2) "X" sections, (3) "Y" sections, (4) "Z" sections, and (5) classes for the "educable mentally retarded." The criteria for the differential placement of pupils include intelligence (IQ), scores on standardized achievement tests, past academic performance, and teacher judgment. (See Table 13 for summary of selection criteria.)

The working definition of an "interest" might be expressed, "interests . . . represent a tendency to select one activity or thing in preference to something else . . . interests are likes."[2] Jager and Froelich have described four methods for collecting information about a pupil's interests: "(1) observing the individual, (2) getting his expressions of interests, (3) studying the activities in which he has engaged, and (4) measuring his interests by means of an interest inventory."[3] Teachers used the first three of these methods to assess the sample of pupils studied. Prior to filling out interest rating forms for each pupil, in-service training sessions were conducted for

---

[1] Rice, J.P.: A comparative study of academic interest patterns among selected groups of exceptional and normal intermediate children. *California Journal of Educational Research,* 14 (No. 3):131-137, May 1963.

[2] Froelich, C., and Hoyt, K.: *Guidance Testing.* Chicago, Science Research Associates, 1959.

[3] Jager, H., and Froelich, C.: Guidance tools for vocational shop instructors. *Vocational Instructors' Shop Handbook,* 7:12-14, Fall 1947.

TABLE 13

SELECTED DESCRIPTIONS OF THE GROUPS STUDIED
INCLUDING MEAN IQ AND IQ RANGE

Group	Description	Mean IQ	IQ Range	Sex Ratio Boys/Girls	N
"Gifted" grades 4-6	School grades typically high. IQ above 130. Attend special gifted classes. Teachers highly recommended.	140.1	131-160	1.00 (19:19)	38
"X" sections grades 4-6	School grades typically high. Accelerated classroom work. High teacher recommendations.	122.1	105-138	1.00 (15:15)	30
"Y" sections grades 4-6	School grades average to above average. Classroom work mediocre to good. Teachers rate as "average worker."	108.4	95-116	1.00 (15:15)	30
"Z" sections grades 4-6	School grades below average. Classroom work unpredictable. Teachers rate as "slow-plodding."	94.2	81-107	1.50 (18:12)	30
"EMR" Intermediate sections	Educable mentally retarded. Special training classrooms. Have psychological diagnosis of "retarded."	70.3	57-80	3.00 (27:9)	36

the participating teachers in order to encourage the use of uniform rating techniques.

The following general techniques for rating pupils' interests were suggested during these training sessions: (1) systematically disregard proficiency or achievement when rating interests; (2) base the greatest share of your rating on an objective long-term observation of the pupil in your classroom; (3) interview all pupils utilizing concise questions concerning their academic interests (e.g. Do you like to read? Is reading your favorite subject? What subjects do you like better than reading?); (4) in your final rating weigh such factors as the pupils' hobbies, clubs he belongs to, and sparetime activities.

The academic interest areas, such as "reading, arithmetic, science, class activity, etc.," were common terms in which teachers habitually think. The nine interest areas studied were discussed during the in-service teacher meetings in order to assure some common agreement. Utilizing a simple checklist, the teachers were asked to rate the pupils as "high, average or low" in interest for nine academic areas and rank each pupil from 1 (most interested) to 9 (least interested) for the nine interest areas.

Undoubtedly, wide differences existed among the pupils' perceptions of the interest areas studied. In general, the teacher was instructed to focus upon the pupils' activities. For instance, a desire to sing and enthusiastic participation in chorus might be one index of interest in "music." An interest in "social studies" would be indicated by active participation in community studies, projects as well as the pupil's positive admission that he "liked social studies." An interest in "art" would manifest itself in activities such as drawing. Teachers were encouraged to hold a student conference prior to filling out the questionnaire in order to reflect the pupil's self-appraisal in their ratings of him.

Discussion of Findings

Table 14 indicates the proportion of teachers who rated the academic interests of children in the various groups from high to low. The interests are listed in Table 14 in the order that teachers rated gifted pupils from high to low. In general, it can be seen that the gifted pupils tended to display more interests in the academic areas while the less talented children displayed more interest in non-academic areas such as class activity and physical activity. Gifted pupils as well as EMR pupils were rated as highly interested in class activity.

Table 15 indicates the composite rank assigned to pupils in the various sections by their teachers. Again, the table is set up based upon the rank order of the interest areas of gifted pupils. The gifted pupils were ranked as most interested in reading and were ranked 9 or least interested in social studies. Table 16 indicates the rank order correlations among these various group interest patterns. It can be seen that the interest configuration of gifted pupils does not resemble that of any other group while the interest patterns of the less talented students tend to be similar.

Teachers tended to rate gifted and "X" section pupils as "highly interested" far more often than teachers rated "Y," "Z," or "EMR" pupils as highly interested in any area. The following specific comments seem indicated by the findings:

1. *Reading.* Interest in reading showed a distinct pattern from gifted down to EMR pupils. The more talented the pupil, the more interested he was in reading.

2. *Class Activity.* Interestingly, this area shows a double peak for gifted pupils and for "EMR" pupils. For reasons not readily understood, "X" section pupils were rated as being relatively uninterested in this area. Subsequent discussion with teachers revealed that "class activity" meant to teachers such activities as class recitation, participation in group learning activities, and working on group projects. This finding tends to refute the notion that gifted pupils often do not readily participate in class activities.

3. *Arithmetic.* Only the gifted group indicated substantial interest in arithmetic. The other groups were characterized by mild interest in this area.

TABLE 14

PROPORTION OF TEACHERS RATING ACADEMIC INTERESTS OF CHILDREN AS HIGH, AVERAGE AND LOW

Interest	Gifted N=38			X N=30			Y N=30			Z N=30			EMR N=36			Chi Square[1] X^2
	High	Av.	Low	High	Av.	Low	High	Av.	Low	High	Av.	Low	High	Av.	Low	
Reading Class	84	13	3	70	23	7	23	60	17	13	47	40	11	39	50	89.85***[2]
Activity	61	37	3	37	50	13	47	50	3	30	43	17	64	22	14	27.75**
Arithmetic	58	39	3	37	53	10	37	40	23	20	40	40	17	42	31	30.29**
Science	58	31	11	67	23	10	27	63	10	17	57	27	—	39	61	72.23**
Writing	55	37	8	27	50	13	17	53	30	17	50	33	11	44	44	44.35**
Music	53	34	13	47	40	13	37	47	17	17	57	17	50	39	11	17.69*
Art	47	45	8	57	43	—	53	33	13	43	53	3	61	33	6	8.42
Physical Activity	42	37	21	50	33	10	70	27	3	40	53	7	67	25	8	28.39**
Social Studies	37	37	26	50	30	20	30	53	17	10	63	27	8	25	67	66.91**

[1] "Expected" figure based on weighted sample of X, Y, Z pupils.
[2] Significant at 5% (*) and 1% (**) level with 8 degrees of freedom.

TABLE 15

TYPICAL ACADEMIC INTERESTS OF CHILDREN AS RANKED BY
TEACHERS FROM MOST INTEREST (RANK 1) TO LEAST INTEREST (RANK 9)

Interest Area	Gifted	X	Y	Z	EMR
Reading	1*	1	8	8	7
Class Activity	2	8	3	3	2
Arithmetic	3	7	5	5	5
Science	4	2	7	6	9
Writing	5	9	9	7	6
Music	6	6	4	4	4
Art	7	3	2	1	3
Physical Activity	8	4	1	2	1
Social Studies	9	5	6	9	8

* Composite rank or rank order of the mean ranks.

TABLE 16

RANK ORDER CORRELATIONS AMONG INTEREST PATTERNS OF
GROUPS STUDIED

Groups	X	Y	Z	EMR
Gifted	0.000	−0.383	−0.150	−0.133
X		0.017	−0.050	−0.300
Y			0.867	0.833
Z				0.850

4. *Science.* As in the case of reading, interest in science showed some tendency to drop off with less talented pupils.

5. *Writing.* This area of interest tended to be rated and ranked relatively low for all types of pupils. However, gifted pupils were the only group to have a majority (55%) rated as "highly interested" in this area. There was a marked tendency for this interest area to be related to academic talent: the higher the talent, the more interest in writing.

6. *Music.* This interest area, as in the case of class activity, indicated higher interest among gifted and "EMR" pupils for reasons not readily understood. It may be that "music" has different meaning to teachers of gifted and EMR pupils. Follow-up study indicated that the teachers of the gifted tend to consider musical concepts and rigorous study of musical form while EMR teachers consider classroom singing and other nontheoretical activities as "music."

7. *Art.* Interest in art indicated some tendency to be more popular among less talented pupils. Here again, as in the case of "music" there may be some tendency for teachers to interpret the term "art" differently at different academic levels.

8. *Physical Activity.* This area was consistently rated and ranked highly for less talented pupils. "Physical activity" meant to most teachers par-

ticipation in sports, physical education, playground activity, and other outdoor functions. Some disinclination toward participation in this area was indicated for more talented students, particularly gifted students.

9. *Social Studies.* Interestingly, all groups indicated relative disinterest in this area. This may reflect the lack of formal subject matter treatment at this level in the view of the teachers interviewed afterward.

The results of this study indicated very clear differences among the intellectual groups of pupils studied. Each group was found to be unique in terms of its particular hierarchy of interests, although average, dull, and retarded children shared more interests in common than did bright and gifted pupils. A majority of bright and gifted pupils were found to be highly interested in reading, arithmetic, science, writing, and music; only a minority of average, dull, or retarded pupils were interested in these academic areas.

As the gifted child advanced from elementary to high school level, his interests will begin to crystalize sooner than is the case with normal students. Many of the standardized inventories of interests or values may be useful for use with gifted children, on an experimental basis, at earlier age levels. However, we should depend on face-to-face discussions with gifted students when we wish to find out what they are interested in doing or what they value. Remember that the gifted student will be more articulate, sure of himself and capable of reflection than will be the normal student. Therefore, the use of published inventories or structured devices may be unnecessary, since the information we seek may be directly related to us by the intelligent student using his own insight about himself.

UNDERSTANDING AND INFLUENCING INTERESTS AND VALUES

A growing child's inclinations may be as important as his endowment for the determination of his future adjustment. Yet, educators have tended to neglect the assessment and development of children's interests, values, and ultimate sense of mission. It is a mistake to assume that children are solely interested in the "academic" subjects that schools emphasize. A broader context for the study of interests is indicated. While the teacher should inquire into the existing inclinations of his students, he must also help the child to develop new interests and values.

It might be useful to think of interests, values, and life missions as progressively mature sorts of motivational orientations.[4] Observation indicates to us that the inclinations of children develop from emotional to rational levels as they mature. The inclinations of the infant are obviously related to his bodily needs and can be described as impulsive. The inclinations of

---

[4] Hurlock, E.: *Child Development.* 3rd ed. New York, McGraw, 1956, p. 440.

the child seem to emerge from his growing storehouse of emotional likes and dislikes.[5] The child can usually explain why he was "interested" in an activity, but the analysis follows the act. The youth becomes aware of "principles, precedents and morals" which prescribe certain activities and censure others. The youth's interests mature to values. Later, the man will consolidate and unify his values. He will attempt to comprehend life and death, Gods and men, and order and chaos in terms of an integral philosophy. The man will subscribe to a mission in life.

Since the emotionally loaded interests of the child form the roots for the values of the man, we must try to understand the process of attitudinal formation. Attitudes tend to reinforce and intensify inclinations.[6] We might define the three main points along the *inclination continuum* as follows:

1. *Interests:* simple inclinations and preferences; activities a person likes to participate in; emotional at inception, interests may be described and understood in rational terms; however, interests are rarely analyzed deliberately by the individual; upon inquiry, he is likely to report, "I (wanted to, felt like, liked) doing it."

2. *Values:* conscious priorities; the hierarchial system of appraisal by means of which a man chooses; behavior is preceded by rational or moral commitment; values cause men to assign differential worth to their activities and the behavior of others.

3. *Mission:* philosophical determinism; the master plan for living a man formulates to find fulfillment; the combination of value orientations toward an integrated understanding of life and its meaning; missions represent complexes of values and may be thought of as the highest callings of men.

In order to constructively influence the emerging interests and values of the child, adults must avoid the pitfalls of misinterpretation, interference, or criticism. Following are some of the most common reasons why adults fail to objectively understand the interests of children:

1. Adults ascribe their own more sophisticated interests to children.

2. Adults allow their feelings and judgements to censure or approve interests of children without reference to the child's feelings or needs.

3. Adults may be impatient. Accurate observation of a child's interests takes time and should include a number of episodes.

4. Adults may overinterpret or overestimate childish interests. All children are curious. They will try most activities at least once. Interests are more than transitory inclinations or impulses.

---

[5] *Ibid.*, p. 441.
[6] *Ibid.*, p. 444.

5. Adults may not approach the study of children's interests with a framework. Some system for the periodic recording of interests should be used. Some list of possible interests children display should be available.

The interests of early childhood are difficult to categorize. Each new activity may have a flavor all its own for the child. We know that he is fascinated by animals, narcissistic images, tangible objects he can possess, play activities, and his mother—for he tells us so as soon as he can talk. The young child's interests are fleeting. It is only when he becomes more aware of his intellectual capability for description, reason, and evaluation that he will acknowledge that he is "interested" in given activities or things. But, these early exposures to objects, surroundings, and general cultural adornments profoundly affect the future ways in which a given child's values will emerge.

The classification of children's interests, which appears below, was derived empirically from the ratings of fifty elementary schoolteachers. Initially, academic interests were studied as reported earlier in this chapter. The broader classification resulted as a by-product when the entire case studies, cumulative records, and evaluations of teachers were analyzed. This classification is not intended to be all inclusive. Moreover, children's interests vary according to their intellectual and maturational levels.[7]

Alphabetically, here are some of the main interests that gifted children between the ages of six and eleven were found to express in their activities and verbalizations:

1. *Body and Growth.* The child is intrigued by his own growth, bodily functions, and physical characteristics. Gifted children want and should obtain accurate knowledge about their anatomy and physiology.

2. *Entertainment.* Fun and enjoyment are ends in themselves for children. Such subjective descriptions of childish activities as "they are useless and silly" only reflect the prejudices of the adult perception. Adults should control entertainment by timing, not by blanket restriction. "Entertainment" for gifted children includes aesthetic experience, nature study, as well as normal play activities.

3. *Fads and Fashions.* Out of their need to identify, children copy the fads of their time. Today, gifted eight-year-olds emulate behavior that was deemed adolescent a generation ago. The adult must tolerate, within common sense limits, such things as silly decorum or outlandish coiffures in the knowledge that these will pass. The eye for detail possessed by the gifted child may exaggerate or accelerate his flair for fashion.

---

[7] Tyler, L.: The relationship of interests to abilities and reputation among first grade children. *Educational Psychological Measurement,* 11:255-264, 1951.

4. *Family.* The older child asks about his forebears. He is concerned with heritage, clannish identity, and the exploits of his ancestors. What he learns will profoundly affect his morality. The gifted child grasps his relationships to national and social identities sooner than normal children.

5. *Games and Sports.* Essentially physical, these interests also involve competition and the development of controlled responses. The gifted enjoy competitive games of all varieties (e.g. chess, various sports, cards).

6. *Heroes.* Children are inclined to interpret history and their own times in terms of heroes. Learning about heroes provides models toward which they may aspire. Anticipating the "self-ideal" model a child should develop, the teacher ought to elaborate upon the faults and failures as well as the accomplishments of heroes. The gifted tend to identify with intellectual, artistic, and political heroes (e.g. Einstein, Beethoven, Lincoln).

7. *Life and Death.* The early considerations of life and death are naive and serene. It is a pity that most children acquire dread for this topic because of the fearful evasions of adults. This concern will be lifelong. The question of the child, Why was I born?, is also the question of the mature philosopher. The gifted indicate desire for philosophical discourse early in childhood.

8. *Mechanisms.* The child's interest in motion and structure is more than a "mechanical interest." The creation of machines must be preceded by studies of power, motion, space, and time. The child asks, What makes it go? The man will ask and answer, How can I make it go better?

9. *Nature.* No one communicates more fully with the secret ecological workings of nature than the gifted child. But alas, we sometimes reward his exhilaration in the outdoors with confinement and his tendency to explore with inhibitions. Given the opportunity, the gifted child begins to integrate his interest in nature with religious and aesthetic experience.

10. *Religion.* Supernatural forces exist for the child. This primitive realization may be supported by faith and guidance and become the belief of the adult, or it may be ridiculed and become the cynicism of the unbelieving adult. The contamination of religious belief by such pagan idolatries as Santa only confuse the child and detract from his ultimate reconciliation of belief with intellectual maturity. Gifted children tend to be highly critical of our irreverent treatment of such religious holidays as Christmas or Easter.

11. *School.* Generalized interest in "going to school" may be thought of as a motivational entity. However, the academic interests of the child very shortly come to resemble our superimposed notions of "subjects." So, the child reports "I'm interested in reading, arithmetic, writing, music, art or social studies," with differential enthusiasm. At first, interest

in school is associated with broader feelings such as "love of learning" or "exploration."

12. *Science.* Although subsumed under "school interests," science has acquired a relatively important status which places it in a class all its own. Right or wrong, we emphasize the importance of science to children quite early. Some children may confuse mere technology with science. Therefore, we need to avoid superficial explanations and present science, even to young children, for what it really is—a method for the collecting, codifying, and applying of bodies of knowledge.

13. *Selfhood.* Children are interested in themselves in down-to-earth ways. They enjoy flattery, they admire themselves physically, and they like to be the central characters of stories. Self-assurance will lead to capabilities for leadership. Slowly, the narcissistic concern of the child will be transformed into the empathetic outlook of the adult. The articulateness of the gifted child enables him to insert himself into adult activities with ease; hence, he may be misdiagnosed as "conceited" or "vain."

14. *Sex.* Identification with boys or girls leads to a role. This role soon becomes reinforced by desires. Questions compound. Orderly discussions of reproduction, morality, emotions, or puberty cannot be avoided with gifted children. Usually, their interest in sex will be more objective or scientific than the puerile concerns of other children.

15. *Vocational Activity.* Gifted children attempt to identify with different vocations quite early. Gifted children should be provided as much information about professions as they can comprehend, early in elementary school. The gifted child comprehends status, socioeconomic and educational differences in occupations.

As we watch the child's interests grow, we note that he becomes more reflective. He consciously chooses certain activities over others. Measures of worth are introduced into his decisions, in short, he begins to formulate a personal system of values.

The *Study of Values*[8] based upon the work of Spranger's *Types of Men*[9] provides a useful basis for a classification of human values. However, Spranger's attempt to classify the motives of men into six types of values, including the theoretical, economic, aesthetic, social, political and religious, has certain shortcomings. Allport notes that "Spranger . . . holds a somewhat flattering view of human nature. He does not allow for formless or

---

[8] Allport, Vernon: *Study of Values:* A Scale for Measuring the Dominant Interests in Personality, 3rd ed. Boston, Houghton, 1960.

[9] Spranger, E.: *Types of Men.* New York, Stechert, 1928. (Translated from Lebensformen, 5th edition by P. Halle Pigors: *Max Niemeyer Verlag.*)

valueless personalities, nor an expedient or hedonistic philosophy of life. . . ."[10]

Any consideration of the full range of value orientations would need to consider primitive, evil, or sensual motives as well as the more acceptable values. History abounds with intelligent people who have been recidivistic, nihilistic, hedonistic, or materialistic as a matter of philosophical *choice*. As we consider a tentative classification of human values, the following factors must be borne in mind:

1. *Human values may be constructive or destructive*. For example, as we speak of humanitarianism, so, we can contemplate its opposite, "anti-value" of misanthropy.

2. *Men may choose to ignore their values for the sake of expediency, survival, or unconscious pressures.*

3. *Men do not necessarily adhere to certain values at the expense of others*. Some men may be exclusively "aesthetic," others may be theoretical, political, or religious in varying combinations.

4. *Maturity in values does not develop uniformly*. Men may mature rapidly and broadly in values or they may fixate or regress in certain areas while developing in others.

Stated in terms of the philosophical code it will become, here are some of the main value orientations gifted youths may adopt based upon extensive interviews with high school level gifted youths:

1. *Aestheticism*. Appreciation of what is beautiful is the main goal of the aesthetic man. In addition to the fine arts, diverse fields such as mathematics or even athletics may be interpreted in terms of the aesthetic modalities of form, harmony, and style.

2. *Altruism*. Service and devotion to others, as opposed to domination, are the goals of the social man. Strong emotions such as love and sympathy help to motivate the altruistic man, although "altruism" for the gifted is essentially and intellectual determination based upon recognition of the needs of mankind.

3. *Domination*. The exercise of power and the tendency to view other men as objects for manipulation characterize the methods of the dominating man. Ordinarily, such men seek power through political or economic domination.

4. *Hedonism*. The pleasure seeking man has his counterpart in the ascetic man, which might be viewed as the "anti-value" for hedonism. The apparent need to indulge the gratification of sexual and sensual needs motivates these persons. Possession of this value orientation

---

[10] Allport, *op. cit.*, p. 3.

may help to explain much of the behavior of the so-called underachieving gifted.

5. *Materialism.* The doctrine advocating that material well-being supersedes all other ethical considerations has certainly gained popularity. Unfortunately, materialism as a way of life tends to divorce itself from appreciation, metaphysical considerations, or moral outlooks. Among more scientific men, materialism may take the form of naturalism.

6. *Moralism.* Moralistic, mystical, and rationalistic types of man are all contemplative. Any of them may or may not be "religious." Moralism concerns itself with legalistic interpretations of good and evil. Conduct, precedent, and conscience guide the moral man. Among gifted youth, the moralist may be viewed as a "drag" by his peers. His tendency to condemn others may be accomplished by ritualistic conformity on his own part.

7. *Mysticism.* Spiritual men rely upon revelation and belief as opposed to reason. They are less dependent upon their environment and may be viewed as "other worldly" by their peers. The mystical man's devotion to his causes is always intense but may appear enigmatic to others. Some of the current youthful cults are excellent examples of mystical people lacking religion.

8. *Nihilism.* Although inarticulate, many of the activities of modern youth display destructive nihilism. The notion of total destruction may be particularly dangerous in our age when it cannot be easily controlled. The hostile ethics of the nihilist may color other value orientations. For example, the dominant man many become the tyrant. The extent of nihilism among gifted youth may be a problem worthy of national concern.

9. *Practicality.* The practical man is concerned with usefulness; he is a doer. Truth is equated with function and the nineteenth century ethical codes for defining work or utility may be appealing to him. Although a comparatively rare value orientation among gifted youth, "practicality," nevertheless, tends to be reinforced by schools.

10. *Rationalism.* Truth, factuality or conclusions may be sought for their own sakes. Reason rather than beauty, feelings, or tradition is thought to be the main source of knowledge. The theoretical man may be subsumed under this type. Although the theorist is more speculative, his abstract principles have to be related to reality by means of applied rational methodologies. Rationalism is popular among today's gifted youth.

As youth struggles toward maturity, values tend to unite to form higher concepts we call "missions." Youth is rarely content with merely copying the ethics of his times. He chooses to add to, not just repeat, his heritage.

His sense of mission defines his goals. To be a scientist means to apply experimental techniques toward the solution of human problems. Rational, altruistic, and practical values merge into a new synthesis.

We cannot dedicate ready-made missions for others. We educate, we do not indoctrinate. But, we can note the progressive development of our students' inclinations and be certain that they are widely exposed to the disparate value orientations of Western civilization, as well as other civilizations. It would be impossible to categorize "types of mission." Literally, every great man represents the living embodiment of the unique mission his particularistic set of values drove him to acquire:

Winston Churchill: dominant, moral and rational, yet traces of aestheticism and hedonism appear also;

Albert Einstein: eminently rational, but aesthetic, altruistic, and moral also; or

Adolph Hitler: essentially nihilistic with strong domination tendencies, he displayed an odd combination of materialistic, moralistic, and mystical values.

We have reviewed some of the dimensions of inclination which should be of concern to educators as they try to understand and influence their gifted students. We must consider more than the fleeting interests of the young child, because the motivational and attitudinal orientations of the child will culminate in the sense of mission, or lack of it, in the adult.

In order to implement the understanding and development of sound values, it is suggested that schools consider subscribing to the following program:

1. A philosophy of education should contain specific commitments to democratic, rational, moral, and aesthetic values. These positive values notwithstanding, liberal exposure to diverse, conflicting, and foreign values should be tolerated and encouraged.

2. Teacher training should include study of the motivational basis for behavior and decision making. Teachers should know how to assess inclinations as well as other personality variables.

3. The interests and values of students should be periodically studied. Interviews, checklists, inventories, objective observation, and standardized instruments can all be used to accomplish a better knowledge of the students' interests and values.

4. Students must be systematically exposed to diverse values and yet learn to choose. Teachers from different disciplines should attend periodic seminars during which they compare their content and discuss ways in which subject matter lends itself to value formation and integration.

5. Through follow-up, teachers should evaluate their affect upon the

destinies of students. It would be difficult to think of a teacher's mission without altruism.

The amoral scientist or the nihilistic politician have their roots in the failures of childhood. Educators must not only impart knowledge, they must also interpret the ethical codes with which knowledge can be applied.

OPINIONS OF GIFTED STUDENTS REGARDING SECONDARY SCHOOL PROGRAMS

The San Diego Unified School District has developed diversified and exemplary programs for mentally gifted students since 1948. Periodic assessment of the special scholastic problems and needs of students with IQ's in excess of 150 have resulted in the establishment of such experimental programs as ungraded classes in the elementary schools and special groupings and seminars in the high schools.

This study[11] included 119 junior and senior high school students, all of whom were interviewed with a view toward gathering their opinions and recommendations for changes in their current academic programs. Essentially, these students were asked open-ended questions designed to (1) ascertain the way in which they would design their own courses of study; (2) contrast existing curriculum offerings with their ambitions, interests, and aspirations; (3) discover whether or not students are afforded sufficient opportunity to think; (4) assess current outlets for creative and intellectual expression; and (5) answer a number of controversial issues, such as Do gifted students prefer to be in segregated classes?

Student interviews were conducted by utilizing a pre-arranged list of discussion questions. A consultant acted as recorder with occasional administrative personnel attending some of the sessions as objective observers. In addition to oral interviews, students were invited to submit written answers; approximately 75 percent of the 119 students submitted some sort of written comment which was considered in the overall compilation of the findings.

In compiling the findings, an attempt was made to distinguish among the responses of gifted versus highly gifted students, boys versus girls, and junior high versus senior high school students. However, responses among these groups tended to be consistent with exceptions to be noted in the findings.

Objective measurements of course choice and philosophy of education were obtained by administering specially prepared sets of checklists. A "Checklist for Academic Course Choices" was empirically structured from

---

[11] Rice, J.P., and Banks, G.: Opinions of gifted students regarding secondary school programs. *Exceptional Child*, —:269-273, Dec. 1967.

TABLE 17

HIGH SCHOOL COURSES RATED BY GIFTED STUDENTS

English	Science	Social Science	Mathematics	Foreign Language	Business	Industrial Arts
Communication Skills	Aeronautics	American History	Advanced Placement Mathematics	Chinese	Advertising	Aeronautics
Composition	Biology	American Institutions	Algebra	French	Bookkeeping	Audiovisual Machines
Creative Writing	Botany	American Problems	Calculus	General Foreign Language	Business Economics	Automotive Mechanics
Debate	Chemistry	Ancient History	College Mathematics	German	Business English	Comprehensive General Shop
Dramatics	Earth Science	Asian History	Elementary Analysis	Hebrew	Business Law	Drafting
English	Electronics	California History	Elementary Functions	Italian	Business Mathematics	Electricity-Electronics
Humanities	General Science	Civics	Geometry	Latin	Business Work Experience	Forestry
Journalism	Life Science	Current History	Introduction to Advanced Math	Pre-Language	Consumer Economics	Graphic Arts
Leadership	Photography	Economics	Mathematics, Analysis	Russian	Consumer Mathematics	Handicrafts
Library	Physical Science	European History	Mathematics, Business	Spanish	Cooperative Distributive Work Experience	Home Mechanics
Literature American	Physics	Freshman Problems	Mathematics, Consumer		Merchandising	Industrial Science
Literature English	Physiology	Geography	Mathematics, Industrial		Cooperative Office Training	Junior Engineering
Literature Modern	Radio	Government	Trigonometry		Dictation and Transcription	Metalworking
Literature World	Zoology	International Relations			Economics, Commercial Geography	Photography
Newspaper		Latin American History			General Business	Shop
Play Production		Problems of Democracy			In-school Business Work Experience	Stagecraft
Publications		Psychology			Library Business Practice	Surveying
Public Speaking		Senior Problems			Office Machines	Upholstery
Radio and Tele-vision Speech		Social Studies			Office Practice	Woodworking
Reading		Sociology			Record Keeping	
Speech Arts		Student Government			Retailing, Merchandising	
Speech and Drama		World History			Salesmanship	
Stagecraft		World Affairs			Shorthand	
Year Book		World Culture			Typing	
		World Problems				

lists of courses offered by all high schools in California. This exhaustive checklist of academic high school course offerings included any academic course actually being offered by any high school in California. Lists of high school courses were presented to students in alphabetized lists. Students rated each course in terms of (1) whether or not it should be offered by their high school, (2) would they take the course, and (3) priorities among courses, which were listed by the student. The courses presented to students are listed in Table 17. A "Checklist of Possible Purposes for Your School" was directly adapted from an earlier checklist used to study

TABLE 18

CHECKLIST OF POSSIBLE PURPOSES FOR YOUR SCHOOL

Following is a list of possible purposes for your school. Read all of thees purposes in order to judge their importance. Then, place an "X" in front of each statement to indicate the importance of each purpose using your own opinion.

Check each purpose as (1) an essential purpose of all schools, (2) a recommended, but secondary or minor purpose, or (3) as not being a purpose.

Essential	Recommneded	Is Not		Rank
( )	( )	( )	A. It prepares young people for homemaking and family life.	( )
( )	( )	( )	B. It promotes self-understanding and good mental health habits.	( )
( )	( )	( )	C. It provides specific vocational education.	( )
( )	( )	( )	D. It provides preparation for further formal education.	( )
( )	( )	( )	E. It helps the student develop and appreciate creativity.	( )
( )	( )	( )	F. It helps the student to realistically choose his life's work.	( )
( )	( )	( )	G. It promotes social development and maturity.	( )
( )	( )	( )	H. It promotes the democratic way of life.	( )
( )	( )	( )	I. It provides help for the student in solving personal adjustment problems.	( )
( )	( )	( )	J. It provides general orientation and guidance programs.	( )
( )	( )	( )	K. It teaches basic skills for everyday living.	( )
( )	( )	( )	L. It provides academic counseling and guidance.	( )
( )	( )	( )	M. It provides a program of adult education beyond high school.	( )
( )	( )	( )	N. It promotes international understanding and peace.	( )
( )	( )	( )	O. It promotes the development of aesthetic skills and appreciation.	( )
( )	( )	( )	P. It helps develop sound moral and spiritual values.	( )
( )	( )	( )	Q. It emphasizes the use of the intellect and promotes critical thinking.	( )

Beginning with the most essential purpose that you feel your school should stand for, rank all of the 17 purposes in order from (rank (1) most essential), (rank (2) next most essential), and so forth down to (rank (17) the least essential purpose).

junior college students (see Table 18). Students rated and ranked seventeen simply stated purposes for a school in terms of their essentiality. This resulted in an hierarchal list of philosophical purposes for the existence of a school as determined by gifted students which could be compared with similar lists from college students and teachers.

Throughout the interview sessions, special attention was paid to the observation of differences between extremely mentally gifted students (Binet IQ 155 and up) and the academically gifted (Binet IQ between 130 and 154). In a more informal manner, the interviewer and observer were watchful for any other possible subgroup differences as, for example, differences between boys' and girls' responses.

In general, interviewers and objective observers agreed that the techniques used resulted in an objective survey of the thinking and opinions of secondary school gifted students.

Since the population of San Diego is cosmopolitan and represents a nationwide sample of emigrees, it should be possible to generalize from these findings.

Actual Responses of Gifted Students

It can be assumed that all of the following statements represent a majority opinion or recommendation of the entire group of gifted unless otherwise noted. Where differences in opinion or recommendation occurred among subgroups, this will be specially noted. Otherwise, it can be assumed that boys and girls, gifted and extremely gifted, junior high school and high school students were all in majority concurrence concerning the point or issue stated.

Given freedom, how would gifted students redesign their own curriculum?

1. Students expressed a desire for more freedom in course selection from the seventh grade up.

2. Much dissatisfaction with physical education, home economics (girls), and shop (boys) was noted. Opinions were strong and varied and ranged from suggestions from elimination of the subjects or putting them on a voluntary basis to completely redesigning these courses to better meet the needs of these students. Constructive suggestions included such ideas as more flexible scheduling of gym periods utilizing weekly or double sessions; coordinating home economics courses with family studies, cultural embellishments such as flower arranging and foreign cuisine; and the adapting of shop courses to the intellectual interests of the students such as the making of high fidelity units or laboratory equipment.

3. An emphatic plea for more literature courses was noted.

4. Requests for more fine arts courses, music, and dramatics were noted.

5. Junior high school students almost unanimously requested more freedom, flexibility, and choice in their academic program with early specialization. Conversely, senior high school students endorsed the "general education concept." High school students were willing to defer specialization until college.

6. Some significantly different outlooks on the part of girls versus boys included the following:

Girls were more critical of their required courses such as home economics than were boys of their required courses. Girls more often expressed feelings of being "manipulated" into courses they would not choose on their own. Girls were less definite about career choices and expressed considerably more frustration when talking about their educational planning for the future. Highly gifted girls voiced more openly critical or hostile comments than did highly gifted boys. In general, it appeared that the gifted girls were less comfortable with the knowledge of their giftedness than were gifted boys.

7. Junior high school students differed significantly from high school students in the following ways:

Junior high school students were critical of the social studies; high school students tended to favor the social sciences as course choices.

More complaints about grading and the emphasis upon grading were detected among junior high school students.

High school students voiced the need for college level work, consultation with outside experts, and the utilization of resources outside of the school.

Junior high school students requested changes in their existing program such as "more flexible scheduling, more time for study within the school day, more time for individual project activity on school time, and more choice of course patterns."

Senior high school students indicated a comprehension of the goals of general education. However, they emphasized the need for more specific subject matter treatment at the high school level. They were very complimentary when describing team teaching experiments they had participated in. High school students were more critical of teachers.

8. Combining all responses, the following composite word picture of the "idealized program" gifted students would design for themselves might be stated as follows:

Scheduling, choice of courses, study times, and grade level placement would be flexible. No student would be arbitrarily held to a grade level or "social level" assignment. Literally, each student would operate intellectually at a level best suited to his individual learning needs.

A culturally enriched and diversified curriculum of subject matter offerings would be about equally divided among the sciences, mathematics, fine arts, foreign languages, social sciences, and literature.

At the junior high level, interdisciplinary seminars and discussions would relate, for example, the sciences to the social sciences. At the high school level, subjects would be pursued in great depth and detail to a level now construed as "college level."

For the extremely gifted student, opportunity would be afforded, at any developmental level, for advanced placement. The need for advanced placement was especially stressed at the high school level.

Qualitatively new subject matter material, such as psychology or sociology, would be introduced at the high school level according to these students. Fundamentals already mastered at the high school level could be readily challenged by examination.

Thus, two essential changes in the existing program would be implemented: flexible programming at all grade levels and qualitative content changes in the subjects offered. More emphasis upon culturation and depth in subject matter treatment would be implemented. Such program restructuring would obviate the general objection to "too much drill and undue review" voiced by most students.

Do existing programs fit the aspirations, goals, and values of students?

1. The great majority (90%) believed that the existing curriculum was preparing them for college very well and constituted an excellent general education program. Among the few dissenters were those high school students who had not made career choices and indicated dissatisfaction with themselves and their progress toward a career choice. This might indicate a need for intensive vocational-professional counseling for selected groups of the gifted.

2. Few junior high school students indicated clear career choices when polled. Even among the high school groups, approximately 30 percent indicated that they had not chosen a career. The extremely gifted student was noted to be more apt to have a firm career choice.

3. In terms of developing their personal values, high school students voiced the need for more open discussion into controversial issues.

Among courses now available, what are the popular academic choices of gifted students?

The following academic courses are listed in the order of priority actually chosen by the gifted students through use of the checklists. In general,

75 percent or more of the students tended to choose the courses listed first and no course is listed unless 50 percent or more of the students indicated that they wanted to take the course:

Foreign language priorities: French, German, Russian, Spanish, and Latin;

Language arts priorities: humanities, creative writing, American literature, English literature, modern literature, and oral arts (debate or dramatics);

Mathematics priorities: geometry, algebra, calculus, and trigonometry;

Science priorities: chemistry, physics, and zoology;

Social science priorities: psychology, American history, economics, international relations, and ancient history.

What are the unpopular courses?

The results from the business or industrial arts courses were not discussed because, in general, only a minority of gifted students indicated that they would like to take the courses. An important exception to this statement was in the area of business courses. Seventy-five percent or more of the students indicated that they would like to take typing. Also, 75 percent or more of the seventh grade students indicated that they would like to take shorthand.

In general, both seventh and twelfth grade groups tended to check a majority of the courses in the column "Should be offered by my high school." Thus, they indicated preference for a wide-range curriculum and the "comprehensive high school" concept. Many of the courses, such as "composition, journalism, leadership, library, electronics, general science, physical science, current history, bookkeeping, drafting, and metal working," were checked by 75 percent or more of the gifted groups as needed course offerings in the high school. However, less than a majority of any group would take the courses themselves. These gifted groups appeared to be cognizant of the general needs of other students, while at the same time realistic and selective about their own academic needs.

Below, differences are noted between seventh and twelfth grade groups in their choice of unpopular courses:

75% of 7th Graders Did Not Mention:	*75% of 12th Graders Did Not Mention:*
English and Language Arts Courses	
Radio and television speech	Leadership
	Library
	Radio and television speech
	Stagecraft
Science Courses	
Earth science	Botany
	Earth science

75% of 7th Graders Did Not Mention: *75% of 12th Graders Did Not Mention:*

Social Science Courses
   American institutions   American institutions
   Freshman problems   California history
   Senior problems   Civics
                                              Freshman problems
                                              Geography
                                              Latin American history
                                              Social studies
                                              Senior problems

Mathematics Courses
   General math   Industrial math

Foreign Language Courses
   Hebrew and pre-language   Hebrew and pre-language

Business Courses
   Consumer economics   Business English
   Consumer mathematics   Work experience in merchandising
   Merchandising work experience   Office training
   Office training
   Retailing and merchandising

Industrial Arts Courses
   Upholstering   Forestry
                                              Industrial science
                                              Junior engineering
                                              Surveying
                                              Upholstering

Of course, all groups added courses not printed on the form. Courses such as "probability theory, astronomy, philosophy or political science" were mentioned. Twelfth grade groups indicated certain write-in choices with amazing regularity. For example, among English and language arts courses 75 percent or more of the twelfth grade group listed poetry, and more than half mentioned Grammar and Great Books as being courses which should be offered by a high school. Also, such courses as "Ocean-ography, Biochemistry, Computer Mathematics, Logic and Reasoning, and Greek and Latin" were mentioned.

Does the school provide possibilities for communication in order to stimulate and challenge thinking?

1. This question elicited more negative opinions than any of the other questions. Over 80 percent of the high school students polled answered "no" to this question.

2. Junior high school students, also reacting negatively to this question, stated that their existing educational program included too much "drill, review of fundamentals and teacher dictated curriculum."

3. General criticism was directed toward state textbooks. Students, at

all levels, alleged that many teachers "taught chiefly from the textbooks in order to cover rigid requirements and cover prescribed curriculum." The criticism of state textbooks was more severe among the junior high school students.

4. Senior high school students volunteered more constructive criticism of teachers and their preparation. These students felt that teachers with "adequate training" were in a better position to stimulate and motivate the thinking processes.

5. Junior high school students felt that the thinking processes were best stimulated in their mathematics courses. Senior high school students mentioned the social sciences and English courses predominantly when praising teachers for the inclusion of thinking processes in their course content. Interestingly, no group mentioned the sciences.

Are there sufficient outlets for creative and intellectual student products?

1. Polls indicated, almost unanimously, that there were not sufficient opportunities for displaying or being recognized for creative or intellectual products. Science fairs were most often mentioned as the only outlet. School publications were criticized because they "systematically excluded controversial or avante-garde material." In fact, it was interesting to note that some enterprising pupils had published a clandestine publication!

2. All felt the need to create something. A majority indicated that they had already produced some worthwhile product for which they could find no outlet for display, dissemination, or recognition. The kinds of products ranged from inventions, scientific equipment, and writings all the way to musical composition and artistic creations.

3. At the high school level the groups complained about "teachers who discouraged creative work in controversial areas." The students indicated that they wanted to study or analyze such areas as "atheism, birth control, communism, and nonconformity."

4. Among high school students there was a majority opinion that the existing outlets were loaded for the mathematics and sciences. The students desired a much wider range of opportunities to include "dramatics, musical composition, art displays, trade fairs for the display of inventions and debate societies."

5. The extremely gifted appeared to be more concerned with the lack of stimulation of the thinking processes and the lack of suitable creative outlets than were the gifted. The high school students were more concerned than were the junior high school students.

6. Junior high school gifted felt that there was more need for a situation in which to create, rather than outlets for the product. As examples of what they meant by a "situation" they cited such examples as "more

time to think alone . . . less emphasis on the repetition of basics, or, . . . opportunities to create are restricted to what the school wants created."

7. High school gifted, and the extremely gifted, emphasized that there was "too much emphasis on rote learning, drill and a tendency to deal with purely practical applications." These groups lamented the lack of "opportunity to think." Some indicated that the "high school campus is not the best opportunity for intellectual stimulation." These groups felt that teachers "emphasize quantity, as opposed to quality, most of the time."

8. The high school groups more often mentioned the need for opportunities to express one's self in writing. Most felt that literary magazines would be more effective if run by the students themselves.

Should students with different abilities be in classes together or separately?

1. In general, all groups favored some separation of gifted students during the school day for selected instructional activities.

2. The extremely gifted students were almost unanimous in their opinions that totally separate education was necessary.

3. Among the gifted groups (Binet between 130 and 154), there was more difference of opinion. However, the majority felt that some separation was necessary, especially in advanced subjects such as mathematics.

4. All groups felt that courses such as physical education, arts and crafts, or foreign language might be shared with normal groups of students.

5. The extremely gifted groups did not appear to be impressed by the "social motive." They felt little motivation toward assistance to students with lesser ability. The gifted groups felt this motive more keenly, however.

6. The extremely gifted students seemed to be more aware of their high mental ability, freely discussing their intellectual prowess during the interviews. They felt that this extreme difference from other students warranted extreme differences in the educational provisions they were afforded.

7. Few in any group mentioned the need for special tutoring, foreign schooling, or acceleration. When acceleration was mentioned, it was on a subject by subject basis. Most students felt that they should not be held back in any subject matter area.

8. Junior high school gifted students tended to request classes separated on the basis of achievement, more often than high school students.

What other suggestions or ideas do you have for program changes?

1. Buildings and plant layouts were criticized for lack of air conditioning, large rooms, different sized rooms for individual and small group

activities and the lack of variation in rooms designed for laboratory, library, and other functional purposes.

2. Students at all levels indicated interest in pursuing their own projects on after-school time as opposed to what they construed as an "over-assignment of homework."

3. A majority of students, at all levels, expressed curriculum needs in the areas of fine arts, music and art appreciation, literature, foreign languages, and subjects usually reserved for the college level.

4. Almost all students indicated that more flexibility in programming was called for. For example, one student suggested intensive one semester, as opposed to year-long courses.

5. Students at all levels indicated the desire to have access to books at a wider range of interest and intellectual levels.

What do gifted students deem to be the "essential purposes for their high school"?

Ranked in the order of essentiality and priority, the gifted high school students would state the philosophical purposes for their high school as follows:

1. It provides preparation for formal education.
2. It emphasizes the use of the intellect and promotes critical thinking.
3. It promotes social development and maturity.
4. It helps the student develop and appreciate creativity.
5. It helps the student to realistically choose his life's work.
6. It provides academic counseling and guidance.
7. It promotes self-understanding and good mental health habits.
8. It teaches basic skills for everyday living.
9. It provides general orientation and guidance programs.
10. It helps develop sound moral and spiritual values.
11. It provides help for the student in solving personal adjustment problems.
12. It promotes the development of aesthetic skills and appreciation.
13. It promotes the democratic way of life.
14. It provides specific vocational education.
15. It prepares young people for homemaking and family life.
16. It promotes international understanding and peace.
17. It provides a program of adult education beyond high school.

Roughly, the first nine priorities listed above received at least a majority endorsement by the gifted students. Proceeding from rank 10 through rank 17 the endorsement becomes lesser until by rank 17 only about 20 percent of the gifted students would agree.

The configuration of purposes chosen by the gifted students in this sample resembled the configuration of priorities agreed upon by college and high school teachers and curriculum specialists. It is quite different from the typical statement of educational priorities stated by junior college students, normal students, or school administrators. Typically, these latter groups place more emphasis upon such priorities as the "democratic way of life, vocational education or homemaking" than do the gifted students. In general, school administrators or normal students arrive at priority configurations approximately reciprocal to those outlined above for gifted students.

Conclusions and Recommendations

It has been shown that gifted students are capable of providing meaningful insights into the nature of their educational programs. Moreover, gifted students represent an essentially untapped reservoir of imaginative suggestions for program innovation and change. Inspection of their opinions reveals a close resemblance to suggestions made in the literature for programs for the gifted. Substantial unanimity was observed among the gifted concerning basic questions about their education.

Based on these findings, school districts planning programs for the gifted might consider the following recommendations:

1. Special groupings of gifted students during the school day including special activities as well as accelerated contents.

2. Carefully assessing the needs of the local gifted population.

3. More utilization of psychometric data such as achievement test scores for the proper scholastic placement of gifted students.

4. Attitudinal disparities among subgroups of the gifted warrant special counseling and interview services for the study and treatment of developmental problems which appear to disturb the gifted just as frequently as any other student group.

5. The establishment of seminar settings in which controversial issues and problems may be discussed with a view toward clarification and value analysis.

6. The worth of non-academic work such as physical education needs to be reevaluated in the light of the true needs of the gifted.

Chapter 6

BUILDING MODEL CURRICULUMS FOR
SPECIAL EDUCATION

O NLY two elemental curriculum models need be contemplated for education of the gifted:[1]

1. *Differentiated curriculum:* designed expressly for given talented students and built to the requirements of higher level mental processes or

2. *Supplemental curriculum:* especially enriched or accelerated regular curriculum emphasizing quantitative or additive approaches.

In practice, school districts tend to combine these models; special classes may be set up at certain grade levels, followed by enriched or accelerated courses. At the high school level, regular courses may be augmented by special (e.g. "honors") courses or courses not ordinarily offered to other students.

Ideally, most agree that all students should have a "differentiated" curriculum designed especially for them and implemented through tutorial teaching methods. As a practical reality, "individual instruction" may not be as "idealistic" as one might first conclude. Recent technological advances in computors and data processing equipment coupled with the development of "computor language programs" make direct interaction of individual students with vast storehouses of collected material quite feasible. Diagram 1 illustrates the typical inputs and generated information derived from computor based instructional models. As we become more proficient at programming for stimulation of the higher intellectual processes, "computorized instruction" will undoubtedly profoundly affect the nature of the teaching-learning system.

Meanwhile, we must design curriculums with sufficient specificity for identifiable groups of talented students; such curriculums have to contain sufficient applicability for general usage to justify the effect devoted to their construction. Hence, curriculums for the gifted may be considered to be "models" in two respects:

1. Curriculums for the gifted should be built to the specifications of the intelligent mind; such curriculums, in their totality, present a tangible picture or "model" of the fully-developed human mind.

---

[1] (These curriculum models ought not to be confused with the administrative program prototypes discussed elsewhere.)

146

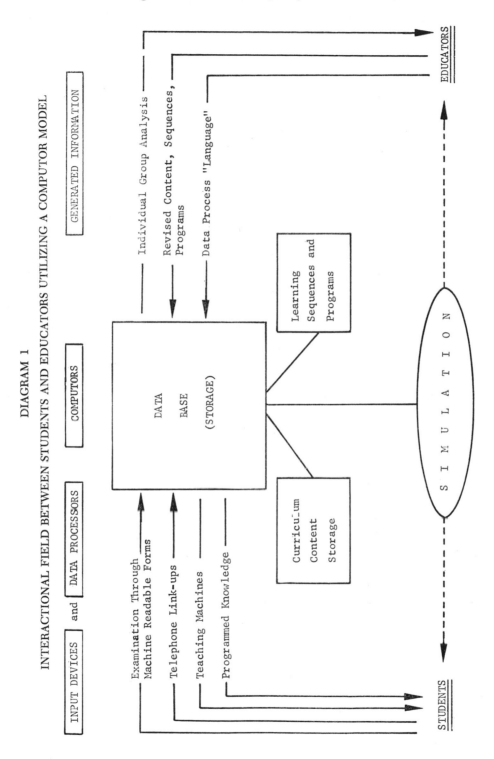

DIAGRAM 1

INTERACTIONAL FIELD BETWEEN STUDENTS AND EDUCATORS UTILIZING A COMPUTOR MODEL

2. Such curriculums represent ideal prototypes or "models" for lesser curriculum design. While it is a mistake to attempt to force these curriculums on ordinary students, they can nevertheless serve as operational *goals* for general education on the assumption that the entire population tends to upgrade itself and increase in mental skills.

In conceptualizing curriculum structure, it is impossible to ignore objectives, What are the purposes of the specific contents? What nature of human product is desired following exposure to particular sequences of learning? Therefore, it seems logical to interrelate descriptions of intellectual functioning with the ordering of educational goals. Perhaps the most widely-used source for curriculum construction, Blooms' *Taxonomy of Educational Objectives*, does combine the concept of "classification of classroom objectives" with that of "analysis of kinds of learning." Other theorists (e.g. J.P. Guilford) have addressed themselves directly to the "structure of the human intellect." Overall, most contemporary educational theorists appear to agree that curriculum building should begin by analyzing how learning and thinking occur. Curriculum activities and contents should stimulate and parallel cognitive processes. Table 19 represents a composite summary of mental operations and products; the table is structured in hierarchical fashion proceeding from simple (i.e. Reception) to complex (i.e. Innovation) levels of mental work.

Relevance for curriculum building is understood when it is realized that much contemporary teaching aims to implement Levels I. Reception and II. Knowledge. Levels III. Thought and IV. Innovation are frequently left to the student to exercise on his own. Of course, the actual cognitive process is fluid and spontaneous, not rigid and orderly as Table 19 might imply. Thus, a student may, though unobserved by the teacher, conceptualize answers to problems while simulating methodological inquiry by his overt behavior. This may explain why so many gifted students do not adjust well to "laboratory" periods which call for routine plodding toward conclusions which they easily anticipate intuitively. Unfortunately, much higher level cognition is viewed as surreptitious by teachers who do not recognize the thinking (as opposed to learning) pathways to knowledge.

Moreover, the situation is further complicated by observing that Levels I. Reception and II. Knowledge constitute a potentially closed logical system of learning. It is literally unnecessary to "think or innovate" in order to gain and utilize all of the methods and knowledge of the civilization. Under such circumstances, knowledge would tend to become static and stylized; this is precisely what has happened to certain civilizations preceding us. "Methodological inquiry" is often rigged by teachers to cause students to come to preordained conclusions. Regrettably, most so-called science laboratory work is of this kind. The most damaging aspect of this

TABLE 19

HIERARCHY OF MENTAL OPERATIONS AND PRODUCTS

Levels	Mental (Cognitive) Operations	Products or Outcomes
IV. Innovation	12. Integration: unifying; comprehending existence and function beyond the self	Universal understanding of relationships
		Unlimited extension of self
	11. Production: create; intuit	Invention, literature, art forms, insights
III. Thought	10. Evaluation: judge, determine, rate	Values, theories, priorities, convictions
	9. Synthesis: reorganize; combine	Systems, new ideas, predictions
	8. Problem Solving: compare, analyze, calculate	Tentative solutions, empirical truths
II. Knowledge	7. Conceptualization: reflective thinking	Abstract ideas, hypotheses, summaries, generalizations
	6. Methodological Inquiry: apply learned tools, methods, formulas, explore, pose problems	Experimental designs and mathematical models arrived at by precedent
	5. Retrieval: define; codify	Classifications, relationships
	4. Symbolization/Storage: memorize, acknowledge	Associations; comparisons; images
I. Reception	3. Perception: interest; discriminate	Choice of action; meaningful responses
	2. Reception: accept/reject; attend	Differentiation; recognition
	1. Sensation: feeling or sensing internal external stimuli	Unmediated (raw) stimulation (data)

closed process occurs when students believe that they are thinking or problem solving, when, in reality, they are merely rehearsing precedents.

It is possible to convert the "hierarchy of mental operations" outlined in Table 19 into a behavioral rating scale for use in classroom observations of teacher-pupil discussions. Typical episodes and activities tend to characterize each level as follows:

Level I. Reception: students observe (e.g. "smell, see, touch"); emphasize accuracy and repeatability of stimulus descriptions; uniformity of response is stressed.

Level II. Knowledge: students recite, define, "tell it like it is"; teachers drill, interrogate, authorize, prescribe, and authenticate; accuracy, validity, reliability, and thoroughness are stressed.

Level III. Thought: students formulate, experiment outside of prescribed limits, apply learning in unique styles, judge and arrive at individual conclusions; teachers allow wide latitudes in discussion; co-mingle subject matters, do not prescribe "the" solutions and guide students toward present and future orientations (as opposed to precedent); speculation, multiple hypotheses are stressed.

Level IV. Innovation: students *and* teachers meditate, philosophize,

TABLE 20

PERCENT OF DISCUSSION TIME DEVOTED TO VARIOUS LEVELS OF MENTAL OPERATIONS

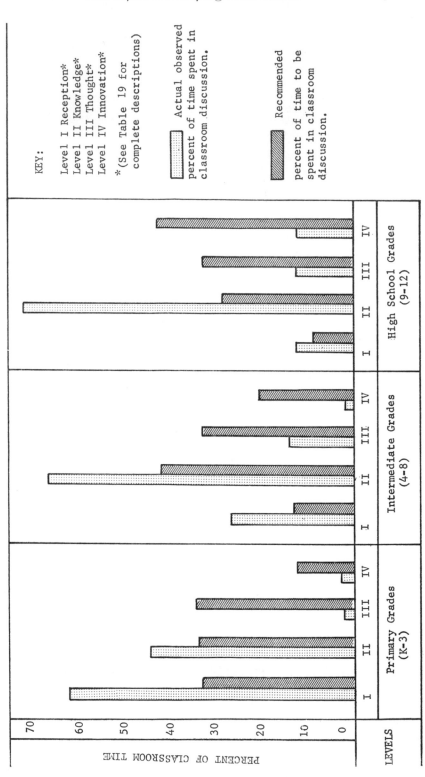

theorize, and produce tangible products; uniqueness of response is prized, ordinary barriers to thought (e.g. mores, standards, rules) tend to be disregarded.

Observations of twenty primary classrooms, twenty intermediate classrooms and fifteen high school classes (primarily in the social sciences) were pooled and Table 20 is the result. All classrooms contained a "cluster" of gifted students and observations lasted at least a half hour. It can be seen that actual classroom discussion is heavily loaded with "knowledge transmittal," usually in an authoritarian circuit from teacher to student. This phenomenon appears to increase in the higher grades. Although the "recommended percents of time" advocated tend to be speculative, some study was made of special classes in which teachers were expressly trained to stimulate more discussion of thought provoking topics. Such classrooms were observed to approximate the "recommended" amounts advocated in Table 20. An actuarial record of numbers of instances of typical levels was also kept; when converted to percentages, these data were not equivalent to the "time spent" on discussion of topics at various levels of cognitive operation because the number of discrete questions and answers handled in an authoritarian "information giving" session tends to be far greater than the number of topics handled in situations in which maximum discussion is allowed.

These observations (i.e. Table 20) lead to the conclusion that two basic teaching-learning paradigms are competing in today's classrooms. The overwhelmingly popular paradigm could be summarized as follows:

PARADIGM 1

DIRECTIVE TEACHING

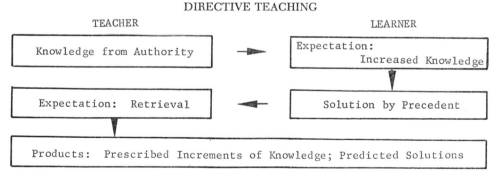

Directive teaching depends upon rote memory mechanisms and renders students exclusively dependent upon precedent, tradition, and authority. Many, if not most, older scholars have been taught in this mode; it may be observed that academically gifted students may thrive in such an environment. It cannot be said, however, that creatively or psychosocially gifted students thrive in such settings. Moreover, we cannot begin to calculate the loss of productive outcomes, forthcoming from academically gifted students, who though scholarly, never reach productive or innovative levels for want of opportunity.

The second paradigm, implied in the recommendations of Table 19, might be represented as follows:

PARADIGM 2

PRODUCTIVE TEACHING

TEACHER   LEARNER

Knowledge Through Reason →	Expectation: Exercises in Thinking Processes
Expectation: Evaluation and Feedback ←	Solutions by Application of Problem-Solving Techniques
Products: Improved Methods; Shared Solutions; Interpersonal Involvement with Students	Products: Individual Cognitive Style; Repertoire of Methodologies; Self-reliance; Increased Productivity

Productive teaching emphasizes methods for discovering or constructing knowledge. Knowledge is viewed as a transitory product of civilizations, subject to change. Emphasis is placed upon independence of interpretation. If students utilize existing methods and adopt traditional knowledge, they do so because their independent investigations have verified such methods or knowledge.

Three indispensable ingredients need to be considered as we construct curriculums for the gifted:

1. descriptive educational models which combine the goals of education with a valid picture of the learner;

2. appropriate teaching methodologies designed to implement the goals of the educational model adopted; and

3. subject matter contents, sequences, and related materials which are tailored to the educational model and teaching methodologies used.

METHODOLOGY TAKEN SERIOUSLY

Proceeding on the assumption that the gifted student will call upon the teacher to employ a variety of teaching methodologies in order to meet his vast learning demands, such teachers would do well to study all of the available strategies, methodologies, and techniques available for the instruction of children. An excellent source book for such a background study is the *Handbook of Research on Teaching,* edited by N.L. Gage and published by the Rand McNally Company of Chicago in 1963. It is generally agreed that the teacher fulfills many roles when he plays the part of a teacher in a free society. For example, Havighurst and Neugarten[2] have developed a classification of the roles teachers play both in relation to other adults in the school system and community and with reference to students. They note that the teacher plays at least five roles in relationship to students:

1. mediator of learning
2. disciplinarian
3. parent substitute
4. confidante
5. surrogate of middle-class morality.

We will be concerned with the first two roles; and, more specifically, we will explore the various methodologies which can be applied to serve the role of a mediator of learning. It may be that the role of "disciplinarian" is an artificial category necessitated by the expectations of the society to enforce particularistic modes of conformity. An argument can be made for the case that learning itself is "disciplinary." It may be that an advanced system of teaching-learning would incorporate sufficiently potent methodologies to obviate the need for superimposed "punishments" for the infraction of extraneous rules pertaining to the community and not to the specific demands of learning.

Most historical methods of teaching view the teaching act as a direct expression of the personality and wisdom of the teacher. The personality of the teacher, therefore, is viewed, more or less, as the beginning and ending of the teaching episode. "Methodology" was viewed as various styles of presentation, imparting of wisdom or influence on the student. Implicit in the application of dialectics, scholasticism, or other approaches was the assumption that the teacher was the focal point for learning. Little if any diagnostic consideration entered into the design of the teaching act.

While modern teaching methodologies tend to divide attention between the readiness of the learner and the preparation of the teacher, the main emphasis still remains upon the capability of the teacher to apply a certain methodology in order to accomplish direct and well-defined changes in the learner. Of course, a number of modern educators are beginning to shift the focus completely to the learner as a person (e.g., refer for example to the methods and settings accomplished at Summerhill). Thus far in our development of differential methodologies, only two receive widespread attention in the literature. On the one hand, there is a group of di-

---

[2] Havighurst, R.J., and Neugarten, Bernice L.: *Society and Education.* Boston, Allyn & Bacon, 1957.

rect authoritative methods sometimes referred to as "telling methods" in which the teacher directly imparts to students knowledge, truths, or values deemed to be, more or less, absolute in the sense that the student is to recall them at the teacher's will and present them as facts. On the other hand, a group of modern heuristic methods are being developed in which the teacher tends to impart methods for the discovery of knowledge rather than the knowledge itself. These latter methods tend to result in a wider possible variation in the actual knowledge, facts, truths, or values learned by the students.

Such methods complicate the classical methods of pupil evaluation. While it is possible to evaluate the way in which the pupil applies and benefits from the methods taught to him, it is not logical to assume that all students will eventually decide upon the same knowledge, facts, truths, or values. Therefore, the teacher's task becomes far more complex and difficult. The teacher must trace the student's application of methodology and decide whether or not the knowledge arrived at was logical in terms of the methodologies applied. Interestingly enough, heuristic methods may be far more "directive" than some of the advocates would currently admit. For example, the student is called upon to emulate given methodologies which are valued or prized and referred to as "inquiry, scientific methodology" or the like. What if a given student seriously wanted to apply an ancient method of revelation? He might be referred to the school psychologist. Such "modern trends" may be just as authoritarian and breed just as much conformity as the more ancient methods. Somewhere along the line educators will need to ask themselves deep questions of personal concern, such as Do we really want to allow pupils to apply and benefit from methodologies, however disparate these methodologies may be from current acceptable techniques, to the solution of their problems and for the collection of knowledge which is meaningful to them?

It may be that currently practiced methodologies of teaching can be classified into three main categories including authoritarian methods, heuristic methods, and indirect methods utilizing planned exposures to the artifacts of learning rather than a specific person-to-person teaching technique.

It is obvious to any observer of school classrooms that the first alternative is, by far and away, the most commonly applied teaching methodology. The word "authoritarian" was deliberately chosen over the word "authoritative" since the typical teacher presents knowledge as absolute, frequently neglecting to validate this knowledge with historical evidence or experimental proof. Such methods as exist in cases where the classroom teacher merely reads a book to students and calls upon them to parrot the information back exactly as it was read to them can be labeled nothing but "authoritarian." We will use the more lenient term "authoritative," however, in the classification of teaching methodologies which will follow. Actually, even a cursory exploration of the variety of possible teaching methodologies available to teachers will reveal that a simple two-way classification is simply inadequate. Therefore, we might speculate about a wider classification for the methodologies of modern teachers. An eight-way classification of existing methodologies of teachers follows. We will consider authoritative, attitudinal, diagnostic, dialectical, developmental, heuristic, inclinatory, and remedial methodologies. A presentation, including a brief explanation and some possible examples of the teaching method involved, follow.

Authoritative Methods

When applying authoritative (defined from Webster as ". . . proceeding from authority; entitled to obedience, credit or acceptance") methods, the teacher directly or by inference poses as an absolute authority. The teacher may reveal, indoctrinate, or impart knowledge, laws, values, or facts directly to students. It is notable that the student has little if any opportunity to challenge such imparting of facts except by reference to higher authority. Some examples of authoritative methods might include

direct lecturing enforcing notetaking;
drill emphasizing retention and recall;
systematized programming of materials such as so-called programmed instruction;
mechanized instruction such as televised lectures or teaching machines;
directive skills training as for special applications such as music, art, and the like; and
simple indoctrination.

Attitudinal or Motivational Control

Here, the teacher's attention is focused upon current attitudinal and motivational concerns of the student with definite motives to change or redirect such attitudes and motivational patterns toward given learning and value outcomes. Typically, the teacher attempts to create an accepting social environment in which the teacher displays outward emotional concern for individuals in the group and encourages behavior conducive to group cooperation and participation. The teacher stresses social ethics, primarily by example. The teacher assumes that learning will occur incidental to the desire, on the part of the student, to conform to the group, learn more about the group, and express himself individually. Examples for this kind of teaching methodology are difficult to cite because considerable cultural bias has been developed for and against such methodologies by the usage of disparaging terms such as "progressive education, life adjustment education, and the like." A few examples of this sort of teacher-imposed environmental manipulation and attitude control follow:

1. "Life Adjustment Education." This recent trend, now becoming less popular, is difficult to formulate in a sentence or two. Essentially, each student is viewed as a "total personality" and educational methodology attempts to facilitate the personal adjustment of the student to the demands of his school and society at large. It is characteristic for such programs to incorporate guidance, orientation, or adjustment seminars, classes, or classroom projects.

2. Social Studies Centered Curriculum. Again we are dealing with a trend of the past decade which may or may not withstand the current criticisms leveled against it. The social studies curriculum as a core area for study in the overall curriculum of the student has been developed in widespread applications at the elementary school level. The curriculum usually centers about "key concepts" concerning the study of man and his environment. Frequently, role playing in simulated social settings is incorporated into the activities of the classroom. Other subject matter tends to be related to the study and operations of man as a social animal. Although neglected in the literature on this subject, it is apparent to even the casual observer that definite social ethics are implied in the instruction and activities the students are called upon to interact with. Since the student must conform to the activity and implied social role he has little choice concerning his autonomous personal development.

3. Psychotherapeutics. A small but significant group of school districts offer adjustment classes or other forms of psychotherapeutic teaching designed for students who might otherwise be lost to the schools for reasons of emotional or behavioral malfunctioning. Classes have been recently developed, for example, for emotionally and neurologically disturbed children. School districts in such states as Illinois and Massachusetts cooperate with child guidance clinics for the individual treatment of children. Such individual or group treatment developing out of the specific symptomatology of the child would have to involve individualized instruction and especially chosen learning materials. Hence, this kind of approach can be easily distinguished from authoritative and other methodologies.

Diagnostic Methods

Of course, most of the methods described in this classification involve "diagnostic" elements such as ascertaining the capability, interests, and motivational patterns of the students before and after given methodologies are applied. However, it is possible to segregate out of the various methodologies those which utilize the diagnostic understanding of the student as the main or focal element of the educational program. Such methods would have to be eclectic since the diagnostic needs of the student would vary individual to individual and call for a wide application of teaching methods, materials, and settings. Several examples of diagnostic methods follow:

1. Individualized conferences, counseling, tutoring, or instruction may be designed to ascertain the special needs of individual pupils and provide feedback for the classroom teacher if he is different from the special individual tutor, counselor, or teacher. Such individual methods would ordinarily involve systematic and periodic psychometric evaluation of pupils. Such psychometric evaluations would form the basis for a specific individual plan of learning for the student.

2. Group counseling, seminars, or instruction may be designed for special groups such as "underachieving students." Such group programs would be identical in intent to the individual programs designed above except that they would incorporate the more efficient utilization of professional staff by discovering and grouping students with special needs.

3. Individual diagnostic educational programming can occur by the use of a wide variety of achievement and psychological tests in conjunction with computers for individual student programming.

Dialectical Methods

Stemming from the teachers of antiquity, we note the existence of teaching methodologies which utilize logical systems for the design of the teaching act and for the determination of what knowledge is imparted to the student. Ordinarily, such methods emphasize the "art of disputation" and encourage the student to discriminate fact from fiction, truth from error. Many modern teachers are rediscovering the need for a systematized approach to dialectics. This is especially important because of the growth and influence of the mass media. The modern student is called upon to discriminate among many forms and levels of propaganda, advertising, and political haranguing. A meaningful classification of dialectical methods would be as long as the individual teachers advocating particularlistic systems of logic. Therefore, no attempt will be made to specify examples. It is sufficient to know that such philosophers as Socrates advocated a dialectical approach to teaching and that a number of new systems of teaching utilize the application of special disciplinary logical approaches such as mathematical, theological, or inquiry-oriented systems of scientific investigation.

Developmental Methods and Models of Instruction

A number of new schemes for the design of teaching have been advocated lately. Some of these schemes have been designed to describe the differential developmental and learning capabilities of children (as Piaget's), others have attempted to design structures of the intellect which can serve as models toward which to develop the minds of students (Guilford), and still others have advocated taxonomies for the classification of teaching objectives (Bloom). The utilization of such paradigms is exciting since it calls upon the teacher to act as a true developer of human intellect and personality as well as a mere repository for knowledge. Moreover, the utilization of such paradigms and systems of teaching call upon the teacher to plan the teaching act in terms of more meaningful and complex dimensions. Some worthwhile models for consideration follow:

1. Piaget[3] has analyzed the ways in which children develop levels of concept formation. His isolation of five main levels of concept formation including (1) the sensory motor, (2) the preoperational thought, (3) the intuitive thought, (4) the concrete operations, and (5) the propositional or formal logic, enables the teacher to plan a specific teaching-learning strategy based upon the level of thinking the student is at during a particular developmental period.

2. Guilford[4] has described a theory for the structure of human intellect. This structure will be dealt with in more detail elsewhere. Suffice it to say at this point that his differentiation of learning into the "contents, operations, and products" of learning enables the teacher to design a curriculum differentially focusing upon contents, operations, and products. Also, Guilford's recognition of a number of levels of operation as the human intellect works including "cognition, memory, convergent thinking, divergent thinking, and evaluation" enables the teacher to design, plan, and relate various levels of content for the specific interplay of the level of intellectual operation desired.

3. Bloom[5] and others have developed and are developing various taxonomies of educational objectives. To date they have described the cognitive and affective domains. Eventually they will design a taxonomy of

---

[3] Piaget, Jean: *The Psychology of Intelligence,* 1st ed. London, Routledge & Kegan Paul Ltd., 1950.

[4] A more complete list of J.P. Guilford's work may be found in the bibliography. The "Structure of Intellect Model" was elaborated in Guilford, J.P., and Morrifield, P.R.: The structure of the intellect model: Its uses and implications. *Reports from the Psychological Laboratory,* No. 24. Los Angeles, University of Southern California.

[5] Refer to Bloom, B.S. (Ed.): *Taxonomy of Educational Objectives: Handbook I: Cognitive Domain.* New York, McKay, 1956; and Krathwahl, D.R.; Bloom, B.S., and Masin, B.B.: *Taxonomy of Educational Objectives: Handbook II: Affective Domain.* New York, McKay, 1964.

educational objectives for the psychomotor domain. Again, the deliberate planning of curriculum to enhance more than the simple accumulation of knowledge and to deliberately guide the student toward "comprehension, application, analysis, synthesis, and evaluation of knowledge" should enrich the teaching act to the extent that it develops meaningful intellectual tendencies on the part of the pupil as well as spelling out various complexities of the types of knowledge taught.

4. Bruner has also described the nature of intellectual processes in his book, *The Process of Education.* Bruner describes the acquisition, transformation, and evaluation of knowledge. Here again, it is possible to have the teacher design curriculum, as will be treated in future treatments of this topic, according to a specific developmental plan.

Heuristic Methods

Historically and currently many teaching methodologies have been developed to cause the student to discover knowledge for himself. Most heuristic methods attempt to stimulate the student to investigate for himself following some demonstration of the methods we would wish him to apply. In one sense, these methods are "indirect" in the sense that they call upon the student to rely more upon his own resources for the discovery, application, and modification of knowledge. Some examples follow:

1. Inductive methods of teaching as described by Henderson[6] involves "(1) presenting instances of the item of knowledge to be taught in order to enable the students to form hypotheses, (2) presenting evidence . . . serving either to confirm or disconfirm the various hypotheses student state. . . . (3) stating or having a student state the item of knowledge which is warranted as an inference from steps 1 and 2."

2. Deductive methods utilize the use of authoritative statements, particularly rules of the operations called for to solve given problems.

3. Certain new methods such as the so-called inquiry methods, while thought to be "inductive," may be viewed in a category of heuristic methods by themselves. This is true since "inquiry training" does not necessarily employ the formal steps of inductive methodology described above nor is it necessarily an imparting of authoritative procedures for the deductive collection of knowledge. It is possible to suppose that the student will uncover or invent an atypical methodology for the solution of the problem. To some degree the new inquiry-oriented methodologies may be viewed as pragmatic. In another sense they may be viewed as a throwback to the eighteenth and nineteenth century emphasis upon

[6] Gage, N.L. (Ed.): *Handbook of Research on Teaching.* See Henderson, Kenneth B.: Research on teaching secondary school mathematics. Chap. 19, 1014. Chicago, Rand McNally, 1963.

discovery as the cornerstone of all science. It may be stated that the inquiry methods may rely too much upon the limitations imposed by the human sense modalities. Literally, the pupil is hemmed in or cut out, as the case may be, from data not discernible through his sense modalities. Also, considerable mental groping, not designated as "introspection," is involved.

Inclinatory Methodologies

It may be that the meaning of "inclinatory" could be construed to be "permissive." In applying these methodologies, the teacher attends to the individual inclinations including the interests and values already possessed by the student. The curriculum, literally, becomes a reflection of the inclinatory needs of the student during differing periods of his development. Perhaps the Summerhill School is a case in point. Here again, no attempt will be made to classify inclinatory methods. It is possible to note, however, that such methods frequently involve a "cafeteria" approach to learning. The student is surrounded with a myriad of supplies, outlets, settings, and environmental stimulations. It is assumed that the student will pick and choose from this kaleidoscope of learning opportunities those most related to his internal needs and interests.

Remedial Methods

It is necessary to stress that even gifted and talented students frequently require "remedial teaching." Of course, remedial teaching could be considered a part of the diagnostic methodologies discussed above. However, in view of the fact that remedial instruction is necessitated because of gaps in learning or developmental lagging on the part of students, we could view it in a category by itself. Remedial instruction could be classified in terms of specific subject matter areas (e.g. mathematics, science, social science and the like) or it could be viewed in terms of newly-discoverd methodologies for the exacting remediation of a given student problem such as "remedial reading." Each remedial area, therefore, could be found to possess its own rationale, methodologies, and applications.

APPLYING DESCRIPTIVE EDUCATIONAL MODELS TO CURRICULUM CONSTRUCTION AND TEACHING METHODOLOGY

Educational models for use in curriculum construction could be derived from various disciplines and approaches; for example:

1. *Developmental psychology* (e.g. the work of Piaget)
2. *Mental health and maturity studies* (e.g. A.H. Maslow's concept of "self-actualization")
3. *Educational psychology; theories of cognition* (e.g. J.P. Guilford's "Structure of Intellect" model)

4. *Educational philosophy* (e.g. B.S. Bloom's "Taxonomy of Educational Objectives")

5. *Studies of educational process* (e.g. J.S. Bruner's discussions on "The Process of Education") or

6. *Behaviorism* (e.g. B.F. Skinner's "reinforcement models" as outlined in *Walden II*).

While all of these sources have proven useful for the development of general education programs of instruction, in particular, the works of J.P. Guilford, B.S. Bloom, and J.S. Bruner have proven adaptable for the production of working curriculum models for the gifted, as will be shown in the illustrations which follow.

The Structure of Intellect Model[7]

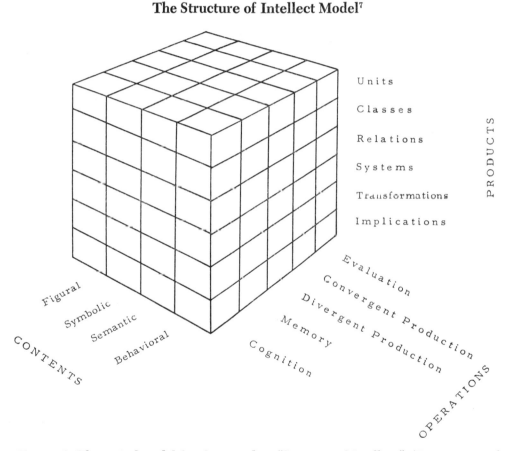

FIGURE 2. Theoretical model for the complete "Structure of Intellect." (Department of Psychology, Projection on Aptitudes of High-level Personnel, University of Southern California, October 1961.)

---

[7] Guilford, *op. cit.*

A three-dimensional model of the intellect, as proposed by J.P. Guilford, is represented in Figure 2. This construct hypothesizes that the totality of human intellect may be understood in terms of (1) *mental operations* or progressively complex activities of the mind, (2) *ideational contents* or the "stuff" that thoughts are made of, and (3) the *products* or outcomes of thoughtful processes. Among these three dimensions, mental operations would be of particular importance to curriculum constructors since teaching methods should coincide closely with the kinds of activities the student's mind is capable of. Intellectual contents would be of importance when determining the form that learning inputs should take (e.g. study materials). Products are anticipated outcomes of a given intellectual operation utilizing a given content category. For example, *memory* may be used to assimilate *symbolic contents* (perhaps a table or graph) to result in a learned class of related items. Or, *convergent production* may be applyed to *semantic contents* (e.g. a book) and result in the learning of given *systems* of information (e.g. biological taxonomies). Thus, when classifying a given intellectual process, all three components (e.g. operation, content, and product) should be identified.

Definitions of categories in the "Structure of Intellect" model follow.

OPERATIONS: major kinds of intellectual activities or processes; what the organism does with the raw materials of information.

Cognition: immediate discovery, awareness, rediscovery, or recognition of information in various forms; comprehension; understanding.

Memory: retention or storage of information in any form.

Convergent Production (Thinking): generation of information from given information, where the emphasis is upon achieving conventionally accepted outcomes. Single, rather than multiple, outputs, conclusions, or products are sought.

Divergent Production (Thinking): generation of information from input information, where the emphasis is upon variety and quantity of output from the same source; involves elements of creative operations.

Evaluation: reaching decisions or making judgments concerning the correctness, suitability, adequacy, or desirability of information.

CONTENTS: varieties of information; the raw materials of thought.

Figural Content: information in concrete form, as perceived or as recalled in the form of images. The term "figural" implies some degree of organization or structuring. Different sense modalities may be involved (e.g. visual, auditory, kinesthetic).

Symbolic Content: information in the form of single signs, having no significance in and of themselves; such as letters, numbers, or musical notations; primarily elements of codes, languages, and other systems of meaning.

Semantic Content: information in the form of meanings to which words commonly become attached, hence most notable in verbal thinking and in verbal communication.

Behavioral Content: information, essentially nonverbal, involved in human interactions, where awareness of the attitudes, needs, desires, moods, intentions, perceptions, or thoughts of other persons are important.

PRODUCTS: results or outcomes of the organisms processing information.
Units: isolated, segregated, or circumscribed unitary items of information having tangible character.

Classes: sets of items of information grouped by virtue of their common properties.

Relations: recognized connections between units of information based upon variables that apply to both of them.

Systems: organized or structured aggregates of items of information; complexes of interrelated or interacting parts.

Transformations: changes in existing or known information or in its use; usually the result of a productive thinking operation.

Implications: extrapolations of information, in the form of expectancies, predictions, antecedents, concomitants, or consequences.

Guilford's theoretical "mock-up" of the intellect has developmental as well as structual implications. Does the more complicated processes of divergent production or evaluation occur in young children? What is the role of practice in eliciting these complex mental processes? Obviously, a child must first store up sufficient memory traces (e.g. figural, symbolic, or semantic contents) before he can generate meaningful relationships or organize systems of information. Table 21 summarizes a developmental curriculum design in three different subject matter areas; complexity of intellectual operations are logically escalated over the span of three grade levels from cognition (simple inputs) to divergent production (creative products) and evaluation (values, judgments). It can be seen that the "structure of intellect model" is useful in two ways: (1) it helps the teacher to classify and interpret the mental components of specific learning episodes, and (2) it implies developmental learning goals which lend themselves to objective observation and measurement.

Of course, at the curriculum construction stage, the "structure of intellect model" is useful for prescribing the sorts of subject matters appropriate for succeeding grade levels. For example, the more primative operations of cognition and memory are stimulated to work most efficiently through

TABLE 21

INCORPORATION OF STRUCTURE OF INTELLECT MODEL INTO A CURRICULUM MODEL

General Sequential Objectives and Operations	CONTENTS AND ANTICIPATED PRODUCTS		
	Fine Arts	*Scientific Discovery*	*Literature*
4th Grade Develop a background of knowledge.	Historical studies: (1) Knowledge gathering by listening and viewing. (2) Each historical period is studied to provide maximum exposure. (3) Vocabulary, terminology and symbols of art and music.	Observation: (1) Learning the techniques of observation. (2) Terminology, vocabulary, the scope of science. (3) Introduction to equipment and materials.	Maximum exposure to literary forms: (1) Myths (2) Legends (3) Fantasies (4) Poetry (5) Short stories
Use: (Cognition) (Memory) (Convergent Production)	(Essentially) figural, symbolic contents working toward units, classes and relationships.		
5th Grade Theory building and applying methodologies; applying knowledge.	Learning and applying structure and form of music and principles of art: (1) Philosophical definitions of aesthetic forms. (2) Survey of art forms and techniques (e.g. architecture, sculpture, printing). (3) Physical properties of light (e.g. shading, color mixture). (4) Physical properties of sound (e.g. pitch, timbre, volume). (5) Forms of music (e.g. sonata, fugue). (6) Instruments of orchestra.	Scientific methodology: (1) Inference (2) Prediction (3) Classification (4) Measurement (5) Control of variables (6) Communication (7) Data interpretation	Thematic approach to understanding: (1) Analyze, compare literary forms. (2) Read critically and analytically. (3) Acquire an awareness of literary elements within each form (e.g. characterization, background, time and place, foreshadowing, theme plot).

Use: (Memory) (Convergent Production)	(Essentially) semantic content leading toward systems of information.	
6th Grade Individual projects, creative endeavors, brainstorming sessions and experimentation.	Opportunity to be productive, to exercise selectivity, and to concentrate upon application of structure and form of music and art.	Emphasis upon rigorous application of methodology to experimentation; generation of alternative hypotheses evaluation of current explanations. Interpret, apply value judgments, generalize, write creatively, and apply knowledge of literary elements and form in own work.
Use: (Convergent thinking) (Divergent thinking)	(Involves all contents and products) but major semantic and behavioral contents are being transformed to new systems, transformations, and implications.	

utilization of audiovisual inputs (e.g. slides, movies, "drill cards"). Once having stored sufficient data and images, the student is ready to embark upon higher level operations. Table 21 should not be interpreted to mean that only the processes of cognition and memory are stimulated during fourth grade operations are the central foci for the teacher's efforts. In actuality, it is probable that students spontaneously utilize various mental operations to achieve manifold objectives (products) at every grade level.

The hypothetical nature of the "structure of intellect" model should be borne in mind if it is used as a basis for planning sequences of curriculum. Simpler models, it must be remembered, seem to have worked effectively for general educational designs. For instance, an old standby, the simple stimulus-response paradigm has proven adequate for the design of curriculums as well as teaching machines. On the other hand, the "cells" of the "structural cube," representing the components of human intelligence, were arrived at empirically by factor analyzing the intercorrelations of diverse pools of psychological test scores. Therefore, this model should bear considerable resemblance to whatever it is school psychologists claim they are measuring. Moreover, it should be possible to eventually find extremely specific tests to measure each and every component in the "structure of intellect" model. We must hasten to add that such measures do not, in general, exist now.

In teaching, we have customarily thought in terms of two major methods known as the "tell-and-do" and heuristic methods.

The "tell-and-do methods" can be thought of as consisting of the following steps:

1. stating the item of knowledge to be taught,
2. clarifying (by the teacher) the meaning of the sentence used to express the knowledge,
3. justifying the item; for example, establishing the truth of the item if it has a truth value or arguing that it is the means to some acecptable end if it is a prescription,
4. understanding the item, and
5. making a transition to the next item to be taught.[8]

"Tell-and-do" methods seem to fit into the concept of "convergent thinking."

The heuristic methods might, on superficial observation, be thought to involve divergent thinking since they are based on inquiry. However, closer scrutiny of the heuristic methods, both inductive and deductive, indicates that they only involve redefinition and utilize conventional solutions. The student "thinks" with methods provided by the instructor. Therefore, he is locked into a conventional solution (e.g. convergent thinking). The

---

[8] Henderson, *op. cit.*, pp. 1007-1030.

inductive method of teaching and learning involves such steps as "(1) presenting instances . . . of knowledge. . . . (2) presenting evidence . . . (3) stating . . . the *item of knowledge.* . . ."[9] This seems to be "convergent thinking" utilizing conventional or recognized solutions and arriving at conclusions based upon prior knowledge. Therefore, both deductive and inductive methods of teaching may be considered conventional solutions to problems. The student relies ultimately on the authoritative source, namely the teacher. Even in the inductive methods, the presentation of evidence is limited by the specific data fed into the thinking system by the teacher. The process may involve redefinition or transformation of information, but it is convergent thinking. Deductive methods of teaching and learning are, of course, clearly sorts of convergent thinking operations since they directly involve the use of authoritative statements both as concerns the rules of operation, as well as the actual working knowledge used to solve problems.[10]

Using inductive and deductive methods of teaching exclusively, it can be seriously questioned as to whether or not the student really has an opportunity for free inquiry or that he can entertain novel hypotheses. The student must conform to the operations, methods, and actual knowledge fed into his thinking system by the teacher. In summing up this point, the so-called heuristic methods are examples of "convergent thinking" including both inductive and deductive methods.

Therefore, the concept of "divergent thinking" may represent Guilford's most imaginative contribution to our understanding of the human intellect. Divergent thinking is thinking which involves mental search in new and different directions; it is the ability to think in untested ways while deferring final judgment until these new directions can be assessed. Divergent thinking, then, involves considerable scanning of stored information with a critical viewpoint. The divergent thinker is not likely to accept conventions or simple historical precedents as being valid alternative solutions to current problems. Rather, the divergent thinker makes intellectual sorties into uncharted areas of discovery and thought. No doubt, some emotional elements of daringness or courage are involved in this capability for novel thinking which may result in revolutionary conclusions.

Thus, Guilford's "structure of intellect" model is certainly useful for

1. envisioning new teaching teachniques and methods;
2. analyzing existing curriculum in terms of the intellectual operations stimulated;
3. organizing curricular activities to be logically related to the natural operations of the human mind;

---

[9] Henderson, *op. cit.*, pp. 1017-1018.
[10] Henderson, *op. cit.*, p. 1018.

4. suggesting a framework for the total evaluation of a learning program;

5. (experimentally) designing new curriculums to coincide with the dimensional components of the overall thinking processes; and

6. hypothesizing the irreducible number and qualities of discrete mental functions as a basis for developing a finite set of mental measurements.

However, since validation of this model has been slow, in materialization, caution should be heeded when applying it as the sole rationale for building new curriculums. The "structure of intellect" model seems to be more logically applicable to the understanding of the student and the manner in which he operates intellectually.

CLASSIFYING EDUCATIONAL OBJECTIVES

Stemming from antiquity, man has tended to view himself in terms of a tripartite model of organization:

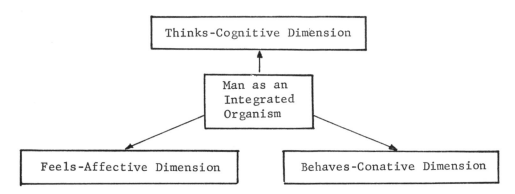

His institutions and mores tend to be structured according to this model: schools have emerged to train, indoctrinate, and educate; family structures and moral codes have been superimposed on the individual to guide, regulate, and channel his emotions; governments, laws, and prescribed outlets for work have evolved which tightly control his options for individual action. Any global set of educational objectives, therefore, would have to identify and relate to this classical image of man as thinker, feeler, and doer.

The ultimate "taxonomy of educational objectives" proposed by B.S. Bloom and associates will address itself to the three main dimensions or "domains" of man:[11]

The *Handbook I: Cognitive Domain* has been widely used throughout the country for two broad purposes : (1) to classify and codify local educational objectives in order to expedite teacher-to-teacher communication and (2)

---

[11] Bloom, *op. cit.*

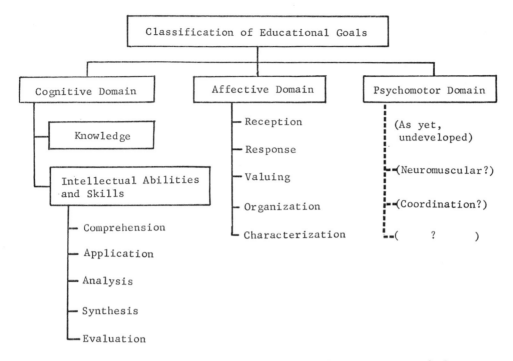

to provide a tool for the classification and actual construction of classroom examinations of students. A third, and more ambitious, purpose is emerging —that of curriculum construction. Perhaps the most potentially dangerous misuse of this, or any other general framework, would occur if educators "rigidified their thinking about education."[12] The "empirical" nature of these taxonomies has been stressed; they are only as useful as their capability for interpreting and their correspondence to objectively observed educational processes. Although many teachers are cognizant of the importance of children's feelings, it is noteworthy that little application has been made of *Handbook II: Affective Domain*. Our understanding of child development might have been dramatically improved if B.S. Bloom and associates had reversed their order of handbook construction (i.e. first, the psychomotor domain; second, the affective domain; and third, the cognitive domain). In fact, this author would advocate study of the affective functioning of students before cognitive interventions are attempted. It might be speculated that many so-called learning disability problems might be averted, if primary grade teachers would specialize their efforts toward nourishment of the attitudinal and motivational orientations of children.

In keeping with this developmental outlook, Table 22 summarizes and correlates the "cognitive" with the "affective" domains; such a combination has been suggested by B.S. Bloom.[13] Curriculum constructors or

---

[12] Bloom, *op. cit., Handbook I*, p. 24.
[13] Bloom, *op. cit., Handbook II: Affective Domain*, pp. 49-50.

evaluators should organize their work in such a way as to simultaneously apply both the cognitive and affective continua, when they attempt to interpret student behavior and plan appropriate curricular activities. Is it possible to discuss the acquiring of knowledge without assessing the student's day-to-day attentive efficiency? Are the mental faculties exercised for "their own sake," or should they be applied toward the organization of personal systems of valuing? The approach to curriculum contruction which would focus entirely upon cognitive operations would seem to be isolated from the realities of totally functioning organisms. Particularly when assessing student involvement in learning processes, it is necessary to analyze affective factors such as attitudes.

TABLE 22

OUTLINE AND INTEGRATION OF THE COGNITIVE AND
AFFECTIVE DOMAINS ADOPTED FROM B.S. BLOOM[14]

The Cognitive Continuum	The Affective Continuum

Knowledge: recall, relating, organizing
  Knowledge of *specifics:* terms, facts
  Knowledge of *methods:* conventions, trends, classifications, criteria
  Knowledge of *universals:* principles, generalizations, theories, structures
	Receiving (attending): sensitivity to stimuli, directing and controlling attention
	  Awareness
	  Willingness to receive)
	  Controlled (selective) attention

Comprehension: understanding
  Translation: to other forms of communication
  Interpretation: explanation, summarization
  Extrapolation: implications, consequences, effects
	Responding: motivated to react
	  Acquiescence: compliance
	  Willingness (to respond)
	  Satisfaction: pleasure

Application: using abstractions	*Valuing:* assessing worth
	  Acceptance (of a value)
	  Preference for a value
	  Commitment

Analysis: clarification
  Analysis of *elements*
  Analysis of *relationships*
  Analysis of *organizational principles*
Synthesis: forming wholes from parts; productive rearrangement
  Production of a *unique communication*
  Production of a *plan,* or proposed *set of operations*
  Derivation of a *set of abstract relations*
	Organization of a system of values
	  Conceptualization of a value

Evaluation: Quantitative and qualitative judgments
  Judgments in terms of *internal evidence*
  Judgments in terms of *external criteria*
	Organization of a (personal) value system

	Characterization by a value or value complex: internally consistent personal hierarchy of values *Generalized set:* selective responding according to inner dictates; the basis for one's philosophy of life

[14] Bloom, *Op. cit., Handbook I: Cognitive Domain* and *Handbook II: Affective Domain.*

Table 23 includes examples of typical subject matter contents which lend themselves to classification according to cognitive educational objectives; these examples are merely intended to be rough reminders that the subject content (e.g. tangible learning) that occurs in classrooms should, in and of itself, lead to high level manipulations. Some subject matters are composed of implied, or self-contained, methodological prescriptions (e.g. math-science). In these cases, it is extremely difficult to indicate where "knowledge of methods or universals" ends and true "analysis or synthesis" begins. By definition, a student would have to already possess the "intellectual abilities and skills" enumerated under "application, analysis and synthesis" before he could demonstrate meaningful "knowledge" of analytical geometry or calculus. Other subject matters imply more rapid development towards evaluation by the student (e.g. social studies) or eccentric sequences of mental skills application (e.g. appreciating literature or the fine arts). The examples in Table 23 represent crude developmental sequences which coincide, roughly, with grade level progress in these subjects. However, it is also possible to apply the *Taxonomy* to subject matters within single graded situations. For example, in a given subject area, the teacher should attempt to pace the student through the appropriate mental operations necessary to accomplish the full range of educational goals (i.e. knowledge should be systematically subjected to analysis or evaluation).

Perhaps the most practical use the *Taxonomy* could be put to is for daily lesson planning, particularly the formulation of teacher questions to the class for the purpose of eliciting higher level intellectual responses from the students. As shown earlier (Table 20), the majority of teachers appear to dwell on classroom discussions which call for the recitation of prior knowledge; they do not aggressively pursue analysis or evaluation of knowledge. Of course, students do think through the implications and applications for knowledge they have learned; but, they must do this on their own or during extracurricular episodes. It is impossible for the teacher to directly ascertain the usefulness of learning unless related intellectual activities are purposefully built into classroom practice. Following are selected examples from a variety of subject areas, of questions teachers have asked students for the purpose of stimulating the use of their higher level intellectual processes:

Teacher's questions designed to assess comprehension:
    What? When? Where? How? Under the following circumstances . . . ?
    Can we restate (the problem, plot, event) in your own words?
    Can we define . . . explain . . . summarize?
    Does the author agree (disagree) with . . . ?
    Can we translate that passage into this (language, idiom, form)?
    Are (principles, laws, rules) alluded to by the author?

Teacher's questions fomulated to stimulate students to apply knowledge:
    Could we solve this problem given these (facts, methods, principles)?
    Can this specimen be grouped with . . . ?
    Which one of these tentative (hypotheses, answers, solutions) seems
       most (feasible, plausible, useful)?
    Can we explain this (discrepancy, exception, oddity)?

Teacher's questions calling for analysis or synthesis:
    Can a general (rule, principle, law) be drawn from our observations?
    Could we utilize more than one methodology to solve this problem?
    Could we (rate, rank) these factors in terms of . . . ?
    Can we state the ways the author interrelated (plot, character, se-
       quence)?
    Can we design a (plan, operation, method, or product) of our own?

Teacher's questions suggesting that the students evaluate:
    How do you reconcile this (fact, theory, proposal) with your own per-
       sonal (wishes, convictions, rights, understandings)?
      Do you feel ready, competent (to rate, grade, criticize) yourself?
    Have you developed some individual (choices, tastes, preferences) for
      (given literature, art, music)?
    Why do you take that stand on this issue?
    Are you able to compare your (outlooks, convictions, feelings) with the
      views of (others, objective criteria)?

Summarizing the *Taxonomy of Educational Objectives,* it is probably the most useful currently available tool for evaluating and constructing curriculum according to an empirically valid framework of learning expectancies. The emphasis upon "intellectual skills" renders the *Taxonomy* specifically important when planning learning activities for the gifted. Parallel possibilities for appraising emotional development is an added asset. The *Taxonomy* has been used widely for analyzing existing curriculum, initiating commonality in teacher communications, suggesting examination items, indicating questions teachers might pose to students, and initial planning of new curriculum to accomplish logical and comprehensive coverage of topics and intellectual skill development. The shortcomings of the *Taxonomy* are shared with all of the other educational models discussed: (1) it lacks specificity for intercategorical talents; (2) it is clearly influenced by and descriptive of only scientific (i.e. experimental, logical, or empirical) procedures (whatever happened to prophetic, intuitive, mystical, or purely aesthetic approaches to knowledge?); and (3) it treats the learning process as if it were sequential, orderly, and segmented whereas introspection reveals the process to be fluid, reversible, spontaneous and, above all, unpredictable.

TABLE 23

EXAMPLES OF SUBJECT CONTENTS ORGANIZED AND ASSESSED
ACCORDING TO THE TAXONOMY OF EDUCATIONAL OBJECTIVES

Content Areas	Knowledge	Comprehension	Application	Analysis	Synthesis	Evaluation
Math-Science	Numbers, symbols, methods	Transpose to tables, graphs, verbal forms	Apply formulas to problem solving	Theorems, differential equations	Unique mathematical expressions, solutions	Probability theory, significance indices
	Biological classifications	Translate classifications to working descriptions of organisms	Classify specimens	Relate species to natural law (e.g. ecology)	Evolution theory, unify disparate classifications	Test limits of taxonomies, propose alternatives
	(Concepts) energy, matter	Define in particular instances (e.g. electricity, motion)	Explain naturally occurring phenomena	Experimental determination of properties	Interrelate concepts (e.g. law of conservation)	Estimate worth of concepts in terms of unexplained phenomena
Language Arts	Literature, differentiated forms (e.g. myth, novel, play, etc.)	Derive enriched meaning through use of metaphor, simile, etc.	Writing reports, interpreting life (current) conditions	Plot, characterization, elemental thema critical essays	Composing, generalizing trends, periods, typologies	Develops rational tastes, personal literary style
Social Science	People, society, culture	Identify cultural-anthropological identities	Explain current events; reinterpret literature	Inventory social needs; test historical hyptheses	Derive universal tendencies of man; political theory	Assess contemporary values of culture; recommend improved institutions
Student Assessment Factors: Cognitive and Affective Domains	Objective examination: multiple choice tests; recitation; measure attention span; reading rate; enthusiasm	Essay tests; class discussion and participation; volunteer projects; expression of satisfaction; richness of associations	Laboratory usage; competitive success; solution of novel instances; use of learned principles; value formation-taking "stands," understanding self	Guiding others to conclusions; objective criticism amount of independent study; statements of positions, ability to probe	Sets of generalizations; summary papers (e.g. term paper); oral exams on total areas; evidence of an emerging value system	Capacity for self-criticism, ability to modify own behavior; emergence of respect of and from peers; tackles universal problems

Chapter 7

APPROPRIATE DEVELOPMENTAL PLACEMENT

A LMOST every school district in our nation has probably practiced acceleration in some form.[1] In spite of the great body of evidence that has been developed in the past twenty years, educators are still skeptical about this process. Such skepticism is often based upon attitudes or hearsay rather than documented facts. For example, one of the more common criticisms of acceleration hinges upon the alleged detrimental social outcomes it produces. Yet, substantial evidence exists to indicate that accelerated pupils match or excel the social development of their grade placement peers.

For example, H.J. Klausmeier recently studied the "Effects of Accelerating Bright Older Pupils From Second to Fourth Grade." His findings indicated that the results of this experiment are interpreted as strongly favorable toward accelerating older second graders. . . ."[2] Heer studied junior high school accelerants in Pennsylvania back in 1937 and found that they kept up with or surpassed regular control groups of all academic variables. Keys, in 1938, studied two groups; one group consisted of Oakland High School accelerants, the other consisted of underage students entering the University of California. Both studies indicated "results favoring acceleration."[3] In 1957, Keys again reviewed the research on acceleration and concluded that we "should accelerate bright students in terms of the research findings."[4] Mirman recently studied pupils who had been doubly promoted in the elementary schools in Los Angeles. He attempted to assess not only the performance of this group but also their attitudes, their parents' attitudes, and their social adjustment. Mirman concluded that "acceleration could be used more widely." He found that "personal adjustment is not appreciably affected by acceleration. . . . This problem can be minimized by allowing the child to skip during the early years of elementary school."[5]

Of course, acceleration is but one of several broad administrative methods by means of which we can meet the needs of gifted pupils. Other methods include special grouping, enrichment, special tutoring, special counseling opportunities, or extracurricular activities.

---

[1] Particularly, if we include advanced curriculum as a "form of acceleration."

[2] Klausmeier, H.J., and Ripple, R.E.: Effects of accelerating bright older pupils from second to fourth grade. *J Educ Psychol,* 53 (No. 2): 1962.

[3] Keys, Noel: *The Underage Student in High School and College.* Berkeley, U. Calif., 1938, pp. 145-272.

[4] Keys, Noel: Should we accelerate the bright? *Exceptional Children,* 23:199-201, Feb. 1957.

[5] Mirman, Norman: A Study of Social Adjustment as It Relates to Grade-Skipping in the Elementary School. Unpublished doctoral dissertation. Los Angeles, University of California, 1961.

One recently developed program of acceleration is the "Individual Place-ment Project for Academically Talented Pupils in the Elementary Schools," developed by the writer. This program calls for the identification of more advanced pupils at the end of the second grade. Such academically ad-vanced pupils are placed according to their individual needs into a summer tutoring program which substitutes for the third grade. During their fourth and fifth grades, periodic evaluations are made to ascertain their progress and special requirements. An individual counseling program supplements their experiences during the fourth and fifth grades. At the end of the fifth grade this advanced individual placement group is evaluated with a view toward placing those pupils with sufficient readiness into a special summer program which substitutes for the sixth grade. This individual placement project develops, demonstrates, and validates a framework for acceleration which enables elementary school pupils to accelerate one or two years without missing any crucial experiences or actual curriculum content. The program will be explained in more detail later.

Why should it come as a shock to some educators to discover that children are individually different? With our modern emphasis upon "difference" one is puzzled to account for all of the generalizations that are made con-cerning young children. Such generalizations as "they tire easily; they need more play activities; their interest in formal learning is fleeting" are not true of *all* children. Of course, such statements are true of *some* children. In an age when knowledge and new concepts are developing by geometric proportions, do we dare to keep the learner lock-stepped in an arbitrary and unilaterally determined framework? We are advocating taking the pressures for remaining an infant away and allowing the child to develop at his own pace and within the more valid framework of his own motivational patterns.

It seems obvious that no educator should advocate "hurrying or pushing" children. It seems just as obvious that no educator should prevent the de-velopmental process of growth to proceed at its own pace.

A DEVELOPMENTAL APPROACH TO PUPIL ACCELERATION

Many educators have advocated the grade level acceleration of pupils on a large scale. Many other educators reject the various methods of accelera-tion. Some argue that undue pressures are inevitably felt by the accelerated student as he attempts to adjust to classes of students who possess higher degrees of maturity, sophistication, and actual achievement. Others have noted that, providing the accelerants are chosen upon valid criteria, the advanced students resemble the older grade peers with whom they are placed more exactly than they resembled their own age peers.

One wonders if this question of acceleration is really an "all-or-nothing" affair. It may be that the two schools of thought on the matter have been overstated, thereby confusing the issues and overgeneralizing the application of both points of view. For example, most educators espouse the philosophy of individual differences. Given such a philosophical framework, it is improbable that hard-and-fast rules can be applied to any group of students without consideration of their particularistic developmental and educational needs.

Perhaps we are ready to face the real issues. If so, we must set aside the oversimplified view that "acceleration" is an isolated administrative method for patching an inadequately challenging educational sequence. Instead, we will need to analyze the developmental realities of disparate student differences as well as the entire structure and content of existing curriculum.

The term "acceleration" will be used even though it is thought that a new phrase such as "proper developmental placement" would be more suitable and descriptive. What we choose to call "acceleration" may not be a change in rate or speed of learning but rather a reassessment of the students' capabilities, with subsequent placement into a more appropriate higher grade level setting. Most school districts in the nation have practiced acceleration in some form. Yet, in spite of the collection of a great body of evidence, educators are still skeptical about this procedure.

Why are educators so skeptical? Perhaps Chapman summed up the case when he stated, "Grade skipping . . . adjusts the child to the system. . . . The child is entitled to a more logical, sustained, planned curriculum than that offered by skipping."[6] He pointed out that acceleration, as an administrative technique, saves money and time and obviates the need for complex programming. It seems obvious that typical programs of acceleration offer considerable financial, administrative, and timesaving advantages. But these advantages may be bought at the expense of the individual child's needs unless a very thorough investigation and case study is conducted before actual advanced placement.

Pressey, after surveying the literature, concluded that "Acceleration may not only give a student more education in a given time, but increase his functioning abilities."[7] Pressey observed that some of the neglected values, such as those of time saving, are being reevaluated by modern educators. Also, he noted the powerful argument that young intellectuals tend to produce their most significant creative contributions early in their professional careers. As if to reinforce Pressey's conclusions, Shannon recently summarized the existing literature on acceleration and concluded that in

		[6] Chapman, Guy: Educational programs in California for the gifted and talented. *The Gifted Child in Elementary School.* Twenty-sixth Yearbook of the California Elementary School Administrators Association, 1954. Burlingame, California, California Elementary School Administrators Association, 1954, p. 21.
		[7] Pressey, Sidney: Educational acceleration: Occasional procedure or major issue? *Personnel and Guidance Journal,* 41 (No. 1): Dec. 1962.

later life accelerated students perform as well as or better than nonaccelerated matched students.[8]

In a more recent study, Mirman studied the effects of double promotion in the elementary schools upon the later social adjustment of these same students in the high school. Mirman concluded that "Acceleration could be used more widely . . . acceleration needs to be an individual matter." Moreover, he found that "Personal adjustment is not appreciably affected by acceleration." He found that girls did not encounter as many problems as did boys. He noted that "Teachers should discuss the accelerant's special abilities and interests. . . . If more children were accelerated, the result would be to make the accelerated child feel less conspicuous."[9]

Klausmeier has conducted a number of studies concerning the effects of acceleration upon bright older elementary pupils. Klausmeier's general conclusion has been that the results of his experiments could be interpreted to mean that "It appears unwise to force bright students to spend twelve years in completing high school and sixteen years in completing the requirements for the Baccalaureate Degree."[10] Summarizing the research, it appears obvious that most well-planned procedures for the orderly advanced placement of pupils result in moderate to good adjustment to the higher grades as well as successful academic achievement.

It seems safe to conclude the following:

1. Acceleration is a safe technique, provided it is implemented by a well thought-out program.

2. More students should be included in acceleration-type programs.

3. Accelerated pupils need more attention, such as special counseling opportunities and the chance for follow-up activities, such as specific tutoring.

4. Accelerated children can be expected to equal or excel their new grade level peers, and even need additional educational enrichment in their higher grade placement.

Acceleration programs in today's schools assume many forms, including the following:

1. advanced classes in subject matter disciplines,
2. ungraded or multigraded classrooms,
3. summer school programs for grade substitution,
4. early entrance to kindergarten or the first grade,

---

[8] Shannon, Dan: What research says about acceleration. *Phi Delta Kappan,* XXXIX, November, 1957.

[9] Mirman, Norman: A Study of Social Adjustment as It Relates to Grade Skipping in the Elementary Schools. Unpublished doctoral dissertation, University of California at Los Angeles, 1961.

[10] Klausmeier, Hubert: Effects of accelerating bright older elementary pupils: A follow-up. *J Educ Psychol,* 54 (No. 3): 1963.

5. combined grades with restructured, accelerated curriculum,
6. high ceiling curriculum with no grade level advancement,
7. simple double promotion, and
8. advanced placement to college.

As they establish different programs of acceleration, educators must keep in mind the fundamental purposes for schools. It is generally accepted that schools have as their primary purpose that of imparting basic intellectual skills and knowledge to children. However, schools must also present appropriate cultural values in order for the student to use his skills and knowledge for useful productivity and socially acceptable ends. In addition, most schools recognize an obligation to encourage and promote the development of creative potentialities. Therefore, schools cannot claim that they have "educated" their students merely because they have trained or indoctrinated them with the stereotyped skills, knowledge, and morals of the past. There is some danger that acceleration programs might degenerate to the level of pure "stimulus-response" learning. If this pitfall is to be avoided, educators establishing acceleration programs must continually reassess their goals for education.

Most of the specific procedures for acceleration listed above lend themselves to the first six years of formal schooling. This is because these forms of acceleration are based upon the rapid acquisition of knowledge and skills. It is assumed that when the student reaches a saturation point for learning, there is no particular point for repetitious activity. It is better to place the student at a more advanced level at which he can acquire more abstract skills of learning and apply himself toward the solution of more complex mental problems. The whole point of the matter is that the student ought to be placed in an educational milieu which contains adequate books, teachers, equipment, classrooms, laboratories, and libraries to cope with his precocious intellectual functioning.

Early entrance to school seems logical in view of the fact that modern children are exposed to formal learning, especially symbol recognition, quite early because of modern communication media. Of course, the child accepted for early entrance should be thoroughly evaluated by the use of individual testing techniques, developmental case studies, counseling, and consultation with his parents. An "early entrance" child placed in an ungraded primary situation may advance quite rapidly and be prepared to enter the fourth grade in a couple of years. The real stumbling block for advanced placement into the fourth grade may be social and emotional factors rather than intellectual. Therefore, teachers of ungraded primaries should be provided with appropriate and valid tools of evaluation. Sociometric scales, locally constructed student rating scales, and psychometric devices are all useful for the study of the total development of the child in the classroom setting. Student assessment should include academic, social, emotional, physiological, and personal dimensions.

Assuming that the secondary school setting is equipped with laboratory, library, and other advanced facilities, there would appear to be little need for actual grade level advancement until the end of the high school experience. Rather, high schools need to reconsider the meaning of "high ceiling curriculums." The great barrier to student intellectual growth in the modern high school is not the problem of learning equipment and settings but rather the reluctance of high school teachers to "let their students go." Perhaps the reintroduction of small group activities, including the popular seminar experience, would be a fruitful approach to the stimulation of bright students in the high school setting. The great ideas of Western Man, as well as his ethics, can be discussed in great depth. Small group experiences can incorporate personnel such as guidance staff.

As the able student approaches the eleventh and twelfth grades, the problem of saturation of learning again presents itself. The possibilities for advanced placement to college are limited only by the imaginations of the professional staff involved.

Perhaps the main error made by school administrators when they establish "acceleration programs" is that they ignore the realities of individual student differences. The schools may create a rigid program and expect students to adjust to it. Instead, the program should be considered flexible. Individual developmental placement of children into an educational situation which is more stimulating and challenging should be considered at any grade level. In order to establish such a master program, it is necessary to enlist the forces of guidance, psychological, parental, and community agencies. The master program should build in provisions for early entrance, ungraded classrooms, summer school opportunities, grade combinations, special classrooms with ceiling curriculums, special individual and group counseling opportunities, subject matter seminars, interdisciplinary activities, and possibilities for advanced placement to college.

In order to implement a master program of developmental placement, a school district would need to consider the following factors:

1. Standard measurements, forms, procedures, and reporting techniques should be developed. In order for teachers to communicate from grade level to grade level, they will need to be provided with meaningful data which is comprehensible. Even complicated reports, such as case studies, may be simplified by the adoption of uniform definitions and rating scales for the use of all professional personnel. Evaluative studies can be easily conducted if forms given to students, parents, and teachers reflect similar definitions, statistical models, and formats. For example, attitudinal case study forms can provide comparative data when

similar forms are given to teachers, parents, and students, and compared for similarity of ratings.

2. Identification of students for advanced programs should be thorough, reliable, and systematic. Teachers should be provided with referral forms and motivated to refer all pupils whom they consider to be prospects for educational replacement. In order to accomplish such professional motivation, teachers' opinions must be genuinely valued. Also, professional guidance consultants should be available for the individual testing and diagnosis of students. Frequent communication should occur between guidance and teaching staffs through certification and placement meetings in which pupils are placed in an advanced program based upon a thorough study of their records.

3. Special counseling and tutoring services should be available for students and their parents. Adjustment problems are bound to occur when students are placed in unfamiliar surroundings. Also, it is logical to expect that modern parents, with their propensity toward competition, may inadvertently "push" their offspring. Therefore, it is necessary to provide special guidance services not only for those students who are accelerated but more particularly for those students whose prognosis for acceleration is poor. Even the most able student may encounter a subject in which he does not succeed at a pace commensurate with his other work. While such situations could not be considered to be "remedial," the student will need compensatory or supplemental tutoring.

4. The curriculum must be viewed as flexible and continuous. The whole key to a successful master program of proper developmental placement of pupils may be the ability of teachers to modify the curriculum needs of the pupil. Unfortunately, the reverse process of forcing all students to adjust to a rigid curriculum structure is the common form in many schools. Teachers at all grade levels should continually reassess the content of their daily lesson plans. Special projects should be prescribed for highly advanced students.

More particularly, teachers need to consider a curriculum model upon which they can base their long-range educational plans. For example, Bloom's *Taxonomy of Educational Objectives: The Cognitive Domain* might serve such a purpose. Once the teachers begin to develop their lessons collectively about a central theoretical structure, they will be able to communicate with one another more effectively. Thus, it will become possible for functional "teaching teams" to operate. One of the main problems will be that of articulation, particularly between elementary and secondary schools. There is no easy solution to this problem. It appears obvious that more articulation committees ought to be formed between the two levels, with a view toward amalgamation of educational philosophies, curriculum structures, and methodologies.

5. Overall program administration should be initiated. In order for a complex master program to function, someone, somewhere, will need to coordinate and supervise its various aspects. Just as school districts have found that a director of special education is needed to coordinate the complex aspects of programs for retarded and handicapped students, so they are discovering a similar and equally pressing need for coordination of programs for students of higher and more individualized educational needs.

It has been observed that a child may be artificially locked into an educational system which expects him to adjust to it, rather than itself adjusting to his individual needs. It has been advocated that educators begin to synthesize the various so-called acceleration programs into a new amalgamated concept of "proper developmental placement of students." In order to accomplish this highly complex task, specialists such as school psychologists will need to cooperate with teachers in the development of a sophisticated master program of advanced placement which incorporates adequate case studies of students, theoretical training of teachers, and the establishment of a diversity of program possibilities.

THE INDIVIDUAL PLACEMENT PROJECT—ACCELERATION DURING SUMMER SCHOOL

The Individual Placement Project for academically talented pupils in the elementary schools is a unique form of acceleration which utilizes the summer school and involves no actual skipping of grades. Academically advanced and talented pupils are identified at the end of the second grade. These pupils are placed, according to their individual needs, into a special tutoring program in the summer which substitutes for the third grade. During their fourth and fifth grades, periodic evaluations will be made to establish their progress and appraise any special requirements they may have. An individual counseling and tutoring program must supplement the experiences of these children during their fourth and fifth grades. At the end of the fifth grade, this advanced placement group will be re-evaluated with a view toward placing those pupils with sufficient readiness into a special program which would substitute for the sixth grade. This project has been field tested in ten California school districts, including the Pasadena City Schools, since 1963.

It should be emphasized that the Individual Placement Project is essentially an administrative device to accomplish acceleration without skipping. However, acceleration is not an end in itself. The main purpose for accelerating children is to place them with a peer group more like themselves in order that they may be adequately challenged, stimulated, and interested in their everyday program. This administrative procedure, even when it is carefully thought out, must be supplemented by other experiences. The talented child who is accelerated does not cease to have highly specialized needs. He may require special counseling, tutoring, special projects, or other enrichment activities in the grade into which he is advanced. He may still need to interact with other gifted pupils with whom he is placed.

Special problems may arise when, in spite of the careful identification processes to be utilized, pupils are still misplaced into the substitute summer programs. These problems will not be so severe if we are entirely forthright with parents, children, and teachers in all phases of this program. For example, if the parents realize that participation in the substitute summer program is not an automatic "ticket" into the fourth grade, they will be able to understand and, hopefully, agree with some new decision that may be reached by the special teacher during the summer program. There is no special formula to avoid disagreement, disappointment, and other unfortunate experiences. If the parents and the child have been intimately involved in the identification, placement, and educational processes of this program, they will probably agree right down the line with any decision that is forthcoming from the certification committees or special summer program teachers.

Some special problems may arise with those children who are not accelerated even though they have been screened. Again, no strategic problems will arise providing we are completely open-minded and forthright with all parents. We have just as much obligation to the parents and children who are not accepted for participation in the program as we do for those who are accepted. We owe the parents of a child who was not included a full and thorough explanation of why he was not included. If the explanation is academically and psychologically sound, the parent will undoubtedly agree with us wholeheartedly. In fact, we would prefer the parents themselves to make many of these crucial decisions.

The cornerstone of the Individual Placement Program is the individual treatment of the pupil. The success of this program depends upon the extent to which local districts thoroughly study and cater to the individual needs of the participating pupils. Make no mistake about it, this aspect of the program may be expensive. However, it would seem that we have a special ethical obligation to see to it that mistakes simply are not made. Mistakes need not be made providing each child who participates is thoroughly studied and receives any special tutoring or counseling which may be necessary for his individual adjustment into the special summer programs and the advanced classes into which he will be accelerated.

Excess costs for this program during the spring semester should take the form of (1) individual identification costs, (2) counseling with the pupil and his parents, (3) tutoring for those pupils with special needs,

(4) in-service training for teachers, and (5) special curriculum development and consultation with teachers, parents, and pupils concerning curricular needs.

Excess costs incurred during the summer will probably include (1) extra instructional costs, especially in the form of special tutoring time teachers devote to the participating pupils after school during the summer, (2) any special counseling necessary for the participating pupils, (3) extra materials such as reading laboratories, spelling laboratories, reference books, and project materials not ordinarily bought, (4) possibly, excess transportation costs, and (5) consultant costs, particularly curriculum consultant costs.

Excess costs will also be incurred during the fall semester when the pupils are placed in the fourth grade and during the fifth grade. These special costs will take the form of (1) any special counseling or tutoring necessary to accomplish the pupil's full adjustment to his advanced class, (2) consultant services for the teachers with whom the participating pupils are placed in advanced classes, (3) follow-up costs including group examination costs, and (4) any special project materials needed by the pupils in their advanced classes.

The extra materials needed to implement and facilitate this program will be determined at the local level and specifically adjusted to meet the needs of the local districts educational philosophy and normal third-grade and sixth-grade programs. The extra personnel needed to expedite this program include the following: (1) a guidance consultant with training the administration of individual tests and with research experience, (2) a curriculum consultant with elementary curriculum development training and an ability to work closely with teachers, psychologists, and others in the individual development of courses of study suited to meet very specialized individual needs, and (3) special summer school teachers whose background and training in education render them "master teachers" with a special skill in dealing with exceptionally talented and creative children.

Providing the special program provisions outlined above are carried out, it has been estimated that this program will cost sixty dollars in excess costs a year per pupil on the average. This figure is based upon an exhaustive study of the ten school districts which offered such programs in California. Moreover, there will be an undeniable saving to the district in terms of providing four or five rather than six years of education to the participating pupils. Of course, this saving is only incidental. We are concerned only with the full development of pupil potentiality.

After a district has decided to participate in the Individual Placement Project, the following specific steps need to be taken in order to launch, facilitate, and implement the program:

Step 1

The district must reevaluate its educational philosophy and make sure that this particular kind of program correlates with their unique situation. Where contradictions or differences of opinion exist, there should be healthy discussion, clarification, explanation, and modification. Perhaps this step is best expedited by a special district-wide committee whose functions would consist of overseeing the entire Individual Placement Program.

Step 2

All of the teachers in the district should be acquainted with the proposed program. This can be done efficiently by means of one or more general in-service meetings. During these meetings, the entire project would be explained to the district professional staff. More specific in-service meetings and training would follow for those persons specifically involved in the project such as the summer school teachers, consultants, and other related personnel. In-service training for the participating personnel should be devoted to (1) understanding and implementing the district's educational philosophy and the goals of the Individual Placement Project, (2) identification techniques and procedures, (3) the nature of the gifted and talented child, (4) the curriculum procedures and materials to be utilized during the substitute summer programs, (5) the development of special evaluative techniques such as report cards, satisfaction rating sheets, progress reports, etc., (6) the development of adequate follow-up procedures and the stimulation of lines of communication between and among consultants, special class teachers, and advanced placement teachers.

Step 3

Nomination forms and procedures need to be developed and distributed to second-grade teachers. Suggested nomination forms have been developed and appear in this chapter, however, a particular local district may wish to modify these forms for its own purposes. Nominations should come from regular teachers in the second grade. The teachers should nominate pupils who in their judgment match certain criteria which would be provided. These criteria should include estimates of the child's intellectual, emotional, social, and physical functioning.

Step 4

From the pool of nominations, the guidance consultants must identify and develop a case study for those pupils who will participate in the special summer programs. This identification and case study process may be summarized in a document entitled "Individual Placement Project Certification and Summary Form." It must be emphasized that the identification case study process does not merely involve individual examination with the

Stanford-Binet or the Wechsler Intelligence Scale for Children (WISC). Rather, it involves the gathering of minimal data in the areas of (1) academic background and proficiency, (2) objective test results, (3) intellectual functioning, (4) personal interests, (5) personality and emotional stability, and (6) social maturity.

Step 5

A placement and certification conference must be held, attended by the guidance consultant, nominating teacher, parents, and an administrative representative. All of the committee members would sign a certification document indicating their approval for the child's participation in the project and, where appropriate, their certification of legal "mental giftedness." This committee would see to it that adequate follow-up, counseling, tutoring, or any other special implementation was forthcoming in the case of a particular child.

Step 6

Special counseling and tutoring should be available for any participating pupil who needs it. This special tutoring or counseling might be needed prior to his participation in the substitute summer program during the summer program, or sometime following the summer program. Perhaps the easiest way to implement this step is to designate members of the professional staff whose assignment would include special tutoring or counseling for pupils needing it.

Step 7

The special substitute summer programs need to be developed with emphasis upon special tutoring for individual pupil needs. Suggested curriculum will be presented later in this chapter. However, a given district may wish to deviate from this curriculum in terms of its own specific educational philosophy. In general, skills, methods, and specific learnings typically offered in the third grade should be emphasized. However, a given pupil may have certain weaknesses as, for example, in the area of arithmetical skills. For this particular student, arithmetic should be emphasized during the summer program. Generally, the research indicates that talented pupils may have relative weaknesses in the areas of language skills (especially spelling and writing), creative writing, and study habits. Generalizing from third-grade programs, the following time breakdowns in terms of percentage of time devoted to a given area follow: (1) language arts including reading, literature, spelling, oral and written expression—40 percent; (2) social studies—12 percent; (3) arithmetical work—8 percent; (4) science and health—10 percent; (5) combined art-music—10 percent; and (6) the rest of the time for planning and evaluation. It is suggested that the six-week summer program be designed on a full-time basis to include five forty-minute periods with at least one twenty-five minute play period.

Step 8

Follow-up and evaluation. Professional personnel need to be designated for the evaluation portion of this project. The participating pupils need to be studied periodically, preferably each year, by means of objective tests, indications of satisfaction, and teacher ratings. The follow-up procedure should also focus upon the individual pupil, offering him special opportunity for tutoring and counseling.

Special Case Study for Individual Placement Project

In general, case study material should be collected, analyzed, and recorded by a school psychologist. Of course, the school psychologist may freely corroborate with social workers, teachers, and other professional workers in the collection of case study material. Any and all case study material should be considered confidential. Extraneous or unnecessary information should not be collected nor recorded. It is a wise policy to keep case study material separately filed in specially designated and locked cabinets. The parents of the child being studied should be informed of the nature of and security arrangements provided for the case study. All persons contributing material to a case study should sign their contributions. Case study material should never be shared with other institutions unless express written permission is obtained from the parents or legal guardians of the child being studied. The case study is the single most important component of an acceleration type of program.

The specific elements of the case study are described below and include such things as academic background, achievement, intelligence, interests, personality functioning, and social maturity. The gathering of an adequate case study enables us to tailor-make an educational program for a given pupil. If the information has been gathered in a conscientious manner, we obtain descriptions of the pupil's needs, motives, attitudes, and intellectual functioning. Of course, no amount of prescription can substitute for accurate, insightful, and emphathetic notes by teachers and others contributing to the cumulative case study of a pupil.

The Certification and Summary Form of the case study is intended to act as a checklist of the factors to be studied. The headings used in the checklist are, for the most part, self-explanatory. The headings entitled "Recommendation for Participation," "Needs Further Study," "Included in Case Study," and "Comments or Reservations" are to be filled with the pupil's prognosis for participation in the Individual Placement Project as the criterion. For example, under the "Recommendation for Participation" column there are three subheadings entitled "Yes," "Undecided," "No."

The guidance consultant should check each of the factors listed as "Yes," "Undecided," or "No" in terms of whether or not that particular factor indicates positive evidence for the particular child's participation in the Individual Placement Project. Under the column entitled "Tests or Sources Used" the guidance consultant should indicate the specific test, person, or record from which the particular factor in question was studied. Under the column entitled "Comments or Reservations," any of the four certification conference participants, including the teacher, administrator, guidance consultant, or parent, should feel free to state any reservations or critical comments they have concerning the placement of the particular child in question into the Individual Placement Project as it relates to the factor listed in the lefthand margin.

The guidance consultant should systematically analyze the pupil's academic record, his cumulative folder, and any other historical data that is available. Anecdotal notes should be kept of the factors studied when recorded in a permanent case study report.

When filling in the "Summary of Case Study Form" the guidance consultant should use the following criteria to determine how to check the "Recommendation for Participation" column. (1) Analysis of Grades—in order to be checked in the "Yes" column, a pupil should have obtained mostly "A" and a few "B" grades. Pupils with any "C" grades would probably be placed in the "Undecided" column and pupils receiving "D" or lower grades in any subject area would probably be placed in the "No" column in this particular area. Under the column "Raw Scores," the guidance consultant should list the typical grade obtained by the pupil and any comments that are necessary for the purposes of explanation. (2) Teacher Ratings—the "cum" folder will have to be studied carefully in order to fill out the case study in this area. Particularly pertinent comments or reservations from the teacher ratings contained in the cumulative records should be briefly recorded in the column on the summary sheet. (3) Cumulative Data—this factor can include an analysis of any records, documents, rating scales, or other evidence of academic achievement not included in the teacher ratings or analysis of grades.

The typical child has not had much standardized testing by the end of the second grade. However, as a minimum standard, there should be at least one test of reading readiness and/or achievement and arithmetic. These tests, with their title and the estimated prognosis for success in the Individual Placement Project, should be checked as indicated on the summary form.

As a minimum standard, the pupil should have been examined with at least one group intelligence test and one individual intelligence test. The group intelligence test may have been administered as early as the kindergarten and still be valid for the purposes of this study. If the Stanford-

Binet is used, the mental age (MA) should be included under the "Score" column. If the Wechsler-Bellevue is used, both the verbal and nonverbal subject raw scores should be listed under "Scores," and all ten subtest scores should be recorded under "Comments."

The teacher, in conjunction with the guidance consultant, should fill in the case study materials having to do with the pupils' interests. We are particularly concerned with the pupils' academic interests as listed on the summary case study form. When the teacher fills out the "Recommendation for Participation" column, she should check "Yes" for those interests which indicate a high degree of potential motivation for participation in special programs. Under the column "Scores," the teacher should rate the pupil as high, average, or low in all of the academic interest areas as compared with his peers in actual classroom activities.

If the teacher or guidance consultant has made observations concerning the child's basic attitudes or if the professional workers have noted any unusual development in the child's system of values, these comments should be recorded in the case study and briefly noted under "Comments or Reservations" on the summary form.

For the purposes of this case study for acceleration, we are not concerned with an elaborate, diagnostic personality workup. We are, however, concerned with the particular child's ability to adjust to new and challenging situations. Under "Recommendations," the guidance consultant and teacher should check "Yes" for participation only when the child's total personality, in their professional opinion, is the type that would benefit from an acceleration program. If personality devices or tests are used, their titles should be indicated and brief summaries of the findings listed under the "Comment" column of the summary report. Detailed analysis of the personality test findings should be written into the case study. Any severe personality malfunctioning would obviate a given child's participation.

The guidance consultant may wish to use the Vineland Social Maturity Scale as the basis for the objective rating in this column. We are particularly concerned that the child has sufficient social awareness to realize the implications of his acceleration. Also, we want to make sure that the child possesses sufficient sophistication and ego-adapting mechanisms to deal with the inevitable frustrations and challenges that acceleration will bring about. Parent ratings should always be included in the summary. Preferably, the same rating scale that is used by teachers and guidance consultants to rate the social maturity of the child should be used by the parent. The ratings of all of the adults can then be compared and any contradictions analyzed.

It should be emphasized that more data than are here listed should be collected in order for a given case study to be thorough. To be worthwhile, any case study must reflect the unique, personal, and particular qualities of the human being that is described.

Some "other factors" to consider for the case study are (1) the child's approach to thinking and ability to use scientific and other methods, (2) the pupil's health, (3) indications of creativity, (4) the pupil's effectiveness in social situations (leadership), and (5) attitudes.

The following forms were developed by the author and staff as part of "California Project Talent" and appear in a publication entitled *Acceleration Programs for Intellectually Gifted Pupils* which is in the Public Domain:

CHECKLIST FOR SCREENING MENTALLY GIFTED PUPILS

First Grade

Date _____

Pupil's name _____   Birthdate _____

School _____   Teacher _____

Note: Since superior pupils exhibit their superiority in many ways, no single test score should be used as the sole criterion upon which such pupils should be identified. Teachers' judgments, evidence of a high level of performance in any of the academic fields, and evidence of high motivation coupled with high test scores can all be used in the identification of potentially superior students.

Check if in evidence:

_____ 1. Large vocabularies which are used easily and accurately
_____ 2. Asks many penetrating questions; wants to know causes and reasons for things
_____ 3. A wide range of interests, but may concentrate heavily on one
_____ 4. Quick to recognize relationships and understand meanings
_____ 5. Expresses himself well
_____ 6. Is willing to spend time beyond the usual assignments or schedule on things that interest him
_____ 7. Spends much time on special projects of his own, such as constructing, collecting, and writing
_____ 8. Tendency to figure out what is wrong with an activity and show how it can be done better
_____ 9. Tendency to give refreshing twists even to old ideas
_____10. Likes to get answers to problems, puzzles, and trick questions
_____11. Usually gets good marks
_____12. Shows less patience than most pupils with routine procedures and drills
_____13. Other pupils tend to turn to him for ideas and suggestions when something must be decided
_____14. Likes to read and find satisfaction in thinking about and discussing what has been read

Check the items which describe this pupil's performance in the subjects listed:

Arithmetic

____ No interest
____ Uses simple counting
____ Understands simple processes
____ Understands and uses complex processes

Art

____ Meaningless production
____ Representation (child interpreted)
____ Meaningful representation (simple)
____ Detailed, complex representation

Language Arts

____ No contribution
____ Contributes occasionally
____ Contributes better ideas than most
____ Dictates detailed stories individually

Music

____ Little participation
____ Participates on level of class
____ Use of original, creative ideas

Science

____ No participation
____ Works at level of class
____ Contributes better ideas than most
____ Contributes to class through independent research

Social Sciences

____ No participation
____ Works at level of class
____ Contributes better ideas than most
____ Contributes to class through independent research

Comments: _____

PRELIMINARY CONSIDERATION OF PLACEMENT
OF GIFTED PUPIL IN ACCELERATION PROGRAM

Date _____

Pupil's name _____ Grade _____ Birthdate _____

School _____ Teacher _____

TEST DATA:

Intelligence Tests

Name of Test	Date test taken	IQ

Achievement Tests

Name of test	Date test taken	Score (Grade level or percentile)		
		Reading	Arithmetic	Composite

Other Matters to Be Considered

Matter to be evaluated	Well above average	Above average	Average	Below average
Size relative to age				
Emotional stability				
Academic motivation				
Work habits				
Creativity, originality				

Matter to be evaluated	Well above average	Above average	Average	Below average
Gets along with others				
Attendance				
Health				
Energy				
Home interest in child's school progress				
Reading comprehension				
Word attack skills				
Arithmetic concepts and problem-solving ability				
Arithmetic computation				
Spelling				
Handwriting				
Speech and vocabulary				

Parent attitude toward acceleration for this child:

☐ Favorable   ☐ Unfavorable

Comments: _____

_____

_____

_____

_____

_____

_____

CASE STUDY FORMAT

Part I
BACKGROUND INFORMATION

| Confidential Information |

Date _____

Pupil's name _____ Sex: M F   Birthdate _____

Father's name _____ Mother's name _____

Address _____ Phone _____

1. Summary of School Experience

School	Location	Dates	Grades	Age

2. Parents

Type of information	Father	Mother
Educational background		
Occupation		
Special interests and aptitudes		

Description of Family Unit

Marital status, deaths, other adults in home, and the like	Date

Siblings in Home

Name	Age	Sex	Academic potential	Date

CASE STUDY FORMAT

Part II
HEALTH RECORD

Pupil's name _____

1. Data relevant to Physical Development (nutrition, description of body build, appearance, posture, handedness, and the like)

Grade	Data	Entry by	Date

2. Energy Level

Grade	Low		Moderate		High	Rated by	Date
	1	2	3	·4	5		

3. Current Problems or Handicaps (speech, hearing, vision, and the like)

Grade	Description	Entry by	Date

4. History of Illnesses or Problems

Age	Description	Entry by	Date

5. Health Tests and Measurements

Grade	Age	Height	Weight	Teeth	Hearing	Vision	Entry by	Date

6. Results of Medical Examinations

Grade	Results	Entry by	Date

CASE STUDY FORMAT

Part III
SCREENING AND NOMINATION FORM

Pupil's name _____   Teacher _____

Birthdate _____   School _____

Grade _____   Date _____

Test Data

1. Academic Achievement Tests

Name	Results	Grade	Date

2. Group Ability Tests

Name	Results	Grade	Date

3. Individual Intelligence Tests

Name	Results	Grade	Date

4. Other Tests or Examinations

Name	Results	Grade	Date

Intellectual Functioning

Disregarding test results, would you rank this pupil in the upper 5 percent of his class in academic performance? In your opinion, is this child "mentally gifted"? Is classroom performance consistent with results of standardized tests?

Upper 5 percent?		"Mentally gifted"? (by state criteria)		Performance consistent with tests?	
Yes	No	Yes	No	Yes	No

Check the column which best describes the child's intellectual functioning. These items include a range of possible characteristics or objectives. A child is not expected to be high on all of them.

Item to be evaluated		Little 1	2	Moderate 3	4	Much 5
1. Knowledge and skills (Possesses a comfortable knowledge of basic skills and factual information)						
2. Concentration (Has ability to concentrate; is not easily distracted)						
3. Enjoyment of school (Enjoys academic pursuits and assignments; likes school)						
4. Persistence (Has the ability and desire to follow through on work; concerned with completion; able to see a problem through)	In own interests					
	In assigned tasks					
5. Responsiveness (Is easily motivated; responsive to adult suggestions and questions)						
6. Intellectual curiosity (Pursues interests primarily to understand or satisfy curiosity; questions the common, ordinary, or the unusual; wants to know how and why; generates questions of his own, in connection with personal interests or group concerns)						
7. Challenge (Enjoys the challenge of difficult problems, assignments, issues, and materials)						
8. Perceptiveness (Is alert, perceptive, and observant beyond his years; aware of many stimuli)						
9. Verbal facility (Shows marked facility with language; uses many words easily and accurately)						

Item to be evaluated	Little 1	2	Moderate 3	4	Much 5
10. Fluency of ideas (Produces a large number of ideas or products, often very quickly)					
11. Flexibility (Is able to approach ideas and problems from a number of perspectives; adaptable; able to find alternative ways of solving problems)					
12. Sensitivity to problems (Perceives and is aware of problems that others may not see; is ready to question or change existing situations and suggest improvements)					
13. Originality (Often uses original methods of solving problems, is able to combine ideas and materials in a number of ways, or creates products of unusual character or quality)					
14. Imagination (Can freely respond to stimuli with the production of mental images; may "play" with ideas or produce remote, fanciful associations or insights)					
15. Reasoning (Is logical, often generalizes or applies understanding in new situations, expands concepts into broader relationships, or sees parts in relation to the whole)					
16. Scientific method (Can define problems, formulate hypotheses, test ideas, and arrive at valid conclusions)					
17. Independence in thought (Inclined to follow his own organization and ideas rather than the structuring of others)					
18. Independence in action (Able to plan and organize activities, direct action, and evaluate results)					
19. Independence in work habits (Requires a minimum of adult direction and attention; possesses research skills to facilitate independent work)					
20. Elaboration (Concerned with detail and complexity; often involved with a variety of implications and consequences)					
21. Aesthetic appreciation (Enjoys and is responsive to beauty in the arts or nature)					

22. Describe any unpredictable behavior which interferes with study; e. g., wandering away from seat without apparent purpose:

_____
_____
_____
_____
_____
_____

23. Describe any unusual preoccupations such as "daydreaming" or "flights into fantasy" which lessen the pupil's learning efficiency:

_____
_____
_____
_____
_____

24. Describe any learning characteristics which seem outstanding or would especially facilitate this child's progress in a challenging educational program:

_____
_____
_____
_____
_____

25. Describe any learning difficulties the child might have in particular areas--difficulties which could hinder progress in such a program:

_____
_____
_____
_____
_____

26. Describe any examples of the child's creative productivity:

_____
_____
_____
_____
_____
_____
_____

The following list of subjects and activities is to be checked for (1) the child's apparent interest, judged by your observations of his classroom behavior; (2) performance, judged either by grades or quality of products or actions; and (3) the grade level at which the child seems capable of functioning.

Subject	Interest					Performance					Capability
	Little 1	2	Moderate 3	4	Much 5	Low 1	2	Average 3	4	High 5	Grade level
Art											
Construction or manipulation											
Dramatic expression											
Language arts Foreign language											
Handwriting											
Oral expression											
Reading											
Spelling											
Written expression											
Mathematics											
Music											
Physical activities											
Science											
Social science											

Comment on any intellectual characteristics you have observed which are not included in the preceding items:

_____

_____

_____

_____

_____

_____

Physical Development

Item to be evaluated	Little 1	2	Moderate 3	4	Much 5
1. Physical expression (Indicates that physical activities are a comfortable, enjoyable area for self-expression)					
2. Physical ability (Coordination, timing, agility, and ability to participate satisfactorily in organized games)					
3. Energy level (Has available resources of pep and vigor for carrying on most activities)					
4. Physical appearance (Appears neat, well-groomed; has appropriate clothes for age and group)					

5. Check the spaces which best describe the child's physical build and posture as compared with the rest of the class:

Physical build: Posture:

   Small stature _____   Good _____

   Medium build _____   Average _____

   More physically developed than most _____   Poor _____

6. Describe any important aspect of the pupil's health or physical development which **might** affect participation in a challenging educational program:

Social Development

Check the column which best describes this child's social development.

Item to be evaluated		Little 1	2	Moderate 3	4	Much 5
1. Popularity (Others seem to enjoy and want to be with this child; frequently seen interacting with others in a social, friendly manner)	With same sex					
	With opposite sex					
2. Acceptance of others (Relates to others with genuine interest and concern; enjoys others; seeks them out; shows warmth)						
3. Status (Assumes public roles and leadership positions or enjoys considerable status in peer group)						
4. Social maturity (Able and willing to work with others; can "give and take"; is sensitive to the needs and feelings of others; shows consideration; observes rules of social conduct)						
5. Sense of humor (Ability to laugh at himself; gets enjoyment and pleasure from lighter moments in school day; laughs easily and comfortably)						
6. Sense of well-being (Seems self-confident, happy, and comfortable in most situations)						
7. Rapport with teacher (Two-way communication which seems to bring enjoyment to both child and teacher; relatively open and relaxed)						

8. Describe any characteristic of social behavior which you feel could interfere with this child's educational progress:

_____

_____

_____

_____

9. Comment upon the child's apparent capabilities for forming friendships and identifying with groups such as Boy Scouts, YMCA, and the like:

_____

_____

_____

_____

Emotional Development·

Check the column which best describes this child's emotional development. Please note that a high score may not be desirable on all of the items which follow.

Item to be evaluated	Little 1	2	Moderate 3	4	Much 5
1. Emotional stability (Is able to cope with normal frustrations of living; adjusts to change with minimum of difficulty)					
2. Emotional control (Expresses and displays emotions appropriately; emotional outbursts rarely occur)					
3. Openness to experience (Appears to be receptive to new tasks or experiences; seems able to take reasonable risks; can respond naturally to unusual or unexpected stimuli)					
4. Enthusiasm (Enters into most activities with eagerness and wholehearted participation; maintains enthusiasm for duration of activity)					
5. Self-acceptance (Seems to understand and accept self; able to view self in terms of both limitations and abilities)					
6. Independence (Behavior usually is dictated by his own set of values; is concerned with the freedom to express ideas and feelings)					
7. Conformity (Behavior is influenced by expectancies and desires of others) — Influence of adults					
Influence of peers					
8. Anxiety over achievement (Seems anxious about achievement; worried or concerned about schoolwork or the impression any performance makes on others)					
9. Competitiveness (Has high standards for performance, usually desiring to do as well or better than peers)					
10. Dominance (Asserts self with influence in a group situation)					
11. Aggressiveness (Acts with apparent intent to hurt others)					

12. Describe any emotional immaturity or other personality characteristic which could hinder this child's development:

_____

_____

_____

_____

_____

_____

CASE STUDY FORMAT

Part IV
PARENT INVENTORY

Pupil's name _____ Date _____

School _____ Grade _____

Birthdate _____

1. Summary of Child's School Experience

Location	Dates	Grades	Age

2. Parental Background

Type of information	Father	Mother
Educational level completed		
Occupation		
Special interests and aptitudes		

3. Description of Family Unit (marital status, step-parents, other adults in home, and the like)

_____

_____

_____

_____

4. Significant Conditions or Stresses Which Might Influence School Performance

_____

_____

_____

_____

5. Description of Early Indications of Superior Ability (e. g., speech, interests, physical development)

_____

_____

_____

_____

6. Activities in Which Family Engages

Activity	Little	Moderate	Much
Taking trips			
Attending concerts			
Visiting museums			
Visiting art galleries			
Attending plays			
Picnicking			
Going to movies			
Visiting friends			
Attending lectures			
Camping			
Fishing			
Hunting			
Boating			
Swimming			
Other sports ( )			
Other activities ( )			

7. Describe any problems your child has had (e. g., speech, emotional, hearing): _____

_____

_____

_____

8. Describe any important aspect of the pupil's health or physical development which might affect participation in a challenging educational program (serious illnesses or handicaps):

_____

_____

_____

_____

9. What special talents or skills do you feel your child has? _____

_____

_____

10. What examples can you give of your child's creative productivity? _____

_____

_____

_____

11. What are your child's vocational aspirations? _____

_____

_____

_____

12. What are your educational and vocational expectancies for your child? _____

_____

_____

_____

13. Child's reading interests (favorite books, type of book):_____

_____

_____

14. Reading materials available for child's use (e. g., encyclopedias, magazines): _____

_____

_____

_____

15. Amount of child's reading per week (estimate): _____

_____

16. What special lessons, training, or learning opportunities does your child have outside
    of school? _____

_____

_____

_____

17. Child's hobbies and special interests (e. g., collections, dancing, making models,
    swimming, singing, painting, cooking, sewing, drama):_____

_____

_____

_____

_____

18. Discuss your child's attitude toward school (e. g., activities enjoyed or disliked, enthusiasms, criticisms, relations to adults): _____

_____

_____

_____

19. What kinds of development do you feel are most important for your child? _____

_____

_____

_____

_____

20. What suggestions can you give for meeting your child's needs in school? _____

_____

_____

_____

_____

Check the following items from 1 (little) to 5 (much) as best describes your child as you see him or her.

Item to be evaluated		Little 1	2	Moderate 3	4	Much 5
21. Enjoyment of school (Enjoys academic pursuits and assignments; likes school)						
22. Persistence (Ability and desire to follow through on work; concern with completion; ability to see a problem through)	In own interests					
	In assigned tasks					
23. Intellectual curiosity (Pursues interests primarily to understand or satisfy curiosity; questions the common, ordinary, or the unusual; wants to know how and why; generates questions of his own--in connection with personal interests or group concerns)						
24. Perceptiveness (Is alert, perceptive, and observant beyond his years; aware of many stimuli)						
25. Fluency (Produces a large number of ideas or products, often very quickly)						
26. Flexibilty (Able to approach ideas and problems from a number of perspectives; adaptable; able to find alternative ways of solving problems)						
27. Sensitivity to problems (Perceives and is aware of problems and inconsistencies that others may not see; is ready to question or change existing situations and suggest improvements)						

Item to be evaluated	Little 1	2	Moderate 3	4	Much 5
28. Originality (Often uses original methods of solving problems, is able to combine ideas and materials in a number of ways, or creates products of unusual character or quality)					
29. Imagination (Can freely respond to stimuli with the production of mental images; may "play" with ideas or produce remote, fanciful associations or insights)					
30. Elaboration (Concerned with detail and complexity; often involved with a variety of implications and consequences)					
31. Aesthetic appreciation (Enjoys and is responsive to beauty in the arts or nature)					
32. Independence in thought (Inclined to follow his own organization and ideas rather than the structuring of others)					
33. Independence in action (Able to plan and organize activities, direct action, and evaluate results)					
34. Physical expression (Indicates that physical activities are a comfortable, enjoyable area for self-expression)					
35. Physical ability (Coordination, timing, agility, and ability to participate satisfactorily in organized games)					
36. Energy level (Has available resources of pep and vigor for carrying on most activities)					
37. Popularity (Others seem to enjoy and want to be with this child; frequently seen interacting with others in a social, friendly manner)					
38. Acceptance of others (Relates to others with genuine interest and concern; enjoys others; seeks them out; shows warmth)					
39. Social maturity (Able and willing to work with others; can "give and take"; is sensitive to the needs and feelings of others; shows consideration; observes rules of social conduct)					
40. Sense of humor (Ability to laugh at himself; gets enjoyment and pleasure from lighter moments in school day; laughs easily and comfortably)					
41. Happy qualities (Seems self-confident, happy, and comfortable in most situations; usually has a cheerful, pleased, or satisfied look on his face; does not seem to worry too much)					
42. Emotional stability (Is able to cope with normal frustrations of living; adjust to change with minimum of difficulty)					
43. Emotional control (Expresses and displays emotions)					

Item to be evaluated	Little 1	2	Moderate 3	4	Much 5
44. Enthusiasm (Appears enthusiastic about life; enters into most activities with eagerness and wholehearted participation)					
45. Self-acceptance (Seems to understand and accept self; able to view self in terms of both limitations and abilities)					
46. Independence (Behavior usually is dictated by his own set of values; is concerned with the freedom to express ideas and feelings)					
47. Dominance (Asserts self with influence in group situations)					
48. Aggressiveness (Frequently acts with apparent intent to hurt others)					

- -

Parental Permission

School_____

Date_____

If you are in agreement with the recommendations made for your child,

_____, and wish him/her to participate in the

_____Program, please sign below.

Signature_____

Reason for granting permission:_____

_____

_____

_____

_____

CASE STUDY FORMAT

Part V
TEACHER SUMMARY

Pupil's name _____

What SPECIAL PROVISIONS have been made to meet this pupil's INDIVIDUAL NEEDS; e. g., enrichment, individual project, acceleration, special class, counseling?

Grade	Entry by	Date

What CHANGES have you seen in this PUPIL since the start of the year; e. g., attitudinal, behavioral, appearance, functioning?

Grade	Entry by	Date

What RECOMMENDATIONS can you make for CURRICULUM PLANNING designed to meet this pupil's INDIVIDUAL NEEDS?

Grade	Entry by	Date

Anecdotal Records

A file of anecdotal record cards kept in chronological order can provide valuable data for determining behavior change over a period of time, in a variety of situations, and through the eyes of multiple observers. The following is a sample of a card for use in making such observations:

Name _____   Teacher _____

School _____   Date _____ Time _____

Recorded by _____

Activity _____

Description of behavior:

If the teacher has ample cards easily available, he can make brief notes during a class period and complete the description when he has more time. An event should be described specifically as: "He knocked Mary's books to the floor," "He picked Mary's books up for her," or "He talked to Jim during study period when instructions had been given to work independently." Observations should be made to show the child's interactions in many situations. Contrasting and comparing such data can provide valuable insights into characteristic behavior patterns. Since people tend to perceive somewhat selectively, it is wise to have anecdotal records made by as many adults in the school environment as possible.

To have such records typed periodically and filed with other case study data would be helpful in setting up goals and programs for individual children or appraising their development. Categories such as the following might be established:

- Classroom behavior
- Behavior with adults
- Behavior with special friends
- Behavior with large groups of children
- Behavior with small groups of children
- Playground behavior
- Behavior in different subject areas

- Unusual achievements
- Evidence of learning characteristics
- Accounts of learning difficulties
- Areas avoided
- Use of free time
- Evidence of special interests
- Significant comments

The simplest way to analyze anecdotal records probably would be to develop a color code for desired categories. Underlining key descriptions would facilitate interpretation.

Confidential Information

Individual Placement Project
CERTIFICATION AND SUMMARY FORM

Pupil's Name_____ School_____

Pupil's Age_____ (M)_____ (F)_____ Grades Completed: K 1 2 3 4 5 6 7 8

Parent_____ Siblings (number) M___ F___ (ages) M___ F___

Address_____ Phone_____ Date_____

CHECK OR FILL IN ALL ITEMS THAT APPLY:

Factor	Tests or Source of Information	Scores	Recommendation for Participation			Needs Further Study		Incl. in Case Study		Comments Reservations Data
			Yes	Undec	No	Yes	No	Yes	No	
Academic										
Grades										
Teacher Ratings										
Cum. Data										
Achievement Tests										
Reading										
Arithmetic										
Other ( )										
Total Scores										
Intelligence										
Group Test										
Indiv. Test										
Interests	Rank	Hi Av Lo								
Arithmetic										
Art										
Interpersonal										
Music										
Outdoor										
Physical Act.										
Science										
Soc. Studies										
Reading										
Writing										
Other ( )										
Personality										
Interview										
Tests Used										
Other ( )										
Social Maturity										
Teacher Rating										
Parent Rating										
Objective Rating										
Other ( )										
Other Factors										

Identified as gifted: Yes____ No____ Date Certified as gifted_____

We certify and approve_____ for participation in the
(pupil's name)
Individual Placement Project.

_____ _____ _____ _____
(Teacher)   (Administrator)   (Guidance Consultant)   (Parent)

Curriculum Development for Special Summer School

Perhaps one of the most important innovations of the Individual Placement Program is the utilization of the summer school. This special summer school opportunity has many unique opportunities which might be overlooked including (1) an opportunity for talented pupils to have a special class outside of the regular school year, (2) the opportunity for talented pupils to embark upon special projects including an introduction to preliminary research methodology, and (3) the precedent for subsequent summer school sessions for the talented for purposes other than acceleration.

It can be safely assumed that most of the carefully selected pupils included in the third-grade program will possess skills and learning far in advance of the third-grade curriculum. Therefore, we are not primarily concerned with an information-giving process. Rather, we should focus our teaching upon the development of reading, writing, arithmetical skills, more sophisticated study techniques and habits, and the development of such intellectual disciplines as critical thinking. Certainly, class size should not exceed twenty-five for the purposes of this special summer school program. With class size kept at a reasonable level, the teacher should have ample opportunity to individualize instruction and help to develop the specific case study of each child begun in the spring.

The six-week, third-grade summer program can be divided into three phases:

1. *Examination and assessment* (one to two weeks). Teacher systematically examines basic expected third-grade skills and learnings, especially in the areas of reading with comprehension, general language development, and arithmetical skills. Individual pupil projects are started by interpreting the pupil's interests and advising him to proceed along indicated interest lines. For example, a given pupil may have an interest in astronomy. The teacher and parents would help the child discover materials at his reading level. Perhaps simple experimentation, including observation of the heavens, would help to implement his exploratory "project." At this age level, most "projects" would be exploratory rather than experimental in nature. However, we cannot discount the possibility that a level of sophistication may be found warranting the utilization of simple experimentation, especially in the sciences.

2. *Rapid review of third-grade curriculum* (two to three weeks). Based upon the preliminary findings, the teacher must design an impromptu curriculum for this period emphasizing those skills and learnings in which the class has been demonstrated to have relative weaknesses. For example, during the examination period, it may have been

discovered that a particular class had weaknesses in spelling. For this class, more time might be spent working with an SRA Spelling Laboratory. It is suggested that this period of time be divided into subject-matter areas with appropriate scheduling and periods devoted to science, social studies, the arts, arithmetic, and reading.

3. *Expansion and evaluation* (one to two weeks). Toward the end of the summer school session sufficient time should be devoted to expanding and beginning to explore the concepts ordinarily offered in the fourth grade. During this period, the teacher would deliberately "test the limits" in order to judge the specific capabilities of each pupil. In addition to the "grading" of her pupils, this special summer school teacher should write subjective evaluations for each pupil with copies to the new fourth-grade teacher and the parents. This subjective evaluation should be based upon each child's potentiality in terms of his skills and capabilities for individual study. It is during this final period that the child should finish and report to the class or to the teacher in writing his "project" begun during the first week of the summer session.

No part of the special summer program should include "rote" learning or repetitious activities. The main purpose of the summer session is to evaluate the child's progress and prognosticate concerning his ability to understand and assimilate the content of the fourth grade. Many excellent curriculum guides exist elaborating upon and demonstrating some of the methods for the content of the elementary school. We assume that the summer school teacher is an experienced third-grade "master teacher" who is thoroughly acquainted with third- and fourth-grade curriculum.

By way of example, in the area of arithmetic, the child should be expected to have mastered such skills as multiplication to four or five places, understand how to use small fractions, and understand our systems of measurement. During the first week or two the teacher would design examinations spot-checking the ability of her children to perform these and other typical third-grade tasks. During the middle part of the summer school, she would review and elaborate upon those particular skills in which the class as a whole has demonstrated weaknesses. Special attention should be devoted to the development of a wide vocabulary, not only in arithmetic but in other areas as well. It is recommended that the books used for reading include interest area volumes in arithmetic, science, and the arts.

Since the gifted child tends to become intellectually productive, it is of special importance that we emphasize the traditional skills and framework in which he must operate. In the teaching of reading and writing, we have splendid opportunities to impart to the child the "rules of the game." For example, during the summer session, the teacher would do well to check each child's ability to perform such important functions as recognizing the syllabic division of words, alphabetizing, dividing polysyllables by rule, etc.

During the screening and examination of the pupils for this program, we should have involved the parents to supplement and implement the summer program in order to cover all of the rich experiences ordinarily contained in a typical third-grade setting. Since the pupil will have to be exposed to important basic skills and spend much time being evaluated, some areas are bound to be neglected by default. Music, art, and possibly social studies, particularly as it relates to an understanding of the community, are areas which may not be fully developed. These are areas in which parents can be invaluable assets in implementing the "total program" of the pupil. The parents should be intimately involved during the summer with moderate amounts of "homework" assigned to the child and proposed "field trip" assignments for the following year.

Toward the end of the summer school, during the time in which the teacher is subjectively as well as objectively evaluating the pupils, recommendations should be drawn up by the teacher for extended experiences to occur during the remainder of the summer and the following school year. Some of the recommended experiences might include field trips normally taken by third graders to community facilities; cultural activities including community concerts, visits to museums and other points of interest; and outdoor or "nature trips."

Some teachers may wish to accomplish this "parent assignment task" by holding a group meeting of all of the parents involved and having them develop this projected "assignment list." This would be a healthy way to involve the parents and at the same time help to compensate for the obvious handicap of the short time period of the special summer third-grade program. In addition to the general recommendations for program "enrichment," each parent should receive some specific recommendations which seem particularly important for the particular child in question.

Preferably, teachers with experience in dealing with talented children should be chosen for the summer school assignment. The teachers should definitely have third-grade experience. The teachers must be aware that they are dealing with the upper 2 to 5 percent of the pupil population and cannot, in all fairness, grade the pupils according to some arbitrary format such as the so-called normal curve. It seems obvious that most of the children should receive "B's" and "A's" or something has been radically the matter with the selection process. The teacher should objectively grade the pupils according to a strict interpretation of what is expected from a *typical* third-grader, academically. It is in the suggested subjective evaluations to be given to the fourth-grade teacher and the parents that the summer school teacher will have an opportunity to express the finely differentiated or *relative* strengths and weaknesses of a particular pupil.

As the teacher and the curriculum consultant develop the outlines for the six-week summer school, lists of supplemental materials should be made. By way of general suggestion, the following materials seem especially useful for the purposes of this program: (1) SRA Reading Laboratories (particularly laboratories IIa and IIb), (2) SRA Spelling Laboratory IIb, (3) SRA Graph and Picture Study Skills and SRA Math Discovery Board, (4) individual books and materials for pupil projects as they are requested by the pupil himself and approved by his teacher, (5) a basic set of elementary school encyclopedias such as the youth editions of *Britannica* or *Americanna*, (6) a "special interest library" including such volumes as *The Answer Book* series or the *Illustrated Encyclopedia* (both published by Grosset and Dunlap), and (7) special subject matter equipment such as magnifying glasses, laboratory equipment, specimen cages, art materials, listening equipment, and tapes or records.

The individual placement program should provide supplemental services including special counseling, tutoring, consulting, and testing services during the summer. It would be wise to assign specific staff members from the central office of the district involved to perform these functions. Some of these services might include the following:

1. *Counseling for Pupils or Parents.* During the summer session, special problems are bound to arise for some pupils. For example, the adjustment to a rapidly developing curriculum might generate pressures for the child. Special counseling services to discuss these problems with the child and his parents are important to the success of the program.

2. *Special Tutoring Services.* Any special tutoring needed by the participating pupils should probably be provided by the classroom teacher. However, if the child has special problems, particularly relating to this individual project, he might need the services of other summer school teachers serving in that district.

3. *Consulting Services.* It is to be hoped that the curriculum for this program is considered dynamic in nature. During the summer an elementary curriculum consultant should work closely with the summer school teacher in developing and refining the curriculum used.

4. *Testing.* Psychological or psychometric help should be available during the summer for any special diagnostic problems which arise. Such personnel should have time provided for teacher, parent, and pupil conferences.

Evaluation of the Individual Placement Project

In a publication entitled, *Acceleration Programs for Intellectually Gifted Students,* published by the California State Department of Education in

1968, the Individual Placement Project summer school acceleration programs are fully described and evaluated. In general, this document supplements a rich literature on the acceleration process and verifies the feasibility and usefulness of acceleration programs.

Based upon an intensive study of ten California school districts, with particular study upon the Pasadena City Schools and the Ravenswood Elementary School District in the Palo Alto area, the following generalizations were reached:

Generalization 1

Efficient screening and accurate identification are the keys to successful acceleration programs. It is imperative that high IQ not be the only factor considered in screening children for identification. Our studies of accelerates indicate that the following factors are also important when considering acceleration of a child: (1) *age*, older children in a criterion class are more likely to be successful in the advanced placement situation than are younger classmates; (2) *sex*, twice as many girls as boys met the rigid screening criteria used by the California acceleration centers, this finding is in conflict with some other acceleration studies indicating about equal prognosis for success for boys and girls; (3) *physical characteristics*, taller, more energetic children indicated a higher prognosis for success than did their physically smaller classmates; (4) *support of the family*, the home environment may be supportive to or detrimental for the accelerate depending upon the degree to which the home supports and intellectually influences the child's educational growth; (5) *personal and social relationships*, children who are more adaptive to new surroundings and are capable of forming new friendships more readily adjust to the advanced class; shy or taciturn children might be counseled away from acceleration programs, and (6) *independent attitudes*, accelerates must be capable of competitive behavior; they cannot be easily discouraged by new classmates who may be equal in ability.

Generalization 2

Before they are advanced to the higher grade placement, potential accelerates should demonstrate mastery of all important academic skills and learning necessary for adequate scholarship in the next grade level. We have found that otherwise highly intelligent and high-achieving accelerates who possess specific comparative weaknesses in such academic areas as arithmetic, spelling, or cursive writing will face much increased difficulty and frustration in the advanced grades than will accelerates who do not possess such comparative weaknesses. Even though all other factors indicate acceleration, relative low achievers in specified academic subjects should not be accelerated.

Generalization 3

Even though individually-selected accelerates possessed similar characteristics, a wide range of individual differences was observed in summer school classes. Within the high IQ group chosen for acceleration, achievement levels vary considerably. Therefore, such individual differences in achievement must be treated appropriately, in a diagnostic and remedial way if necessary, during the summer school session.

A corollary to this generalization was found: much variability in intellectual functioning and skills was found within the psychometric profiles of individual accelerates. Contrary to former research studies indicating that "positive characteristics tend to corollate positively," many of our accelerates were found to have widely divergent scores when measured on a wide spectrum of mental and achievement capabilities.

Generalization 4

Acceleration programs will succeed only if accompanied by administrative procedures designed to help the accelerated child to be accepted in the new classroom and the community at large. For example, the receiving teacher at the higher grade level must obtain special in-service training to cope with the inevitable difficulties and frustrations that accelerates face when confronted with the competition of the advanced grade level work. Also, the concept of "accelerating pupils" needs to be constantly discussed and reassessed by *all* teachers and parents in order to accommodate the changing needs of new groups of accelerates.

Generalization 5

Most accelerates require individual or group counseling at some point during the acceleration process. Although accelerates differ in terms of the intensity and/or duration of the adjustment period, most need some sort of special help in order to answer such questions as Will I make it in the next grade? A certain amount of insecurity generated by a break with the traditional system should be anticipated.

Generalization 6

Assuming appropriate and thorough selection, most accelerates achieve well in the advanced grade, are highly rated in terms of their abilities and adjustment by both parents and teachers, appear better suited to their new older social peers, and rapidly approach, and later surpass, the par academic levels of their new classmates.

EARLY ADMISSION PROGRAMS

Most of the "general benefits" enumerated above for acceleration programs are realized in so-called early entrance programs which allow precocious children to enter school at a younger age. Likewise, most of the "general problems" enumerated above are mitigated or circumvented through this procedure. Although early entrance programs occur at the beginning of formal schooling and advanced placement programs occur at the end of the public school career, they share in common the advantage of allowing the student to pursue an otherwise normally-sequenced educational program.

Worcester has summarized the research on programs of early admission as follows:

1. Early entrance has the advantage of any other form of acceleration in that it saves a year of the pupil's life. . . . The child has the regular number of years of education with all the possibilities of enrichment. . . .

2. The child will be placed from the beginning with those more nearly his mental and social equal and will, therefore, be less likely to develop habits of dawdling and laziness.

3. His education will be directed (e.g. the mentally ready child will not have to "sit and wait" to benefit from formal schooling).

4. The problem of skipping material in the curriculum is obviated.

5. Teachers are made more aware of the particular needs of bright children by recognizing them at the beginning of their school careers.

6. The school system as a whole becomes sensitive to the problem of the gifted.[11]

Formal and informal programs of early entrance to school are probably practiced in most states. More formal programs have been developed in California, Connecticut, and Pennsylvania. More informal programs probably occur every time a parent exaggerates the age of a bright child in order to get him placed into school. Also, it is well known that many parents circumvent legal entrance restrictions by placing their children in private preschool, kindergarten, and first-grade settings in order to accomplish legal matriculation of the younger children into public schools when they become of legal age. Of course, it is unfortunate that many psychologists and parents must resort to subterfuge and outright fraud in order to accomplish a worthwhile end.

Birch has conducted extensive programs of screening and early placement of children in Pennsylvania. His ambitious programs involved the examination of all criterion children in a given community between the ages of three years and nine months and four years and eight months of age. Birch has used multiple criteria recommended by earlier researches and including the following "major bench marks":

---

[11] Worcester, D.A.: *The Education of Children of Above Average Mentality.* U. of Nebr., 1956.

A. Individual intelligence quotients approximately 130 or higher . . .

B. Social maturity approximately one year or more above standard, based on the Vineland Social Maturity Scale . . .

C. Sound and well-developed personality, as judged by the examining psychologist from observation of the child's parents . . .

D. Physical characteristics not likely to limit the child. . . .[12]

Interest on the part of parents in early entrance procedures has caused a few states to enact permissive legislation to allow for the early entrance of children into kindergarten or the first grade. For example, California *Education Code* Section 5302 allows:

> A child who has been lawfully admitted to a public school kindergarten in California and who is judged by the administration of the school district . . . to be ready for first grade work may be admitted to the first grade at the discretion of the school administration of the district and with the consent of the child's parent or guardian regardless of age.

However, according to this same California *Education Code,* the child must be four years and nine months of age on or before September 1 of the current school year before he can be admitted to the kindergarten. Therefore, there is still a rigid limit upon the age at which a child may be formally admitted to school.

Summarizing the experiences gleaned from states which have practiced early entrance (e.g. California, Connecticut, and Pennsylvania), it is possible to outline a general sequence of early entrance program development as follows:

Step 1. District or Communitywide Screening

Preschool population is tested.

Criteria for screening include high intelligence, marked social maturity, and physical readiness.

Parental and community attitudes are assessed and evaluated.

Projections are made for portion of preschool population ready for advanced placement.

Step 2. Parental and Community Involvement

Early entrance program is interpreted through public media and community organizations such as PTA.

Participation and support of professional physicians, psychologists, and educators is actively sought.

---

[12] Birch, Jack W.: The Effectiveness and Feasibility of Early Entrance to School for Mentally Advanced Children. Presentation and mimeographed paper at the July 4, 1962 meeting of the National Education Association at Denver, Colorado.

Legal and regulatory barriers are eliminated through proposed legislation and regulatory changes.

Step 3. Pupil Candidate Selection, Orientation, and Placement

Approximately 5 to 10 percent of the target population is chosen for early entrance to kindergarten or the first grade.

Prior to early entrance or advanced placement, pupils, and their parents are thoroughly oriented.

Sufficient pupil and parent counseling is available to deal with problems.

Pupils are actually placed early in the kindergarten or advanced to the first grade.

Step 4. Teacher Preparation

During the summer or preschool institutes, kindergarten and first grade teachers are thoroughly briefed on the implications of the early entrance program

All teachers, throughout the grade sequence, are informed of the program.

Case study techniques are emphasized in teacher preparation and in-service training.

Step 5. Demonstration Program for Trial Period

A single district or community within a region or state practices the program for a trial period.

Demonstration district invites visitors and critics.

Prototype program is modified according to results of pupil progress and teacher criticism.

Step 6 Follow-Up and Evaluation of Prototype Program

Following a two- to three-year trial period, the prototype program is thoroughly evaluated.

Pupil progress and case study information is vital to thorough program evaluation.

Prototype program is disseminated to other districts and communities.

In summary, early entrance programs constitute a true form of "appropriate developmental placement." These programs are not true acceleration programs since the pupil conforms to a normally-paced educational sequence following placement in school at an earlier age. Interstate results have demonstrated the feasibility and practicality of this approach. Since the students follow an uncomplicated sequence of schooling and social interaction, many of the drawbacks contained in other forms of "acceleration" are alleviated. Unfortunately, states have been slow to enact permissive legislation to allow early entrance to school.

SUMMARIZING ACCELERATION PROGRAMS

What we have loosely referred to as "acceleration" in education, actually may refer to four or more distinctly different procedures applied at different developmental levels:

1. Based upon manifest developmental maturity, we may place children into school earlier. Thereafter, they follow a normally-placed educational sequence of grades.

2. Pursuant to intensive case study findings indicating high achievement and mental maturity, we may advance a child one or more grades at any point, K through grade 12; this procedure does not actually accelerate course content sequences but merely places a child at an educational level he demonstrates he has already attained on his own.

3. *True acceleration* programs expose children to speeded up subject content sequences; for example, the summer school may be utilized to offer a compressed grade level sequence of subject matter; or, several grades (e.g. grades 4, 5, and 6) may be programmed for accomplishment in two calendar years. Also, given subjects may be offered in shorter time periods.

4. After a normally-paced education in kindergarten and grades 1 to 10, a student, subject to examination, may be placed in college level courses (so-called Advanced Placement), or may actually skip completion of high school courses and go directly to college.

Some models for acceleration of the education process are outlined in Table 24. It can be observed that certain procedures emphasize speeded up processes at earlier developmental levels (e.g. Early Entrance Programs), while other procedures speed up advancement at the end of the public school sequence (e.g. Advanced Placement Programs). True acceleration programs tend to encompass the whole educational sequence, advancing the student strictly in accordance with his manifest achievement and developmental readiness.

In general, all types of acceleration programs conform to the general education process more readily than special programs for the gifted which require a differential curriculum and total separation of the student from ordinary settings and processes. In fact, all programs for the talented might be classified into two main prototypes:

Prototype 1—Differentiated Special Education

    Examples—Full-time special classes with atypical curriculums and sequences
        —Individual tutorial education

TABLE 24

MODELS FOR ACCELERATION OF THE EDUCATIONAL PROCESS

Age	3	4	5	6	7	8	9	10	11	12	13	14	15	16	17	18
"Normal Pace"	Nursery School		K	Primary Grades		Intermediate Grades			Junior High School			High School			College	
(Grades)			K	1	2	3	4	5	6	7	8	9	10	11	12	College
								[Standard Pace]								
Early Entrance	K	1	2	3		4	5	6	7	8	9	10	11	12	College	
							[Standard Paced Sequences]									
Individual Placement			K	1	2	(3)	4	5	(6)	7	8	9	10	11	12	College
					[Actual Acceleration]				[Standard Pace]							
Advanced Placement			K	1		2	3	4	5		6	7	8	9 10 (11)—College		
													(Flexible entrance to College subjects)			
						[Standard Pace]		[Actual Acceleration]								
Nongraded							Primary Experiences Basic Skills				Intermediate Academic Subject Matters			High School Advanced Subject Matters		College

(length of grade school experiences
dependent upon individual development)
[Actual Acceleration]

Prototype 2—Supplemental-Integrated Education
    *Examples—*Selected acceleration of regular subjects
         —Subject embellishment (e.g. course enrichment)

Of course, few school districts offer "pure programs." Pupils may be accelerated in the primary grades, be placed in special classes during the intermediate grades, and, as a result of this confused sequence, require special counseling for the remainder of their school career. It is important for the total school system to decide upon a coherent educational philosophy and stay with it through the whole education sequence. Alternate objectives should be available to pupils and their parents, since family philosophies vary widely as to the relative importance of early childhood play experiences versus scholastic achievement in youth. It is significant to note that the only unanimity of opinion concerning acceleration to be found in the research, occurs for early adolescence (i.e. most researchers agree we should *not* accelerate during this period).

Assuming a school district prefers an acceleration program, the best specific program would offer individual pupil options for acceleration at any grade level coupled with arrangements for ungraded subject matter contents at all grade levels. The main problem, inherent in any acceleration program, is that of correlating actual advanced grade level placement with the realities of overall developmental readiness. It is probable that *any*

TABLE 25

BENEFITS AND POTENTIAL PROBLEMS FOR ACCELERATION OF STUDENTS AT DIFFERENT PERIODS OF THEIR EDUCATION

Period of Acceleration	*Justificational Benefits*	*Potential Problems*
Preschool (Education by parents)	Gifted verbalize early Can learn rules for independence Reading is self- rewarding, ego enhancing Verifies parental hunches of giftedness	Check all mental abilities to establish par developments Do not drive child toward premature experiences Other (play) activities should also be provided Stimulate full range of creative activities
Early Entrance (K and Grades 1 and 2)	No problem of skipping curriculum units Gifted ready for advanced work Avoid boredom, provide initial motivation Begin education with (older) peer group Introduce scholarly habits from beginning	Incomplete case study or prognosis should not be used as basis for early entrance Failure to enlist child's consent may result in lack of effort Child should perceive himself a part of older peer group Must provide balanced attitudes toward work and play
Primary Grades (Grades 1-3)	Rapid learning rate during this period Comparative flexibility of young children Lack of fixed friendship patterns Eagerness, unrestrained motivation	Pedantry must be avoided Acquiescence to adult decisions may be regretted later Watch for asocial tendencies Must build in capability for judgment in time management
Intermediate Grades (Grades 4-6)	Avoid subject content repetition Advanced cognitive skills (e.g. abstract reasoning) Creates readiness for high school subjects Need for intellectual stimulation through discourse	Rote learning proficiency sometimes confused with comprehension Lack of valid measurements for higher level mental abilities Do not mistake aggressiveness for inquiry
Junior High (Grades 7-9)	(In general, least advantagious period for acceleration due to personal adjustment problems presented by puberty); yet, General need for advanced work may be apparent	(*General problems:* Rigidity and insecurity related to adolescent period; overemphasis of peer group identifications; transitory loss of intellectual interests.)
High School (Grades 10-12)	Resurgence of intellectual ambitions Formation of career goals Capability to perform research, advanced work Lessened dependence on peer group	Idealism may obscure practicality, all professional preparations require painstakingly detailed contents
College (Advanced Placement)	Need for productive outlets Readiness for career skills Identification with goals of higher learning	Very young professions May not be accepted by practitioners

student with an IQ over 150 could be sequenced through advanced subject matters well above his chronological grade placement; it is doubtful that most of these same students could adjust to the social levels of sophistication demanded by normal students three or four years older than themselves. The social-emotional aspects of overall adjustment cannot be ignored. Ostracism could precipitate severe personality problems which would far outweigh any academic benefits of acceleration. The fact remains that a significant minority of academically gifted students possess an overall personality configuration of social, emotional, physical, and intellectual precocity. Such students thrive on advanced placements.

Proper developmental placement of students can be accomplished only if up-to-date case study records are maintained throughout the student's schooling. While it is possible to generalize about certain optional periods for accelerating children (e.g. primary grades or high school), it must be remembered that individual children may develop erratically. For example, even though readiness for acceleration is evidenced by most potential accelerates before they reach the third grade, nevertheless, a number of so-called late bloomers do not perform well until they reach high school or college. Only by keeping adequate developmental records can the individual maturity rates of children be kept track of.

Recognizing the inherent dangers in overgeneralizing, it is still possible to identify "special benefits and potential problems" for acceleration programs during given educational periods. Such "benefits and problems" are summarized in Table 25. It may be observed that acceleration procedures appear to be more feasible and safer, both early and late in the educational sequence; of course, individual differences may alter this rule. Whenever acceleration programs are discussed, there is the tendency to view the educational process too narrowly in academic terms. If "education" consisted of academic components exclusively, the educational process involved psychosocial, psychomotor, and affective components as well. During the primary grades, psychomotor lags may obviate acceleration; for example, lack of small muscular precision may preclude cursive writing. In higher grades, the psychosocial component may present formidable problems in the form of exaggerated peer group identities.

Before considering the specific programs of *early* and *advanced* placement in more detail, it might be advisable to review the *general* benefits and problems inherent in *any* form of acceleration.

General Benefits of Any Acceleration Program

1. The whole school system becomes involved in the program, since accelerates are distributed among ordinary classroom settings; hence, the whole system becomes more aware and, hopefully, more sensitive to the special needs of gifted students.

2. Accelerates, if chosen appropriately, are more nearly matched in personality and cognitive characteristics with older children; hence, overall social adjustment, productivity, and cooperative behavior should be enhanced by their advanced placement.

3. With only one life to live, timesaving should still be considered a virtue. Given the vast scope of intellectual activities available to the gifted mind, it seems pointless to condemn the person to mundane activities.

4. Likewise, effective and efficient productivity should remain a cherished virtue. History shows that a majority of worthwhile productivity has occurred during the youth and early adulthood of the producer; in the fields of invention, scientific investigation, and poetry writing this appears to be especially true. By deliberately retarding the pace of development of our gifted are we inadvertently shutting off intellectual productivity?

5. Many of the resources, being unwisely devoted to providing repetitious educational activities for the gifted, could be diverted to more meaningful use for work with slow learners.

6. In view of the national need for high level professionals (e.g. Ph.D.'s), general programs of acceleration would produce more doctoral students especially among women. Currently, many intelligent women forsake higher education for marriage. Due to economic pressures, many young men settle for master's degrees and a moderate paying job.

General Problems of Any Acceleration Program

1. During prior periods, educators have accelerated students on the basis of insufficient case study; hence, many parents have formed negatige attitudes with reference to acceleration based on their personal experiences. No acceleration should occur in the absence of a complete case study which investigates all aspects of the candidate's personal and educational development.

2. Adults may seek vicarious satisfactions from the success of their children. Well-meaning parents may pressure children to compete for higher grade placements, without taking into account the child's desires or his liabilities. Adult pressure should be completely removed as a possible basis for acceleration.

3. Advanced grade level placement should be based upon the observation that a student has already attained developmental and educational levels similar to students older than himself. Unfortunately, legal and social barriers exist which do not admit to developmental differences (e.g. drivers' licenses, marriage laws, voting rights). The realities of legal and social inhibitions should be considered, before any child is accelerated, and might preclude advancement of more than three grade levels.

4. Even though a student sanctions his own acceleration, he still may harbor self-doubts which could jeopardize his future adjustment. In part, two important mores (or social expectations) are violated when a student is accelerated: (1) the individual fails to *conform* to group practices, and (2) he fails to "do his full job" in everyday terms of actual work output. Both of these "failures" force a confrontation of the accelerate with his acquired value system. Some accelerates, otherwise fully adequate to the advanced placement, show signs of "guilt" over "getting something for nothing." All acceleration-type programs should build in counseling opportunities and/or sequenced units of work to assure the accelerate "full measure" of educational experiences.

5. By implication, the typical accelerate will be oriented toward high scholarship, intense study habits, and a competitive outlook. These qualities may lose their survival value in the adult world of "job-love-and play." Hence, accelerates may need "life adjustment counseling" more urgently than do normal students. We must be assured that high scholarship does not degenerate to exclusiveness; intense study habits to seclusiveness or narrow living habits; competitiveness and compulsive perfectionism.

Chapter 8

INTEGRATED GUIDANCE AND INSTRUCTIONAL PROGRAMS

A RTICULATION of guidance and instructional programs has been stated as a fundamental goal of education. Yet, as programs of guidance and curriculum grow, they tend to diverge and produce separate roles within school districts. While teachers have adopted many guidance practices (e.g. group testing, orientation courses, or career guidance services), professional guidance workers seldom enter into the teacher-pupil interaction.

We will discuss such topics as the diverging roles of professional guidance and instructional staffs; the need for leadership training programs; some practical ways in which these separate professional groups can come together in common tasks of instruction; the special guidance needs of gifted students; and some suggested programs for cooperative guidance and instructional programs.

Leadership programs, for students with psychosocial giftedness, should represent a logical starting point for guidance-instructional programs. Currently, leadership qualities emerge in our society, but not by design. Guidance services are provided after problems become manifest; little is done to participate actively in the educational process for talent and leadership development. In theory, on the other hand, we have ample reason to believe that our potential leadership in all fields can be universally exposed to our democratic heritage of diverse values, while being trained to accept and act upon the responsibilities of manhood.

To understand the dynamics of leadership, one must apply the most complex models of personality theory. Guidance personnel should be the most logical agents for such studies. Moreover, the counselor can advise the young leader concerning models with which he my obtain better understanding of hismelf and others. Counselors can be of immeasurable service to teachers by supplying program feedback in the form of student reactions and objective evaluation. Teachers and counselors interacting in a planned sequential process of education can be mutually reinforcing and contribute specialized functions of which the other may not be capable.

By entering into the learning process directly, guidance workers can better fulfill their roles. Gaining insights, making comparisons, resolving conflicts, relating affect to symbols, introjecting subject content into one's system of personal values—all are part of the educational process. Such functions are known to occur more effectively in small-group interactions with trained guidance help. Guidance services would be upgraded to the level of active, direct influences as opposed to their curent status of indirect, diagnostic services which are laregly "afterthoughts."

GUIDANCE AND INSTRUCTION AMALGAMATED

Guidance is ordinarily thought of as the process which "helps the individual develop satisfactorily in terms of personal potentialities, environmental opportunities, social needs, and moral values. . . ."[1] It is commonly accepted that this guidance process is administered by professional agents, who "assist the individual, through counsel, to make wise choices, adjustments and interpretations in connection with critical situations in his life in such a way as to insure continued growth in ability for self-direction."[2]

In the orthodox view of guidance services, there is a tendency to think of such services as distinct from instructional programs and processes. Thus, guidance services and professional guidance workers have become stereotyped as specialists who collectively apply scientific, psychological procedures to accomplish the solution of personal, education, or moral problems. The distinction between psychologists and guidance workers becomes blurred when one follows these observations through to their logical conclusions.

Obviously, a worker dealing with standardized testing and delving into the personal problems of students requires considerable training and is, in fact, a "specialist." However, guidance functions must be articulated with teaching in order to adjust the student with academic problems back into a classroom setting. Moreover, guidance specialists are the best prepared persons to interpret learning theory and apply diagnostic findings to the reorganization of educational programs.

As the "general education" movement became widespread in American education, the idea of a philosophical wedding between guidance services and instructional functions became apparent.[3] In this movement, it has been accepted that the teacher can play a guidance role not only in the counseling process but in diagnosing student's learning needs and adjusting his program accordingly. Instructional and guidance services can be amalgamated toward the single goal of accommodating each students' educational development. Thorough guidance services can provide immediate feedback to classroom teachers. Teachers can modify curriculum, while utilizing guidance services for scientifically planned evaluation studies.

Jones has voiced the opinion that guidance and education are indistinguishable in theory: ". . . separation is impossible; it violates the essential

---

[1] Mathewson, Robert H.: *Guidance Policy and Practice*. New York, Harper, 1949, p. 118.

[2] Jones, Arthur: *Principles of Guidance*. New York, McGraw, 1945. Frontispiece.

[3] Present and former members of the faculty: *The Idea and Practice of General Education*. Chicago, U. of Chicago, 1950, Chapter 12.

nature of education and guidance. . . . Teaching conceived as assisting a learner to choose ends or methods is guidance."[4] Hollinshead has noted that if the teacher possessed special training, he might be the best person to render certain guidance services: ". . . teachers are expected to help develop young people by . . . giving them personal, social, academic, and vocational guidance. . . . If the teacher has some background of technical knowledge in guidance . . . he may be the best person to give academic counseling."[5]

Thus, we find that professional guidance workers have already considered the problem of merging the functions of the guidance worker with those of the teacher. Still, they have persisted in clearly demarcating counseling versus teaching roles. Guidance experts have failed to exploit their most useful capability, that of facilitating the learning process by applying the laws of learning and remedial activities as may be appropriate to expedite scholarship. While they have suggested that the teacher become involved in guidance processes, they have insisted that the teacher must become a professional counselor. For example, Brown has elaborated upon the teacher's usefulness in the guidance process, while still distinguishing between the specialties of guidance and teaching.[6] Brown made reference to the teacher's potential usefulness as an objective observer and recorded in the overall process of collecting information for the guidance agency. In other words, he views the teacher as an agent for the guidance agency instead of the other way around.

In summarizing the traditional view of guidance services, the following may be stated:

1. Guidance and teaching have been viewed as mutually distinctive and specialized professional entities.

2. The tendency has been to view the teacher as an agent for the guidance services to facilitate the feedback of information concerning personal, vocational, and educational problems of students. The counselor has remained aloof from classroom observation. Counselors have not participated in the development of curriculum.

3. Counseling services have come to resemble clinical psychological services. Thus, counseling services focus upon pathological problems. "Diagnosis and therapy" have become bywords. Students are referred to counseling services only when they require remediation, therapy, or readjustment of some sort.

4. The separate professional preparations of counselors and teachers has widened this gap. For example, most states have stringent requirements for obtaining counseling, psychological, or other guidance creden-

[4] Jones, Arthur: *Principles of Guidance.* New York, McGraw, 1945, p. 68.
[5] Hollinshead, Byron: *Who Should Go to College.* New York, Columbia, 1952, p. 111.
[6] Brown, Robert: The teacher as a guidance worker. *Journal of Education,* 139:3-12, April 1957.

tials. Thus, the image of the guidance worker as a "specialist" has been intensified.

5. The preparation of guidance counselors rarely includes course work in learning theory, applications of strategies of learning to classroom operation or curriculum development techniques. As a result, counselors do not participate actively in curriculum building.

6. It is commendable that the more recent trends in guidance services have stressed the role of the teacher as an objective observer and contributor of information. However, the objective observation of students by counselors and psychologists has not been reciprocated to any marked extent.

At the elementary school level, guidance services are being reevaluated, and redesigned. Some have advocated a program of guidance for the young child which utilizes the classroom teacher as one who supports the child in terms of his emotional health as well as learning.[7] Also, educators have recognized the necessity for interdisciplinary cooperative services between guidance personnel and curriculum developers.[8]

With an emphasis upon child study, elementary guidance has been defined as "a planned program involving those materials and procedures that deal specifically with the social and emotional welfare."[9] Elaborating upon this definition, Martinson and Smallenburg noted the following:

1. All functions of a guidance centered school are pointed toward the best welfare of the child.

2. Guidance activities are carried on through the classroom teacher, or in full cooperation with her.

3. Resource persons, if any are available, apply their special training toward better understanding of children and their needs.

4. Persons directly concerned with the child plan together to make use of all possible knowledge and special skills.[10]

At the elementary level, then, responsibility for conducting guidance services has been delegated to other professional personnel and especially teachers.

The concept of organizing "guidance committees" within schools has been proposed by the Los Angeles County Superintendent of Schools Office. Such committees function to observe and deal with student problems such as ". . . improving acceptance for a child who seemed to have no friends . . . studying a highly intelligent child who is working much below his

---

[7] Heffernan, Helen: *Guiding the Young Child.* Boston, Heath, 1959.

[8] Kelly, Janet: *Guidance and Curriculum.* Englewood Cliffs, Prentice-Hall, 1955.

[9] Martinson, Ruth A., and Smallenburg, Harry: *Guidance in Elementary Schools.* Englewood Cliffs, Prentice-Hall, 1963.

[10] *Ibid,* pp. 2-3.

ability . . . studying an extremely hyper-active youngster . . . selecting the best grade placement for several children. . . ."[11]

In addition to studying individual children, guidance committees perform such functions as "planning a district testing program . . . evaluating effectiveness of certain curricula experiences . . . studying the out-of-school influences upon children's achievements . . . considering the uses of cumulative records . . . formulating placement and promotion policies . . . revising methods of reporting children's growth . . . and . . . developing with teachers and children a written code for discipline in the school."[12]

Cooperative guidance and instructional programs can be inaugurated in the public schools; but first the professional staffs must reconsider their traditional roles and attempt to rework their activities into amalgamated functions. Partly, this change involves redefinition of tasks. Modern educational tasks call upon teachers and guidance workers to share common training and preparation for professional service. Sharing of educational tasks enable guidance-instructional staffs to design hybrid programs which incorporate the best ideas of guidance and teaching. For example, programs such as "guidance through literature" expose children to specific kinds of literature designed to stimulate appropriate kinds of value development. As a by-product, the student is affirmed opportunity to find bibliographical sources to answer his own problems.[13]

This amalgamation of guidance and instructional services should occur at elementary, secondary, and college levels. However, at the secondary level, we tend to find more orthodox viewpoints concerning the role of the counselor versus the role of the teacher. The traditional development of guidance services has paralleled freudian psychology. As Freud focused upon pathology in the problems of man, so guidance workers have focused upon the manifest problems of youth.

Instead, we should advocate "preventive educational guidance." We should adopt an educational psychology which emphasizes prophylactic guidance and promote instructional services which spend as much time dealing with the achieving learner as they do with the remedial learner. Of course, every child, healthy or abnormal, bright or dull, with or without special social or emotional problems, could benefit from coordinated guidance and instructional services.

In order to implement the establishment of cooperative guidance and

---

[11] Los Angeles County Superintendent of Schools Office. *Guiding Today's Children* (A Guidance Book for Teachers and Administrators of Elementary Schools). Los Angeles, California Test Bureau and the Los Angeles County Superintendent of Schools Office, May 1959, p. 205.

[12] *Ibid*, p. 206.

[13] Rogers, Wilma S.: *The Annotated Bibliography for Guidance Through Literature.* Instructional Materials Center, Alpine, Nevada, Placer, and Sierra Counties, California, January, 1961.

instructional programs, the following interdisciplinary professional problems need to be studied by school districts:

1. Administrators need to redefine the roles of teachers, counselors, and psychologists. We should envision professional roles as overlapping, rather than being exclusive and distinctive, one from another. For example, there are obvious overlaps in the kinds of roles teachers and counselors play or between the kinds of roles counselors and psychologists play.

2. What are the theoretical differences, among such educational activities as seminars, individual tutoring, individual counseling, group counseling, or psychotherapy?

3. Should taboos be superimposed upon relationships among counselors, teachers, and students? Modern mental hospital staffs have come to realize that patients can sometimes more easily discuss their deep problems with nurses; is it not possible that students will seek out persons with whom they are emotionally comfortable rather than going to persons who are professionally competent?

4. In-service training programs for interdisciplinary personnel, sharing common frames of reference, can lead to more efficient observation of the behavior of children. Who will develop and share child study and objective observation techniques? Someone must clarify the differences among child studies by teachers and psychological workups.

5. Design testing programs which are useful for individual diagnosis of student progress as well as providing feedback for the evaluation of academic programs; design systematic and periodic evaluation programs for the feedback of learning outcomes to teachers, curriculum developers, and students.

6. School personnel need to establish new experimental roles. It may be that peers are more appropriate in the role of evaluators; it might be useful for teachers to visit one another's classrooms and compare observations. Or, professional psychologists may be used. In this fashion, "evaluation" would cease to be equated with a teacher's job security. Evaluation would come to be understood as a necessary adjunct to teaching.

7. New hierarchies of roles might be introduced. For example, the station of the "teacher leader or master teacher," supervising a team of teachers, may evolve.

8. The ideal of individually-programmed instruction for every child may be within our reach. Possibilities for computerized student programming and storage of knowledge in data banks exist now. It is possible to design an individual program for each student according to his unique individual needs at the present time.

At any level, students require large group, small group, and individual learning and counseling activities. Although the problems differ for children as compared with youth, appropriate programs can be based upon accurate development observations. Good practice indicates that emotional problems, for instance, can be best diagnosed and remediated at an earlier developmental level. Counseling-instructional programs wed developmental observations with appropriate pedagogical theory and practice. As we re-design amalgamated roles for teachers and guidance workers, we might consider the following guiding principles:

Modern guidance service ought to

1. provide the traditional individual and group counseling services for eductional, vocational, moral, social, and emotional counseling;

2. establish and provide individual and group counseling opportunities at all grade levels;

3. periodically measure student achievement and evaluate the effectiveness of curriculum accordingly;

4. institute and operate special seminars for both students and teachers, in combined groups or separately (Such seminars should be addressed to the development of values in man. Discussion should center upon the ways new knowledge changes one's philosophy of life, attitudes, and emotional well-being.);

5. with teacher cooperation, help to design innovative teaching techniques based on learning theory and test these methods according to valid research designs;

6. provide periodic visits to all classrooms for the purposes of observing teacher and student behavior;

7. offer specific recommendations for specialized programs such as the acceleration of advanced students;

8. cause schools to adopt uniform case study procedures, beginning in the kindergarten, which incorporate developmental criteria for the study of children and youth;

9. establish committees for the evaluation of terminology used, to assure that teachers at all levels can communicate one with another;

10. make frequent surveys and studies of the community and cultural milieu; offer hypotheses to explain unusual group behavior; invite the participation of other professional disciplines such as anthropology, sociology, and psychiatry for the understanding of the total environment of the teacher and the student;

11. participate in the development of criteria for the selection of all professional staff; help appraise mental health and capability; cause administrators to emphasize prevention rather than remediation;

12. build, modify, and criticize curriculum on the basis of student assessment, teacher observation, and the application of modern schemas;

13. under certain controlled conditions, such as cooperation with a university clinic, offer specialized outlets for both staff and students who require special help such as psychotherapy; and

14. design, reevaluate, and maintain strict codes of ethics with safeguards for confidentiality of information; help to institute professional penalties for teachers or guidance workers who are unethical in their behavior.

New instructional roles and tasks for the teacher include

1. taking responsibility for understanding the process of learning and the developmental problems of children at various grade levels; acquiring sufficient subject-matter preparation to meet the diverse needs of the gifted;

2. learning to objectively observe one's own teaching act, the behavior of students, and the teaching act as performed by other teachers; sharing such observations with other professionals in objective, nonhostile ways;

3. learning to accurately report, in terms of anecdotal notes, the behavior of students; communicating those observations which will be most important at the next grade level; practicing succinct, behaviorally-oriented case study recording;

4. envisioning grade spans rather than particular grades to enhance curriculum articulation;

5. seeking and utilizing feedback from standardized tests and reports from other professionals; redesigning daily lesson plans to match overall curriculum goals;

6. continually looking for ways in which given subject matter can be related to other disciplines and designing interdisciplinary seminars, classes, and contents;

7. practicing team approaches to teaching; and

8. viewing the teaching-learning system as a two-way process; teachers can learn from students; both may learn from a third source.

GUIDANCE SERVICES FOR THE GIFTED

Writers, addressing themselves to the subject of guidance services for the gifted student, have stressed the same kinds of guidance services as required by ordinary students, such as vocational or personal counseling.[14] In addition, they have stressed the particular needs of academically tal-

---

[14] See for example, Drews, Elizabeth M. (Ed.): *Guidance for the Academically Talented Student.* Washington, D.C., National Education Association, joint publication with the American Personnel and Guidance Association, 1961.

ented students, such as "personal needs, including the problem of acceptance encompassing self-understanding and self-acceptance. . . . Educational
needs such as developing independent study habits, acquiring efficient
learning techniques, orienting oneself to the methods of research and
problem solving, developing one's special talents and encouraging creative
thinking, emergence of human concerns, such as humanitarianism and the
development of adequate communications skills. . . ."[15]

Gowan has described the work of the counselor with the gifted child as
involving: "helping to identify gifted individuals. . . . Providing the educational experience the gifted need. . . . Helping with the vocational guidance
of the gifted. . . . Help in various problem areas, such as realizing their intellectual potentialities. . . . The counselor can, with the cooperation of
the school administration, help teachers to a better understanding of the
gifted. . . . Help create a favorable environment for the gifted child. . . .
Assist the teachers with vocational guidance units. . . ."[16]

Special problems may be encountered by gifted children simply because
they have more comprehension and sensitivity to current problems. It is
possible for gifted children to be misdiagnosed as "psychological problems"
when they relate to parents, teachers, or counselors that they are strug-
gling with such questions as Does God exist? Gifted children will begin
to consider such searching problems earlier than will normal children.
Moreover, gifted children with creative propensities will be more apt to
seek out problems, dilemmas, ambiguous situations, and controversial issues. Counselors may be tempted to make superficial diagnoses and blame
"personal problems" for the ideas an individual talks about. However, such
"problems" may not be construed by the children as "personal problems"
at all. It is important to ascertain the extent to which the child has been
able to differentiate between personal, emotional involvement, and intellectual consideration of a problem or conflict. We should expect gifted
individuals to think deeply about their own philosophies and styles of
living. Therefore, it is important that individual and group counseling
services be made available to deal with "problems" in the more scientific
definition for the word (e.g. "problem: . . . questions proposed for solution." From Webster).

We will assume that the ordinary guidance services such as imparting
information concerning colleges and scholarships, vocational counseling,
academic counseling, administering aptitude, interest or other tests, or
counseling for self-understanding are available to the gifted child. In addition to these regular guidance services, we should establish guidance
services specifically required by gifted child programs such as:

---

[15] *Ibid,* pp. 46-50.

[16] Gowan, John Curtis, and Demos, G.D.: *The Education and Guidance of the Ablest.*
Springfield, Thomas, 1964, pp. 252-254.

1. identification services for the differential diagnosis of various kinds of talented students along with the availability of appropriate individual and group tests, adequate case study procedures, and full-scale follow-up studies for students;

2. surveys and other studies conducted periodically to indicate the success or failure of given kinds of talented students in advanced programs, and later in vocational and professional work;

3. special testing services to measure the outcomes of the curriculum as well as the design of special tests and evaluate instruments; along with this responsibility would be the education of teachers to such concepts as "validity, reliability, norms or standardization of devices";

4. planned sequences of individual instruction for each student utilizing program materials, special seminars, or programmed learning devices;

5. individual counseling for intellectual, philosophical, religious, and other problem areas unique to the intellectually gifted student;

6. group counseling opportunities to discuss such questions as self-actualization, maturity, or the responsibilities of leadership;

7. in-service education for teachers in such areas as learning theory, models of intellect, curriculum construction, or theories of personality;

8. parental and community involvement in the overall development and exploitation of talent in the community;

9. daily reinforcement of learning theory by classroom visitations and subsequent interviews with teachers to demonstrate ways in which learning theory can be applied to the development of daily lesson plans, curriculum, and the understanding of student behavior;

10. conducting seminars and classes for teachers in such topical areas as the psychology of adjustment, marriage and family living, vocational and professional choice, or guidance and education of the gifted; and

11. conducting basic and applied research for an understanding of special subgroups among the talented and for the validation of educational tests and programs developed within the school.

Some of the learning problems of gifted students may be different in kind that the problems encountered by normal students. Gifted students may be plagued with overzealous parents and teachers who overinterpret the gifted child's endurance without taking into consideration such variables as the child's personal goals. As a consequence, many of the learning problems of the gifted child stem not from any lack of ability but from misapplied or misunderstood motivation. Since poor study habits or personal problems may occur with gifted students as with any other student, it is necessary to provide adequate counseling services.

Table 26 couples the unique characteristics of gifted students with the concomitant problems which may arise as a result of these very character-

TABLE 26

CHARACTERISTICS OF THE GIFTED AND CONCOMITANT PROBLEMS

Characteristic of Gifted	Possible Concomitant Problems
Critically observes, analyzes; skepticism	Teachers feel threatened; peers censure, try to silence discussion; argumentative
Emphatic response to people; leadership capabilities	Rejection causes intense reaction (e.g. depression or hostility); may seek to dominate rather than understand others
Independent perception of self and world	Egotism; alinenation; odd interpretations of reality
Individuality; search for freedom	Isolation; loneliness; combativeness; lack of socially acceptable identities
Intellectual interests; intellectuality	Snobbishness; limited recreational outlets; boring to others; intolerance for lesser capabilities
Intense application of energies; persistence	Obsession with problem tasks; compulsivity; obstinacy; overwork toward physical exhaustion
Large vocabulary; verbal facility; high retention	Inappropriate level of communication; dominates class discussion; unnecessary elaboration
Originality	Perceived as "off the subject" by others; impracticality; frequent breaks with tradition; radicalism
Scholarliness	Anti-intellectual reaction by peers; stuffiness; pedantry
Theoretical-aesthetic mixture of interests	Simulated masculinity in girls, effeminacy in boys; overemphasis of importance of science; escape into art forms
Thinks with logical systems; objective, rational problem-solving	Disregard for intuitive, retrospective, or subjective solutions; rejection of belief, revelation as methods
Unusual, esoteric subjects appealing	Eccentricity; gullibility; mysticism; attraction to untryed avant-garde causes

istics. This information should be of value to teachers and counselors wanting to anticipate the possible emotional, social, and motivational problems likely to occur among groups of gifted students in the classroom.

Table 27 summarizes the special kinds of major problems likely to be encountered by various groups of talented students. It is apparent that the typical kinds of problems encountered by a student possessing high mechanical aptitude will be different from the problems of a dramatic performer. As counselors design counseling strategies for talented students, implementation for a wide variety of problem contingencies must be accounted for.

TABLE 27

SOME MAJOR PROBLEMS ENCOUNTERED BY VARIOUS TALENTED STUDENTS

Type of Talent	Elementary							High School					
	K	1	2	3	4	5	6	7	8	9	10	11	12
Academic Verbal Mathematical Scientific	(Getting into school early)—Getting properly placed with one's intellectual peers . . . repetitive work with accompanying frustration . . . (Getting advanced placement) Problems of precocity: wanting you to act like a child, yet expecting endurance and application from you								Lacking intellectual stimulation Conforming to adolescent peers who may deride "eggheads"				
Creative Inventive Innovative Revolutionary					Autonomous behavior may be misdiagnosed as "odd," confused with rebellion Few outlets for creative energy				Creativity likely to be equated with nonconformity, not tolerated				
Kinesthetic Athletic Dance				Poor physical education programs (if any) Equation of physical education with "play games"		No emphasis on physical fitness, exercise, body development		Equation of physical prowess with brutishness, raw competition Little support for nonsport athletic programs Equation of dance with effeminacy Segregation of physical education with other disciplines					
Psychosocial Political Social Profession				No organized expression outlets for real leaders except outside of school (gangs) Domineering teachers, children are supposed to be passive, obedient, compliant (indig. leaders opposite)					Few opportunities for real responsibility, leadership (Educators over appraisal seniority, age/disallow young leadership Student governments important (when conflict with administration they are dissolved (general autocratic attitude in schools				
Performing Art Music Drama					Embarrassment being perceived as "show-off" by others Possible exploitation by adults				Finding appropriate outlets for talent in high school Folklore pegs artists as "characters, avant-garde, racy," causing some compulsion to play the part				
Mechanical Technical Industrial				Few, if any, mechanical outlets, pursuits Rigid association with male activities					Snobbish attitudes concerning trades, crafts (socioeconomic association with lower classes). Lack genuine recognition and reward				
Manipulative Craftsmanship				General disuse and degeneration of handicrafts Isolation from folklore, craftsman					Lack of economic demand for craftsmanship Equation of craftsmanship with leisure time activity Association with retarded, left-over activity which everyone could do if had to (they couldn't)				

Total leadership preparation should include individual counseling services which differ both in the kinds of counseling rendered and in the frequency of that counseling. Academically or creatively-talented students may encounter philosophical or intellectual problems which other children may not perceive at a given age. They grapple with problems which much older students evade. Gifted students require additional counseling services which include frequent, knowledgeable, and extensive discussions of such matters as developing one's philosophy of life, integrating one's personal values into the folkways superimposed by society, or discussing ways in which specialized or unique talents can be adapted to the realities and demands of the outside world.

Our traditional notions of "academic and vocational counseling" may be limited in their application to the gifted. The counselor for the talented may need to be different from regular counselors as teachers for the gifted are different in kind from the teachers of normal children. Counselors for the talented will need to be well prepared in such areas as psychology of giftedness or advanced theories of learning and thinking processes. Currently, we tend to reserve counseling services for those who have already developed personal, academic, emotional, or other serious problems. Counseling services for the gifted are based upon the assumption that talented individuals will undergo a process of "self-actualization."

The following list of problems summarizes some of the ways in which seemingly typical developmental problems affect those with superior endowment.

Learning Problems, Study Habits

Particularly preschool and primary gifted children far surpass peers in actual academic skills. As a consequence, they may receive mixed signals from parents and teachers alternately advising them to study and learn (from parents) and to "slow down and enjoy their childhood" (from teachers). This problem may lead to more serious difficulties, such as confused or insecure motivational patterns.

Teachers may assign inappropriate or unsuitable tasks to gifted children. For example, the child may be forced to review learning skills in the primary grades when his reading rate is already many grade levels beyond his chronological peers. Hence, the child becomes bored, unchallenged, and finally frustrated with tasks which are of no practical importance to him.

The tendency for gifted children to work rapidly and to shift easily from one subject to another may be falsely diagnosed as poor application or short attention span by unobservant parents and teachers. Teachers need to evaluate the output of gifted children over a longer time period. Actual long-term outcomes and tangible results rather than daily classroom procedures should be emphasized.

At the secondary school level, the gifted student may react unfavorably to the philosophical discontinuity between elementary and secondary school philosophies of education. After being prompted to slow down and keep step with his peers during the elementary period, he may suddenly be referred to as an "underachiever" in high school. Teachers may falsely diagnose the problem as one of "poor study habits." The problem, of course, is actually motivational and directly attributable to the contradictory environments he has been exposed to during his development.

Emotional or "Psychological" Problems

Gifted children are more apt to receive confused, disconnected, contradictory, or incorrect advice than are normal students. This is due to the tendency of adults to underestimate their comprehension. They may be provided with childish explanations for profound philosophical questions, leading to disbelief in later life.

Gifted students may be placed in the position of a "double-bind" by receiving discrepant emotional and/or intellectual signals from adults. A mother may verbalize her desires for scholarly behavior from her child while at the same time her emotional reactions convey clearly that she desires a normal child with all that the term infers. Acquiescence to her wishes for expected kinds of childhood dependencies may be impossible by virtue of the child's superiority.

Adults sometimes convey disparate or contradictory demands for the student. As a consequence, the gifted child may become confused as to what kind of role the society wants him to play with resultant emotional disturbance. For example, adults may demand that the child be "intellectually independent and free." Subsequent "free" behavior may be violently condemned as "degenerate or radical" (e.g. current college protest movements).

Growth in intellectuality may far outstrip concomitant growth in general developmental maturity. Hence, the society may incorrectly expect mature behavior from the gifted child who is incapable of producing adultlike reactions in all aspects of his behavior. Such disparities between intellectual and maturity levels may cause adults to perceive the behavior of the highly gifted child as freakish. Such incongruent behavior may cause adults to incorrectly refer to the child as "immature." In time, the child may come to believe that he is emotionally or socially backward resulting in withdrawn or asocial behavior.

Gifted children may overemphasize the use of ego defense mechanisms in their overall adjustment to life: due to the intellectual abilities of the gifted child, he may resort to "intellectualism" as a means of insulating himself from hurtful emotional occurrences or to explain all of life's problems. Or, he might distort or cut off the emotional from the intellectual aspect of a hurtful situation ("insulation"). Intellectual activity may come to have an isolated, even delusional, meaning all of its own.

Statements of the philosophies of others may be used to "explain away" guilt-laden unethical feelings or behavior ("rationalization"). The individual may parrot such a philosophy as "the cultural relativity of ideas" to explain why he has conformed with his company's policies instead of his own personal set of ethics. Such ego defense mechanisms as rationalization may be used with greater facility, due to the special ability of the gifted person to construct verbal justifications or actual fabrications.

Special Problems of Social Maladjustment

The gifted child will be called upon to adapt himself to play activities which he is personally uninterested in. For example, the elementary school pupil may be called upon to participate in playground activities when he actually wants to read. His honest desire to read may be misinterpreted as "isolation or withdrawal." Eventually, such differences in interest may lead to the child's being perceived as a "loner or nonconformist."

As a consequence, the child may have to play a deceptive role in order to appear to conform to the wishes of teachers and age peers. This artificiality may be perceived by others as condescension. The gifted child is in a position of being "damned if he does and damned if he doesn't."

The gifted student may be the brunt of a special kind of prejudice. In a sense, intellectually gifted students represent a definable "minority group." He may be construed by others to be "different" in a society which cultivates conformity. The everyday use of such colloquialisms as "egghead" bear witness to this kind of anti-intellectual prejudice. This prejudice is particularly pronounced during the adolescent period when the "others" are participating in group activities and responding to fads which the gifted student may ignore or react adversely to.

"Social maladjustment" has special meaning for the gifted girl. The diminishing visibility of gifted girls after puberty is one general indication of the way in which they may choose to conform to psychosexual expectations rather than exploit their intellectuality. Common folkways demand feminine, attractive, and permissive behavior from all women. Such attributes are inimical to expressions of intellectuality. Hence, intellectually expressive women are commonly referred to as "masculine, domineering or aggressive." The gifted woman must make a dramatic choice. Such choices are not made without taking a great toll of their emotional well-being.

Motivational "Inadequacies"

Due to the extensive background of knowledge a gifted student brings to any given academic situation, it is probable that he will make individualistic interpretations of new subject matter. As a result, teachers may interpret that he is paying attention to other subject matter than that on the table. Actually, he may be paying attention to remote or highly-involved aspects of the problem presented to him.

In his overall motivational pattern, the gifted student may be "attending to a distant drummer." For example, the church or some other institution may be perceived by him as the center of his intellectual life, not the school. William Saroyan has reported that the Fresno County Library was the important scholarly reality in his young life, not the schools. Jean Paul Sartre attended to the visiting friends of his grandfather, not his tutors. Winston Churchill's schoolboy days have become legendary, due to his nonconformity and poor performance as a student.

Without thinking, do we superimpose the puritanical values of our society on all individuals? So far, this discussion has implied that a gifted individual ought to be "motivated." Who actually experiences the disgrace of having a beachcomber in the family? Is the beachcomber himself really an unmotivated rogue? Or, is he motivated by a set of values at variance with those that his society holds so dear? Unnumbered gifted individuals have chosen strange motivational patterns during their lives. Arthur Koestler chose a fantastic array of menial callings from beggar to ship's steward. Eric Hoffer, in spite of his reputation as philosopher and lecturer, still enjoys being known as longshoreman. The seemingly strange callings of some intellectuals should cause us to wonder whether or not some kind of genius can only emerge in unusual circumstances.

The gifted frequently possess linear intense interests as opposed to universal ones. We sometimes discourage the gifted student who may wish to pursue a highly specific area of interest over a long period of time.

Special problems require special counseling. In addition to conventional guidance services, the gifted need access to (1) gifted adults from varying backgrounds, (2) counselors familiar with the unique problems of the gifted, (3) wide ranging philosophical discussion, (4) the challenge of critical disputation (e.g. interdisciplinary seminars), and (5) materials describing psychological theories of learning, thinking, and psychodynamics.

In addition, there are special programs for the gifted which require organized inputs from guidance personnel: accelerated courses, special classes, cooperative guidance-instructional seminars, or group counseling experiences.

Concerning the selection and placement of students into *high level subjects or seminars,* some of the following specific questions should be asked:

1. Has the student matured in emotional, social, and psychological ways at a level commensurate with his intellectual growth?
2. Does the student possess sufficient personal security to discuss high-

ly controversial or ambiguous topical areas with a group of individuals who are apt to be probing and critical in their pursuit of truth?

3. Does the student possess defensive mechanisms which would inhibit his active participation in small group seminar activity?

4. How much do we know about the student's prejudices, values, and attitudes which can help us understand the interpretations he will make concerning social issues?

5. Are such factors as emotional stability, or "openness" to suggestions, sufficiently mature to enable the student to benefit from free and open discussions of topics designed to enhance his self-understanding?

6. To what extent is the student "pedantic" as opposed to being "scholarly"? To what extent would he benefit from new or unusual theories, ideas, and knowledge?

7. Are we taking into consideration the developmental level of the child? What is his capability for understanding, in depth, certain kinds of literature? For example, is he ready to study, analyze, and discuss materials of a psychosexual, socially controversial, ethically ambiguous, or revolutionary nature?

8. How much do we know about the student's personal values? How tolerant is he of different or opposing values to his own?

9. To what extent will this student attempt to emulate the customs or new knowledge he discovers in the world around him?

As we select students for guidance and instructional leadership programs, we should apply more varied criteria. Leadership potentiality may be the kind of talent least well correlated with general intelligence. Therefore, we cannot select leadership training groups exclusively from the pool of academically talented students. When selecting potential leaders, guidance personnel might look for the following kinds of qualities:

1. significantly high scores on interest or value inventories in "social, leadership, or service" areas;

2. indigenous student leaders who emerge by being selected by their classmates, their performance in extracurricular activities, and their spontaneous assumption of responsibility as need arises;

3. experimental use of sociometric techniques designed to discover students who are respected by and interact with their peers more than other students;

4. nomination by fellow students of other students whom they consider to be potential leaders;

5. study of the aspirations of students, even their fantasies, concerning participation in great events or episodes which will influence others;

6. utilize the findings of projective techniques (e.g. indices of empathy, cooperativeness, maturity); and

7. include students who appear to be maladjusted due to overactive or unacceptable behavior; include "frustrated leaders" or "gang leaders."

As we select students for "creativity" programs, such as "brainstorming seminars" or innovative projects, the following additional questions might be asked:

1. Has the student demonstrated higher level cognitive processes (e.g. originality, judgment, flexibility, or evaluative skills)?

2. Is he comfortable with ambiguity, unsolved chronic problems, or complexity?

3. Is he meditative, independent, and autonomous as opposed to withdrawn, autistic, or isolated?

4. Is he spontaneous and self-assured instead of eccentric or self-centered?

5. Has he produced worthwhile products which are useful, beautiful, or represent intelligent departures?

6. Can he spontaneously generate viable alternatives or divergent hypotheses when problems are posed?

7. Does he fear the unknown or react to new problems as challenges?

Thus, the task of identifying students for programs involving cooperative guidance and instructional elements results in three main subgroups: (1) those with leadership potential, (2) those with academic potential accompanied by special needs for self-understanding, social awareness and values, and (3) those with creative talent who need guidance toward methods for controlling their inventiveness, revolutionary activities, or unusual interpretations of problems.

UNDERACHIEVEMENT—A SPECIAL PROBLEM COMPLEX

There does not appear to be a consistent definition for the "underachieving" student. In common educational usage, teachers usually refer to students whose grades are low and tested potentialities high as "underachievers." There is a kind of "technical" underachievement which appears in test record discrepancies; a given student's intelligence quotient may be a standard deviation or more higher than are his reading, arithmetic, or other achievement scores. However, even in such seemingly clear-cut situations, there is much room for misuse of the term "underachievement." Perhaps the abilities being measured by standardized tests in no way predict capability for earning grades in a given subject. Some standardized achievement tests are known to be highly correlated with intelligence; other achievement areas are dependent solely upon one's exposure to a given subject matter content. Since educators appear to universally agree that there is such a case as the "underachieving student," we need to discuss ways in which counseling-instructional programs can be of specific benefit for the student who teachers have designated, rightly or wrongly, as being an "underachiever."

In terms of definition, we find as much difference of opinion among the experts as we do among teachers as to who qualifies as an underachieving student. Some definitions are quite general defining underachievement as ". . . failure to go as far in education as one's abilities would justify."[17] Other definitions seem to imply an equation between measured potentiality and achievement in the classroom, "An underachieving, gifted student . . . achieves below his potential. . . . Potential is generally defined in terms of intelligence and achievement by teacher grades or standardized tests."[18] Other experts have attempted to specify underachievement in terms of class standing: "The underachiever is . . . the pupil who ranks in the upper tenth or upper quarter of his class in terms of ability, but whose course grades are average or below."[19]

Other experts have added the notion of motivation when viewing underachievement and refer to underachievement as "a stopping short of one's capacity . . ."[20] or ". . . one who indicates no desire to achieve the academic success of which he is capable."[21]

It is possible to reserve the term "underachievement" for children whose apparent inability or unwillingness to perform in school may be related to physical, psychological, or neurological damage.[22] Any case tentatively diagnosed as "underachievement" should be referred for a complete psychological workup which ought to include individual testing in the reading, perceptual, and intellectual areas.

There are a number of environmental variables which complicate our understanding of the underachieving student. For example, teachers applying rigorous disciplines may superimpose upon their classes unusually high, strict, severe, or unrealistic standards for performance. Some forms of "underachievement" may be the result of hostile responses to the demands of such teachers.

Following puberty, during the adolescent period, some students, especial-

---

[17] Havighurst, Robert J.: Conditions productive of superior children. *Teachers College Record*, 62:303, April 1961.

[18] Durr, William K.: *The Gifted Student*. New York, Oxford U. P., 1964, p. 42.

[19] DeHaan, Robert, and Havighurst, R.J.: *Educating Gifted Children*. Chicago, U. of Chicago, 1961, p. 333.

[20] Abraham, Willard: *Common Sense About Gifted Children*. New York, Harper, 1958, p. 67.

[21] *Education for the Gifted, The Fifty-Seventh Yearbook*, Part II, National Society for the Study of Education. Chicago, U. of Chicago, 1958 (Article by Kough, p. 43).

[22] Strauss, Alfred A., and Lehtinen, Laura: *Psychopathology and Education of the Brain Injured Child*. New York, Grune, 1951.

ly boys, may challenge and rebel against adult authority as a way of life. In such cases, underachievement in school may be symptomatic of a much deeper developmental problem. Incidentally, most researchers agree that more than twice as many boys as girls are diagnosed as underachievers.[23]

Societal prejudices, such as anti-intellectualism, tend to precipitate under-achievement in gifted students. Goldberg elaborated upon societal biases for the gifted as follows: "Evidence of intellectual or artistic gifts may be a handicap, a threat to happiness and to social adjustment, and may evoke such epithets as egghead, long-haired kid genius or brain."[24] Goldberg ob-served that such unsavory labels may be heard, "in a wealthy suburban community as well as in the mill town or rural area."[25] Mead summarized this viewpoint as follows: ". . . Any degree of outstanding success is repre-sented as cutting off from the group. . . . It becomes fashionable not to get better grades than the others, not to go up too fast. These pressures for keeping on all fours with one's classmates, neighbors, business associates . . . are increasing in American life . . . especially in the case of the child who shows intellectual or artistic gifts."[26]

A common cause of underachievement may be the upbringing, home and family background of the student. For instance, some observers have noted that ". . . underachievers tend to come from homes where parents have less education . . . their values tend to be either neutral or negative with respect to education. . . . Parents of underachievers not only appear to demand less in the way of specific performance from their children but also tend to make demands at a later date than parents of achievers usually do."[27] The opposite type of home environment also cause underachieve-ment; the child may be "subjected to relentless harassment at home from an ambitious mother or father who insists he achieve at levels higher than his ability."[28]

Some research has uncovered a common family pattern in the homes of the underachiever which indicates the presence of a "dominant and ag-gressive mother and a weak and ineffectual father."[29] Domineering parents

[23] Shaw, Merville C.: Definition and identification of academic underachievers. *Guidance for the Underachiever With Superior Ability*, DE 25021, Bulletin 1961, No. 25, Superinten-dent of Documents, United States Printing Office, Washington 25, D.C.

[24] Goldberg, Miriam: Factors facilitating or impeding talent development. *Problems in Moti-vation*, p. 5. Project on Guidance and Motivation of Superior and Talented Students, 5454 South Shore Drive, Chicago 15, Illinois.

[25] *Ibid*, p. 5.

[26] Mead, Margaret: The gifted child in the American culture of today. *Journal of Teacher Education*, 5:211-214, Sept. 1954.

[27] Shaw, *op. cit.*, pp. 22-23.

[28] Harris, Irving: *Emotional Blocks to Learning*. Chicago, Free Press of Glencoe, 1961, p. 145.

[29] National Education Association: *Guidance for the Academically Talented Student*. Wash-ington, D.C., The National Education Association, 1961, pp. 38-39.

may exploit the child by demanding advanced skills such as rapid reading capability in order to enhance the prestige of the parent. Such early exploitations of the child have been known to act as "inhibitors of outstanding adult performance."[30]

Other parents may be troubled because their child is in any way unusual. Such parents may feel inadequate to cope with the child's questions or to provide him with intellectual stimulation. As a consequence, they may demand "normal" kinds of adjustment, such as play activities or acceptance of peer group activities, which are not necessarily best suited for this particular child.[31]

Cultural or economic deprivation may form the basis for future underachievement. The results of such socioeconomic and cultural deprivation are well known. When a student from a lower-class family background reaches high school, he is most often under pressure to get out and earn money; he gets little financial support from the home and such thoughts as going to college may be, for him, purely illusionary.[32] His vocabulary, his ethics obtained in the home, and his style of living may be so disparate from the typical middle-class school system, that he may find the system meaningless or hostile.[33]

Another broad area of causation of underachievement may be that of neurological handicap or psychological disturbance. Some writers have directly associated certain forms of underachievement with "learning disability or emotional disturbance."[34] Emotional disturbance may be viewed as an underlying factor percipitating underachievement as a symptom. We should take into account that many underachievers, especially boys, display considerable hostility, aggressiveness, and rejection of the school as an agency of authority. This hostility may also find its expression in ". . . attitudes toward other people . . . general distrust and lack of faith in others."[35]

Underachievers seem to be oriented in the present, they typically fail to make plans for a vocation.[36] In part, this shortsightedness in educational and vocational planning may result from an inadequate self-image, or lack of an "ego ideal": ". . . far too many gifted pupils have neglected to . . . build an ideal of self or choose an individually appropriate vocation."[37]

---

[30] Goldberg, *op. cit.*, p. 6.

[31] Goldberg, *op. cit.*, p. 106.

[32] DeHaan and Havighurst, *op. cit.*, p. 131.

[33] Harris, *op. cit.*, p. 145.

[34] D'Evelyn, Katherine: *Meeting Children's Emotional Needs.* Englewood Cliffs, Prentice-Hall, 1957.

[35] Shaw, *op. cit.*, p. 24.

[36] Hurtz, John J., and Swenson, Esther: Factors related to overachievement and underachievement in school. *Educating the Gifted,* edited by Joseph L. French. New York, Holt, 1960, p. 440.

[37] Witty, Paul: Who Are the Gifted? *Education for the Gifted,* The 57th Yearbook, Part II, National Society for the Study of Education. Chicago, U. of Chicago, 1958, p. 46.

Schools tend to superimpose upon human personality rigorous disciplines, work schedules, and academic subject matters. Teachers seldom recognize that many students possess talents which are not necessarily developed in such rigid academic settings. For some students "book learning" is inimical to self-actualization. Such students would rather be doing something with their hands or performing other skills more in keeping with their native endowments. Hurtz has noted that such students "would rather be out of the classroom situation, not necessarily because of indolence, but because of disinclination for academic activity."[38]

Studies of the incidence of all forms of underachievement in schools indicate percentages from 10 to as high as 40 percent.[39] Some school districts find great disparities between the proportion of underachievers at the elementary school and secondary school levels. For example, a study by the San Diego Unified School District reported underachievement as a problem for 8 percent of their elementary school students and 15 percent for secondary school students.

Experimental programs designed to alleviate the symptoms of underachievement have been generally disappointing. For example, an experimental program conducted at the DeWitt Clinton High School in New York City found that "underachievers who had shown improvement as the result of a year's membership in a warm, accepting, and flexible group would not sustain their gains when held to uniformly high standards, both of conduct and achievement."[40] The DeWitt Clinton researchers noted the following:

1. Academic underachievement appears to be a symptom of a variety of more basic personal and social problems.

2. Underachieving students who improved were able to identify with a teacher who was consistently supportive and interested in them. These students received assistance in mastering the skills of learning which they and other underachievers failed to acquire in the earlier grades.

3. It seemed advisable to the DeWitt Clinton group to separate teaching and guidance functions. The person who worked closely and personally with the students was found to be more effective if this person was not the same one who had to grade or evaluate the students.

4. The teachers found that the practice of grouping students in a subject matter class was not wise. Underachieving students tended to

---

[38] Hurtz and Swenson, *op. cit.*, p. 410.

[39] Freehill, Maurice F.: *Gifted Children: Their Psychology of Education.* New York, Macmillan, 1961.

[40] This DeWitt Clinton High School study has been reported in DeHaan, Robert F., and Robert Havighurst, *Educating the Gifted Children.* Chicago, U. of Chicago, 1961; and Passow, Harry A., and Goldberg, Miriam L.: A study of underachieving gifted. *Educational Leadership,* 16: Nov. 1958.

give negative support to one another and this group behavior could not be adequately handled in a regular classroom.

The Fresno City Unified School District has tried several varieties of experimental classes, seminars, and counseling situations including individual and group activities for underachievers. One program established a sort of "buddy system" for pairs of high-achieving and low-achieving high school students. It was assumed that association with a high-achieving student would motivate the low achiever in the pair. A variation of this program brought together teams of high-achieving upperclassmen from the high school and junior college with low achievers from the junior high school. This latter activity added the possibility for identification, on the part of the younger student, with an older and more successful student.

The Fresno programs met with modest success as measured by slightly increased grade point averages, on the part of the younger or underachieving students. However, as in the case of the New York or San Diego Programs, once the student was withdrawn from the program, he tended to lapse back to his underachieving habits.

A similar type of program for underachieving junior high school students was inaugurated at the Pasadena Unified School District. The Pasadena program included underachievers drawn from economically deprived or minority groups. It was found that disruptive sociological factors complicated the administration of a counseling program for underachievers of this type. Counselors and teachers became preoccupied with wider social and political implications. The special programs tended to be relegated to secondary importance. When underachievement is due to much deeper sociological forces, no amount of educational implementation may be capable of alleviating the difficulty. Solution for such forms of underachievement may rest with other institutions, such as governmental agencies, which have the power and authority to deal with primary *causal factors*.

We have seen that the term "underachiever" is applied to students having more basic *problems* of social, emotional, physical, academic, perceptual, or motivational origin. Therefore, instructional-counseling programs designed to work with underachievers ought to be based upon thorough preprogram diagnosis. It will probably be found that a single counseling-instructional program for all kinds of underachievers would be inadequate. Rather, we will need to think in terms of a slate of specialized counseling-instructional programs for dealing with the specific problems of underachievement. Some of the special programs should be remedial in nature and offer specialized kinds of instruction. Other programs may need to be connected with agencies outside of the school in order to offer help for those students with deep-seated emotional disturbances requiring psychotherapy.

The composite classification for underachievers which appears below includes the broad causes of underachievement generally included in the literature. There may be considerable overlap of the categories within this classification; a given student may have negative attitudinal orientations, emotional disturbance, family problems, and severe motivational inadequacies—all at the same time. Following each category are some suggestions for possible instructional-counseling programs to deal with the particular problem.

1. *Instrumental Overinterpretation of IQ, Achievement Tests, and School Grades*

    Comparison of test scores over the complete academic career of the student

    Talks by psychologists to explain the meaning of high IQ's in a given student

    Programs which focus upon teacher training and understanding of students

2. *Attitudinal Problems Including Rebellion, Hostility, and Over-Reaction to the Changes of Adolescence*

    Individual counseling

    Increased extracurricular activities particularly those involving social missions, such as service clubs or church work

    Seminar activities to acquaint the student with models of conduct from the study of the lives of others

3. *Emotional or Psychological Disturbance*

    Referral for psychotherapy

    Individually assigned work to be performed under supervision

    Special classes for the emotionally handicapped

4. *Family Problems and Conflicts*

    Evening sessions for parents including lecture series on parenthood

    Opportunities for parent counseling

    Courses for teachers incorporating studies of personal adjustment for students with family problems as their topic

5. *Socioeconomic Disparities*

    Total push programs of cultivation

    Classes emphasizing the basic learning skills

    Seminars held by professionals and community leaders of one's own race, cultural background, or socioeconomic level

6. *Learning Disabilities*

    Intensive psychological, neurological and psychiatric diagnosis

    Specialized learning settings involving special application of teaching machines, reading aids, and prescriptive teaching

    Special classes for learning disability groups

7. *Limited, Specialized, or Rare Talents*

Opportunities for exploiting one's special talents through theatre groups, musical organizations, handicrafts, or other very specialized activities

Design of individual programs with some subjects at remedial levels with others at advanced levels

School time devoted to special projects or studies with opportunities for special credit and recognition

8. *Specific Subject Matter Difficulty*

Individual and group counseling designed to discover why certain subjects cause fear or are more difficult

Counselor-teacher conferences

Classroom visitations by counselors to diagnose any personality conflicts between teachers and students

Special remedial classes

Pairing low-achieving students with high-achieving students for study activities

Redesign classes to include new teaching techniques

Select teachers for special classes who possess such qualities as empathy for underachievers

9. *Deficient Work Habits, Lack of Basic Learning Skills*

Remedial classes

Annual orientation classes to introduce students to expected work habits at the next level

Special seminars to study the nature of and techniques for the learning process

Films and film strips dealing with proper study and work habits

10. *Motivational Inadequacy Including Lack of Interest or Sense of Purpose*

Vocational and personal counseling

Identification of subject areas in which student performs well

Seminars and group counseling sessions devoted to studies of the development of human preferences and values

Increased association with students or professionals with whom the student should identify

GUIDANCE-INSTRUCTIONAL PROGRAMS FOR THE GIFTED

If cooperative guidance and instructional programs are to become a reality, it will be necessary for the traditional roles of both guidance workers and teachers to be changed. The guidance worker will have to become more directly involved in the teaching-learning process. Counselors will have to provide individual counseling and guidance services, observations in classrooms, appropriate feedback to classroom teachers, as well as conduct seminars and special classes such as "preparing for leadership" for teachers and students. The teacher will have to apply the research in child study and show that he objectively understands children through clinical analysis of their behavior.

The following are some assumptions made by school administrators contemplating guidance and instructional programs:

1. Counselors are universally available in the elementary schools of the district.

2. Counselors have minimal teacher training and experience, and conversely teachers have minimal guidance training, including study of the guidance process, testing, child study procedures, and learning theory.

3. Teachers and counselors deliberately design subject matter contents which lend themselves to guidance-oriented seminars and counseling activities.

4. Teachers, counselors, and administrators voluntarily meet on a planned basis to compare, evaluate, modify, and reconstruct aspects of cooperative counseling and instructional programs.

5. The administrative climate of the school district is "open" (i.e. roles are well defined leading to open discussions of all educational concerns with no intrigues among professionals allowed).

6. A philosophical tolerance for controversy exists. Possibilities exist for uninhibited and forthright discussion of all topics.

7. A high degree of professional sophistication allows for hierarchies of professional workers to function. Teachers accept guidance workers' technical understandings of group processes and go to them, on occasion, for advice. In turn, counselors admit their limitations and refer difficult personal or learning problems to psychologists.

8. Professional staffs develop and live up to strict ethical codes of professional conduct which describe and limit relationships between professional educators and students.

Table 28 summarizes some of the major counseling and instructional services and functions performed at various grade levels. By reviewing the counseling, seminar, and classroom activities going on simultaneously at various grade levels, we can envision ways in which articulation between counseling and instructional endeavors takes place. For example, as students begin to study the social sciences in depth at the high school level, we have ample reason to offer special seminars in such topical areas as "ethics applied to science and social science" or "political leadership and responsibility." Also, teachers and counselors working in teams can establish special seminar programs which deliberately cut across subject matter boundaries thereby enhancing integration and synthesis of concepts and generalizations.

TABLE 28

MAJOR COUNSELING—INSTRUCTIONAL FUNCTIONS PERFORMED AT
VARIOUS GRADE LEVELS

Level	*Primary*	*Elementary*	*Secondary*	*College*
Grade	K 1 2 3	4 5 6 7 8	9 10 11 12 13	14 15 16

Counseling (individual as indicated)
  Adjusting to special program
    (e.g., acceleration, special classes) ——————→
  Coping with physical disabilities————————————————————————→
  Learning problems, study habits——————————————————————————→
      Emotional problems—————————————————————————→
          Social maladjustment————→
          Motivational inadequacy————————————————→
          Moral inadequacy ———→

Group Counseling (5-10 students)
  Frequent small group activities —→
  Learning to live in groups ——————→   Understanding group processes →   Self expression—→
  (Orientation to new institutions):   ←(JHS)→   ←——(HS)——→   ←——(College)——→
    Study habits——————————→
    Self-Understanding———————————————————————————→
        Creative thinking————————————————→
        Philosophy of life——— ——————————→
    Special counseling groups
      (e.g., Underachieving)———————→

Seminars (10-12 students)
  Student Government, Democratic processes————————————→
  Interrelating Subjects, common principles——————————————→
    Great Ideas of Man   Ethics applied to science, social science
    Values of Mankind   Political leadership and responsibility
    Adjustment redefined   Aesthetics in our times
    Theories of Learning   Religion and disbelief
    (Seminars by subject)   Mathematical models and man
              Literature and controversy

Classes (general outline)
  (Accelerated) (basic skills)   (Subject matter)   Great books   Social sciences
  Aesthetic acculturation   (differentiation)   philosophy   Genuine research
         Languages   Sciences   advanced subjects————————→

Regular counseling services ought to be available to aid gifted children on the same basis that they are available to aid any child. In addition, it is possible to think in terms of special categories of counseling services such as helping students adjust to special programs or help for accelerated gifted children whose frustrations may emerge while adjusting to older children and more demanding work. Also, counselors will need to become sensitive to the unique ways in which gifted children may perceive problems.

Guidance-instructional programs should especially select potential students for inclusion in leadership training programs:

1. students who have demonstrated leadership capability in terms of their service to the school;
2. students selected for social or political leadership roles by their peers;
3. students whose prognosis for potential leadership roles is indicated by high scores on such devices as standardized interest or value tests in "social or leadership" areas; and
4. those students whose style of living demonstrates unique potentiality for filling leadership roles, as indicated by a study of their aspirations or self-appraisal leadership potential.

In general, leaders undertake to guide, command, influence, change, oppose, or reinforce the behavior of others. This influence upon others may be expressed in intellectual, social, religious, scientific, artistic, as well as political ways. Leadership is not confined to direct action, it may be subtle as well as bold, democratic as well as totalitarian. Therefore, the leader's philosophical aims determine the degree to which his direction will lead others toward social usefulness and constructive cultural contributions. Unfortunately, the converse dimensions of these qualities (e.g. nihilism) may be adopted by the leader. "Greatness in leadership is clearly associated with greatness of purpose."[41]

The designers of leadership programs, therefore, should base the selection of students upon very thorough case histories which delve into such matters as attitudes, beliefs, philosophical orientations, and social maturity, as well as the usual intellectual and achievement factors.

The degree of political astuteness or social sophistication a student possesses should help to determine whether or not he is ready for inclusion in seminars or classes in which controversial issues are freely discussed. It is particularly important to assess the student's value orientations. The main goal of leadership training programs should be to help students determine what they believe in. Students should also ask themselves how their values integrate one with another within their own philosophical systems. Moreover, students should ask themselves how these values jibe with those held by and conformed to by the society at large.

Since the twentieth century has witnessed the rise of the "Fuehrer Prinzep" (i.e. leadership principle), professional educators are morally responsible to question the motives and values of potential leaders. Leaders can drastically affect the lives of other men when they are strategically

---

[41] Tead, Ordway: Leadership. *Encyclopaedia Britannica*, Vol. 13. Chicago, William Benton Publications, 1957, pp. 824-825.

placed in political positions of power. Therefore, it is imperative that all potential leaders, in whatever field of endeavor, comprehend the nature and pitfalls of power. It would seem logical to train the leader to engage in continual self-criticism, self-analysis, and self-improvement; he should consciously aim toward the principles of self-actualization.

Since human values may motivate individuals toward constructive or destructive behavior, the humanitarian has his counterpart in the misanthrope; the political man may degenerate to the level of the nihilist. Even if youths are exposed to healthy values and respect the demands of society, they still may choose to ignore these values for the sake of expediency or social survival. Mere knowledge of the values of human society are not sufficient for guaranteeing that the leader will become ethical in his behavior. In addition to acquiring a basic set of values, he must also develop the courage and emotional stability with which to defend and perpetuate these values.

It is necessary to consider possibilities for individual as well as group counseling when designing leadership programs. The potential young leader must understand values and ethics intellectually; he must also learn to accept his values emotionally. For some, the incorporation of one's values into a consistent philosophy of life will not be easy. It is possible that a number of values which society chooses to introject into the philosophies of potential leaders may not be acceptable to these leaders. Modern societies have already witnessed student riots and other challenges to the traditional establishment by students whose values do not conform to those currently held by the society. The student could probably resolve many of these conflicting personal and societal values earlier in his educational career, if schools would permit free discussion of controversial issues, problems, and conflicts.

The school attempts to implement two potentially disparate goals when establishing leadership programs: (1) sufficient freedom of thought and expression must be allowed in seminars, classes, and counseling to insure that the individual student discovers, develops, and incorporates a unique system of values into his own view of life, and (2) the school is responsible to the society as a whole for the perpetration of acceptable mores, laws, and values.

Therefore, the school should present to students the traditions, heritage, and collective value judgments of civilization as they have evolved through history. These two major goals are not always in consonance. The school, as the repository of all civilized knowledge, has a higher obligation to perpetuate those values which maintain the civilization. Therefore, it is important for teachers to engage in considerable philosophical discussion concerning hierarchies of values and the relative importance of the individual's values, the collective values of the state, and those of minorities within society. Educational programs must clearly identify for students the ethics, mores, folkways, and laws of society which form the raw materials for the development of personal values.

As we design guidance-instructional programs in leadership preparation, we might bear in mind Bruner's concept of a "vigorous pluralism."[42] We are not attempting to create a homogenous society in which all individuals and groups possess similar values. On the contrary, we deliberately want to encourage "pluralism," if for no other reason than that it will spawn new ideas, innovations, and dialogue.

While educators frequently assess students' interests and values, they rarely grapple with the process of influencing and contributing to their students' values. Sometimes, educators become vaguely aware that they may have overemphasized one value orientation over another. For example, there has been an overemphasis on science due to current interest in modern technology. Such revelations are usually followed by equally mistaken overemphasis on other compensatory values. Perhaps our overconcern with the humanities might become detrimental to the development of science. Educators must expose students to the whole range of human interests and values, leaving it up to the student to choose those interests and values with which he can identify.

Fortunately, "there is extensive experience to prove that those who direct others can be trained not only to direct better, but to rise above command or mere order-giving into the manifesting of true leadership."[43]

In addition to imparting the technique for self-assessment, arranging for the discussion of values and conflicts, and guidance of youth toward appropriate social goals, we can also train them to perform leadership functions efficiently, effectively, humanely, and ethically. Seminars and classes can be designed around the central topic of leadership. In such classes, the nature of leadership should be discussed along with its responsibilities, problems, and temptations. Such classes might involve the "laboratory" use of clubs and other student organizations for the study and practice of acceptable leadership techniques.

Group counseling aspects of an overall guidance-instructional master program should begin at the primary level. Group counseling programs for young children should go beyond the concept of "learning to live in groups." Young children need to become sensitized to the necessity for communicating their ideas and feelings to others. The dynamics of group processes need to be understood through intimate and frequent contact with others.

Teachers and counselors should anticipate the common learning problems

---

[42] Bruner, Jerome S.: *The Process of Education.* New York, Vintage Books, 1963, p. 20.

[43] *Encyclopaedia Britannica, op. cit.,* p. 824.

talented children encounter, and they should organize special counseling sessions accordingly. The dynamics inherent in the group counseling sessions should not differ substantially from the seminar activities described earlier. It would be difficult to distinguish between processes which change one's values in a social science seminar from the experiences which occur during group counseling processes. We are dealing with the kind of developmental psychology which emphasizes mental health and progress toward self-realization.

Others have advocated informal discussion with a small group ". . . as the most effective procedure to use with young children."[44] Getting the young child accustomed to open-ended, probing discussions of problems should lead to a growing awareness of the relationships among the various concepts he must understand in order to be an effective intellectual. By the fifth or sixth grade level, group counseling should be structured in terms of important personal concerns of students such as effective study habits, anxiety reactions as generated by school related frustrations, self-understanding, relating social data to one's personal values, social outlook, and interrelating contradictory, controversial or different beliefs with one's personal values.

By the secondary school level, students ought to be ready to accept guidance in such areas as creative thinking and cultural contribution. Thorough "brainstorming" sessions, as well as formalized discussion of one's philosophy of life, should be related to planning one's destiny. Specialized group counseling settings should be maintained for identifiable problem areas such as underachieving in school, inability to conform to social expectation, or inability to apply one's self to the demands of a professional preparation.

Counselors and teachers should discuss institutional goals in terms of expected behavioral outcomes for their students. Following are some of the possible goals counselors and teachers might agree upon as bases for developmental group counseling-seminar sessions for students:

1. *Self-Actualization and Self-Understanding.* Seminar programs can be constructed which arrange exposures of the student to discussions of differential values for living. Perhaps such discussions might focus upon the various possibilities for typing men into value groups. It must be emphasized that men are basically different with reference to the attitudes, interests, and values they adopt. These discussions ought to stress the need for tolerance for the discrepant values of others. The topic of "Understanding One's Self" might begin with a study of the analytical approaches to the study of man including the work of Freud, Jung, Maslow, or other personality theorists.

[44] Heffernan, Helen (Ed.): *Guiding the Young Child.* Boston, Heath, 1959, p. 67.

2. *Self-Analysis of the Learning Process.* We do not spend enough time in the ordinary school setting teaching students theories of learning or procedures and practices of efficient study habits. In order to obtain optimal motivation from students, they need to have some insight into the nature of learning, its objectives, and an analysis of their own personal attitudes and feelings toward school. Such discussions should lead to consideration of the inherent values of learning, as well as its practical applications for professional preparation. The counselor should cite examples of productive versus inefficient scholarship. Studies of the lives of eminent men would be appropriate to reinforce effective learning habits.

3. *Taking Inventory of Personal Assets and Liabilities.* The student must develop an awareness of his assets and liabilities. In the process, he will learn that objectivity begins with an understanding of one's self. Personal inventories, interpretation of psychological test results, and the subjective understanding of one's feelings should be the subject of individual and group counseling sessions.

4. *Evaluation and Adoption of Socially Prescribed Values.* The school certainly prescribes morality. This is not to say that the school unilaterally superimposes a morality upon the student. Rather, the school clearly identifies prevailing morals, ethics, and values for their students.

Group counseling or seminar activities are not established for the treatment of serious problems. Rather, they are set up to accomplish positive productive objectives. The student should not be conceived as a silent partner in the establishment of such programs. From the primary grades to the higher levels of schooling, the theories and procedures involved in the counseling programs should be explained to the student in keeping with his high level of comprehension. The student must believe that he is an equal partner in the educational process. As time progresses, the student may elect to take a far more aggressive role in the planning of his own study activities.

Designing and implementing counseling-instructional programs calls upon the professional staff to undergo group processes not unlike those the students themselves undergo. We cannot expect a professional staff with diverse backgrounds to unanimously agree upon this type of program without deliberation. Therefore, before the actual program is started much discussion of program design, time scheduling, objectives, and methods of evaluation must ensue. At least five stages of program development should characterize the construction of a counseling/seminar program in a school system:

1. *Inventory of professional staff members.* Search for staff with preparations such as learning theory; group dynamics; curriculum develop-

ment; tests and measurements; or general liberal arts preparation across subject-matter categories. Attempt to create a professional team with different skills that can be put to use in cooperative program efforts. If certain skills are lacking in a given staff, attempt to acquire new staff members with needed skills, or prepare existing staff by providing appropriate in-service training programs or re-education.

2. *Philosophical deliberation and debate.* No time limit should be placed upon discussion of such topics as staff attitudes concerning the gifted, controversial topics in curriculum, or interrelationships among subject-matters. Staff should critically analyze their existing philosophies of education. Does the prevailing philosophy of education contain glib generalizations or axiomatic truisms? If so, it will need to be rewritten in such a way as to be practical and meaningful for the goals of a counseling-instructional program.

Do educators really value personal commitment, the study of controversial issues, or the understanding of disparate political beliefs? If so, possible outcomes of open discussion and debate on the part of students ought to be realistically recognized. If we decide that free discussion of controversial issues ought to be open to older students, they may acquire unacceptable beliefs or political philosophies. Such questions need to be honestly discussed by professional staffs and some resolution made before the program is actually inaugurated.

Limitations upon free expression might be agreed upon. In such a case, staff would need to critically analyze the effects upon the behavior, attitudes, and expressions of teachers and students. As we tolerate, or do not tolerate, specified kinds of expression on the part of the students, so we need to apply these limits, or lack of limits, for the professional staff. We should not underestimate the extent to which adults introject their own values, attitudes, beliefs, and outlooks upon students.

3. *Alternate designs for different forms of counseling-instructional programs ought to be implemented.* Such implementations as rescheduling of class periods must accompany the design of programs which include frequent small group and individual activities. Such designs must reschedule assignments for teachers and counselors within the school day; some teachers will need to serve large group activities (e.g. lecture or television teaching) while other professionals devote their time to small group activities. Scheduling of students should be viewed as a daily affair rather than a semester or yearly counseling operation. The ultimate success of the program will depend upon flexibility of scheduling. Hence, the school system may need to adjust its scheduling procedures to computerized approaches.

A complete slate of different counseling-instructional program possibilities ought to be scheduled for students (e.g. various subject matter seminars, group counseling activities along with special classes). Programs should not be based upon single subjects or problems.

4. *Informational feedback to teachers, counselors, administrators, and students should be accomplished through systematic communication.* Communication among staff members and students should be facilitated by the development of special forms and routines for this purpose. It is not enough to advocate that "teachers ought to meet with counselors to obtain feedback from their students." Instead, weekly or daily sessions should be scheduled between counselors and teachers to specifically discuss problems, issues, and ideas for improvement. This is the program evaluation phase, which should lead to program improvement and reassessment.

5. *As the financial and professional resources of a school district grow, it should aim toward the ideal of individual instruction and counseling.* Programs must be viewed as tentative applications of professional procedures and knowledge. Periodic staff meetings should result in continual changes in both curriculum content and teaching and counseling methodologies. The Staff assumes that any group program is only an interim step toward the ideal of individual instruction. As the school becomes more accustomed to utilizing scientific approaches and utilizing individual learning techniques, it should slowly retool its whole educational program toward individualization of instruction.

It should be emphasized that group counseling programs should never become substitutes for individual counseling services. The total development of various kinds of talent is predicated upon the assumption that individual psychodiagnostic and counseling services will be made available to students throughout their schooling. When problems of a personal nature appear in group counseling or seminar situations, the counselor ought to terminate discussion and advise the student that the problem ought to be brought to an individual setting. Admittedly, seminars designed to discuss deep matters may make it difficult to determine the line of demarcation between personal and group concerns. Guidelines have to be established to determine that point at which emotional involvement begins and philosophical disputation ends. The professional preparation and experience of counselors and teachers involved in special counseling-instructional programs will directly influence the effectiveness of such guidelines.

Listed below are examples of problems and discussion topics which seem to be appropriate for group counseling or seminar activities:

1. Intellectual, philosophical differences of opinion
2. The general nature of intellect, talent, and eminence
3. Occupations appropriate for the talented
4. General interpretations of tests, inventories, or statistical findings

5. Any subject matter material
6. The general ethics of teaching and learning
7. The application of learning theory, procedures, and individual approaches to learning and scholarship

The following types of problems should be referred to individual counseling settings:

1. Guilt deriving from personal attitudes, prejudices, or values
2. Personal problems involving the home or emotional entanglements
3. Choice of a profession when in conflict with family
4. Individual study of attributes and weaknesses
5. Relationships with individual teachers; complaints
6. Any personal problem involving maladjustment

The two foundations for counseling-instructional programs should be (a) participation by students in school governmental activities down to the elementary school level and (b) sequential series of seminars and group counseling activities devoted to discussions of subject matter. All aspects of the program should be participated in by groups of students, teachers and counselors. Immediate feedback of academic problems, conflicts, and misunderstandings should occur.

Current student participation in school activities tends to be passive and important. While educators mouth platitudinous objectives for the development of democratic ideals, student governmental activities tend to limit themselves to discharging the mandates of school administrations. Rather, they should be discussing political problems of immediate concern to students. If student governmental activities are to lead to adult political responsibility, then student leadership activities should include the whole range of political experience. The whole social and political structure of the school should be revamped to resemble the society at large. The school should be a simulated democratic structure for resolving immediate social and political problems.

At the high school levels, special seminar settings should be organized to discuss topics which cut across subject matter boundaries. Also, topics of current concern to students should be included. Of particular importance are seminars devoted to discussion of ethics, esthetics, or religion. Seminar settings ought to be arranged for students with special kinds of talent. For example, we might establish separate settings for potential political leaders, dramatists, industrial trainees, or artists and craftsmen to discuss topics of particular interest to their special group.

Of special concern in counseling-instructional programs should be leadership selection and preparation. Currently leadership qualities tend to emerge in our society on their own, not by any design. Hence, we see signs of frustrated leadership in our youth. Some youths are forced to lead others clandestinely because no meaningful outlets for their leadership capability exist in the school or community. In theory, we have ample reason to believe that our potential leadership talent can be trained to accept and act upon the responsibilities inherent in our heritage of Western Civilization. In order to accomplish the realization of full leadership potentialities, we must universally expose them to the diverse values of our democratic heritage. In addition, the young person should be afforded the opportunity to emerge with a unique philosophy of life which incorporates freely chosen beliefs and values.

To control the development of leadership, educators must apply modern understandings of personality theory and group dynamics. Specially trained counselors are logical agents for such applications of theory and studies of students. In performing such tasks, counselors will need to relinquish the traditional viewpoint that educational counseling is an afterthought devoted to the solution of problems already manifest. The new roles of the counselor should include selection of potential leaders; utilization of diverse models of leadership; historical studies of men of eminence; or exposure of the student to modern personality theory and theories of learning. Counselors should not only become group leaders for counseling and seminars, they should also enter the teaching-learning episode by contributing subject matter.

The inauguration of full-fledged counseling-instructional programs ought to reunite teachers, counselors, and students into an educational team. The artificial typologies of "teacher" versus "learner" should merge. In an educational setting everyone "teaches"; everyone "learns."

Chapter 9

STAFFING PATTERNS AND TEACHER
QUALIFICATIONS

STAFFING patterns for talent development programs are complicated in proportion to the degree to which integration with the regular education occurs. Special classes, tutoring, or counseling programs call for comparatively simple staffing arrangements similar to any other education program. Enrichment, differentiated curriculums in regular settings or other forms of programs which mix students of varying capabilities call for complicated programming of materials, instructional services, and extra-classroom specialists.

Staff qualifications, though complex, may be envisioned more readily. One is tempted to answer "yes" to the taunting question of general educators, Do you think that the gifted ought to get all of the best teachers? But, who would be saddled with the "other" teachers? It is clear that retarded children need and get teachers who are highly specialized both in training and personal qualifications. Teachers of average children must possess considerable patience and perseverance in order to teach effectively even a fraction of currently adopted curriculums. In short, all modern teachers are specialists; they should be chosen as "best" for given specific teaching tasks. In addition to mastery of appropriate subject matters, they must be able to cope with the needs of children with categorical characteristics. Thus, it is unnecessary to force the issue of who gets the "best" teacher. The question becomes, Who gets the teacher best qualified to instruct him effectively and efficiently according to his unique configuration of learning capabilities?

For the gifted student, it is important to maximize such learning inputs as thinking strategies, uncommon knowledge, and sophisticated methodologies. Hence, it is necessary to find instructors who are equipped to handle such learning inputs. Since no individual teacher could be expected to possess all of the skills necessary to provide the full range of inputs, it is important to utilize teams of resource experts, tutors, and masters. Staffing patterns are complicated by such factors as scarcity of resource specialists (rural areas especially), lack of time on the part of highly productive intellectuals to devote to personal interaction with the gifted, or failure of professional education to capture its share of intellectuals.

Ideally, we should disregard traditional formulas for teacher-pupil settings and ratios when educating the gifted. Unfortunately, the realities of integration with the whole public school population forces us to recognize and work with existing conditions. Perhaps the most useful advice, given these conditions, is the simplest; let us call it "the scatter-gun pattern." In "normal" educational circumstances (e.g. "self-contained" elementary classrooms and "departmentalized" high schools), it is necessary to intersperse as many special resource persons, places, and things as money and conditions will allow. In order to fully ultilize these resources, students must be allowed radically flexible opportunities to avail themselves of unique, personalized experiences. At present, the main enemy of such an arrangement seems to be state-imposed regulations which prescribe courses, time schedules, and attendance requirements. The dedicated teacher of the gifted is sometimes forced to choose between programming resource opportunities throughout the regular school day to the loss of basic content coverage or asking the students to forego part of their leisure time for after-school and Saturday activities. Of course, the administrative option of special classes is always available for those willing to make clear-cut, but controversial, decisions.

On a minimum basis, any program for the gifted should have the following professional services available to it:

1. full-time or intermittent supervising teachers with the following qualifications—one or more academic majors at the master's degree level; six school hours or more graduate level course work on the psychology and education of the gifted;

2. school psychologists who, in addition to full pedagogical training, are experienced in identifying the gifted and are capable of advising teachers on learning theory as applied to program construction;

3. curriculum specialists in all major academic areas, persons who can really write curriculum and demonstrate its application;

4. lists of community experts from as broad a spectrum of professional backgrounds as possible; these experts should be available for personal student interaction as well as curriculum construction;

5. school counselors possessing special training in conducting group seminars and counseling; counselors who understand and relate to the unique personal problems of the gifted; and

6. overall coordinators capable of orchestrating all the variables toward the end of total talent development.

Overall program coordinators, at the school district level, may be drawn from the ranks of teachers or they may be career supervisors. It is important that coordinators maintain a program focus on curriculum building, dissemination and evaluation. Program coordinators should be "action-oriented," frequently visiting classrooms and personally participating in demonstrations of exemplary teaching techniques.

In discussing staffing patterns, we will emphasize two roles: the consultant (as program coordinator) and the teacher. It is an educational axiom that all programs depend ultimately upon the teacher for their successful execution. However, the strategic role of the program builder must not be overlooked. Individual teachers may produce outstanding classroom results, but district or regional excellence in educational programming can only be accomplished through advanced management methods applied by consultants operating on an inter-classroom basis. Only by realizing some degree of standardization of program excellence can we hope to guarantee equivalent opportunities for all talented students.

THE CHANGING ROLE OF THE CONSULTANT

This section will attempt to relate the emerging role of the district consultant to the changing requirements posed by new educational programs. The need for professional consultant services for educational program development has been accelerated by the proliferation of special student requirements.

The sweeping obligations of county superintendents of schools such as "enforcing courses of study, supervising schools by visiting them, and supplying direct services to smaller districts" might be expanded into more meaningful consultant services to school districts. While large counties have tended to expand consultant services with indirect services such as workshops, in-service training, the development of new courses and the like, state legislatures have authorized no new indirect services, and have consistently discouraged regional offices by the curtailment of funds. Hence, it is vital to encourage the growth of direct consultant services at the school district level.

The stylized use of such terms as "direct service" or "indirect service" have confused issues and subverted attempts by conscientious state and local education agencies to organize and administer adequate consultant services. Therefore, more precise, objective definitions will need to be written. For example, "expenditures for instruction" might be defined as "all activities dealing directly with the teaching of pupils, improving the quality of teaching, or aiding in the adjustment of pupils to the educational program."[1] Such disparate costs as "principals' salaries, supervisors' salaries, and certain consultant fees" should be considered "direct expense." It seems logical that consultant services designed to generate new curriculum for students should be construed as "direct expenses." Once this point is well clarified and accepted, the following recommendations for consultant services could proceed unhindered.

The underlying assumption upon which all consultant services are based is that one person cannot envision, hypothesize, design, refine, try out,

---

[1] *California School Accounting Manual.* California State Department of Education, Sacramento, 1966.

collect information about, and modify modern total educational programs. This immense task may best be performed by teams of specialists coordinated by specially-trained consultants. Individual teachers are both members of the "specialist teams" and aspire toward consultant roles.

The following five-stage outline describes typical tasks and roles of consultants; this outline is intended to be generalized and should be applicable to any situation which involves district, county, state, or national level consultant work.

Step 1. Make Preliminary Assessment of Agency to Be Worked With

Analyze readiness of agency for
 conducting established programs;
 educational innovation
 educational research, criticism, and program modification; and
 organizational change.
Study appropriate lines of communication
 line-staff-field relationships;
 open channels of communication between line and staff; and
 existing mechanisms for communication.
Review legal authority
 study and interpret assumed prerogatives outside of the law;
 define unstated or ambiguous areas of authority; and
 evaluate need for new law or regulations.
Evaluate organizational efficiency
 review past record of successes and failures; and
 informally assess effectiveness of staff with conducting programs and
working with lower level personnel.

Step 2. Inaugurate Study and Training Programs

Arrange exploratory surveys of populations to be served
 describe student population thoroughly;
 from description of student population, derive learning needs of subgroups
 survey professional population noting availability of specialists; and
 survey parent population along with community human resources.
Survey and describe all available educational supplies, equipment, and
facilities
 pay special attention to library with emphasis on variety and scope of
books;
 survey and classify appropriate community facilities such as special
laboratories with timetables for availability.
Establish professional workshops
 in-service training programs for teachers;

in-service training for pupil personnel workers and other specialists;
offer liaison with local colleges for special training for professionals, and
offer unique in-service programs for the special needs of the agency
being worked with.
Organize working committees within the agency
explain role of the consultant and groom local person to assume such
role;
organize working committees along lines of demonstrated professional
needs of agency; and
help institute realistic work schedules which will enhance morale.
Collect, interpret, and disseminate recent research
prepare appropriate bibliographies;
recommend particularly useful bibliographical sources for purchase for
professional library;
prepare and distribute résumés of research; and
help design and publish local newsletter services.
Study and report back existing programs and standards
rationale and effect of grading policies;
grouping and selection policies;
evaluate effectiveness of existing special programs with objective data;
and
share methods of evaluation for recurring use by agency.
Promote public understanding and support
inaugurate information service to public;
encourage specialized parent organizations; and
instruct district personnel concerning proper sharing of confidential information on students.

Step 3. Organize Action Programs

Study existing goals, philosophy, and standards
study and describe existing goals, philosophy, standards;
compare existing goals, philosophy, and standards with other agencies
and literature;
evaluate standards in the light of literature and other criteria; and
recommend revised goals, philosophy, standards.
Help to organize uniform programs of special education
advocate proper screening procedures;
review identification standards for students and enforce same;
advocate certification standards and appropriate placement; and
emphasize advisability of specialized curriculum development for
special programs.
Integrate counseling and guidance services with instructional programs

    establish pilot individual and group counseling programs;

    instruct staff in methods of articulation of guidance and teaching staffs;

    demonstrate use of feedback operations utilizing counseling staff;

    review meaning of psychometric scores and their use with students;

    review referral procedures both inside and outside the agency;

    define teacher's place in guidance; and

    review and refer to references on specialized counseling opportunities and results.

Help develop efficient procedures for program operation

    appropriate forms for special program and referral;

    mechanisms for rapid communication through hierarchy; and

    clear-cut procedures for student referral, evaluation feedback, requests for consultant services.

Demonstrate steps needed for curriculum development

    define clearly who does what work;

    promote agreement upon format for curriculum writing;

    open channels for teacher contribution of written curriculum;

    inaugurate pilot programs for unique curriculum tryout;

    establish clearly defined methods for the evaluation of units of curriculum; and

    create instruments and train personnel for the specific job of curriculum dissemination to other classrooms after it has been tried out and evaluated.

Establish effective study programs for teaching methodology

    stimulate discussion of disparate teaching methods;

    promote and defend freedom for open discussion and the presentation of disparate points of view; and

    instruct staff on latest developments in teaching procedures, grouping and the like.

Help design experimental model programs

    emphasize definition of and ethical use of "experimental programs" with students;

    encourage systematic use of matched groups and comparative evaluative procedures for study outcomes;

    emphasize the need for definition of "validity" with reference to education programs; and

    define point at which "experimental program" becomes "operational" and ready for export to other classrooms.

Step 4. Supervision, Enforcement and Follow-Up

Continue to advise upon and enforce law, codes, regulations.

Continue to advise on standards, goals, philosophy

    specifically review effect of existing standards upon growth of students;

keep agency aware of emerging goals and standards of other districts and areas; and

keep agency "reality-oriented" by systematically comparing standards with performance, differences of opinion, usefulness of standards and philosophy for the definition of operational educational programs.
Observe teachers and programs in operation

evaluate with intellectual honesty and critical integrity;

encourage uniform observation and evaluation of forms and standards; and

encourage experimental use of confidential rating techniques particularly by peer groups (e.g. teachers observing and rating their fellows confidentially).

Explore, advocate, and support interagency cooperation and contractual relationships.

Continually suggest appropriate called for changes
in curriculum and special programs;
teacher training and selection; and
mechanisms for constructive criticisms and feedback.

Supply agency with thorough description of one's own methods of operation as a possible model for use by district level consultants.
Make immediately available any evaluations, criticisms or suggestions by higher level agencies.

Step 5. Evaluation

Maintain up-to-date, accurate, useful records of consultation services, changes, and new program developments in agencies work with.

Develop, administer and interpret devices for self-evaluation
utilize format, such as the one presented here, for model against which to assess services;
possible use of rating scale for services; and
objectively assess, sometimes refer to other consultants for assessment, correspondence, ancedotal notes, and testimonial feedback.

Design, explain, and help to carry out scientific programs of research at the agency level

encourage basic theoretical research at local level;
outline methods for comparative research;
promote experimental research in all of its forms along with appropriate warnings and evaluate comments; and
encourage innovation in hypothesis generation including such novel methods as "brainstorming."

Establish systematic continuing programs of research and evaluation
   for constant feedback for existing programs;
   for the testing of pilot and model programs; and
   for the continual testing of school standards.

Continue individual study and research with particular emphasis upon the study and understanding of new learning theory and its applications

   design and apply practical applications for new learning theory developments.

The foregoing outline of recommended consultant services may be considered sequential. For example, before action programs are contemplated, it is necessary to make preliminary assessments of existing programs and follow this by the inauguration of specialized study programs. Of course, supervision, enforcement, and follow-up are all-encompassing phases of the consultant service beginning with the first visit to an agency and never ending. Likewise, the function of evaluation should be contemplated during the earliest preliminary assessment of an agency to be worked with and continued to be applied through to the end of work with the agency. For the most part, except for supervision and enforcement, all of the phases of the consultant's operation are for the benefit of the agency he is working with. Such programs might be inaugurated by the agency itself without outside consultant help. The outside consultant supplies the organization, motivation, and technical skill to bring the overall program development function to fruition.

PROFESSIONAL INVOLVEMENT AND LEADERSHIP AT THE SCHOOL LEVEL

The implementation of programs for talented students depends upon the utilization of varied staff skills within a given school. Adequate program planning and administration demands upon cooperation of the entire faculty with supplemental resource personnel and agencies. In general, four main kinds of personnel are required at local levels: school psychologists, school counselors, resource specialists including curriculum consultants, and teachers from all subject matter disciplines. Each professional staff member is called upon to discharge a unique role in keeping with his specialized preparation. In addition, professional staff members share common tasks to which they must all cooperatively contribute. These unique and common tasks are submitted in Table 29.

It can be seen that a number of unique roles are clearly related to the specialized preparation of the staff member in question. For example, the school psychologist should be the only one expected to render intensive psychodiagnosis of talents in view of his background and credentials. By

TABLE 29

UNIQUE ROLES AND COMMON TASKS OF PERSONNEL IN
TALENT DEVELOPMENT PROGRAMS

Unique Roles	Common Tasks	Unique Roles
Psychologists	Research and Evaluation	*Resource Specialists or Curriculum Specialists*
Psychodiagnosis	Instrument Standardization	Curriculum Content
Individual Testing		Design for Curriculum
Interpretation of Complex Personal, Social Phenomena	Define Roles in Ethical Terms Curriculum Development	Try-out and Validation of Curriculum
Design of Teaching-Learning Strategies	Student Observation, Case Study and Records	Recommend New Curricula Models and Child Development Models
	Student Rating or Grading	
Counselors		*Teachers*
	Communication of Test	
Provide Counseling	Results, Student Progress to Parents	Definition of the Teaching Act
Group Testing		
	Public Information, Parent	
Classroom Observation	Conferences, Community Involvement	Methods of Self-Evaluation
Explanation of Learning Behavior, Problems		Application of Learning Theory to Lesson Planning
		Use and Customized Adaptation of Curriculum Outlines to Daily Classroom Use

the same token, we should expect a steady flow of suggestions from curriculum consultants concerning the application of newer designs for the construction, evaluation, and modification of existing curricula. These specializations notwithstanding, there still needs to be considerable sharing of common tasks toward the ultimate development of viable programs of instruction.

Professional "isolationism," particularly between counselors and teachers, may pose a formidable barrier to the success of programs. Perhaps the most expeditious way of overcoming this segregation of the two professions may be to redefine the role of the teacher and the counselor in the areas where their roles overlap. Counselors providing direct student services within the classroom through the conducting of seminars or observation of student performance should enhance the integration of counselor and teacher roles. Under such circumstances, counselors would come to be viewed as an integral part of the teaching-learning process. Likewise, as teachers become more proficient in interpreting student classroom behavior, they will come to be viewed as more generally competent by counselors. In the process, the artificial distinctions between counseling and teaching will diminish.

Conference, classroom, and counseling interrelationships and interpersonal dynamics should merge.

A fundamental reason why educational application has lagged behind basic research is the lack of operational plans for the utilization of research findings. The common tasks of "research and evaluation, instrumental standardization or curriculum development," shown in Table 29, refer to the practical tasks of interpreting, reverifying in a local setting, developing actual curriculum, and redefining basic research for use in the overall educational program. In order to expedite this process, initiatives must be made by all levels of personnel. The staff should look to the school psychologist for seminars, college or university level courses, and systematic in-service training for counselors and teachers related to the types of teaching-learning strategies accepted by the district. Resource specialists, such as curriculum consultants, need to design methods of operation, conduct meetings, and generally direct services in the classroom. As we expect counselors to enter the classroom for the purpose of behavioral observation, so we should expect the curriculum consultant and psychologist to visit classrooms periodically for the purposes of assessing the efficiency of new teaching-learning strategies, demonstrating new approaches, and actually participating in the try-out of new concepts of teaching. We must deliberately emphasize the merging of professional roles.

The common tasks for psychologists, counselors, resource specialists, curriculum consultants and teachers, listed in Table 29 represent an order; the tasks listed toward the top are more approximately participated in by more highly-trained personnel such as psychologists or resource consultants, while the tasks listed toward the lower end of the list are more appropriately carried out by personnel such as counselors or teachers who are in direct contact with students and the public. All levels of personnel, highly and modestly trained, should participate in all of these common activities:

1. *Research and Evaluation.* Assessing the need for additional research and evaluation should be the task of district level personnel with responsibilities beyond single classroom involvements. However, the ideas for such research and the actual conducting of the research will need to be done by counselors and teachers. Such a common task might be equitably divided in terms of assessment, theoretical design, and suggested procedures for the accomplishment of the research by high level staff; actual gathering of the findings conducted by classroom level staff; and eventual evaluation and drawing of conclusions ought to be a common task involving personnel from all levels.

2. *Instrument Standardization.* Assessing new tests, measurements, examinations, or rating scales is a complicated and technical task. In this

sense, it is best carried out by a school psychologist or researcher with background in research design and statistics. However, if these instruments are to be useful in a practical classroom setting, they will need to be based upon and related to the curriculum goals of the school. Therefore, curriculum consultants ought to be involved in the design of any instrument which will be used in making judgments, evaluations, or drawing conclusions about curriculum. Instruments designed to evaluate programs will be only as useful as counselors' and teachers' capability of understanding them in the first instance and respecting the results drawn from them in the second instance. Therefore, personnel from all levels ought to contribute items to such instruments, participate in their standardization, and actively contribute to the ultimate judgment as to whether such new instruments are valid and reliable for use in the local setting.

3. *Curriculum Development.* The development and continuing evaluation and modification of a district's curriculum is the best single example of a common task to be shared by all of the professional staff. Unfortunately, in all too many schools "curriculum" is a somewhat mysterious connotation attached to certain writings which tend to be locked somewhere in a district's files. Here, we are assuming a more organic and fundamental meaning for "curriculum development." We are agreeing with the New York Board of Education when they think of the curriculum as including "all of the activities, experiences and materials involved in the instruction of students." Curriculum development, then, is the very core for the institutional meaning of the school. It is the organized activities, experiences, and materials accumulated and incorporated into the curriculum that constitute the difference between the school as an institution and, for the sake of comparison, the home as an institution.

Basic to the overall public evaluation of the school should be well-structured and organized materials, plans, described activities, extracurricular activities, and all of the other dimensions of the school that we collectively refer to as the "curriculum." This broad and somewhat unwieldly concept needs constant clarification, redefinition, and modification. The leadership for such complex coordination of human behavior needs to be administered by personnel with the highest possible competencies; they require understanding of learning theory, exceptional breadth in the assimilation and understanding of subject matter content, and training and experience in the procedural and methodological implication of demonstrating, trying out, evaluating, and changing the behavior of students and teachers alike.

In order to understand how local school personnel might function in an operational program, following are some of the unique tasks performed by various specialized personnel with a school district:

1. *The school psychologist*
   certifies all talented students at the outset of program;
   diagnoses and refers cases involving emotional or other problems;
   calls for the help of other agencies to deal with problems;
   writes research reports, position papers, memorandums designed to
      stimulate the understanding and use of modern learning theory;
   meets, on request, with groups of teachers, intermixed with coun-
      selors, who are encountering special problems with students
      which they are unable to resolve themselves;
   proposes formats, outlines, and items for examinations, rating scales,
      and evaluation devices;
   is available, on an individual consultative basis, to work out pro-
      fessional problems such as designing teaching-learning strategies;
   "talks out" individual problems involving teacher-to-teacher, stu-
      dent-to-student, or student-to-teacher conflicts;
   utilizes his professional training to judge the usefulness of proposed
      items purporting to measure or evaluate human behavior, such
      as teacher rating scales, pupil rating scales or the like;
   conducts courses, for district professional growth credit, for coun-
      selors and teachers in such areas as "characteristics of the gifted,
      interview and counseling techniques, or the psychology of ex-
      ceptionality";
   meets with seminar groups of students, teachers, or counselors, at
      their request, to help define or understand certain group dynamics
      or technical problems which puzzle the group and inhibit their
      group interaction.

2. *School counselors*
   promote, provide and appropriately disseminate to teachers the
      findings from individual and group counseling sessions with stu-
      dents;
   administer all group and, where qualified, individual, psychometric
      devices;
   prepare and interpret the individual and group results of such
      testing to students, parents, and teachers;
   divide their work on a basis of subject matter content competency
      as well as counseling competency and distribute their services
      in student and teacher seminars accordingly;
   actively participate in periodic classroom observation of all students
      involved in seminars and group counseling;

act as chairman for weekly teacher conferences to discuss findings from student observations, special counseling sessions, and integrated seminar experiences;

generally coordinate the counseling and instructional programs of the school by investigating and redefining the goals of the programs;

observe the everyday outcomes of the programs and elaborate upon suggestions for more efficient administration of the programs;

participate in parent-teacher-student conferences when invited;

hold group conferences for the investigation of problems referred by teachers which cannot be handled in an ordinary parent-teacher conference;

conduct systematic in-service training programs for teachers with special emphasis on "the application of group dynamics techniques, standards for student rating and grading, elementary statistics, and understanding testing and measurement results";

observe, tentatively interpret, and refer conflicts, problems, maladjustments, misunderstandings and inefficient practices, techniques and materials to psychologists and resource specialists for their study and subsequent solution.

3. *Resource specialists and curriculum consultants*

study the growing body of literature describing child development, models for curriculum development;

prescribe new ways to present curriculum to students;

convey new developments to teachers by way of frequent memoranda, and curriculum circulars;

contemplate, design, write-up, and demonstrate specific blocks of curriculum content for classroom teachers by actual participation in the teaching act in the classroom;

redefine and administer new concepts of supervision involving changes in teacher behavior;

provide objective and fair feedback based upon agreed standards for teacher appraisal;

review new curriculum developments in other districts and agencies, apply these for use in the district only when they are appropriately remodified to fit in with the existing district philosophy and standing curriculum practices;

involve teacher committees and provide feedback from classroom try-outs and demonstration of proposed new curriculum units;

act as a clearinghouse for the relocation of teachers to expedite new attempts at team teaching, interschool observation by other teachers, the hiring of substitutes for released time activities, and committee curriculum writing;

adopt from the literature validation designs and standards for new curriculum practices;

assess and evaluate the validation or standardization offered by commercial firms for their "packaged curriculum materials";

propose and refine standards for final curriculum adoption;

such standards must include objective measurement of the effectiveness of a given body of content as gauged by changed student behavior.

4. *Teachers*

participate in the dynamic redefinition of the teaching act;

pay special attention to the preparation of the teachers;

suggest objective methods for the measurement of the effect of teacher behavior upon students;

contribute items for curriculum building, student rating, and self-evaluation;

suggest and try out novel adaptations of curriculum;

write, for practical everyday use, daily lesson plans;

participate in group seminar activities across subject matter boundaries for purposes of content articulation;

emphasize broad generalizations in the curriculum which cut across subject matter lines;

keep daily records of apparent changes in student behavior, attitudes, manifest skills, and knowledge;

periodically reassess their entire approach to their subject by a thorough analysis of the feedback from the counseling program bearing upon student feelings, changes in students, such as psychometric or achievement testing results;

serve on curriculum development committees, in-service training activities;

apply group process in actual student seminars.

The incorporation of a uniform code of ethical standards is of strategic importance to a successful program. This is because new roles and tasks will have to be assumed by teachers, counselors, psychologists, and others without infringing upon existing legal, moral, ethical, or professional standards. This may not seem like an easy marriage of interprofessional ethics at first. Some professions, as for example psychologists, have developed highly-specialized standards for ethical behavior, while other professional groups, as teachers, have evolved, at best, only vague statements of their general ethical purposes.

Some of the ethical standards of psychologists, such as public responsibility, client relationships, standards in teaching, standards in research, and standards in professional relationships, may have direct applicability to our discussion of interprofessional ethical relationships.[2] The teacher in actuality may be a psychologist; thus, many of the standards are written in such a way as to have direct applicability for the teaching profession. The role of the psychologist, as teacher, is clearly reflected in the following statements of ethical standards: "As a teacher, the psychologist should recognize his affiliation not only with the profession of psychology but also with the profession of teaching (Principle 1.11-2) . . . the psychologist's ultimate allegiance is to society . . . the welfare of the profession . . . is clearly subordinate to the welfare of the public. (Principle 1.12-1)"[3]

Listed below are selected statements of ethical standards of psychologists which seem to have particular appropriateness for guidelines in the development of ethical standards for professional participants in counseling-instructional programs for the gifted:

(Principle 1.32-1): A psychologist should insist on highest ethical standards and professional competence in persons with whom he is directly associated.

(Principle 1.42-4): An author of books, tests, and similar materials published or distributed by an organization should take every precaution to insure that the organization representing him adheres to the spirit of these principles in its promotional activities.

(Principle 2.12-1): The psychologist should refuse to suggest, support, or condone unwarranted assumptions, invalid applications or unjustified conclusions in the use of psychological instruments or techniques.

(Principle 2.16-1): When a psychologist becomes aware of practices likely to result in the offering of inferior professional work . . . he should exert what influence he can to rectify the situation.

(Principle 2.21-1): A cardinal obligation of the . . . psychologist is to respect the integrity and protect the welfare of the person with whom he is working.

(Principle 2.22-3): The psychologist should not guarantee easy solutions or favorable outcomes as a result of his work.

(Principle 2.32-1): Psychological information, such as the results of tests . . . should be given to a client in a manner likely to be instructive in his effort to solve his problem.

(Principle 3.11-1): The teacher . . . should respect the right of the student to maintain his privacy.

(Principle 3.12-2): A teacher (the standards refer to teachers of psychology) who becomes aware of an adjustment problem in a student . . . should assist the student to find . . . help if it is available.

(Principle 3.13-2): Evaluative data and judgments concerning students . . . should be shared only with persons who need and will use them in confidence, and for professional purposes.

---

[2] Discussion which follows will be based upon *Ethical Standards of Psychologists*, Washington, D.C., The American Psychological Association, 1333 Sixteenth Street, N.W., Washington 6, D.C., 1953.
[3] *Ibid*, pp. 4-7.

(Principle 3.32-4): A teacher is expected to instruct his students in the content of the course rather than the specific items which happen to be included in a test instructed to measure mastery of the course content.

(Principle 3.24-1): Students should be admitted to courses, and permitted to continue study in a field, only if there is good reason for believing that they have legitimate reasons for taking the course, that they have the theoretical and technical background needed, and that they are likely not to misuse what they learn.

(Principle 4.11-1): The psychologist is responsible within the limits of his knowledge, competence, and facilities for planning his research in such a way as to minimize the possibility that his findings will be misleading.

(Principle 5.11-1): Administrators are expected to take or be given credit for authorship of professional reports only when they have made significant contributions to the conduct of the research or to the writing of the report.

(Principle 5.12-1): Credit should be assigned to all those who have contributed to a publication, in proportion to their contributions, and only to these. . . .

(Principle 5.41-1): Tests and diagnostic aids should be released only to persons who can demonstrate that they have the knowledge and skill necessary for their effective use and interpretation. . . .

(Principle 6.11-2): A psychologist's professional relationships involve multiple loyalties: to society, to his client, department, supervisor, and colleague. When there is a conflict among professional workers, the psychologist should be concerned primarily for the welfare of the client involved and only secondary with the interests of his own professional group.

(Principle 6.11-3): The psychologist should not attempt to gain favor by making personal comparisons damaging to colleagues nor should he belittle the services of ethical professional workers.

(Principle 6.12-1): As a matter of professional courtesy, a psychologist who plans to initiate professional activity likely to encroach upon a recognized field of work of a colleague in the same institution is expected to consult with his colleague before proceeding.

(Principle 6.12-2): A psychologist in a school, college, or university should be free to help students in areas in which he is competent. However, professional courtesy suggests that in offering assistance outside his assigned area, he should be careful not to interfere with the instruction or research of another staff member.

(Principle 6.12-3): A psychologist who wishes to conduct activities in an organization in which he is not connected should, as a matter of courtesy, clear not only with the head of the organization, but with all the officials immediately concerned before beginning his work.

It can be seen, just by inspecting a code of ethics from one of the professions involved, that the design of an overall code of ethics for the entire school staff will not be an easy job. It is suggested that the task of writing an operational code of ethics for all the staff members involved in the school district's counseling and instructional programs should proceed as follows:

1. Each professional role must be described in entirety and detail; a separate list of all of those common tasks which must be participated in

by staff members with different preparations and experience should be drawn up.

2. A deliberate search for duplication, conflict, or ill-defined roles should be made; the search for conflict should involve a thorough study of all existing ethical codes from the separate professions involved; the policies and practices of the local, state, or national jurisdictional agency should follow.

3. The district can then draw up its own operational code of ethics including a specific description of the roles and tasks performed by various professional workers and common tasks to be contributed to and participated in by all staff members.

The code of ethics should include standards for confidentiality. The private lives of students must be protected. The discussion of problems, conflicts, or controversies brought up in group counseling sessions should be confidential and discussed with teachers only in general terms. Counselors and psychologists, particularly, should keep confidential any criticisms and inappropriate or false evaluations of teachers made by those unqualified to do so. In the final analysis, professional level conduct can only be accomplished through continual upgrading of professional preparation and accompanying growth in mutual respect among teachers, psychologists, and counselors. Once teachers and counselors become convinced of their own rights and privileges to privacy and objective evaluation, the program should be successful.

There is no rigid design for the development of a code of ethics for a school district. The code of ethics will need to be specific to the school district designing a given program. However, the unique and common tasks shown in Table 29 infer underlying codes of ethical behavior. For example, the common tasks of developing research, standardizing instruments, rating students, or disseminating public information—all require special rules for conduct and communication.

Another sensitive area involving ethical concerns is that of professional evaluation. The clandestine way in which some teachers are "evaluated" is apocryphal. Professional staffs will need to assume that individual members of their team possess minimum qualifications and are capable of behavioral change. It is upon this assumption of behavioral change that an ethical design for evaluation can be constructed. It is likely that teachers in an actual school setting would expose themselves to objective observation by their peers providing such observations and consequent conferences were confidential and not used for "professional growth or pay increments." Clear demarcations will need to be made between competitive evaluations for economic gain, and professional growth evaluations for self-improvement.

In summary, if programs for the gifted are to function, teachers and counselors alike must restudy their respective educational roles and readjust to the new realities of the teaching-learning system made possible by the application of learning theory and personality development. Teachers can no longer avoid the responsibility for understanding the full-range of behavior and maturity. Counselors cannot avoid the responsibility for providing meaningful feedback to teachers and counseling services for students which enhance efficient teaching-learning relationships. It is inevitable that roles must change. New responsibilities necessitate sharing common ethical systems.

SPECIAL PREPARATIONS FOR TEACHERS OF THE GIFTED

Special educational programs for gifted students have grown rapidly over the past ten years. In California alone, over one hundred thousand elementary and secondary students are in such special programs for all or part of their school day. One of the most commonly offered program prototypes is that of special classes for the gifted which requires a full-time teacher with appropriate teaching skills and a wide background of general knowledge.

However, state education agencies have not constructed specific credential requirements for teachers of the gifted in spite of the fact that it has been amply demonstrated that such teachers need to possess special preparation and characteristics, skills, and knowledge. The general characteristics of current teachers of the gifted, some suggestions for teacher-training program possibilities, and a discussion of some special teacher preparation patterns will follow.

It has been estimated at the national level, that about two million students or 4 percent of the school population can be considered as "academically talented."[4] Since our national "talent pool" contains many other kinds of specific talents in addition to academic ones, the total number of students requiring special educational provisions must be far greater than the two million reported above.[5]

Approximately thirty states have assigned personnel for the development of such programs. A number of states, including California, Illinois, Minnesota, New York, and North Carolina, among others, have developed full-fledged programs for the special education of gifted students.[6]

In California alone, it is estimated that over four hundred special coordinators of programs for the gifted students currently work at the local

---

[4] Health, Education, and Welfare Indicators. Education for the Gifted. April, 1964. Washington, Superintendent of Documents, U.S. Government Printing Office.

[5] *Ibid*, p. XXVII.

[6] Personnel and Activities for Talent Development, 1964. U.S. Department of Health, Education and Welfare, Office of Education Publication OE-35054. Washington, Superintendent of Documents, U.S. Printing Office.

school district level. More than 5,500 teachers are now specifically assigned to work exclusively with groups of gifted students in California. Local districts are asking for criteria for teacher selection. While a number of higher educational institutions have already proposed possible teacher education majors or minors in the area of the gifted child, no general pattern has yet emerged. Consequently, teachers must obtain special preparation on a "catch as catch can" basis.

Special programs for gifted students are complex. Such programs need to be well planned and based upon outcomes reported in a vast pool of current informational sources. Teachers in this field must be acquainted with the literature and be able to translate research findings into practical program design. In review, commonly offered special program designs for gifted students which teachers must be familiar with include

1. *Special Grouping*
   Special classes, total segregation of the gifted
   Cluster grouping of gifted in classrooms with high achievers
   Homogeneous grouping of all students by IQ cutoff points

2. *Enrichment in the Regular Classroom*
   Special student projects in selected subject matter disciplines
   Supplemental learning kits, reading libraries, programmed materials, audiovisual laboratories
   Enrichment of the curriculum by special subjects not ordinarily offered, such as fine arts in the elementary school
   Teacher specialists exchange presentations (e.g. "team-teaching")
   Group work or seminar activities in the classroom
   Large group activities for educational TV, lectures, or political events
   Field trip activities, camps, community involvement

3. *Advanced developmental placement or acceleration*
   Advanced classes in subject matter disciplines
   Ungraded or multigraded classrooms
   Summer school acceleration programs
   Early entrance to kindergarten or the first grade
   Combined grades with reconstructed and accelerated curriculum
   "High ceiling" curriculum with student remaining at chronological grade level
   Simple double promotion
   Advanced placement to college

4. *Special settings, tutoring, or counseling*
   Group counseling for commonly-shared problems

>Integration of guidance services with instruction, such as special seminar activities
>
>Special seminars outside of the regular school day
>
>Individual tutoring by subject matter involving resource teachers, experts, or older students
>
>Travel, including foreign and domestic trips and student exchanges

Before the teacher can assign the gifted student to an appropriate educational program, he must understand the student's learning needs as well as his developmental background. Therefore, the prospective teacher of the gifted must have a thorough understanding of the characteristics of gifted children as well as identification techniques and procedures. The rationale, definitions, and purpose for selection of the gifted child for special education programs need to be understood. The teacher needs to understand the procedures for certification and placement of the gifted student into an appropriate educational program. Also, the teacher needs tools of assessment with which to make evaluations of students, given program prototypes, and themselves.

While most of the existing special educational programs for talented students emphasize purely academic content, it is known that gifted students may actually require new kinds of curriculum design for their special needs. Such special qualities as intellectual curiosity, fluency of ideas, originality, independence of thought, or conceptual elaboration will require a qualitatively different curriculum to challenge and satisfy the student. Therefore, the prospective teacher will need to be familiar with modern advances in learning theory and evolve a particular approach to curriculum construction of his own.

Unfortunately, most of our gifted teachers appear to migrate toward the higher educational levels.[7] In fact, approximately half of Ginzberg's sample went into college teaching with research; about half of this group entered into the humanities and social sciences indicating no particular bias for the physical sciences.[8] We will need to lure more intellectual teachers into elementary and secondary school settings.

Margaret Horton of the Escondido Union Elementary School District has carefully analyzed the current literature in order to derive a list of definitive characteristics describing the teacher of the gifted student.[9] Horton discovered that more than thirty characteristics were listed in the various studies but these seemed to fall into four broad categories including in-

---

[7] Ginzberg, Eli, and John, Herma: *Talent and Performance.* New York, Columbia, 1964.

[8] *Ibid*, p. 45.

[9] Horton, Margaret: Special Report to MAL Administrative Committee Selecting Teachers for More Able Learners. Unpublished mimeographed paper, Escondido Union School District, Escondido, California.

tellectual traits, personality traits, teaching techniques, and education or general knowledge. Horton analyzed the research reported by Brumbaugh, Conant, Cruickshank, Davis, Dunlap, Fliegler, Newland, Strang, Witty, and Worchester, among others.

> Horton found that among the intellectual traits, those most frequently mentioned were curiosity, intellectual agility, high intellectual potential as indicated by intelligence test scores, and intellectually wide interests.
>
> Among the personality traits most mentioned to describe the teacher of the gifted child were patience, sense of humor, firmness, fairness, enjoyment of teaching, emotional security, high energy level, interest in pupil problems, good disposition, consistent behavior, and pleasing personal appearance and personality.
>
> As concerns teaching techniques, teachers of the gifted were most likely to possess the following: ability to establish social responsibility in students, ability to foster group discussion, ability to develop a classroom atmosphere conducive to good mental health, a tendency to make clear assignments and not interrupt students once they have commenced, more than two years' successful teaching experience, attitudes which reflect cooperative and democratic outlooks, flexibility, tendency to foster creativity, ingenuity in suggesting projects and materials, and skill in teaching with a problem-solving approach.
>
> Teachers of the gifted were ordinarily reported to have an educational background which included broad cultural exposure, specialized subject matter knowledge, knowledge of twentieth century research, and an understanding of the conceptualization process.

Summarizing from correspondence and personal contact with many actual programs, the characteristics of teachers assigned to gifted child classrooms tend to include the following:

1. They possess a high level of enthusiasm.
2. They have demonstrated an ability to perform individual research and may have published articles or other literary products.
3. They have demonstrated interest in intellectual pursuits as opposed to other activities.
4. They demonstrate diversified value patterns with several intense interest areas pursued in considerable depth through hobbies or other activities.
5. They have a tolerance for ambiguity.
6. They are flexible and adaptive.
7. They are inquisitive and tenacious when pursuing the solution to an unsolved problem.
8. They are in sympathy with gifted human beings and are capable of empathizing with the needs of the gifted child.

In 1964, French surveyed colleges throughout the nation and found that only sixty-four institutions offered course work in the area of the gifted child.[10] The majority of these institutions offered only one course with a title derived from the following: "Education of Gifted Children." French found that when one course was offered, it centered around the dual theme of education and psychology of gifted children. When a second course was offered, it was either a workshop or a course in curriculum and materials development. In short, instruction in the area of the gifted child was divided between characteristics and curriculum development. Few institutions offered more than two courses. Since 1965, several universities have started to offer master's and doctoral degree programs in gifted children education (e.g. University of California at Los Angeles, University of Illinois, University of Southern California).

The Professional Standards Committee of the Council for Exceptional Children has suggested professional standards for both college teachers and teacher candidates preparing to teach gifted children. These standards, somewhat edited, appear below:[11]

> At present, most of the efforts toward improved teaching for the gifted consist of one or two courses at an institution for teacher education, summer courses and workshops, and brief in-service courses. Very few institutions have developed a carefully planned program of studies. Any such program should develop within certain minimal conditions which are necessary to its success.

> *Faculty (College Level)*

> General faculty support and understanding are necessary to the success of any special program, including programs for the preparation of teachers of the gifted. Although one person should be directly responsible, the program should be viewed as multidisciplinary in nature and should recognize and encourage contributions from persons outside the college or university community as well.

> Faculty within the institution should support the four conditions listed below as necessary to the success of a teacher education program for the gifted. Such support is particularly vital within the teacher education faculty itself. There should be

> 1. knowledge of and sensitivity to the unique characteristics of the gifted;

> 2. selection of teacher candidates who demonstrate superior knowledge and ability and who understand the significance of differential capacities in the gifted;

> 3. access to demonstration facilities which provide opportunity for the gifted to learn without unwarranted restrictions, and thus provide for the student trainees an opportunity to observe and understand how the gifted can function when given sufficient and appropriate opportunities;

---

[10] French, Joseph: Where and How Are Teachers of the Gifted Trained? Presentation delivered at the 43rd Annual Convention of the Council for Exceptional Children, Thursday, April 22, 1965.

[11] Professional Standards Committee of the Council for Exceptional Children. Professional Standards for Personnel in the Education of Exceptional Children. *Professional Standards Project Report,* pp. 27-30, The Council for Exceptional Children, National Education Association, 1201 Sixteenth Street, N.W., Washington, D.C., 1967.

4. a learning climate within the college or university which exemplifies that which is appropriate for learning by the gifted, including faculty members actively demonstrating those qualities which are basic to success in teaching the gifted; an environment which provides open opportunities for learning; individually planned programs which are directed toward preparing candidates for the specific task of providing differential education for the gifted; flexible means for evaluation to determine completion of course requirements; opportunities for independent study, demonstration, participation in teaching and research, discussion of issues, and inquiry. . . .

Programs

Assuming that these essential conditions are met, the following more specific provisions should be made to assure an appropriate program of studies.

1. Time and responsibility for program planning and development should be assigned to one person on the faculty. Additional persons will be involved in teaching, but the coordination of responsibility should be specifically delegated. This person should have achieved recognition in the field of the gifted and should have a doctoral degree, except in rare circumstances where the individual has achieved marked recognition in the field.

2. Facilities which provide opportunities for students to work with gifted pupils in varied arrangements should be readily assessible. These facilities should provide means for observation, demonstration, and participation with gifted students as well as for student teaching. Facilities should allow for the complete study of gifted individuals and should center on differentiated curriculum and varied arrangements designed to meet the needs of students with varying talents and abilities rather than on predominantly administrative arrangements. Students should be given rich opportunities for contacts with personnel in and out of school who contribute directly to the education of the gifted and in many ways should be made aware of flexible, diverse approaches which may be necessary in planning appropriate educational experiences for the gifted.

Selection of Candidates

Criteria for identification of promising teacher candidates should be established. These criteria should be based on specific standards, such as assured performance at or beyond specific levels on graduate aptitude and achievement tests, criteria established through research, and demonstrated interest in teaching the gifted. Early identification and orientation of students may occur through course-work taken at undergraduate and graduate levels. Students showing promise should be encouraged toward further study.

Areas of Professional Competence

The teacher-to-be should approach his studies through independent inquiry and research insofar as possible. He should have opportunities in his program to study some topics in great depth, much as the gifted person whom he teaches would approach such study. Specialized work, predicated on the assumption that the student has a sound general background in behavioral sciences, child development, application of learning theory in relation to the gifted, and a consumer's understanding of statistics and research methodology, should be planned individually on the basis of need.

The student should have an understanding of the meaning of exceptionality, not only in relation to the gifted but in relation to all children. This understanding should emanate from the study of the literature, case studies, practicum experiences, knowledge of the concepts in measurement of abilities, and demonstrations.

The student should possess a commitment to differential education for the gifted derived from a study of the literature dealing with the historical roots and precedents of educational efforts for the gifted, the psychology and needs of the gifted, and study in depth of the growth and development of the gifted.

Advanced Preparation

In all cases, advanced preparation for work with the gifted should be based upon the needs of the candidates. Programs for counselors, administrators, and supervisory personnel will require special provisions but should be based upon the competencies delineated in the section above. Special courses and workshops should be planned for community resource personnel. Attention in programs for specialists should be given also to promising innovations, program improvement, and change.

It has been shown that many professionals have thought through the problem of preparing teachers to instruct gifted students. Generalizing from the sources tapped, the following special preparation pattern might be considered:

1. The prospective teacher trainee in the area of gifted child education ought to provide evidence of superior academic or honors work in general education courses including high school work.

2. A general level of high scholastic competency should also be demonstrated by high entrance test performance at the college level.

3. It is logical to presume that candidates for teachers of the gifted ought to be selected from the upper half of the teacher trainee population.

4. Such teachers ought to obtain broad subject matter preparation at the baccalaureate level. A "liberal arts" oriented curriculum might be advisable at the baccalaureate level. Most successful teachers of gifted children are found to possess major areas of preparation in several academic subject matter fields rather than the usual single preparation.

5. Such candidates usually integrate their knowledge of various subject matter fields into unified understandings of their life and times.

6. At the master's degree level, specialized course work ought to be designed including the following: the psychology and characteristics of gifted children; curriculum development and models; research on the gifted child; the techniques of conducting research; practicum in teaching gifted students; literary techniques; modern learning theory; tests and measurements; statistics; and, personality theory as related to the gifted human being.

The creation of a specialized preparation major area in the education of the gifted child, which could be applied as a major or a minor toward a standard teaching credential, should be considered by colleges. The prescription of a sequence of course work, such as that outlined above, could be used. In addition, a system of examinations might be developed which could substitute for any or all of the professional courses in the curriculum. For example, highly intelligent candidates might possess many of the skill areas, such as statistics, without taking formal course work. While a coherent national pattern is being developed for the preparation of teachers of the gifted, summer workshops and assorted practicum experiences may substitute for the more specific course work which would be included in a formal teaching major.

The possibilities for summer workshop opportunities for teachers of the gifted seem especially fruitful. Many teachers are now called upon to instruct gifted children without any special preparation. During an intensive summer workshop program, lasting four to six weeks and held simultaneously with special classes for gifted children, diversified program designs, methodologies, and techniques can be demonstrated and observed. Two basic possibilities for the summer workshop program have emerged in California. One prototype, that developed by California Project Talent in conjunction with Sacramento State College, emphasized the demonstration of differential program possibilities for gifted children in acceleration, enrichment, special classes, and counseling during the summer. Counselors, teachers and administrators can simultaneously attend and benefit from such a workshop. Psychologists and counselors can concentrate upon identification, case study techniques, follow-up, and classroom observation of children in special educational settings. Teachers and curriculum consultants can study the various methodologies called for in differential program designs. During the summer experience they can actually plan their own district's program for the coming fall. Administrators can study broad program designs as well as the organizational and evaluative responsibilities for programs.

Another summer workshop possibility, as exemplified by that developed by Dr. K. A. Martyn, California State College at Los Angeles, seeks to "provide the teacher with an opportunity to increase his understanding and knowledge . . . of gifted children . . . provide a clinical or laboratory setting for the teacher to try out or test the particular methods and materials . . . provide an opportunity for the teacher to develop appropriate curriculum materials for gifted children." Such a teacher-training program leaves the selection of specific courses up to the particular teacher candidate. It becomes possible for a teacher candidate to enroll in theoretical courses, such as the "nature of gifted children," and also in courses designed to enrich the experience and background of the teacher such as advanced geography, history, or mathematics.

In summary, we should develop meaningful teacher-training programs for teachers of gifted children. Perhaps we might begin by encouraging academically able teacher trainees to embark upon specialized graduate level programs emphasizing the characteristics and educational needs of gifted children. Also, colleges might try out various patterns for the preparation of such specialist teachers. Our ultimate goal ought to be the creation of a cadre of specially prepared teachers who will be capable of formulating, instructing, and evaluating special educational programs for gifted children and youth. Ultimately, this group of professional workers ought to provide leadership for the upgrading of the general teaching curriculum. Such specially trained teachers will form the talent pool from which needed supervisory and administrative positions in the area of the education of the gifted can be drawn.

Chapter 10

STRATEGIES FOR PROGRAM DEVELOPMENT AND ADMINISTRATION

A BEWILDERING array of variables faces the educator planning special programs for gifted students. There are different administrative plans and policies to be sorted out. The general curriculum has to be analyzed in terms of its usefulness for the gifted. The suitability of existing classrooms and equipment for the advanced needs of the gifted has to be assessed. Inventories should be made of the availability of teachers with broad preparation backgrounds. The larger community should be studied as a cultural environment and exploited accordingly. Someone has to coordinate all of these variables and build an integrated, logical, and total education program out of the pieces. But, where does he begin? What are some of the basic elements of a model program for the gifted?

At the core of special programs for the gifted is subject matter content. This content should differ in quantity, quality, sequence, and level from typical curriculum. The quantity of knowledge, details, and embellishments presented in a given subject area will be greater because the gifted tend to possess those qualities of learning capability and motivation which demand greater content coverage.

Since the gifted demonstrate the use of higher mental operations much earlier than others, their curriculum should contain problem-solving, logical systems and methodological content from the outset. Typical curriculum is based on assumptions made by observing normal children. Hence, much content is envisioned as memory units which are repeated in logical sequences until the child demonstrates a capability to recall and systematically relate the knowledge learned to prior knowledge and future situations.

The gifted do not rely on memory but utilize their problem-solving faculties to generate knowledge. This phenomenon may have led ancient philosophers (e.g. Plato) to conclude that men were born with "ideal knowledges" already imprinted in their minds. Observing the nimble mental operations of a gifted child, as manifested by his rapid solution of problems posed to him, might lead the observer to conclude that the child possessed prior knowledge. This is probably not the case. Careful analysis of the situation will usually reveal the use of higher level mental operations toward the solution of problems posed. Instead of searching for precedent or memorized solutions, the gifted child will apply reasoning. Specifically, the curriculum for the gifted should contain qualitatively different content calling for the use of higher level mental operations.

Thus, the program planner should consider the variety of mental operations used by the gifted child before subject matter content is sequenced. For example, the postponement of experimental methods or higher mathematical computations until high school is clearly contraindicated for the gifted. When it is said that the "gifted frequently go unchallenged," we do not mean that he lacks work to do but rather that he is not allowed to use his mind to full advantage.

In Chapter 5, it was shown that the gifted student desires a variety of qualitatively different content. At the elementary level, he wants knowledge to understand science, sex, or literature. At the secondary level, his inquiring mind leads him to wonder about psychological, economic, or intercultural relationships. For the specifically gifted musician or dancer, the situation is further complicated by the necessity for intense practice and specialization at an early age. The overall program of the school must reflect these diverse student needs. While "core programs" may be planned for the mastery of basic skills and general cultural education, enough flexibility must be built into the program to allow for early specialization at one extreme, to prolonged general education at the other extreme.

As we study existing programs, it is possible to discriminate among three main administrative approaches (or prototypes):

1. *The Acceleration Model.* Here the key ingredient is access to advanced content. The child may be physically placed with older groups or remain with his peers. Traditional or typical content is ordinarily used in this model. Little new content is produced. The main advantage of this model is the preparation of the gifted for productivity earlier in life.

2. *The Enrichment Model.* Relying on the typical curriculum as a skeletal structure, the main thrust of enrichment programs is supplementation. The supplemental content may take one of two main forms: (1) additive knowledge which embellishes upon basic concepts (so-called horizontal enrichment) or (2) qualitatively different or advanced topics not ordinarily dealt with at a given grade level (so-called vertical enrichment). This model represents the only compromise between general and special education.

3. *The Special Settings Model.* Special classes, individual tutoring or foreign schooling may be designed to educate the student uniquely. Radically new methods, contents, sequences of subjects, or levels of learning may be introduced. Special settings may range from the starkly traditional (e.g. foreign school) to the wildly experimental (e.g. self-programming). This is the only model capable of accommodating totally different curriculum expressly designed for the gifted.

The teacher, along with his ancillary services (e.g. school psychologist, curriculum specialist), is the focal point for the programming of students through an appropriate sequence of learning activities and experiences. In order to program students with diverse abilities through planned episodes of learning, the teacher must perceive new roles for himself. He becomes an educational diagnostician who therefore teaches by prescription. Evaluation of learning outcomes is his direct responsibility. Only by directly measuring the effectiveness of his teaching and the efficiency of the student's output can the teacher modify educational prescriptions.

The teacher must manipulate concrete and abstract variables in this process called "prescriptive teaching." The entire process of the "teaching-learning system" may be understood in terms of the following paradigm:

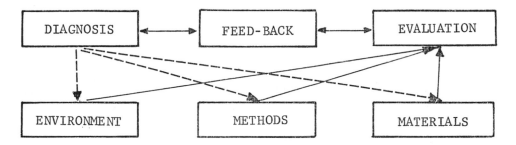

The teacher first undertakes a complete diagnosis of the student's needs. Specific environments, techniques (methods), and materials (books, programmed learning materials, aids, etc.) are then prescribed and programmed. Each of these variables can be measured in terms of their contributions to effective learning. Evaluation results in modifications of a logical cycle of diagnosis—prescription—and measurement of outcomes.

Most educational policy is based upon unilateral program choices (e.g. acceleration versus enrichment) or monolithic use of media. A more eclectic position is possible. School districts might promote differential plans for education and support multidimensional media for teaching. Being spectacular in their differences, the gifted require flexible and varied program frameworks. Possibilities for acceleration, enrichment, and special settings can coexist. Books, television, programmed materials, or laboratory experience may be individually prescribed irrespective of the overall program prototype a student happens to be enrolled in.

In order to pull all of the aforementioned variables together into coherent and operable total education programs, two remaining conditions must be accounted for:

1. Educators must incorporate technological and logistical changes into their overall (strategic) planning. For example, new data processing techniques open avenues for such innovations as daily individualized reading-programs, daily evaluations with immediate feedback, or simulated teaching experiments which avoid mistakes with children. The dif-

ferential program concept does not lend itself to fixed settings. Self-contained classrooms are obsolete. Buildings must be opened; classroom space should be viewed as plastic.

2. Teachers do not work alone. They are members of teams of specialists. Some excel in given subject matters, others manipulate media well, still others easily manage changing settings (e.g. classroom rearrangement, grouping individually programmed instruction). As new curriculums are constructed for the gifted, it must be assumed that they will be implemented by teams of teacher specialists working in concert.

In connection with teachers, professional specialists must be available as resources for curriculum planning, evaluation experts and educational "engineers." Hence, a large part of administrative planning must be devoted to programming special consultants in such a manner as to maximize overall program development.

DIFFERENTIAL EDUCATION PROGRAMS

Ideally, thoroughly individualized academic programs, based upon a definite evaluation of the student's learning potential, should be designed for every pupil. Short of this ideal, differential programming offers a compromise between mass homogenized education and individual instruction. When a school district establishes a slate of different program possibilities for talented pupils, they significantly increase the possibility for placing each pupil into a program sequence best suited to develop his individual talents.

School district personnel planning differential programs should discuss disparate educational philosophies. Monolithic philosophies must be discarded since such philosophies would preclude alternative practices for the establishment of programs with multitudinal objectives. The philosophy of education of such a district is eclectic, experimental, dynamic, and free.

The professional attitudes of participating school personnel are crucial. Educators must act effectively, sometimes aggressively, rather than reacting to educational needs. Differentiated program possibilities for able and talented youngsters must be conceived as their basic program; supplemental or additive program patchworks may only serve the purpose of mediocrity.

The variables which must be taken into account when planning differential programs are extensive. Vast individual differences in achievement, potentiality, and creativity among students must be accommodated. In order to expedite the appropriate placement of students into suitable educational programs, teachers may have to call upon other professionals such as school psychologists or subject matter experts from the community. In implementing a slate of differential program possibilities across grade levels, teachers will find that the old-fashioned notion of a "self-contained educational environment" is no longer valid. The variables are simply too complex to be dealt with by one teacher in a single educational setting utilizing sparse educational tools and techniques. Instead, the modern teacher may have to reassess the entire teaching-learning system. The teacher will probably discover that complex modern educational demands require a more systematized and specialized teaching episode.

Some of the new roles that the modern teacher must fulfill include those of

1. educational diagnostician and learning theorist;
2. environmental manipulator with expertise in school planning, classroom setup, community resources utilization and the like;
3. content and educational materials programmer;
4. educational technician with current knowledge of modern educational machines, hardware, and sundry materials; and
5. educational evaluator, experimenter, and program modifier.

It may be that the profession will choose in the next few decades to specialize according to a breakdown of job tasks such as that outlined just above. It is certain that a single individual could not master nor apply all of the implied skills made by the demands of the modern student. Therefore, if the profession does not specialize, it may need to look at such interim techniques as team teaching or the utilization of extraprofessional technicians and experts.

Perhaps the key role of the emerging modern teacher is that of edcational programmer. In order to program students through appropriate subject matter content according to their specific individual learning needs, the teacher must first view himself as an educational methodologist. The particular and unique teaching strategies and tactics adopted by the teacher will necessitate or imply the adoption of synchronized learning environments and teaching aids. Moreover, the specialized program of evaluation decided upon will be dependent upon the predictability or divergency of the educational methodology applied. For example, traditional methodologies calling for highly predictable amounts of learning input such as achievement lend themselves to traditional, even stereotyped, methods of evaluation. Newer methodologies advocating the development of higher level mental functions, such as analysis of data or the maturity of the individual toward a codified system of values, will require entirely novel methods of evaluation which will have to be designed concomitantly with the educational program itself.

In order to form a philosophical foundation for differential programming, we need to recapitulate the rationale for special programs for gifted and talented students. Some of the major purposes for establishing such special programs include the following:

1. to promote intellectual attainment and excellence; to utilize the

full spectrum of American talent for the betterment of American society;

2. to provide equal opportunity for each talented individual in terms of his unique potentialities;

3. to generate cultural, scientific, and literary innovation; research and upgrading of the society at large;

4. to reaffirm the main tenets of Western Civilization; to reaffirm the fundamental search for knowledge and truth; to support Western Man's social concept of cultural plurality;

5. to destroy indigenous American anti-intellectualism and open the way for a genuine American renaissance;

6. to generate our own breed of American intellectuals thereby reducing our dependence upon the importation of foreign intellectuals; and

7. to stimulate the democratic process of social mobility by helping our indigenous talented individuals within minority and culturally deprived groups to develop to their full potential and contribute to the betterment of their subsocietal groups.

In order to conform to such a diverse grouping of philosophical demands, schools will need to speculate about educational alternatives. The luxury of maintaining dogmatic, rigid, or monolithic philosophies of education is a thing of the past. Since we are profoundly aware of the fantastic diversity represented by the personalities of men, we can no longer pontificate with assurity that any single educational goal is justifiable. We must now provide multiple objective possibilities for the varied needs and demands of our students.

"Differential Programming" might be defined as "the establishment of varied program patterns and multiple subject matter content sequences within a single school district." Thus, a school district purporting to offer differential programming possibilities for students must be able to tolerate differing, even disparate, educational points of view. The traditional educational battles must be resolved and a number of cherished cliches discarded.

Arguments between proponents of the special class versus the heterogeneous class will no longer have appropriateness or meaning since all program possibilities must be tried or offered. Differential programming should offer an objective frame of reference for open-minded educators. The main concern of educators will shift from parochial concerns to more valid considerations of real student needs. The questions teachers will ask should include such considerations as What is best for the student in terms of his unique developmental needs? rather than What particularistic educational philosophy do I adhere to?

Existing philosophies of education have a tendency to focus upon some single aspect of the teaching-learning system rather than attempting to encompass all of the aspects of the complex teacher-learner-environment-complex.

Listed below are five educational foci of existing educational theory and practice:

1. *Focus on Content.* Many educators view all learning in concrete terms. They imagine that the outcomes of education can be inventoried in quantitative terms. They use such adjectives as "basic, fundamental, subject matter oriented, or skills" to describe their major concerns. Unfortunately, there may be some tendency to disregard such important factors as the development of human values or the extent to which higher level mental functions accompany the mere acquisition of knowledge.

2. *Focus on Method.* Other educators emphasize teaching methodologies and techniques. In its pure form "methodological teaching" can be as ludicrous as pure "content teaching." We are able to find some modern programs which train children to apply esoteric systems of logic to non-existent problems. A highly-gifted sixth grade boy recently summarized this problem when he said, "Our program in mathematical logic really has no practical application, it is a kind of mental masturbation."

3. *Focus on Educational Setting.* A smaller group of educators, including mostly school administrators or Board of Education members, tend to place inordinate reliance upon the physical school setting for accomplishing the ends of learning. While the classroom structure with its array of equipment constitutes an indisputable ingredient in the overall functioning of the teaching-learning system, yet, the mere presence of expensive school buildings and equipment cannot be shown to culminate in desired outcomes by themselves. If this were the case, the ancient buildings of our venerable institutions could not result in the high level educational outcomes that can be demonstrated for them.

4. *Focus on Materials.* Another group of educators actively promotes the use of prepared materials, hardware, kits, and other materials as a sort of curriculum in and of themselves. Of course, commercial firms are tending to exaggerate the usefulness of manufactured educational bric-a-brac as the sole ingredient in educational programming. Obviously, educational materials must be related, to the broader developmental demands of school curriculums. However, it is possible to view the educational aid, such as a subject matter learning kit, as the entire teaching process including implied methodology, teaching outcomes and mechanics of instruction.

5. *Education as an Application of Scientific Method.* A newer group of educational theorists and experimenters have received prominent publicity in professional journals and the press. Educational experimenta-

tion and innovation is spectacular since it is in stark contrast with the existing traditional educational programs. Recent attempts to classify educational goals, correlate educational programming with student outcomes, diagnosis of learning potential, or attempting to individually program each student through the use of computerized planning are all examples of this latest trend. It is with this scientific trend that a philosophy of differential programming must identify.

Some of the major goals of a working philosophy of differential programming would include the following:

1. to cultivate professional attitudes of objectivity, eclecticism, and freedom of investigation;

2. to withhold all judgment pending the collection of sufficiently reliable and valid evidence to warrant tentative conclusions about a person or program;

3. to emphasize program revision, modification, and longevity as opposed to professional faddism;

4. to individually weigh the importance of such factors as environment, methods, and use of materials for each separate education program;

5. to define all terminology precisely and to avoid ambiguous or misleading claims for programs;

6. to test every separable aspect of a new program with proper scientific and research methodologies and by utilizing adequate control groups and to link the claims for a given program strictly to the experimental findings;

7. to adopt a code of ethics which clearly interprets teachers and experimenters prerogatives and the rights of pupils to such privileges as privacy;

8. to tolerate genuine differences of opinion while stimulating professional understanding of all of the programs set up by the district;

9. to encourage specialization of teachers by content and methodology while at the same time insisting upon completely open lines of communication and understanding;

10. to support administrative policies which attract only the highest level of teacher through adequate pay scales and definitions of professional preparation;

11. to supplement the acquisition of a highly-trained professional staff with in-service training programs designed to adapt teachers to the varying demands of separate differential programs;

12. to encourage the widest possible acculturation for students and teachers alike including all aspects of the interests and values of man with encouragement for individual productivity and creativity;

13. to maximize the possibilities for individual expression by teachers

or pupils by incorporating as much individual study and project time as possible into the educational programming possibilities; and

14. to base the entire development of differential programming upon scientific methodology and the application of experimental techniques for the validation of new programs and the continuing evaluation of existing programs.

School personnel willing to tolerate differential educational programs in their midsts should discipline themselves to avoid the acceptance of sweeping generalities or assumptions. For many decades, some educators have conducted the development of educational programs along the lines of religion. They have convinced, or cajoled as the case may be, their followers into accepting sweeping philosophical assertions. Once these assumptions were accepted (e.g. "education builds the total child" or "the child requires the nurturance of the self-contained classroom") little argumentation could follow without challenging a glittering generality which resembles such other cultural generalities as "momism" or patriotism. Reliance upon such sweeping generalities within education has proven to be dangerous. As a consequence, educational programs have been developed by "experts" working in the isolation of their particularistic philosophies. Their power has been based upon the extent to which they can convince followers of their worthiness, lovingness, and loyalty, rather than the utility of their philosophies.

To sum up the case, modern education must become "scientific education." That is to say, all outcomes of the educational process must lend themselves to measurement and evaluation. If a given projected goal of the educational process cannot be measured, or someone claims it cannot be measured, it ought to be thought of as suspect and analyzed to the point where it will lend itself to definition, analysis, and measurement. In short, modern education must adopt the philosophical frame of reference of empiricism.

The traditional steps of scientific or experimental method might be used as a format for the development of steps in the process of validating differential educational methods or programs. If an entire educational program is to be evaluated, it seems clear that the components of the program need to be separately defined, treated as hypotheses, and tested individually. It is unfortunate that many educational programs, which include a number of separable variables, are rejected by school districts due to the failure of only one or a few of the variables to result in positive findings. For example, if a newly-introduced subject matter unit into a regular classroom does not result in demonstrable achievement, such a lack of growth may be due to (1) the basic design of the program, (2) the teacher may have been ineffective, (3) the specially prepared materials may have been nondescript, (4) the educational setting may have been uncommonly distracting, or (5) the defect may be more subtle or complex and involve organizational failures. The point here is that each separate variable within a newly-designed educational program ought to be separately measured and evaluated.

Teachers willing to evaluate new programs, processes, and methods according to an experimental design might proceed according to the modified scientific method described below:

1. Upon recognition of an educational problem, define it in terms of probable causes, observed dimensions, and interrelatedness with other factors.

2. Utilizing the literature, personal experience, and other observed programs, speculate as to possible solutions to the problem at hand. View each educational program in terms of its separate qualities. Each of these separate qualities represents an hypothetical solution, remedy or variable. Each of these variables must be tested separately. For purposes of simplification, a four-way classification of variables might include *students* (as understood by systematic educational diagnosis); the *educational environment* or setting; the particular *educational method* or technique to be applied; and, the *specific educational mechanism*, aid, supply, equipment, or material to be used.

3. Design an operational plan to try out the newly-designed educational program in such a way that all of the variables may be separately evaluated in terms of their contribution or effectiveness. Utilize established research methods and incorporate sufficient controls necessary to arrive at unambiguous conclusions.

4. Collect data during the experimental trial of the program and its variables with utmost objectivity and impartiality. Apply predetermined systems of data collection being careful to avoid premature conclusions and ruling out systematic biases in the collection of the data. Employ methods of statistical collection and treatment of the data which are simple, convincing, accurate, and repeatable.

5. Test the various operational hypotheses entertained by analyzing the data collected according to accepted statistical tests.

6. Accept, modify, or reject each working component by formally stating it as an hypothesis. Do not generalize your findings to other variables nor to the program as a whole. Avoid rejecting or condemning similar classes of variables or programs in the same classification as the program under scrutiny. For example, many would-be researchers made sweeping statements rejecting acceleration as a method because a particular form of acceleration program may not have resulted in student growth.

Overall administrative plans for the validation of educational programs might be summarized in the following fashion:

Stage 1. Curricular and Program Development

Curriculum and materials are imported by benefiting from manufacturers, other studies and the retention of a research staff.

Materials are designed by careful application of the research findings and study of current trends.

Unique materials are written by consultants working directly in classrooms and benefiting from firsthand working tryouts of novel materials, methods, or settings.

Stage 2. Curricular and Program Tryout

Novel program is first considered "pilot program" and is tried out in a casual workaday basis in one or two classrooms being modified as the program evolves.

Reasonably finished program is experimentally tested in terms of all of its variables in the number of classrooms necessary to result in clear statistical findings.

The program is validated or rejected with carefully modified inclusion of questionable variables.

Final preparation of program occurs incorporating findings, modifications, and recommendations.

Stage 3. Program Export

Program is offered for export to other classrooms within the district.

New follow-up data is collected concerning the effects of the new program on other programs, teachers, and students; program is modified accordingly.

Program is offered for export in finished form to other school districts along with sufficient descriptions, guides, and recommendations for study of the program in new settings to afford the program good survival value outside the district of its invention.

As educators begin to focus upon measurable outcomes, it will be seen that the teaching-learning episode is really part of an interactional system of processes, events, and changes. Therefore, we have referred to the teaching process as the "teaching-learning system." This system may be viewed as analogous to such systems as the "nitrogen cycle" in nature. All of the forces and events which enter the system may be viewed as forces in equilibrium. As each force is changed, or new forces are introduced, the entire nature of the system may change. From this point of view, we are no longer able to view the student or the teacher, however individually im-

TABLE 30

THE TEACHING-LEARNING SYSTEM

	Diagnosis of students (Personal and social assessment of teachers and pupils)	Environments (School and community settings)	Methods (Teaching strategies, tactics, and techniques)	Mechanisms (Teacher aids, supplies and equipment)	Evaluation (Data feedback for program evaluation and modification)
Factors Variables:					
Explanations:	The teacher is an educational diagnostician using standardized measures to assess ability, readiness and motivation of students in order to select and administer appropriate techniques, educational settings and evaluations to generate optimal learning.	The teacher is an environmental manipulator selecting the physical setting most suitable for the kind of learning to take place. There are internal and external environments to be considered. Therefore, the teacher controls personal student factors such as attitude or physical well-being.	Methods should be based on valid theoretical frameworks describing learning and utilizing strategies which include definitive descriptions of daily tactics as well as overviews of total sequences and expected outcomes.	Materials, equipment, machines and fixtures must be selected, set up, and modified in such ways as to serve as efficient tools for the teaching strategy being applied. No mechanism is ever an end in itself; teaching devices always serve the ends of a given methodology.	Learning outcomes must be evaluated. A number of elements need to be separately assessed: the reliability of the original educational diagnosis; the suitability of the created environment; the efficiency of the techniques applied; and, the usefulness of the mechanisms used.
Factors the Teacher Controls:	Preparedness Insightfulness and Empathy Knowledge of tests and statistics	Structure of classroom: seating arrangements, study areas, settings Use of school facilities: library, labs Use of community: field trips, museums, industry	Professional education Skills as teachers Knowledge of learning theory Repertoire of techniques Time for preparation	Availability of materials pool Catalog study and ordering Experimental tryout Development of novel tools	Plans to try out, evaluate, techniques, materials Development of standardized case study forms, record keeping and reporting

Factors the Student Controls:	Aptitudes Attitude-Interest Emotional Condition Readiness	Psychological and social maturity Physical maturity Energy and endurance Past exposures	Openness to new approaches Sophistication Attention span Self-reliance Perception	Skill in use of tools Variability of interests Cognitive style	Fear or security in face of examination Use of information to modify his own plans, behavior and self-image
Aids:	Standardized Measures Examinations Sociograms Psychological Services	Different furniture set-ups Equipment placement Cultural embellishments Current displays	Curriculum Committee Resource Consultants Teacher teams Direct use of specialist Tutoring or counseling	Teaching machines Audiovisual aids Manufactured kits and materials Texts and resource books	Use of outside behavioral raters Teacher constructed examinations Standardized Achievement Tests Parent-teacher-pupil mutual ratings

portant they may be, as separate functioning entities. Even the word "teaching" becomes somewhat meaningless when viewed in isolation. "Teaching" may be someone talking in a social vacuum. The physical features of the teaching act must be directly compared with the resultant outcomes in student behavioral change. Perhaps it would be better to say, "students may learn from teachers" rather than "teachers instruct or teach students." Such a restatement enables us to isolate the various components of the teaching episode involved. In this way it becomes possible to accurately locate a "short circuit" in the teaching-learning process.

Table 30 entitled "The Teaching-Learning System" represents the variables a teacher needs to consider when planning a teaching episode. The delineation of these variables should lend themselves to individual assessment during an evaluation of a given program. Also, the teacher could use this system to contemplate some of the variables which need to be considered for each of the main five variables of any educational program including student diagnosis, educational environmental setting, educational methodology, educational mechanisms, and program evaluation.

The teacher should view the teaching-learning situation as a system of interdependent variables. Five global variables have been identified including:

1. the individual diagnosis of student learning needs;
2. the educational environment both in the school and community settings;
3. the deliberately designed teaching strategies with their accompanying tactics and techniques;
4. all of the sundry mechanisms used and exploited by teachers to accomplish given learning outcomes such as aids, supplies, and equipment; and
5. the program of evaluation designed to collect feedback data for validation of the program and its variables in the first instance and continued follow-up and modification of programs and pupil behavior in the second instance.

Each global variable, in turn, is composed of separable factors which influence it. For example, the individual diagnosis of a teacher's readiness to teach or a pupil's readiness to learn is dependent upon the factors which feed into the diagnosis. Therefore, as a teacher considers a diagnosis for an individual pupil or a whole class of pupils, he must first assess such factors as his own capability and preparedness to administer, interpret, and arrive at prognostications based on standardized tests.

ADMINISTERING PROGRAMS AT LOCAL LEVELS

Our understanding of the administration of programs may be enhanced by studying the practical kinds of problems school personnel encounter when they attempt to design and implement an actual program at the local school level. The description which follows is based upon a composite of anecdotal records from several actual school settings in which professional staffs have designed, implemented and evaluated programs.

As observed from the viewpoint of an outside consultant, school personnel progressed through some fairly discrete stages of development as they envisioned, formulated, implemented, and evaluated their programs. The stages included (1) *inspiration*, (2) *assessment*, (3) *formulation*, (4) *formal planning*, (5) *initiation and implementation*, and (6) *evaluation*.

Stage 1. Inspiration

It would be difficult to pinpoint the exact moment a school's teaching staff decides to study and inaugurate a program for the talented. Perhaps their inspiration is born during a lecture by a professor or state consultant dwelling upon the possibilities and feasibility of such programs.

The inspirational period gains momentum as teachers begin to take a second look at their current philosophical outlooks and activities of their talented students. Teachers begin to realize that their time is being devoted to the marginal student, the unproductive student, and the problem student. Talent develops by happenstance, while untold time is spent on social, cultural, moral, and legal "losers." Worse yet, as a consequence of this neglect, undesirable moral and social trends are apparent among their intellectually gifted students. The philosophies of young leaders are found to display attitudes of expediency, fatalism, and nihilism. Foreign, irreligious, and subversive philosophies are entertained as alternatives to the accepted values of our society.

A situation or episode occurs which finally crystallizes the thinking of the teaching staff. Perhaps that episode is the first time the high school staff discovers that a group of "Young Turks" is actually organizing a "cell" of totalitarian and subversive activity in the school. Perhaps it is the moment when a social science teacher discovers, through personal interviews with talented students, that they are simply "playing him along" in the class; they really do not accept the democratic values he advocates in class. Clandestinely, the students entertain notions inimical to these values. Teachers take a second look at the attitudinal and moral development of their students. Staff opinion suddenly becomes crystallized: there is an obvious need for special programs designed expressly for the talented.

Once inspired, teachers discover that other students with distinctive talents are being totally neglected in the workaday school setting. They find that students with psychomotor talents are being totally neglected in the so-called comprehensive high school which, in reality, is not "comprehensive" at all. They find that students with capabilities to become sculptors or folk artists are being neglected and treated as mentally retarded students, shuffled into handicraft and "industrial arts" classes, and relegated to a sort of second-class student citizenship. Upon closer scrutiny, staff discovers that even the academically and creatively talented students are harboring personal problems which they are reluctant to bring to the attention of counselors since this might be construed as a "waste of the counselor's time."

The staff has seen and heard enough! They begin to make preliminary assessments of the need for special instructional and counseling programs. They begin to "brainstorm" in the coffee room. They begin to speculate about the kinds of things they could be doing for their talented students. They speculate about the exciting kinds of workshop and laboratory sessions they could establish for students with dramatic or performing skills, or for students with psychomotor skills. Suddenly, unrecognized academically and creatively talented students come to mind. The need for special programs is keenly perceived.

At this point, astute administrative and supervisory leadership must emerge to generate tangible plans for program development. The excitement of new missions must be translated into practical tasks.

Stage 2. Preliminary Assessment

Now, teachers, administrators, and counselors proceed to poll one another and compare observations. Certain patterns emerge. Rating scales and opinionnaires begin to show that students are as aware of the problems as are teachers. Among student circles, the need for special classes, seminars, and categorical training is demonstrated.

As they interview a variety of talented students, their observations concerning differential needs are also verified. Students with high verbal capabilities are found to desire settings such as seminars and special classes. However, students with nonscholastic talents, and particularly those wanting to use their hands or their performing talents, need more imaginative kinds of programs for self-development and expression. This kind of assessment begins to open new channels of thinking; it can now be seen that special programs cannot end with the establishment of small group verbal activities. workshops, laboratories, and community facilities must be opened for the self-expression of students with more diverse kinds of creative capabilities. The staff may have to call in outside experts to advise them as to the kind of program best suited to meet these diversified needs and also to serve in the program as teachers and tutors.

The assessment now becomes serious and formal. It is necessary to discover what unused skills exist in the teaching and counseling staffs. It is found, possibly to the amazement of the administration, that untapped talents exist in the present professional staff: a counselor indicates that his training has included extensive work in learning theory; a teacher reveals that he has professional acting experience; a shop teacher admits that he spends his spare time studying the indigenous folk cultures and products of other societies; an administrator reveals that he has spent evenings over the last couple of years studying ways in which some of the new models for understanding the human intellect can be applied to the writing and evaluation of curriculum.

Why wait any longer? It is apparent that there exists sufficient special skills in the staff, demonstrable need on the part of the students, and sufficient inspiration and motivation to establish programs to better meet the needs of a wider portion of their talented students. The staff is now ready to formulate an actual program.

Stage 3. Program Formulation

The staff soon finds that basic philosophical issues concerning the role of the school have never been clearly defined. Therefore, they must spend considerable time in formulating an educational philosophy for these programs which emphasizes *free* discussion and the development of multi-dimensional values, while at the same time reinforcing the traditional values and heritage of our culture. This step in program formulation is extremely critical and in some ways may never be thoroughly worked out. A staff with diverse backgrounds can never totally agree among themselves upon a uniform, dogmatic, or unilateral policy. On the other hand, most staff will agree upon the universal need for seminars or small group activities which allow students a wide latitude of expression and freedom to develop their own personal set of values. The staff finds that they are being called upon to contemplate roles, relationships, and subject matter content associations which they should have been considering all along.

From their discussion of differences among themselves, it follows logically that they must assess the attitudes, taboos, and folkways of their own community. In a sense, their approach is anthropological or sociological. In fact, they decide to call upon the professional services of a local university sociologist to help them understand their community with some degree of sophistication. They discover, for instance, that even though their community is urban-sized it is permeated with rather old-fashioned rural values. They find that even though people claim to stand by traditional values in American society, such as free speech and expression, in reality, many influential members of the community inhibit free expression with oblique threats of "subversive activity in our schools." They find many local mythologies (e.g. "There are no slums in our community, only temporary housing for transients."). The job of establishing activities in which students are really allowed to look at themselves and their communities in some degree of depth is found to be a task of working simultaneously with the community and working to upgrade that same community.

To some extent, the reality of current attitudes, political beliefs and folkways will have to affect the development of programs—like it or not. Therefore, the staff decides its definitions must clear and link with the traditions of our American heritage. Also, frequent discussions, including open seminars for the public and board of education, should precede actual program inauguration. The staff does not wait for controversy to develop; it anticipates controversy and welcomes it by open community discussion preceding the actual inauguration of the program. In this way, prospective critics of the program are caught at a sort of disadvantage. They cannot accuse the school of "indoctrinating" their children. No active program has yet been established. The program that *is* established will be jointly set up and will involve the collective viewpoint of the community at large.

Stage 4. Formal Planning and Tryout

Following considerable staff deliberation and planning, coupled with extensive inventories of staff members, students, and the community at large, the administration is now ready to formally plan an instructional program sequence which will represent the synthesis of many points of view. The program decided upon may not be as ambitious as that program envisioned during the first inspirational stages when a few "activist" teachers first thought of the possibility for a special sort of program in which all talented students would be dealt with more directly and personally. On the other hand, it is a program which will mesh with community as well as school expectations and have much built-in survival value.

One of the most important determinations made by the school staff is simple and basic: they decide that the program will never be considered fully formed nor static. On the contrary, it will be a program which is amorphous, flexible, and capable of being added to or detracted from. Any new phase of the program must be considered "experimental for tryout." Aspects of the program must be validated as one validates new tests by observing actual results upon students and measuring behavioral changes.

Planning committees are designed to include members of the counseling, administrative, and teaching staffs as well as community representatives. Membership on such study and planning committees rotates. There is a committee for program design and modification. To preserve objectivity, a second committee considers evaluation, follow-up and general effect upon students and the community. Collectively, the school staff decides upon an entire revamping of the scheduling of students, the use of special reporting forms describing student behavior instead of "report cards," and self-determination on the part of students for the planning of their own programs. Also, much after school and Saturday activity is stimulated by an "open door" policy for the use of school facilities.

A new sort of "liberal attitude" (defined in the historical sense of the word) on the part of the school administration and the community at large is in evidence. Programs, techniques, and materials are being attempted which were not even contemplated prior to the staff's original inspirational period. Administrators actively participate in curriculum planning, reassessment, and modification. Released time for teachers and counselors for the purpose of content preparation, the study of students, and special seminars among professional staffs become a part of the professional planning for staff time. New concepts from modern education begin to permeate the thinking of all members of the staff. Spontaneous episodes of "team teaching" begin to be observed. Teachers from disparate disciplines begin to get together for the purpose of interrelating their subject matters. Overall, the school no longer perceives itself as an isolated institution but sees its roles in society as merged with other institutions. The school calls upon these other institutions for the design and actual implementation of these programs.

The staff decides upon the following program for the fall semester which will involve *all* teachers in grades 7 through 12:

1. Weekly subject matter seminars will be held for honors students, in addition to their regular classes, for the purpose of discussing controversial issues, conflicts among subject matter disciplines, and general discussions of the incorporation of learned concepts into one's personal philosophy of life. Such seminars will be conducted weekly by an interdisciplinary group of teachers on a rotating basis.

2. A counseling-instructional program will focus upon literature, the social sciences, and the humanities. Group counseling sessions will be coupled with weekly meetings of all of the teachers who have students attending the special program. During these weekly meetings, counselors report back to teachers obvious kinds of misunderstandings of content and possible dangerous or inappropriate ways students are perceiving and incorporating concepts into their personal understandings and value systems. As a consequence, considerable changes and modifications are expected to occur in curriculum contents.

3. Special college level classes will be established for attendance by *teachers* and *students*. This was deemed to be the best way to "humanize" the student-teacher, teaching-learning continua. Subtly, the teacher should begin to emerge with a new image in the eyes of his students. The teacher will come to be viewed as a partner in scholarship. By observing one another in actual intellectual tasks, students are much more apt to emulate the scholarly behavior of their teachers through emphathy and identification.

4. Those students with creative propensities are encouraged to attend spontaneous, but usually weekly, brainstorming and special project ses-

sions on an individual and group basis. Some of the recent developments in brainstorming techniques are shared with students directly. Students are allowed to diverge into creative areas not ordinarily allowed in the more rigid classroom settings. Special projects for students are as open-ended as local folkways will allow.

5. After school and Saturday availability of laboratories, shops, library facilities, and community facilities are made available for informal and self-designed projects for all kinds of talented students. As part of this program, equipment inventories and lists of volunteer community experts are made available to students for help with individual projects.

6. On an individual basis, all talented students will be considered for appropriate advanced placements (e.g. advanced placement to college, advanced grade levels, or advanced courses).

7. Special curriculum committees will compare the district's course offerings with similar sized districts. Recommendations for (a) new subject areas, (b) accelerated contents, and (c) combined courses will be considered.

The need for unanticipated articulation may become apparent at this point in program development. For example, maintenance of scholarship or vocational files by a placement office may be found to be inadequate for the new demand of talented students. Also, the placement office may need to find creative outlets for student products. All sorts of inquiries will need to be made to industries or patent office personnel to find suitable protections and outlets for student products.

Staff members begin to perceive new roles for themselves. The role of teacher, as information giver, begins to yield to the more sophisticated concept of teacher as an educational programmer. Therefore, new kinds of organizational patterns needed to be designed. Weekly meetings between teachers and counselors begin to eventuate into daily meetings. Some teachers emerge with roles which might be described as "master teachers" or educational programmers. Someone in the program is needed to keep track of progress, program students into appropriate sequences of seminars, and assess outcomes in terms of the student's personal growth: coordinators need to be assigned.

The need for more highly-skilled personnel becomes apparent. School psychologists emerge with new and more challenging roles. At first, the central office school psychologist was called upon to conduct monthly seminars and information giving meetings with counselors. Later, it was seen that this experience might be as useful for teachers as well as for counselors.

Some deeply controversial professional issues begin to emerge. For example, some of the problems besetting students can now be traced to insufficient teacher training. Hence, teacher problems begin to be referred to administrators. Formal teacher evaluation procedures become necessary.

Formal planning and tryout begin to take on a semblance of systematic design. Experimental programs begin to lend themselves to a planned sequence of development, tryout, evaluation, and modification. As the critical attitudes and values of students come under scrutiny, so do the values and attitudes of the professional staff. Changes toward more scientific objectivity, heightened possibilities for communication, and overall pride in the profession begin to be seen among the professional staff.

Stage 5. Program Initiation and Implementation

After trying out several aspects of the program and tentatively assessing their results, the staff decides upon general adoption of proven program components. As the program is widely adopted throughout the school system, many problems emerge which were not envisioned during the preliminary tryout stages.

During the tryout period, the most motivated and best prepared teachers and counselors were recruited. Now, they must include professionals with lesser motivation and more meager training. Hence, the possibility for professional misunderstandings, jealousies, and competitive comparisons become hazardously maximized. Although the staff had been meticulously careful to develop codes of ethics describing the interrelationships among people participating in the program, still gossip developed and unfortunate comparisons among teachers of different capabilities were discussed. The optimistic outlook which emerged as a result of the initial program gives way to more cynical and critical observations.

Perhaps, this is the most critical period of program development for the school administrator. Erick Hoffer has observed, "the most important ingredient in any society is *maintenance.*" How many educational programs have been tried (successfully) yet failed to continue because no one took the responsibility for maintaining them in ever improved condition? Key roles for the school administrator during this period include (a) discouraging educational fads or novelties, (b) acting as a source of security for program continuity, (c) avoiding "change for change's sake," (d) constantly encouraging the upgrading of existing programs, and (e) keeping the original goals of the new programs constantly in the forefront.

Similar problems emerge among student groups as more extensive participation in programs is allowed. Students are found to be relatively unaccustomed to the seminar or small group counseling sessions. Many students confuse small group sessions with "griping sessions." New subject matters may be "overtaxing or too difficult." Much diffuse student activity may be observed such as rambling discussions, excursions into verbal silliness, or uncomfortable discussions of problems which are not really meaningful to students. Students may resort to intellectual subterfuge to "please their teachers."

Following initial misgivings, counselors and teachers begin to spend more time studying the lives of the talented. They discover the sorts of experiences which were most meaningful to the talented in their development toward excellence. The need for extensive in-service training experiences for counselors and teachers becomes quite apparent. Seminars are planned for professional staff on a weekly basis; experts from university and community settings are utilized. Discussion topics include such varied content as differentiating among talented potentialities; what is productive performance?; societal demands for professional and avocational callings; interpreting and motivating the underachiever; utilization of total community resources; or, self-actualization for the talented.

Stage 6. Program Evaluation and Modification

Although the staff had conducted evaluations of the program from the beginning, at this stage "evaluation" takes on a more formal meaning. It is necessary to convince themselves, their students, and the community that measurable changes can be found in students as a result of exposure to the programs.

Global administrative evaluation of the program is not difficult. The many new curriculums developed as a result of student concerns add testimony to the changes in the school's overall design. Likewise, testimonials from parents, students, counselors, and teachers indicate that the programs have resulted in widespread beneficial results. Topics of concern never before discussed within the school setting have been aired; workable solutions have been generated. The unnumbered special student projects, workshops, and practical experiences have resulted in measurable gains in scholarships, invitations to performing arts festivals, offers of job placements, and general public demands for student and teacher talents. Productive performance is being stimulated. Likewise, measurable gains in achievement are easy to assess; it is clear that the programs have caused significant increases in test scores.

However, the measurement of any changes in systems of values, general attitudes, cognitive styles or philosophies of life are far more inaccessible. Of course, the staff attempts to measure values directly utilizing established tools such as *A Study of Values*. But, these are found to be too circumscribed. Moreover, the values that are measured may not be appropriate for understanding an entirely new generation of people who may hold to values not yet contemplated by the makers of older instruments.

How do you interpret marked changes in talented students from values in the theoretical or economic areas toward more aesthetic or religious concerns? Is this "good or bad"? We would have to assume that it was a desirable social gain to have talented students more equally distributed among the various value typologies of man. This staff had accepted Bruner's notion of a "pluralistic society." Hence, from its point of view, it was commendable that the student population of talented students now displayed more varied patterns of value orientations than they displayed when tested several years back. Of course, this point of view would be open to considerable challenge in a community with a scientifically-oriented population. Is the nation more in need of intellectuals with scientific values or aesthetic values?

Perhaps the most fruitful source of program evaluation is the most expensive. The staff found need for individual interviews with the students exposed to the programs. In a sense, such evaluation becomes "a study of lives." Generalizations are almost impossible to apply with this diverse group of talented students. In effect, "evaluation" becomes synonymous with an individual case study of each talented student. "Success" could be equated with the concept of self-actualization; the program is "successful" when individual students demonstrate self-actualization. Success could be deemed equivalent to self-expression, personal fulfillment, individual development, challenge, indices of excellence, and satisfaction.

STATE AGENCIES FOR TALENT DEVELOPMENT

From the national and state levels, it might be wise to consider what sort of agency could best handle the entire spectrum of talent development problems. An agency with "bureau status" could divide its work on the problem of talent development into three main concentrations, including (1) experimental formulation such as the discovery and survey of all kinds of talent, (2) consultation services for the establishment of school and community programs for advanced learners, and talented individuals in the manual, musical and other arts, and (3) workers devoting their time to community talent utilization. The administrative structure for such an agency is outlined below:

1. *Unit for Experimental Formulation—Research in Talent Development*
    Discovery, identification and survey of talent; development of new assessment instruments; validation of existing instruments
    Experimentation with learning theory, thinking processes, and general cognition; corollary development of appropriate teaching methodology; corollary development and tryout of appropriate curriculum
    Basic research in creativity, motivation and personality
    Community experimentation with the utilization and application of various talents

2. *Professional Consultant Services for the Development, Promotion and Evaluation of School and Community Programs for Talent Development*
    Academic programs for advanced learners
    Leadership programs
    Specialized services for the development of unique talent
        for the fine arts
        for the expressive arts
        for the literary arts
        for science and mathematics
        for manual arts and crafts
        for industrial arts
        for linguistics
    The general application of models of creative process to curriculum

3. *Units for Community Talent Utilization*
    Liaison with institutions for higher education
    Development of community art centers and other facilities
    Liaison with the professions, crafts, and apprentice programs
    Stimulation and support of the performing arts

As a state or federal agency phased into a program for talent development, it would be logical to establish the experimental formulation unit a year or two ahead of the other units in the agency. The first job of the experimental unit would be to survey the entire population with reference to all of the qualities of talent sought for. Part of this process would include the evaluation of existing identification instruments and techniques. New instruments for the discovery of talent would need to be contemplated. For example, it is obvious that many raw talents remain undiscovered in our minority populations. "Culture free" tests and measurements will have to be developed to discover the talented individuals contained in our Negro or Mexican-American populations.[1] It is probable that many other kinds of talent should be discovered, encouraged, and educated toward personal fulfillment.

Next, the experimental unit would have to study and summarize existing "learning theory." Curriculum development and tryout with small pilot groups would follow. The definitions of talent developed by this experimental unit would help to clarify the kinds of teaching methodologies and curriculum materials called for. The main contribution of the experimental unit would be to describe ways in which learning theory can be put to practical use in the development and utilization of curriculum materials.

Perhaps the most practical contribution of the experimental formulation

---

[1] Rice, J.P.: Education of subcultural groups. *Schools and Society*, 92(No. 2250):360-362, Nov. 29, 1964.

unit would be the discovery of various techniques for the utilization and application of talent in the community. Different designs for the utilization of talent would need to be experimented with on a pilot basis. For example, the Mexican government has established a federal agency for the subsidization and perpetuation of the folk arts.

The second unit within the agency for talent development would be broad consultant services for the development, promotion, and evaluation of programs in schools and communities. So far, we have concentrated on the development of advanced learner programs only. Given the body of data concerning talent now available, it seems as though three major consultancies would answer the need for program developers at this stage. The first of these consultancies would need to be devoted to the broad category of "advanced learners." This category would include all children whose scholastic performance indicates that they are capable of doing advanced academic work. From the point of view of definition, this would probably include all children with IQ's in excess of 110. These educational programs would be broad and include such implementation as special grouping, acceleration programs, special curriculum units, and special advanced classes.

A consultant staff would develop, try out, and evaluate programs designed to enhance the acquisition of the skills of leadership. This admittedly new area of investigation would need to be designated as "experimental."

The third area for consultant services would be devoted to specific talent development in circumscribed and well-defined areas. For a start, we have listed fine arts, expressive arts, literary arts, science, manual arts, industrial arts, and linguistics. The focus of these consultants would be on programs rather than individuals. For example, the consultant dealing with the expressive arts would attempt to establish and promote programs of talent development in the musical and plastic arts in schools and communities. Among other endeavors, they would attempt to stimulate the development of local musical groups, recitals, and institutes for art.

In all of the specialized talent areas, incentives and rewards would be established for the manifestation of excellence in any field. How many public schools support orchestras, dramatic groups, string ensembles, or other performing groups? Any of these activities would be supported by the specific talent consultant involved.

Of special interest is the neglected area of linguistics. Programs for language study could concentrate upon the development of area institutes in the various language forms. It is unrealistic to suppose that every elementary school within a state can possibly support "experts" in different language capabilities. Through a discovery program for talented children in the linguistics area, regional institutes could be established which could develop audiovisual and other program aids in specific language groups.

Such a system would insure that a rural student interested in the study of, say, Mandarin, could somehow contact an appropriate institute and arrange for summer study, periodic visits to the institute, or programmed materials to be used in his local school setting. We must recognize that some individuals have a special talent for the acquisition of language just as other individuals have other specialized talents.

The third unit of the general agency for the talent development would be that of "community talent utilization." The most obvious service to be performed is that of liaison with higher educational institutions. We now have several programs which bridge the gap between schools and colleges. For example, we have Merit Scholarship Programs, advanced placement to college programs, and so-called Higher Horizon programs for "disadvantaged youth." If the lower grade schools really discover and develop talent then it follows that the higher institutions will receive individuals more highly trained than has been the case previously. Therefore, they will have to "re-tool" and offer significantly advanced programs on their own. This whole process cannot help but upgrade our entire cultural heritage.

The unit on community talent utilization would also need to work with local communities for the development of art centers, museums, and other cultural facilities. Perhaps one of the first work tasks of this unit would be to convince local communities, through a public relations campaign, of the need for "cultural centers."

It would be important for this unit to establish liaison with professions, and crafts which require people of skill. The need for apprenticeship programs would be widespread. Statewide lists of interested professionals could be kept in order to bring together interested pupils with successful individuals in the profession of their choice. Close identity with one's professional choice could begin much earlier than is now the case.

It is important to encourage local communities to devote more attention to the performing arts. Circulation of exceptional musicians, dancers, actors, and artists could be promoted by the circulation of lists of availability. It is conceivable that local school districts could request certain exceptional student performers as they request the appearance of school marching bands today. Whole assembly programs for pupils could be developed around the "availability lists" of exceptional performing pupils from their regional areas.

We have explored some of the possibilities for a unified state or national agency which would devote its time to the entire range of talent development. The agency would contain the professional staff necessary to formulate its own experimental findings, establish and promote appropriate educational programs, and follow through by encouraging communities to utilize the talent being developed. There could be nothing halfway about the endowment of such an agency. It would need to subcontract out working tasks such as basic research to other agencies. Also, it would need to engage in pilot programs which are known to be expensive, such as the endowment of community projects for the performing arts. Such an agency could not be accused of limiting its attention to some specific group within the all-encompassing category of "talent." It would represent society's dedication to the discovery, education and utiliztaion of all of its special talents.

Most of the existing special educational programs for talented students emphasize purely academic content. Measurable gains in knowledge are thought to be appropriate outcomes. Even the interpretation of what constitutes "academic talent" is narrowly defined. Few schools assess such categories of mental maturity as intellectual curiosity, fluency of ideas, originality, independence in thought, or conceptual elaboration.[2] Yet, it has been demonstrated that more complex analyses of students' cognitive processes are possible within the modern classroom setting utilizing a theoretical model such as Guilford's "structure of intellect model."[3] The main reason why such research applications are scarce is the lack of demonstrational agencies for the tryout of novel approaches to educational assessment and curriculum building.

By 1965, eleven states and Puerto Rico had assigned at least one full-time professional consultant at the state level to be responsible for talent development programs.[4] Three states had assigned half-time personnel, fifteen states and the District of Columbia had assigned part-time personnel, but twenty-one states were devoting little or no attention to the problems of organizing, developing, and promoting educational programs for talented children and youth.[5] By 1963, a "Council of State Directors of Programs for the Gifted" had been organized for the purposes of "exchanging information, encouraging research, and promoting programs. . . ."[6] Currently, this group is collecting specimens of research, curriculum and

---

[2] Taken from a Checklist of Intellectual Functioning. *Identification and Case Study*. Sacramento, California State Department of Education, Project Talent, July, 1964 (multilithed).

[3] For example, Dr. Marcella Bonsall of the Los Angeles County Superintendent of Schools Office has adapted Guilford's, "The Structure of Intellect Model: Its Uses and Implications" (Psychological Lab. Report, No. 24, Los Angeles, USC, April, 1960) for use as a rating scale of intellectual processes. Such processes as cognition, memory, convergent production, divergent production, and evaluation are defined and adapted to a five-point rating scale for use by teachers.

[4] Personnel and activities for talent development, 1964. U.S. Department of Health, Education and Welfare, Office of Education publication OE-35054. Washington, Superintendent of Documents, U.S. Printing Office.

[5] *Ibid.*, p. 17.

[6] *Ibid.*, pp. 18-19.

other unique documents in the area of education for the gifted for a sort of national repository. Such efforts should accelerate the distribution and multiple adoptions of special programs. The organization of this group at the national level might be used as a prototype for the establishment of similar groups at the state level. For example, over three hundred school districts in California have specially assigned personnel to administer their gifted child programs.[7] We are currently attempting to enhance their communication by way of a newsletter service and annual regional meetings.[8]

It is interesting to note that Texas was one of the few states to devise a program of talent development which departed from the stereotyped "gifted programs" which are so fashionable. The program emphasized the discovery of raw talent in culturally disadvantaged communities with provisions for compensatory educational activities. The program has, apparently, been dropped. Also notable, are the efforts of North Carolina's summer "Governor's School," which although oriented toward the academically gifted student, sponsors "differential education."[9] In addition to the "academic disciplines," the school integrates the performing arts including instrumental music, drama, and the dance, into its educational experiences.[10] In addition, the school encourages original thinking by emphasizing "general conceptual development, and self-insight into the . . . motivating forces which underlie human behavior."[11]

In California, we are attempting to demonstrate ways in which disparate student needs can be satisfied through the design of master school district programs which incorporate multiple approaches.[12] School districts such as Los Angeles, Pasadena, and San Juan serve as demonstration centers to which interested school officials can be referred for actual observation of different kinds of programs. The task is immense in scope. At the same time teachers in the demonstration situations are themselves learning how to apply some of the new theoretical models to curriculum construction, we must be certain that their students' pressing daily learning needs are met. Our major problem has been program export. Well-intentioned ad-

---

[7] California State Department of Education: County and District Personnel Responsible for Programs for Mentally Gifted Minors, Directory, 1965. Sacramento, State Department of Education, Division of Special Schools and Services (multilithed).

[8] California State Department of Education. The Gifted Pupil (mimeographed newsletter) available quarterly (Vol. I, 1963-1964, three issues; Vol. II, 1964-1965, two issues).

[9] The Governor's School of North Carolina: Staff Report, Theory-Practice-Implementation-Recommendations. Winston-Salem, Salem College, Charles D. Carter, Principal.

[10] *Ibid.*, pp. 33-52.

[11] *Ibid.*, p. 57, pp. 53-60.

[12] Supported by Federal funds, Project D-072: "Demonstration of Differential Programming in Enrichment, Acceleration, Counseling and Special Classes for Gifted Pupils in Grades 1-9. Project duration: April 5, 1963 to December 31, 1966. Project Directors: P.D. Plowman and J.P. Rice, California State Department of Education.

ministrators may return to their districts and pontificate. Rather, they should embark upon systematic programs of in-service training for their staffs, thoughtful evaluation of their existing curriculum, and design of a custom program which will be acceptable locally.

It has been shown that existing programs for talent development typically focus upon academic talent only. Even these programs, with their background of research and tryout, are still subject to subversion by educators who equate "democratic" with "egalitarian." Inaccurate and misleading terminology is often coined in order to fit the huge foot of talent into the narrow shoe of "mental giftedness." Programs are then reworked to be appropriate for such a wide range of capabilities as "creative" children. The end result may be a queer concoction of impulsive expressions (e.g. "creative exercises") with sadistic standards (e.g. "honors programs") which are not suitable for any special group of talented students.

Meanwhile, inestimable human resources remain undeveloped. Far from being cultural centers for their communities, many schools have degenerated to the levels of stockades or arenas. It is appropriate that we begin to envision a much broader context for the development of human talent.

BIBLIOGRAPHY

Abraham, Willard: *Common Sense About Gifted Children*. New York, Harper, 1958.

Adler, M.: A study of the effects of ethnic origin on giftedness. *Gifted Child Quart*, 7:98-102, 1963.

Altich, Richard D.: *Preface to Critical Reading*. New York, Holt, 1962.

American Psychological Association: *Ethical Standards for Psychologists*. Washington, Amer. Psychol. Assoc., 1953.

American Psychological Association: *Technical Recommendations for Psychological and Diagnostic Techniques*. *Psychol Bull*, 51 (No. 2), Part 2, March 1954.

Anderson, H.H. (Ed.): *Creativity in Childhood and Adolescence: A Variety of Approaches*. Palo Alto, Science and Behavior, 1965.

Anderson, H.H. (Ed.): *Creativity and Its Cultivation*. New York, Harper, 1959.

Anderson, Kenneth E. (Ed.): *Research on the Academically Talented Student*. Washington, Nat. Ed. Assoc., 1961.

Applebaum, M.J.: Should gifted students be accelerated? *Calif J Sec Ed*, 36:297-300, 1961.

Astin, A.W.: Differential college effects on the motivation of talented students to obtain the Ph.D. *J Ed Psychol*, 54:63-71, 1963.

Astin, A.W.: Socio-economic factors in the achievements and aspirations of the merit scholar. *Personnel Guidance J*, 42:581-86, 1964.

Ausubel, David P.: The Influence of Experience on the Development of Intelligence. U. of Ill., Bureau of Education Research (mimeogr.).

Ausubel, David P.: *The Psychology of Meaningful Verbal Learning*. New York, Grune, 1963.

Bachtold, L.M.; Plowman, P.D., and Rice, J.P.: Counseling-Instructional Programs for Intellectually Gifted Students (I of California Project Talent Series). Sacramento, Calif. Dept. of Ed., 1966.

Baldwin, J.W.: Teacher judged giftedness and group intelligence tests, kindergarten. *Gifted Child Quart*, 6:153-60, 1962.

Barbe, W.B.: *One in a Thousand*. Columbus, Ohio Board of Ed., 1963.

Barbe, Walter B.: *Psychology and Education of the Gifted*. New York, Appleton, 1965.

Barbe, Walter B.: Study of a gifted family. *Education*, 79:45-48, 1958. (Cf. *Psychol Abst*, 34:976, 1960.)

Barbe, W.B., and Frierson, E.C.: Teaching the gifted, a new frame of reference. *Education*, 82:465-67, 1962.

Barney, W.D.: Early Admission to School for Mentally Advanced Children. Pittsburgh, U. of Pittsburgh, Dept. of Special Ed., 1963.

Barron, F.: Complexity-simplicity as a personality dimension. *J Abnorm Soc Psychol*, 48:163-172, 1953.

Barron, Frank: *Creativity and Psychological Health*. Princeton, Van Nostrand, 1963.

Barron, Frank: Creativity: what research says about it. *Nat Ed Assoc J*, 50:3:17-19, 1961.

Barron, Frank: Originality in relation to personality and Intellect. *J Personnel*, 25:730-742, 1957.

Beggs, David W. III, and Buffie, Edward G.: *Nongraded Schools in Action.* Bold New Venture Creativity Series. Bloomington, Indiana, 1967.

Bereday, G.Z., and Lawerys, J.A., editors: *The Yearbook of Education, 1961: Concepts of Excellence in Education.* London, Evans Bros., 1961.

Bereiter, C.E.: Verbal and ideational fluency in superior tenth grade students. *J Ed Psychol,* Dec. 1960.

Berg, Irwin A., and Bass, Bernard M. (Ed.): *Conformity and Deviation.* New York, Harper, 1960.

Bettelheim, Bruno: Segregation: new style. *School Rev,* 66:264 1958.

Biggs, David W. III: Team Teaching. Bloomington, Indiana, 1964.

Birch, J., and Reynolds, M.C.: The gifted. *Rev Ed Res,* 33:83, 1963.

Bish, C.E. (Ed.): *Productive Thinking in Education.* Washington, Nat. Ed. Assoc., 1965.

Bloom, B.S. (Ed.): *Taxonomy of Educational Objectives Handbook I: Cognitive Domain.* New York, McKay, 1956.

Bonsall, Marcella: Introspections of gifted children. *Calif J Ed Res,* 11:159, 1960.

Bradway, K.P., and Robinson, H.B.: Significant IQ changes in 25 years: a follow-up. *J Ed Psychol,* April 1961.

Brameld, Theodore: *Education for the Emerging Age.* New York, Harper, 1961.

Brandwein, P.F.: *The Gifted Child as a Future Scientist.* New York, Harcourt, 1955.

Brant, Vincent and Keedy: *Elementary Logic for Secondary Schools.* New York, Holt, 1962.

Braun, John R. (Ed.): *Contemporary Research in Learning.* Princeton, Van Nostrand, 1963.

Brickell, Henry: *Organizing New York State for Educational Change.* Buffalo, U. of New York, 1961.

Brown, B. Frank: *The Nongraded High School.* Englewood Cliffs, Prentice-Hall, 1963.

Brown, R.: The teacher as a guidance worker. *J Ed,* 139:3-12 (April) 1957.

Brumbaugh, Florence, and Roshco, B.: *Your Gifted Child: A Guide for Parents.* New York, Holt, 1959.

Bruner, Jerome S.: *The Process of Education.* Cambridge, Harvard, 1966.

Bruner, Jerome S.: *Toward a Theory of Instruction.* Cambridge, Harvard, 1966.

Bruner, Jerome S. and others: *Contemporary Approaches to Creative Thinking.* New York, Atherton, 1963.

Bryan, J.N.: *Building a Program for Superior and Talented Students.* Chicago, North Central Assoc. of Colleges and Sec. Schools, 5454 South Shore Drive, 60615, 1963.

Bryan, J.N.: Talent and Todays Schools. *Superior Student,* 6:1:3-10, 1963.

Burks, Barbara S.; Jensen, Dortha W., and Terman, Lewis M.: *Genetic Studies of Genius,* Vol. III, *The Promise of Youth.* Stanford, Stanford, 1930.

Buros, Oscar Krisen (Ed.): *The Sixth Mental Measurements Yearbook.* Highland Park, Gryphon, 1965.

Burt, C.: The gifted child. *Brit J Stat Psychol,* 14:123-139, 1961.

Burt, C.: Is intelligence distributed normally? *Brit J Stat Psychol,* 16:175-190, 1963.

Burton, William H.; Kimball, Roland B., and Wing, Richard L.: *Education for Effective Thinking.* New York, Appleton, 1960.

California Elementary School Administrators' Association: *The Gifted Child: Another Look.* Monogr. No. 10. Burlingame, Calif. Teachers Assoc., 1958.

Castallan, J.: *Curriculum Adaptations for the Gifted.* New York, Dept. of Ed., Bureau of El. Curriculum Develop., 1958 (Pamphlet).

Cicirelli, V.G.: Form of the relationship between creativity, I.Q. and academic achievement. *J Ed Psychol,* 56(No. 6):303-308, 1965.

Conant, James B.: *The American High School Today.* New York, McGraw, 1959.

Conant, James B.: *Education in the Junior High School Years.* Princeton, Ed. Test. Service, 1960.

Conant, James B., Chairman: The identification and education of the academically talented in the American secondary school. *Report National Education Association Conference.* Washington, Nat. Ed. Assoc., 1958.

Copley, F.O.: *The American High School and the Talented Student.* Ann Arbor, U. of Mich., 1961.

Council for Exceptional Children: *Professional Standards Project Report.* Washington, Nat. Ed. Assoc. Council Except. Child., 1967.

Cox, Catharine Morris: *Genetic Studies of Genius. The Early Mental Traits of Three Hundred Geniuses.* Stanford, Stanford, 1926, Vol. II.

Crow, Lester D. and Alice: *Adolescent Development and Adjustment.* New York, McGraw, 1956.

Cruickshank, William M., and Johnson, G. Orville: *Education of Exceptional Children.* Englewood Cliffs, Prentice-Hall, 1967.

Cutts, N.E., and Moseley, N.: *Bright Children: A Guide for Parents.* New York, Putnam, 1953.

Cutts, N.E., and Moseley, N.: *Teaching the Bright and Gifted.* Englewood Cliffs, Prentice-Hall, 1957.

DeHaan, R.F.: *Accelerated Learning Programs.* Englewood Cliffs, Prentice-Hall, 1963.

DeHaan, Robert F.: *Guidelines for Parents of Capable Youth.* Chicago, Sci. Res. Assoc., 1961.

DeHaan, Robert F., and Havighurst, Robert: *Educating Gifted Children.* Chicago, U. of Chicago, 1961.

Deitrich, F.R.: Comparison of sociometric patterns of sixth grade pupils in two school systems: ability grouping compared with heterogenous grouping. *J Ed Res,* 57:507-513, 1964.

Dennis, W.: Age and productivity among scientists. *Science,* 123:724-726, 1956. (Cf. *Amer Psychol,* 14:457-460, 1958.)

Dereday, G.G., and Lauwerys, J.: *The Gifted Child: The Yearbook of Education, 1962.* New York, Harcourt, 1962.

D'Evelyn, K.: *Meeting Children's Emotional Needs.* Englewood Cliffs, Prentice-Hall, 1957.

Dewey, J.: *Human Nature and Conduct.* New York, Random, 1957.

Drews, E. (Ed.): *Guidance for the Academically Talented Student.* Washington, Nat. Ed. Assoc., 1961.

Drews, Elizabeth, and Montgomery, Susan: Creative and academic performance in gifted adolescents. *High School J,* 48:94-101, 1964.

Duff, O.L., and Siegel, L.: Biographical factors associated with academic over- and under-achievement. *J Ed Psychol,* 51:43-46, 1960.

Durr, William K.: *The Gifted Student.* New York, Oxford U. P., 1964.

Einstein, A.: *Out of My Later Years.* New York, Philosophical Lib., 1950.

Ekstrom, Ruth: Early admission to college. *J. Ed Res,* 7:408-412, 1964.

Endicott, Frank S.: *Guiding Superior and Talented High School Students.* Chicago, Sci. Res. Assoc., 1961.

Everett, S. (Ed.): *Programs for the Gifted: A Case Book in Secondary Education* (15th Yearbook of the John Dewey Society). New York, Harper, 1961.

Farber, W., and Wilson, R.H.L. (Ed.): *Conflict and Creativity*. New York, McGraw, 1963.

Farqubar, W.W., and Payne, D.A.: A classification and comparison of techniques used in selecting under- and over-achievers. *Personnel Guidance J*, 42:874-884, 1964.

Faust, C.H.: Why the new concern for educating the gifted? *School Rev*, 65:12, 1957.

Feldhusen, J.F., and Klausmeier, H.J.: Anxiety, intelligence, and achievement in children of low, average, and high intelligence. *Child Develop*, 33:403-409, 1962. (Cf. pages 83-89) in Ripple, R.E. (Ed.): *Readings in Learning and Human Ability* New York, Harper, 1964.)

Feur, Lewis S.: *The Scientific Intellectual*. New York, Basic Bks, 1963.

Fine, Benjamin: *Stretching Their Minds*. New York, Dutton, 1964.

Findley, W.G. (Ed.): *The Impact and Improvement of School Testing Programs*. Chicago, U. of Chicago, 1963.

Fischer, L.: Social philosophies and the concept of giftedness. *Gifted Child Quart*, 5:93-95, 1961.

Flanagan, J.C., *et al.: The Project Talent Data Bank*. Pittsburgh, U. of Pittsburgh, 1965.

Flavell, John H.: *The Developmental Psychology of Jean Piaget*. Princeton, Van Nostrand, 1963.

Fliegler, Louis A.: *Curriculum Planning for the Gifted*. Englewood Cliffs, Prentice-Hall, 1962.

Frankel, E.: Effects of a program of summer study on the self-perception of academically talented high school students. *Except Child*, 30:245-251, 1964.

Fraser, Dorothy M.: *Current Curiculum Studies in Academic Subjects*. Washington, Nat. Ed. Assoc., 1962.

Fraser, Dorothy M.: *Deciding What to Teach*. Washington, Nat. Ed. Assoc., 1963.

Freehill, M.F.: *Gifted Children, Their Psychology and Education*. New York, Macmillan, 1961.

Freeman, F.S.: *Theory and Practice of Psychological Testing*. New York, Holt, 1961.

French, Joseph L. (Ed.): *Educating the Gifted: A Book of Readings*. New York, Holt, 1960.

French, Joseph L.: Preparation of Teachers of the Gifted. *J Teacher Ed*, 17:69-72, 1961.

Friendenberg, Edgar Z.: *The Vanishing Adolescent*. Boston, Beacon, 1960.

Froelich, C., and Hoyt, K.: *Guidance Testing*. Chicago, Sci. Res. Assoc., 1959.

Gage, N. L. (Ed.): *Handbook of Research on Teaching*. Chicago, Rand McNally, 1963.

Gallagher, J.J.: *Analysis of Research on the Education of Gifted Children*. Springfield, Superintend. of Public Instr., Spec. Study Project for Gifted Child. (n.d.), 1961.

Gallagher, James J.: *The Gifted Child in the Elementary School: What Research Says to the Teacher*. Bulletin No. 17. Washington, Nat. Ed. Assoc., 1959.

Gallagher, James J.: Social Status of Children Related to Intelligence Propinquity and Social Perception. *El School J*, 58:225-231, 1958.

Gallagher, James J.: *Teaching the Gifted Child*. Boston, Allyn & Bacon, 1964.

Gallagher, James J., and Lucito, L.J.: Intellectual patterns of gifted compared with average and retarded. *Except Child*, 27:479-482, 1961. (Cf. *Peabody J Ed*, 38:131-136, 1960.)

Gardner, John W.: *Excellence, Can We Be equal and Excellent Too?* New York, Harper, 1961.

Gavin, Ruth (Ed.): *The Social Education of the Academically Talented*. Washington, Nat. Council Soc. Studies, Nat. Ed. Assoc., 1958.

Gemant, A.: *The Nature of Genius*. Springfield, Thomas, 1961.

Getzels, J.W., and Jackson, P.W.: *Creativity and Intelligence, Explorations with Gifted Students.* New York, Wiley, 1961.

Getzels, J.W., and Jackson, P.W : Family environment and cognitive style: a study of the sources of highly intelligent and highly creative adolescents. *Amer Social Rev,* 26:351-359, 1961.

Gifford, G.R., and others: Creativity, its identification and development. *Curriculum Bull,* 20:244:1-26, 1964.

Ginzberg, E., and others: *Talent and Performance.* New York, Columbia, 1964.

Goertzel, Victor and Mildred G.: *Cradles of Eminence.* Boston, Little, 1962.

Gold, Milton J.: *Education of the Intellectually Gifted.* Merrill's International Education Series. Columbus, Merrill, C.E., 1965, 1966.

Goodlad, John I.: *Planning and Organizing for Teaching.* Washington, Nat. Ed. Assoc., 1963.

Gordon, Ira J.: *The Teacher as a Guidance Worker.* New York, Harper, 1956.

Gowan, John C.: *An Annotated Bibliography on the Academically Talented Student.* Washington, Nat. Ed. Assoc. Project Acad. Talented Student, 1961.

Gowan, John C., and Demos, G.D.: *The Education and Guidance of the Ablest.* Springfield, Thomas, 1964.

Gowan, John C., and Demos, G.D. (Eds.): *The Guidance of Exceptional Children: A Book of Readings.* New York, McKay, 1965.

Gowan, John C.; Demos, George D., and Torrance, E. Paul (Eds.): *Creativity: Its Educational Implications.* New York, Wiley, 1967.

Green, John A.: *Teacher-Made Tests.* New York, Harper, 1963.

Grose, Robert F., and Birney, Robert C. (Eds.): *Transfer of Learning.* Princeton, Van Nostrand, 1963.

Gruber, Howard E.; Terrell, Glen and Wertheimer, Michael: *Contemporary Approaches to Creative Thinking.* New York, Atherton, 1963.

Guilford, J.P.: Basic conceptual problems in the psychology of thinking. *Ann New York Acad Sci,* 1960.

Guilford, J.P.: Creative abilities in the arts. *Psychol Rev,* 1957, 1964.

Guilford, J.P.: Factorial angles to psychology. *Psychol Rev,* 1961, 1968.

Guilford, J.P.: Factors that aid and hinder creativity. *Teachers College Rec,* 389-392, 1962, 1963.

Guilford, J.P.: Frontiers in thinking that teachers should know about. *Read Teacher,* 13:176-182, 1960.

Guilford, J.P.: Human Abilities in Education. *Calif J Instruct Improv,* 1:3-6, 1958.

Guilford, J.P.: Intelligence, creativity and learning. *Pro 1960 Summer Conference.* Bellingham, Western Washington, 1960, pp. 3-46.

Guilford, J.P.: The nature of creative thinking. *Res Bull East Arts Assoc,* 5:5-27, 1954.

Guilford, J.P.: Parameters and categories of talent. In *The Yearbook of Education.* London, Evans, 1962, pp. 115-124.

Guilford, J.P.: The psychology of creativity. *Creative Crafts,* 1:5-8, 1960.

Guilford, J.P.: Some recent findings on thinking abilities and their implications. *Bull Nat Assoc Second School Princ,* 37:3-13, 1953.

Guilford, J.P.: The Structure of Intellect. *Psychol Bull,* 53:267-293, 1956.

Guilford, J.P.: Three faces of intellect. *Amer Psychol,* 14:469-479, 1959.

Guilford, J.P., and Merrifield, P.R.: The structure-of-intellect model: its uses and implications. *Rep Psychol Lab,* No. 24. Los Angeles, U. of Southern Calif., April 1960.

Guilford, J.P.; Merrifield, P.R., and Cox, Anna B.: Creative thinking in children at the junior high school levels. *Rep Psychol Lab,* No. 26. Los Angeles, U. of Southern Calif., 1961.

Harris, I.: *Emotional Blocks to Learning.* New York, Macmillan, 1961.

Havighurst, R.J.: Conditions productive of superior children. *Teachers College Rec,* 62:300-303, 1961.

Havighurst, R.J., and Neugarten, B.L.: *Society and Education.* Boston, Allyn & Bacon, 1957.

Hayes, D.G., and Rothney, J.W.M.: Educational decision-making by superior secondary school students and their parents. *Personnel Guidance J,* 38:26-30, 1960.

Health, Education and Welfare Indicators: *Education for the Gifted.* U.S. Printing Office, Superintendent of Documents, April 1964.

Heffernan, H.: *Guiding the Young Child.* Boston, Heath, 1959.

Hilgard, Ernest R. (Ed.): Theories of learning and instruction. *The Sixty-Third Year-book of the National Society for the Study of Education.* Chicago, U. of Chicago, 1964.

Hill, M.G.: Enrichment: programs for intellectually gifted pupils (IV of California Project Talent Series). Sacramento, Calif. Dept. of Ed., 1969.

Holland, J.L.: Creative and academic performance among talented adolescents. *J Ed Psychol,* June 1961.

Holland, J.L., and Astin, A.W. a): The prediction of the academic, artistic, scientific and social achievement of undergraduate of superior scholastic aptitude. *J Ed Psychol,* 53:132-43, 1962, b): The need for redefining "Talent" and "Talent Loss." *J Higher Ed,* 33:71-82, 1962.

Hollinshead, B.: *Who Should Go to College?* New York, Columbia, 1952.

Holt, E.E.: *A Selected and Annotated Bibliography on the Gifted.* Columbus, Ohio Board of Ed., 1960.

Horton, Margaret: Special Report to MAL Administrative Committee Selecting Teachers for More Able Learners. Unpublished mimeographed paper. Escondido, Escondido Union School District.

Hovery, D.E. and others: Effects of self-directed study on achievement, retention and curiosity. *J Ed Res,* 56:346-51, 1963.

Huck, Charlotte S., and Young, Doris A.: *Children's Literature in the Elementary School.* New York, Holt, 1961.

Hunt, J.: *Intelligence and Experience.* New York, Ronald, 1961.

Hurlock, Elizabeth B.: *Adolescent Development.* New York, McGraw, 1955.

Hurlock, Elizabeth B.: *Child Development* (3rd ed.). New York, McGraw, 1956.

Hutchinson, M., and Young, C.: *Educating the Intelligent.* London, Penguin (Pelican Series A566) 1962.

Jersild, Arthur T.: *The Psychology of Adolescence.* New York, Macmillan, 1957.

Jones, A.: *Principles of Guidance.* New York, McGraw, 1945.

Jones, Marshall R. (Ed.): *Nebraska Symposium on Motivation.* Lincoln, U. of Nebr., 1963.

Karnes, M.B., and others: Underachievement and overachievement of intellectually gifted children. *Except Child,* 28:167-76, 1961.

Karowe, H.E.: Giftedness and creativity. *Gifted Child Quart,* 7:165-75, 1963.

Katz, Robert L.: *Empathy: Its Nature and Uses.* New York, Macmillan, 1963.

Kearney, Nolan C.: *Elementary School Objectives.* New York, Russell Sage, 1953.

Kelly, J.: *Guidance and Curriculum.* Englewood Cliffs, Prentice-Hall, 1955.

Kelly, R.: *Education for the Gifted in New York State.* Albany, New York Board of Ed., 1964.

Ketcham, W.A.: What do we know about gifted children? *High School J,* 48:82-87, 1964.

Keys, N.: Should we accelerate the bright? *Except Child,* 23:199-201, 1957.

Keys, N.: *The Underage Student in High School and College.* Berkeley, U. of Calif., 1938.

Klausmeier, H.J.: Effects of accelerating bright older elementary pupils: a follow-up. *J Ed Psychol,* 54:165-71, 1963.

Klausmeier, H.J., and Loughlin, L.J.: Behaviors during problem solving among children of low, average and high intelligence. *J Ed Psychol,* 52:148-52, 1961.

Klausmeier, H.J., and Ripple, R.E.: Effects of accelerating bright older pupils from second to fourth grade. *J Ed Psychol,* 53:93-100, 1962.

Kough, J.: *Practical Programs for the Gifted.* Chicago, Sci. Res. Assoc., 1960.

Krathwohl, David R.; Bloom, Benjamin S., and Masia, Bertram: *Taxonomy of Educational Objectives.* Handbook II: Affective domain. New York, McKay, 1964.

Krippner, S., and Herald, Clare: Reading disabilities among the academically gifted. *Gifted Child Quart,* 8:12-20, 1964.

Laycock, S.R.: *Gifted Children.* Toronto, Copp-Clark, 1957.

Laycock, S.R.: *Gifted Children.* Special education in Canada (The 1963 Quance Lectures). Toronto, Gage, 1963.

Lehman, H.C.: *Age and Achievement.* Princeton, Princeton, 1953.

Lessinger, Leon M.: Test building and test banks through the use of the taxonomy of educational objectives. *Calif J Ed Res,* 14 (No. 5), Nov. 1963.

Lessinger, Leon M., and Seagoe, May V.: The nature of enrichment for gifted students. *J Ed Res,* 57:142-46, 1963.

Lewis, Gertrude: *Educating the More Able Children in Grades Four, Five and Six.* U.S. Department of Health, Education, and Welfare, Gov. Print. Office, Superintendent of Documents, 1961.

Los Angeles County Superintendent of Schools Office: *Guiding Today's Children.* Los Angeles, Calif. Test Bureau, 1959.

MacKinnon, D.W.: Identifying and developing creativity. *J Second Ed,* 38:166-74, 1963.

MacKinnon, D.W.: The nature and nurture of creative talent. *Amer Psychol,* 17:484-95, 1962.

Manlove, Donald C., and Beggs, David W. III: *Flexible Scheduling.* Bloomington, Indiana, 1965.

Marksberry, Mary Lee: *Foundation of Creativity.* New York, Harper, 1963.

Martinson, Ruth, director: *Educational Program for Gifted Pupils.* Sacramento, Calif. Dept. of Ed., 1961.

Martinson, Ruth, and Smallenburg, Harry: *Guidance in the Elementary School.* Englewood Cliffs, Prentice-Hall, 1958.

Maslow, A.H.: *Motivation and Personality.* New York, Harper, 1954.

Massialas, Byron G., and Zevin, Jack: *Creative Encounters in the Classroom.* New York, Wiley, 1967.

Mathewson, R.H.: *Guidance Policy and Practice.* New York, Harper, 1949.

McClelland, D.C.: *The Achieving Society.* Princeton, Van Nostrand, 1961.

McClelland, D.C. and others: *Talent and Society.* Princeton, Van Nostrand, 1958.

McGuire, C.: Personality Correlates of Creativity. Report No. 13. Austin, U. of Tex., Lab. of Human Behavior, Dept. of Ed. Psychol., 1963.

McNemar, Q.: Lost our intelligence, why? *Amer Psychol,* 19(No.12):871, 1964.

McWilliams, E., and Brown, K.E.: *Superior Pupil in Junior High School Mathematics.*

Bulletin No. 4, U.S. Department of Health, Education and Welfare, Office of Ed. Gov. Print. Office, Superintendent of Documents, 1955.

Mead, M.: The gifted child in the American culture of today. *J Teacher Ed,* 5:211-214, 1954.

Mead, Margaret, and Wolfenstein, Martha (Ed.): *Childhood in Contemporary Cultures.* Chicago, U. of Chicago, 1963.

Meer, B., and Stein, M.I.: Measures of intelligence and creativity. *J Psychol,* 39:117-26, 1955.

Merrifield, P.R.; Guilford, J.P., and Gershon, A.: *Differentiation of Divergent-Production Abilities at the Sixth-Grade Level.* Los Angeles, U. of Southern Calif., 1963.

Mirman, N.J.: A Study of Social Adjustment as It Relates to Grade Skipping in the Elementary School. Unpublished Ed. D. Thesis, Los Angeles, U. of Southern Calif., 1961.

Mitterling, P.I. (Ed.): Programs for superior students in high school. *Superior Student,* 6(1):32-70, 1963.

Morrill, M.B. (Ed.): The superior and gifted student project and Cullowhee: a follow-up study. Cullowhee, Western C. College Guidance Clin., 1964.

Morse, H.T., and McCune, G.H.: *Selected Items for the Testing of Study Skills and Critical Thinking.* Bulletin No. 15. Nat. Council Soc. Studies.

Munn, Norman L. (Ed.): The relation of bilingualism to intelligence. *Psychol Monog, Gen Applied,* 76 No. 546, No. 27. Washington, Amer. Psychol. Assoc., 1962.

Munn, Norman L. (Ed.): Theory and data on the interrelationships of three factors of memory. *Psychol Monog, Gen Applied,* 76 No. 539, No. 20. Washington, Amer. Psychol. Assoc., 1962.

Myer, J.S., and Bendig, A.W.: A longitudinal study of the primary mental abilities test. *J Ed Psychol,* Feb. 1961.

Myers, R.E.: *Invitations to Thinking and Doing.* Minnesota, Perceptive, 1961.

Myers, R.E., and Torrance, E.P.: *Can You Imagine?* Eugene, Perceptive (2795-½ Central Boulevard) 1963.

Myers, R.E., and Torrance, E.P.: *Invitations to Speaking and Writing Creatively.* (Workbook). Eugene, Perceptive (2795-½ Central Boulevard) 1962.

National Education Association: *Planning for Excellence in High School Science.* Washington, Nat. Ed. Assoc., 1961.

National Education Association: *The Scholars Look at the Schools* (A report of the Disciplines Seminar). Washington, Nat. Ed. Assoc., 1962.

National Education Association: *Schools for the 60's.* New York, McGraw, 1963.

National Education Association and National Council of Teachers of Mathematics: *Program Provisions for Mathematically Talented Gifted Students in Secondary Schools.* Washington, Council, 1957.

National Education Association and National Council for the Social Studies a): *Social Studies for the Academically Talented Student in the Secondary School.* Washington, Nat. Ed. Assoc., 1959.

National Education Association and National Council of Teachers of Mathematics: *Mathematics for the Academically Talented Student in the Secondary School.* Washington, Nat. Ed. Assoc., 1959.

National Education Association and National Science Teachers Association: *Science for the Academically Talented Student in the Secondary School.* Washington, Nat. Ed. Assoc., 1959.

National Education Association and Modern Foreign Language Association of America:

Modern Foreign Languages and the Academically Talented Student. Washington, Nat. Ed. Assoc., 1960.

National Educational Association and National Council of Teachers of English: *English for the Academically Talented Student in the Secondary School.* Washington, Nat. Ed. Assoc., 1960.

National Society for the Study of Education: *Education of the Gifted. Fifty-seventh Yearbook, Part II.* Chicago, U. of Chicago, 1958.

Newland, T. Ernest: Some observations on essential qualifications of teachers of the mentally superior. *Except Child,* Nov. 1962.

Newland, T. Ernest, and Meeker, Mary: Binet behavior samplings and Guilford's structure of the intellect. *J School Psychol,* 2:55-59, 1963-1964.

North Carolina Department of Public Instruction: *Materials Being Used in Classes for the Exceptionally Talented in North Carolina.* Raleigh, Dept. of Public Instr., 1964.

Ohlsen, M.M., and Proff, F.C.: *The Extent to Which Group Counseling Improves the Academic and Personal Adjustment of Underachieving Gifted Adolescents.* (CRP No. 623) and Urbana: U. of Ill., College of Ed., 1960.

Orr, D.B.: Project talent: a national inventory of aptitudes and abilities. *Phi Delta Kappan,* 13:237-43, 1961.

Packard, Vance: Do your dreams match your talents? Chicago, Sci. Res. Assoc., 1960.

Palmer and Diedrich: *Critical Thinking in Reading and Writing.* New York, Holt, 1962.

Parnes, S.J.: *Bibliography re Nature and Nurture of Creative Behavior.* Buffalo, Creative Ed. Found. (1614 Rand Building), 1964.

Parnes, S.J. a): Can creativity be increased? *Personnel Administration,* 25(6):2-9, 1962. (See also pp. 185-91 in Parnes, S.J., and Harding, H.F.: *A Source Book for Creative Thinking.* New York, Scribner, 1962.) b): Do you really understand brainstorming? In Parnes, S.J. and Harding, H.F.: *A Source Book for Creative Thinking.* New York, Scribner, 1962, pp. 283-90; c): The creative problem-solving course and institute at the University of Buffalo. In Parnes, S.J. and Harding, H.F.: *A Source Book for Creative Thinking.* New York, Scribner, 1962, pp. 307-23.

Parnes, Sidney J., and Harding, Harold F.: *A Source Book for Creative Thinking.* New York, Scribner, 1962.

Passow, A.H.: The maze of the research on ability grouping. *Ed Forum,* 26:281-88, 1962. (Cf. pp. 238-48 in French, J.L.: *Educating the Gifted, a Book of Readings.* New York, Holt, 1964.)

Passow, A. Harry, and Leeper, Robert R. (Ed.): *Intellectual Development: Another Look.* Washington, Assoc. Supervision and Curriculum Develop., 1964.

Passow, A. Harry, and others: *The Gifted: Digests of Important Studies.* Washington, Nat. Ed. Assoc., Council on Except. Child., 1962.

Piaget, Jean: *Judgment and Reasoning in the Child.* London, Routledge & Kegan, Paul, 1965. (Order from: Humanities Press, Inc., 303 Park Avenue South, New York.)

Piaget, Jean: *Psychology of Intelligence.* London, Routledge & Kegan, Paul, 1947. (Order from: Humanities Press, Inc., 303 Park Avenue South, New York.)

Pielstick, N.L.: Gifted children and learning experiences. *J Ed Res* 57:125-30, 1963.

Piers, E. and others: The identification of creativity in adolescents. *J Ed Psychol,* 51:346-51, 1960.

Plowman, P.D., and Rice, J.P.: *California Project Talent* (V of California Project Talent Series). Sacramento, Dept. of Ed., 1967.

Plowman, P.D., and Rice, J.P.: A progress report on programs for mentally gifted minors in California schools. *Calif. Schools,* 34(3):3-18, 1963, b): Plowman, P.D., and Rice, J.P.: *Evaluating Educational and Counseling Programs for Gifted Children*. Sacramento, Calif. Dept. of Ed. (Project Talent), March 2, 1963.

Plowman, P.D., and Rice, J.P. a): Recent developments in education for gifted pupils in California. *Calif Ed*, 1: Jan. 1964, b): Revised guidelines for establishing and evaluating programs for mentally gifted minors. Sacramento, Calif. Dept. of Ed., (Project Talent), June 1964.

Pressey, S.L.: Education acceleration: occasional procedure or major issue? *Personnel Guidance J*, 41:12-17, 1962. New York, McKay, 1963.

Provus, Malcolm, and Stone, Douglas: *Programmed Instruction in the Classroom*. Chicago, Curiculum Adv. Serv., 1963.

Raph, Jane B.; Goldberg, Miriam L., and Passow, A. Harry: *Bright Underachievers*. New York, Teachers College, 1966.

Reynolds, Maynard C. (Ed.): *Early School Admission for Mentally Advanced Children*. Washington, Council for Except. Child., 1962.

Rice, Joseph P.: California project talent: a unique educational development. *Clear House*, 42 (No. 5), Jan. 1968.

Rice, Joseph P.: A comparative study of academic interest patterns among selected groups of exceptional and normal intermediate children. *Calif J Ed Res*, 14 (No. 3), May 1963.

Rice, Joseph P.: Cooperative guidance and instructional programs for leadership preparation. *Personnel Guidance J* 46(No. 2):967-973, 1966.

Rice, Joseph P.: Differential programming for able and gifted pupils. *Calif Ed*, 2(No. 8), April 1965.

Rice, Joseph P.: Education of subcultural groups. *School Soc*, 92 (No. 2250), Nov. 1964.

Rice, Joseph P.: Opinions of gifted students regarding secondary school programs. *Except Child*, Dec. 1967 (With Banks, George).

Rice, Joseph P.: Screening, examining and programming for mentally gifted pupils. *Clear House*, 38(No. 4), Dec. 1963.

Rice, Joseph P.: Total talent development. *J Secondary Ed*, 42(No. 1):12-16, 1967.

Rice, Joseph P.: Types of problems referred to a central guidance agency at different grade levels. *Personnel Guidance J*, 43(No. 1), Sept. 1963.

Rice, Joseph P., and Plowman, P.D.: A demonstration center with differential programming for gifted pupils in California, grades one through nine. *Calif Schools*, 34:139-54, 1963.

Robeck, M.C.: *Acceleration: Programs for Intellectually Gifted Pupils* (III of California Project Talent Series). Sacramento, Calif. Dept. of Ed., 1968.

Robeck, M.C.: *Special Class: Programs for Intellectually Gifted Pupils* (II of California Project Talent Series). Sacramento, Calif. Dept. of Ed., 1968.

Rogers, W.S.: *The Annotated Bibliography for Guidance Through Literature*. Instructional Materials Center for Alpine, Nevada, Placer, and Sierra Counties, California, 1961.

Rugg, H.: *Imagination*. New York, Harper, 1963.

Sanders, David C. (Ed.): *Elementary Education and the Academically Talented Pupil*. Washington, Nat. Ed. Assoc. and Dept. of Elementary School Principals, 1961.

Sargent, Porter: *The Gifted Educational Resources*. Boston, Sargent, 1961.

Scheifele, Marian (Ed.): *The Gifted Child in the Regular Classroom*. New York, Columbia, 1953.

Scher, Jordan (Ed.): *Theories of the Mind*. New York, Macmillan, 1962.

Shannon, D.: What research says about acceleration. *Phi Delta Kappan*, 34, Nov. 1957.

Shaw, M.C.: Definition and identification of academic underachievers. *Guidance for the Underachiever with Superior Ability*. U.S. Office of Health, Education and Welfare, 25:15-30, 1961.

Shertzer, Bruce (Ed.): *Working with Superior Students: Theories and Practices*. Chicago, Sci. Res. Assoc., 1960.

Simon, Anita, and Boyer, E. Gil: Mirrors for behavior. *Class Interaction Newsl* 3(No. 2), Jan. 1968 (special ed.).

Smith, E.H.: State level educational services for gifted pupils. *J Except Child*, 27:511-16, 1961.

Spearman, C.: *Ability of Man*. New York, Macmillan, 1927.

Spranger, E.: *Types of Men*. New York, Stechert, 1928.

Steckle, Lynde: *Problems of Human Adjustment*. New York, Harper, 1957.

Stein, M.I., and Heinze, S.J.: *Creativity and the Individual*. New York, Macmillan, 1960.

Stoddard, G.D.: *The Meaning of Intelligence*. New York, Macmillan, 1943.

Strang, Ruth: *Helping Your Gifted Child*. New York, Dutton, 1960.

Strang, Ruth: Self concepts of gifted adolescents. *High School J*, 48:102-07, 1964.

Strauss, A.A., and Lehtinen, L.: *Psychopathology and Education of the Brain Injured Child*. New York, Grune, 1951.

Suchman, J.R.: Creative growth and conceptual growth. *Gifted Child Quart*, 6:95-99, 1962.

Sumption, M.R., and Luecking, M.: *Education for the Gifted*. New York, Ronald Press, 1960.

Super, D.E.: *Appraising Vocational Fitness*. New York, Harper, 1949.

Symonds, P.M.: *Dynamic Psychology*. New York, Appleton, 1946.

Taba, Hilda: Opportunities for creativity in the education of exceptional children. *Except Child*, 29:247-56, 1963.

Taylor, C.W.: The creative individual: a new portrait in giftedness. *Ed Leader*, Oct., 1960.

Taylor, Calvin W. (Ed.): *Creativity—Progress and Potential*. New York, McGraw, 1964.

Taylor, Calvin W., and Barron, Frank (Ed.): *Scientific Creativtiy: Its Recognition and Development*. New York, Wiley, 1963.

Taylor, Calvin W., and Williams, Frank E. (Eds.): The Proceedings of the VIth Utah Creativity Research Conference held at Torrey Pines Inn, La Jolla, Calif. New York, Wiley, 1966.

Tead, O.: Leadership. *Encyclop Brit*, 13:824-825, Chicago, Benton, 1957.

Telford, Charles W., and Sawrey, James M.: *The Exceptional Individual: Psychological and Educational Aspects*. Englewood Cliffs, Prentice-Hall, 1967.

Terman, Lewis W., *et al.*: *Genetic Studies of Genius. Vol. I: Mental and Physical Traits of a Thousand Gifted Children*. Stanford, Stanford, 1926.

Terman, Lewis W., and Oden, Melita H.: *Genetic Studies of Genius. Vol. IV: The Gifted Child Grows Up*. Stanford, Stanford, 1947.

Terman, Lewis W., and Oden, Melita H.: *The Gifted Group at Mid-Life*. Stanford, Stanford, 1959.

Thurstone, L.L.: Primary mental abilities. *Psychol Monogr*, No. 1, 1938.

Torrance, E. Paul: *Education and the Creative Potential*. Minneapolis, U. of Minn., 1963.

Torrance, E. Paul: *Guiding Creative Talent*. Englewood Cliffs, Prentice-Hall, 1962.

Torrance, E. Paul (Ed.): *Talent and Education*. Minneapolis, U. of Minn., 1960.

Torrance, E. Paul, and Punsalan, Victoria: *Creativity: A New Dimension of Intelligence.* Washington, Nat. Ed. Assoc., 1961.

Torrance, E. Paul, and Strom, Robert D.: *Mental Health and Achievement: Increasing Potential and Reducing School Dropout.* New York, Wiley, 1965.

Torrance, E. Paul, and others: *Role of Evaluation in Creative Thinking.* Minneapolis, U. of Minn., College of Education, Bureau of Educational Research, Cooperative Research Project No. 725, 1964.

Tyler, L.: The relationship of interests to abilities and reputation among first grade children. *Ed Psychol Measur,* 11:255-264, 1951.

Underwood, Benton J., and Schulz, Rudolph W.: *Meaningfulness and Verbal Learning.* Philadelphia, Lippincott, 1960.

Vane, Julia R.: *The Relation of Early School Achievement to High School Achievement When Race, Intelligence, and Socio-Economic Factors Are Held Constant.* Hempstead, Hofstra, 1964.

Vernon, P.E.: *The Structure of Human Abilities,* 2nd ed., London, Methuen, 1961.

Vinacke, W. Edgar: *The Psychology of Thinking.* New York, McGraw, 1952.

Wann, Dorn Liddle: *Fostering Intellectual Development in Young Children.* New York, Columbia.

Ward, James and others: *Curriculum Integration Concept Applied in the Elementary School.* Austin, U. of Tex., 1960.

Ward, V.S.: *Educating the Gifted: An Axiomatic Approach.* Columbus, Merrill, C.E., 1961.

Washburne, Carleton, and Marland, Sidney P., Jr.: *Winnetka: The History and Significance of an Educational Experiment.* Englewood Cliffs, Prentice-Hall, 1963.

Wechsler, D.: *The Measurement of Adult Intelligence.* Baltimore, Williams and Wilkins, 1949.

White, Robert W.: *The Study of Lives.* New York, Atherton, 1963.

Williams, Frank E.: *Creativity at Home and in School.* E. St. Paul, Macalester, 1968.

Williams, Frank E.: The search for the creative teacher. *Calif Teachers Assoc J,* 60(1):14-16, 1964.

Wilson, R., chairman: *The Curriculum of Secondary Schools Offering Advanced Studies.* London, U. of London, 1962.

Winborn, B., and Schmidt, L.G.: The effectiveness of short-term group counseling upon the academic achievement of potentially superior but underachieving college freshman. *J Ed Res,* 55:109-73, 1962.

Witty, P.A.: A balanced reading program for the gifted. *Read Teacher,* 1:418-24, 1963.

Witty, Paul (Ed.): *The Gifted Child.* Boston, Heath, 1951.

Witty, Paul: *Helping the Gifted Child.* Chicago, Sci. Res. Assoc., 1952.

Wonderly, D.M.: A study of creative females. *Gifted Child Quart,* 8:38-39, 1964.

Woolcock, C.W.: *The Hunter College High School Program for Gifted Students.* New York, Vantage, 1962.

Woolcock, C.W.: *New Approaches to the Education of the Gifted.* Morristown, Silver Burdett, 1961.

Worchester, D.A.: *The Education of Children of Above-Average Mentality.* Lincoln, U. of Nebr., 1956.

Yager, R.E., and Dessel, N.F.: Selection criteria for high ability science students. *J Ed Res,* 57:193-96, 1963.

Yamamoto, K.: Threshold of intelligence in academic achievement of highly creative students. *J Exper Ed,* 32:401-05, 1964.

Yarmolonsky, N.: *Recognition of Excellence*. Glencoe, New Horizon Press, 1960.

Yearbook of Education: *The Education of the Gifted*. London, Evans, 1961.

Ziegfeld, Edwin (Ed.): *Art for the Academically Talented Student in the Secondary School*. Washington, Nat. Ed. Assoc. and Nat. Art Ed. Assoc., 1961.

INDEX